P9-DGJ-539

Reference Guides in Literature

Ronald Gottesman, *Editor*

Flannery O'Connor and Caroline Gordon:
A Reference Guide

Robert E. Golden
Mary C. Sullivan

G. K. HALL & CO., 70 LINCOLN STREET, BOSTON, MASS.

Library of Congress Cataloging in Publication Data

Golden, Robert E
Flannery O'Connor and Caroline Gordon

(Reference guides in literature)
Includes indexes.
1. O'Connor, Flannery--Bibliography. 2. Gordon, Caroline, 1895- --Bibliography. I. Sullivan, Mary C., joint author. II. Title.
Z8640.3.G65 016.813'5'4 76-44334

This publication is printed on permanent/durable acid-free paper
MANUFACTURED IN THE UNITED STATES OF AMERICA

Contents

Flannery O'Connor:
A Reference Guide

Robert E. Golden

Introduction

The aim of this reference guide is to provide scholars and others interested in the fiction of Flannery O'Connor with a convenient guide to reviews, articles, and books about her and her work. Readers of this guide should find it useful for discovering the various interpretations of her works and for tracing the growth and changing nature of her literary reputation. Every attempt has been made to make as complete a listing of the criticism as possible, but in the interests of brevity and usefulness the following items have been excluded: references to O'Connor in standard reference works; reviews of the criticism on O'Connor except when these reviews are major review-articles surveying the scope and direction of O'Connor criticism or when the review also reviews one of O'Connor's works or is in fact an article on her rather than on the criticism; news articles on O'Connor that contain no critical opinions of her work or life or new facts about her; remarks in short story anthologies, except when those remarks are fairly extensive (over two pages) and included in the text itself, not in an instructor's manual; elegaic poems; and reviews of her works that merely describe the contents of a work and offer no critical estimate of those contents. Reprints of articles and reviews are included, but only major reprints, not reprints in short story anthologies or reprints of articles in major newspapers by smaller papers. Foreign language material is listed and annotated, but the listing is limited, with a few exceptions, to those articles or books cited in English language bibliographies.

This reference guide is organized by date of publication of writings on O'Connor, with each year divided into two sections. The first section, "A," lists monographs and full-length books devoted exclusively to O'Connor. The second section, "B ," lists all articles and reviews as well as books only partially devoted to O'Connor. Articles in issues of journals that carry a date of two years, for example 1970-1971, are listed at the end of the "B" section for the earlier year. The works cited for any given year are listed alphabetically by author and are numbered according to their order of appearance in the "A" or "B" section. An article cited as "1966.B12" would be the twelfth article in the "B" section for 1966. This code is employed in the index at the back of this guide and within the text to refer to reprints and scholarly replies.

Flannery O'Connor: A Reference Guide

In this guide, the titles of many journals are abbreviated. Most of these abbreviations are taken from those found in the Modern Language Association International Bibliography. Some additional abbreviations for widely-known journals or for journals cited frequently in this reference guide have been added. A table of these abbreviations may be found on page 7. In addition, a chronology of the first editions of books by O'Connor is located on page 11.

I have tried to make this reference guide as up-to-date as possible, but owing to the time-lag between the appearance of an article and its being listed in the various bibliographies, the list of writings is considerably less complete for 1974, 1975, and 1976 than it is for previous years.

The annotations are intended to be descriptive, not evaluative. They briefly describe the author's argument; no conscious attempt was made to judge the quality of that argument. In the few cases where I was unable to see the article cited or was unable to obtain sufficient information about the article, the article is listed without annotation. These articles, as well as five other references where my annotations are based on sources other than the work itself, have an asterisk before the entry. To avoid any confusion, the reader should note that ellipses are used only within quotations when they are called for, never at the end of quotations.

The listing of published material on O'Connor is followed by a chronological list of Ph.D. dissertations on O'Connor. The guide concludes with an index listing authors and titles of published writings on O'Connor, as well as titles of O'Connor's works and two subject headings: Bibliography and Biography.

I am indebted to the bibliographical work done by various scholars, especially George Wedge, Lewis A. Lawson, Joan T. Brittain and Leon V. Driskell, James Dorsey, David Farmer, and Georgia Ann Newman, whose 1970 Florida State thesis, "Flannery O'Connor: Annotated Bibliography of Secondary Sources," I consulted during preparation of this book. My list of works on O'Connor is based on the work of these scholars, though I have brought my bibliography more up-to-date and have occasionally made corrections in their listings or found new material for the years their bibliographies cover. All the annotations are my own; they are based, with the exception of five entries, on my viewing of the material or on my summations of the translations done for me for some of the foreign language material.

Although it is impossible to summarize adequately the directions of O'Connor criticism in this introduction, perhaps some observations will prove useful to the reader. First, although O'Connor was never ignored as a writer, 1960 was certainly a turning point in her critical reputation. Fifty-nine reviews of The Violent Bear It Away and other articles on her were published in that year, compared with twenty-seven in 1955, the year A Good Man Is Hard to Find was published. The reader should note, though, that O'Connor always received far more attention than most fledgling writers ever hope for or achieve. Much of the early criticism is hostile, but the mere fact that O'Connor was reviewed in prestigious journals like the Kenyon Review and in influential mass circulation magazines like Time indicates that critics saw her as a writer who had to be taken seriously, if not necessarily admired. Second, O'Connor has, especially since her death, drawn an enormous amount of critical attention. There are now eighteen books devoted exclusively to her fiction and sixty-five Ph.D. dissertations that discuss her works. While I have made no numerical comparisons with the amount of criticism written on other postwar writers, it seems safe to say that critical interest in her is as high or higher than it is in almost any other contemporary writer. Whatever time may judge to be her position in American literature, her contemporaries or near-contemporaries have certainly accorded her an enormous amount of attention.

Criticism on O'Connor has dealt with many issues typical of discussions of virtually any writer: the question of the superiority of her work in one genre as opposed to another (in her case, the short story and the novel), the question of her relation to the literature of her region and nation, and the question of her attitude towards and fictional use of the life of her region, to cite but a few. Despite the plethora of issues, there is, however, one that seems paramount in most discussions of O'Connor. The issue is religion, specifically, the relation between O'Connor's stated religious intent and the realization of that intent within the fiction. Since O'Connor, through her numerous essays and lectures on her fiction and on fiction in general, made her conscious intent probably as clear as any writer ever has, the issue is clear-cut and formidable. While critics have enormously diverging opinions on the role of religion in her work, there are, allowing for some oversimplification, four schools of thought on this crucial matter. The first school accepts O'Connor's religious intent as realized in the work and accepts her religious vision as a penetrating view of human life. Such critics often praise O'Connor's religious humanism or praise her ability to probe the shams of secularism. The second school also accepts O'Connor's religious intent as realized in her fiction, but questions the adequacy of her religious vision, often finding it excessively negative and anti-humanistic. Such critics often stress the Jansenist influence on O'Connor and occasionally suggest her protracted struggle with disseminated lupus left her an embittered woman who excoriated the world through her writing. The third school allows that O'Connor's religious intent has some relevance to her fiction, but questions how fully this intent is realized in the work. Such critics suggest various alternative readings of O'Connor, including some that see O'Connor's literary impulse as partly or wholly demonic and some that question whether the fiction itself can bear the weight of the symbolic, religious readings that O'Connor wishes us to give it. The fourth school denies the religious intent completely, preferring to read her work in various other ways: as another example of "southern gothic" and its interest in private neurosis and public degeneracy, as a humanistic cry against the evils of the American South, as O'Connor's way of working out the frustrations of her inner life, or as a closed fictional world, a world in which questions of ideology or belief are not relevant. Much of the early criticism of O'Connor belongs in the fourth school; religious readings of her work increased as her fiction became more familiar and as she increasingly made clear her religious intent, but the fourth school is not silent, occasionally sallying forth against the other schools, especially the first and the second, which are, in terms of numbers of followers, the predominant schools in O'Connor criticism. These four "schools" are more heuristic than descriptive, since any given critic may hold a position that combines elements of two or more schools. As heuristic devices, however, these four categories should help the reader to follow the main directions of O'Connor criticism when using this reference guide.

Many people have helped in the preparation of this book. For the translation of articles from German, Italian, Rumanian, and Hungarian, I would like to thank the following people: Caroline Snyder and Egidio Papa of Rochester Institute of Technology, Charles Carlton of the University of Rochester, Louis Loté of Rochester, N. Y., and Teresa Coletti of the University of Maryland. For help in typing and proofreading, I would like to thank my wife, Barbara Golden, and Constance Downey, and for financial assistance, Dean Paul Bernstein of the College of General Studies of Rochester Institute of Technology. For aid in locating and obtaining material, I am indebted to Gerald Becham of the Ina Dillard Russell Library of Georgia College in Milledgeville, to David Farmer of the Humanities Research Center at the University of Texas, to Phyllis Andrews of the University of Rochester Library, and to Judy Glading and Mary Ann Young of the Interlibrary Loan Department at Rochester Institute of Technology Library. To these last two people especially, I owe a debt of gratitude.

Table of Abbreviations

ABR	American Benedictine Review
AL	American Literature
AntigR	Antigonish Review
AR	Antioch Review
ArQ	Arizona Quarterly
ASch	American Scholar
AUMLA	Journal of the Australasian Universities Language and Literature Association
BB	Bulletin of Bibliography
BUJ	Boston University Journal
CathW	Catholic World
CE	College English
CEA	CEA Critic
CLS	Comparative Literature Studies (U of Ill.)
ColQ	Colorado Quarterly
ConL	Contemporary Literature
ConnR	Connecticut Review
Crit	Critique: Studies in Modern Fiction
EJ	English Journal
Expl	Explicator

FOB	Flannery O'Connor Bulletin
GaR	Georgia Review
HC	The Hollins Critic (Hollins Coll., Va.)
HudR	Hudson Review
JML	Journal of Modern Literature
LanM	Les Langues Modernes
LJ	Library Journal
MFS	Modern Fiction Studies
MinnR	Minnesota Review
MissQ	Mississippi Quarterly
MR	Massachusetts Review
NatR	National Review
NConL	Notes on Contemporary Literature
NRF	Nouvelle Revue Française
NY	New Yorker
NYRB	New York Review of Books
NYT	New York Times
NYTBR	New York Times Book Review
PLL	Papers on Language and Literature
PR	Partisan Review
RANAM	Recherches Anglaises et Américaines
RLM	La Revue des Lettres Modernes
RLMC	Rivista di Letterature Moderne e Comparate (Firenze)
SA	Studi Americani (Roma)
SatR	Saturday Review
SHR	Southern Humanities Review
SLJ	Southern Literary Journal

Table of Abbreviations

SLRJ	Saint Louis University Research Journal
SoR	Southern Review (Louisiana State University)
SR	Sewanee Review
SSF	Studies in Short Fiction
SWR	Southwest Review
SZ	Stimmen der Zeit
TCL	Twentieth Century Literature
TLS	(London) Times Literary Supplement
TSL	Tennessee Studies in Literature
UR	University Review (Kansas City, Mo.)
VQR	Virginia Quarterly Review
WHR	Western Humanities Review
WR	Western Review: A Journal of the Humanities
XUS	Xavier University Studies
YR	Yale Review

Flannery O'Connor's First Editions

Wise Blood. New York: Harcourt, Brace, 1952.

A Good Man Is Hard to Find and Other Stories. New York: Harcourt, Brace, 1955.

The Violent Bear It Away. New York: Farrar, Straus and Cudahy, 1960.

Everything That Rises Must Converge. New York: Farrar, Straus and Giroux, 1965.

Mystery and Manners: Occasional Prose. Edited by Sally and Robert Fitzgerald. New York: Farrar, Straus and Giroux, 1969.

Flannery O'Connor: The Complete Stories. New York: Farrar, Straus and Giroux, 1971.

Published Writings about Flannery O'Connor, 1952 — 1976

1952 A BOOKS - NONE

1952 B SHORTER WRITINGS

1 ANON. "Flannery O'Connor." LJ 77:354.
Brief biographical description of O'Connor. Wise Blood is "about the South, southern religionists, and in the opinion of some readers in the tradition of Kafka."

2 ANON. "Frustrated Preacher." Newsweek (19 May), pp. 114-15.
A review of Wise Blood. O'Connor "is perhaps the most naturally gifted of the youngest generation of American novelists," and the novel has an "imaginative intensity." The reader can find what meaning he will in the novel, though the novel clearly satirizes evangelism and secularism. Probably "there is a subtle parody of Communist soap-boxing in Haze's street sermons."

3 ANON. "May 15 Is Publication Date of Novel by Flannery O'Connor, Milledgeville." Milledgeville Union-Recorder (25 April), p. 1.
An article about the publication of Wise Blood which includes remarks of praise from Caroline Gordon and recounts O'Connor's saying that she got the idea for the gorilla "host" at the movie theater from an advertisement in the Milledgeville Union-Recorder.

4 ANON. Review of Wise Blood. Kirkus 19:252.
A brief review that compares the novel to the work of Truman Capote and ends with this comment: "A grotesque--for the more zealous avantgardists; for others, a deep anesthesia."

5 ANON. Review of Wise Blood. NY (14 June), p. 118.
A capsule review. O'Connor's "dry, withered prose... suits her subject very well but makes the reader wonder if the struggle to get from one sentence to the next is worth while."

1952

6 ANON. Review of Wise Blood. United States Quarterly Book Review 8:256.
In the novel "occasional comedy yields to the grotesque, and the grotesque to horror." Hazel's "virtue...is integrity, and his failure, like that of his world, is lovelessness." O'Connor writes "in a concentrated, severely restrained manner which is basically realistic but which draws effectively, also, upon symbolism and expressionism. This first novel is unusually mature, perceptive, and imaginative."

7 ANON. "Southern Dissonance." Time (9 June), pp. 108, 110.
A review of Wise Blood. The novel is "too far from humanity" and Hazel Motes "is one of the most unlikely dullards ever to grumble through an American novel." Wise Blood often reads "as if Kafka had been set to writing the continuity for L'il Abner."

8 BREEN, MELWYN. "Satanic Satire." Saturday Night (19 July), pp. 22-23.
Wise Blood is "close to blasphemy," but O'Connor's purpose is to attack the perversions of Christianity brought on by evangelism. O'Connor's "deadpan style" and mixture of humor and horror are also mentioned. The novel reminds the reviewer of "the early Evelyn Waugh or Ronald Firbank."

9 BYAM, MILTON S. Review of Wise Blood. LJ 77:894-95.
A capsule review. "In a world in which it is obvious that he is the only Christian, Hazel Motes founds the Church Without Christ." The novel was "penned at deep-freeze temperatures"; it is a "good solid work more concerned with people and moods than story."

10 GOYEN, WILLIAM. "Unending Vengeance." NYTBR (18 May), p. 4.
A review of Wise Blood. O'Connor is praised as a "writer of power" with a "fierceness of literary gesture" and great powers of observation, yet the novel seems like "an indefensible blow delivered in the dark," and this may lead the reader to question "the credibility of such a world of horror." The characters do not seem evil, merely sour, and the novel "does not even define a world of darkness, not even that--for there has been no light to take away."

11 HARTMAN, CARL. "Jesus Without Christ." WR 17:76-80.
A review of Wise Blood. The theme is Haze's failure to find a means of rebellion that will free him. The novel is "a beautifully compact, well-ordered, and effective example" of the use of the grotesque and how it can be employed to

make us see the world by distortion. O'Connor succeeds with the grotesque because of her "deliberate kind of stylization," occasionally reminiscent of Chagall, and her "ironic detachment," which does not preclude her comprehension of the characters. The only weaknesses of the book--the reader's lack of a profound feeling for the characters or "any comforting communion...with the author"--are limitations of the grotesque itself. O'Connor will "go a long, long way" if she moves beyond such limitations.

12 LaFARGE, OLIVER. "Manic Gloom." SatR (24 May), p. 22.
A review of Wise Blood. The novel fails because Hazel Motes is "repulsive" and the tale "gloomy." O'Connor's attempt to relieve the gloom with humor fails because "her idea of humor is almost exclusively variations on the pratfall." O'Connor fails at being either humorous or satirical; perhaps she intended to write a "savage" study of a small town "with special reference to the viciousness of itinerant preachers."

13 ROSENFIELD, ISAAC. "To Win by Default." New Republic (7 July), pp. 19-20.
A review of Wise Blood. O'Connor blurs "the extremely important distinction between religious striving and mania." O'Connor obviously intended the novel to be religious, but the style and the insane characters suggest a completely opposite meaning. The novel is difficult because of its lack of surface and its detached symbolism.

14 SIMONS, JOHN W. "A Case of Possession." Commonweal (27 June), pp. 297-98.
A review of Wise Blood. The novel is praised as a "remarkably precocious beginning," but the characters are mindless, and the world of the novel is "animalistic." In most cases, O'Connor makes her metaphors fit the story, but occasionally "the symbols become detached and seem to be indulged in for their own horrendous sake." The symbolism in the novel may lead the reader to believe that Haze is redeemed, but his redemption is an unlikely possibility.

15 SMITH, MARTHA. "Georgian Pens 'Wise Blood,' A First Novel." Atlanta Journal and Atlanta Constitution (18 May), p. 7-F.
O'Connor is an "extraordinary talent" who has written a novel with "as frightening a set of characters as literature ever produced." The characters seem trapped in their fates, and the novel ends with Hazel's "personal disaster." The review ends thus: "I can hardly wait to read what Miss O'Connor may write about some happy people."

1952

16 STALLINGS, SYLVIA. "Young Writer with a Bizarre Tale to Tell." New York Herald Tribune Book Review (18 May), p. 3.

A review of Wise Blood. The novel is praised for being "at once delicate and grotesque," for convincing the reader of the reality of the strange situation, for comprehending spiritual anguish, and for placing "the fantastic in the specific." Characters like Asa Hawks and his daughter, Sabbath Lily, may seem to derive from "Dogpatch," but they more closely resemble characters in Dostoyevsky.

17 WEBSTER, HARVEY C. "Nihilism as a Faith." New Leader (23 June), pp. 23-24.

A review of Wise Blood. The novel's "characters are symbols," the plot is "slender and plausible," and O'Connor does a good job of showing contemporary man's spiritual dilemmas. Although the novel is marred by contradictions between its realistic and symbolic modes and by a "precious striving for a multiplicity of symbols," it is "an excellent first novel."

1953 A BOOKS - NONE

1953 B SHORTER WRITINGS

1 DAVIS, JOE LEE. "Outraged, or Embarrassed." Kenyon Review 15:320-26.

A review of Wise Blood. In our time any work on religious belief is likely to be such that the "tragic sense... will wear the mask of an irresponsibly sportive nihilism." In Wise Blood O'Connor has unsuccessfully tried to combine the farce of Caldwell, the satire of Waugh, and the allegory of Kafka. She is not yet skillful enough to achieve such a combination, but she does make a brave attempt.

2 LEWIS, R. W. B. "Eccentrics' Pilgrimage." HudR 6:144-50.

A review of Wise Blood and other novels, including Hemingway's The Old Man and the Sea and Ellison's Invisible Man. The novel displays "a curious tension...between a rather horridly surrealistic set of characters and incidents and a remarkably pure, luminous prose." It "has no real plot," and its "characters seem to be grotesque variations on each other." Only the novel's language "echoes the promise of health and reunion extravagantly denied to the characters by themselves." Despite this abundance of grotesquerie, Hazel does resemble the outsiders of the other novels, and "the records of their comic or tragic pilgrimages do communicate among themselves and within the same world."

1955 A BOOKS - NONE

1955 B SHORTER WRITINGS

1 ANON. "Grave and Gay." TLS (2 September), p. 505.
A brief review of Wise Blood. O'Connor is another southern writer "whose gifts, intense, erratic, and strange, demand more than a customary effort of understanding from the English reader." Even Hazel's self-blinding "to express his faith in nothingness" seems to be futile. O'Connor "may become an important writer. She is certainly a serious one."

2 ANON. Review of A Good Man Is Hard to Find. Best Sellers 15:59.
A capsule review. The stories are praised for their "directness and leanness" and for their "unsentimental compassion." Despite the horrors in the stories, O'Connor's "style is simple, characterization seems unerringly penetrating and credible, the imagery often sparkling-fresh and apt."

3 ANON. Review of A Good Man Is Hard to Find. Booklist 51:428.
A capsule review. O'Connor "pities her moral and psychological cripples, without forgetting that grotesqueness and incongruity are part of the human tragicomedy."

4 ANON. Review of A Good Man Is Hard to Find. Bookmark 14:216.
A one-sentence review: "Humor lightens tragedy in distinguished, realistic tales of the South."

5 ANON. Review of A Good Man Is Hard to Find. Kirkus 23:290-91.
A brief review that claims O'Connor's stories are too sketchy and that the longest story, "The Displaced Person," is also the best.

6 ANON. Review of A Good Man Is Hard to Find. NY (18 June), p. 93.
A capsule review. O'Connor's stories have a "lack of depth" because her characters are "mindless." O'Connor has an unreflective compassion for these characters.

7 ANON. "Such Nice People." Time (6 June), p. 114.
A review of A Good Man Is Hard to Find. O'Connor is referred to as "Ferocious Flannery" who writes of a South that is "a sort of up-to-date Tobacco Road paved right into

1955

(ANON.)
town." All of her characters are ignoble, and only in "The Displaced Person" does she, through "arty fumbling," attempt a story of symbolic significance. For a reply See 1958.B5.

8 ANON. "The Summing Up for '55." Newsweek (26 December), pp. 68-70.
A general review of books published in 1955. O'Connor's A Good Man Is Hard to Find, along with works of Eudora Welty, Shirley Ann Grau, and Mary McCarthy, demonstrates the "triumph of feminism," especially in the short story.

9 BORNHAUSER, FRED. Review of A Good Man Is Hard to Find and The Bride of the Innisfallen, by Eudora Welty. Shenandoah, 7 (Autumn), 71-81.
Unlike Welty's, O'Connor's collection is unified by a "dominant ethos," and the effect of the stories on the reader is that "perverseness leads to violence and outrage; these to katharsis; katharsis explodes the truth. Since the truth, when you can find it, really will set you free, it is thus that the light of the hope of salvation is generated in these stories." In O'Connor's stories "everybody is a stranger," which in her vision is connected with perverseness; in Welty this same theme of estrangement is connected with "subjective loneliness." Welty has "greater fluency and ease...as distinguished from the architectonic thrust of detail" in O'Connor. Highly praises "The Artificial Nigger," but feels that the first version of "The Displaced Person" is superior to the collection's version.

10 BREIT, HARVEY. "In and Out of Books." NYTBR (12 June), p. 8.
A report of some of O'Connor's comments on her craft. O'Connor doesn't regard herself as a southern writer. Reprinted 1964.B21.

11 BUTCHER, FANNY. "Ten Pokes in the Ribs with a Poisoned Dart." Chicago Sunday Tribune Magazine of Books (3 July), p. 3.
A review of A Good Man Is Hard to Find. The stories show O'Connor's "sensitivity to the world around her, individual and incisive prose, and almost an obsession with death." O'Connor avoids a nostalgic view of the South, and "the humor is always grotesque." The stories lose some of their effectiveness when read together because "the reader expects ironic violence sometime before the tale is done."

12 CARTER, THOMAS H. "Rhetoric and Southern Landscapes." Accent 15:293-97.
A review of A Good Man Is Hard to Find and Eudora Welty's The Bride of the Innisfallen. Welty's style is "more

dazzling," but her "substance, with one or two exceptions, is trivial." O'Connor has "a firm moral awareness," and her style, which is "lucid, economical, and close to actual speech," is used as "an instrument." O'Connor deals with "fragmentary, incomplete persons suffering from a frustrated or perverted religious impulse," yet her vision is not bleak. She has a "disciplined exuberance of...tone... and her fine humor reflects on her characters a fair share of saving grace." Reprinted 1968.B13.

13 ELDER, WALTER. "That Region." Kenyon Review 17:661-70.
A review of A Good Man Is Hard to Find and Eudora Welty's The Bride of the Innisfallen. O'Connor's "stories are morally absolute. She slams down direct sentence after direct sentence of growing outrage until her people immerse themselves in ignoble disasters." O'Connor "is obsessed with the sin of translating religion into the banal actions required to live," but she does offer a "glimpse of the surface" that suggests a "surpassing peace." "The Displaced Person" and "The Artificial Nigger" differ from the other stories because we sympathize with the characters. O'Connor is superior to Eudora Welty because she deals with the real South, but like Miss Welty she runs the risk of repeating the same story over and over.

14 ENGLE, PAUL and HANSFORD, MARTIN. Introduction to Prize Stories 1955: The O. Henry Awards. Edited by Paul Engle and Hansford Martin. Garden City, N. Y.: Doubleday, pp. 9-12.
The winner of the second prize, "A Circle in the Fire," shows O'Connor's skill at two of her main themes: "the exposition of evil and the celebration of justice." She is probably the most significant young writer in America.

15 FRANCIS, DALE. "Flannery O'Connor." Commonweal (12 August), p. 471.
A letter in reply to James Greene's review (1955.B17). O'Connor's viewpoint arises from her Roman Catholicism, not from one of the schools of southern writing.

16 GORDON, CAROLINE. "With a Glitter of Evil." NYTBR (12 June), p. 5.
A review of A Good Man Is Hard to Find. O'Connor resembles Maupassant in her "precision, density, and...almost alarming circumscription," but unlike Maupassant she does have a moral vision. With O'Connor, "the rural South is, for the first time, viewed by a writer whose orthodoxy matches her talent." O'Connor is "realistic" and "down to earth," but many misunderstand her because they do not see

1955

(GORDON, CAROLINE)
her characters as symbols for spiritual and social aspects of southern life.

17 GREENE, JAMES. "The Comic and the Sad." Commonweal (22 July), p. 404.
A review of A Good Man Is Hard to Find. O'Connor's characters have similarities with those of other southern writers, but they use a "rustic religiosity" to avoid despair. Although the stories suffer from a sameness in the motivations of the characters, O'Connor, "with a direct, detached style" and "a musician's ear," is honest to the mixture of "the comic and sad" in life. See 1955.B15 for a reply.

18 HICKS, GRANVILLE. "Living With Books." New Leader (15 August), p. 17.
A review of A Good Man Is Hard to Find and Eudora Welty's The Bride of the Innisfallen. O'Connor's stories are filled with characters who are physically, mentally, or spiritually defective and who "are confronted with situations to which they are inadequate." O'Connor judges life as an orthodox Christian and finds it "mean and brutish." No younger writer has shown more "originality and power." Reprinted 1970.B24.

19 HUGHES, RILEY. Review of A Good Man Is Hard to Find. CathW (October), pp. 66-67.
O'Connor "does belong to the contemporary Southern school," but her "diamond-hard, diamond-brilliant stories" also contain "a fiery rejection of Bible Beltism." "The Displaced Person" is somewhat murky, but it does make clear that "the critical touchstone is Catholicism."

20 LYNCH, JOHN A. "Isolated World." Today (October), pp. 30-31.
A review of A Good Man Is Hard to Find. O'Connor is ignored by the Catholic literary establishment because she is not pious and saccharine enough for it. O'Connor's tales have "a proper and violent climax," and she attacks "the spiritual isolations of the people of her world."

21 MARSHALL, JOHN DAVID. Review of A Good Man Is Hard to Find. LJ 80:1217.
A capsule review. O'Connor "writes smoothly and well, developing plot and delineating character with much skill."

22 PRESCOTT, ORVILLE. Review of A Good Man Is Hard to Find. NYT (10 June), p. 23.

O'Connor is one of "our most talented young writers" whose "narrative power is exceptional in an era when so many gifted young writers scorn so elementary a virtue as storytelling." Her stories are filled with horror, but the horror is never gratuitous or overdone. O'Connor "retains her sense of proportion and leaves her sordid situations with flashes of acid humor and with a feeling of human compassion." Reprinted 1964.B71.

23 RUBIN, LOUIS D., JR. "Two Ladies of the South." SR 63:671-81.

A review of A Good Man Is Hard to Find and Eudora Welty's The Bride of the Innisfallen. "Where Miss Welty's fiction hovers, where her style is veiled, shimmering, elusive, Miss O'Connor's approach is direct, precise, bounded." O'Connor resembles Erskine Caldwell in subject matter, but differs with him because of her religious concern. She resembles Carson McCullers in her sympathy for outcasts while avoiding McCullers's sentimentality. She is "a distinct, original talent."

24 STALLINGS, SYLVIA. "Flannery O'Connor: A New, Shining Talent Among Our Storytellers." New York Herald Tribune Book Review (5 June), p. 1.

A Good Man Is Hard to Find is praised for its use of the regional to communicate the universal and for its use of "significant detail." O'Connor's "reality is not pleasant," but she "has a fine sense of the comic which transforms the shocking into the funny."

25 STEGGERT, FRANK X. Review of A Good Man Is Hard to Find. Books on Trial 14 (December), 187.

O'Connor is "the most accomplished young American writer of the post-war decade." Some readers may be distressed by the "negative overtones," but O'Connor's situations are "honest and convincing," and "the shock value of her work is the result of the truth of what she has to say." O'Connor does not avoid "moral judgements," though she does not make them explicit.

26 VOGLER, LEWIS. Review of A Good Man Is Hard to Find. San Francisco Chronicle (10 July), p. 19.

Mentions O'Connor's "sardonic compassion," "her special blend of grotesque humor and tragedy," and "the uncomfortable immediacy" her stories achieve. O'Connor does not resemble McCullers or Welty as a writer, but her talent "requires comparison" with theirs.

1955

27 WYLIE, JOHN COOK. "The Unscented South." SatR (4 June), p. 15.
A review of A Good Man Is Hard to Find. O'Connor has "a sophisticate's eye view of the Deep South" and writes with detachment and control about the horrors in her stories. O'Connor is in the "first rank" of young, female American writers, but she most closely resembles Erskine Caldwell, though she is a much better artist.

1956 A BOOKS - NONE

1956 B SHORTER WRITINGS

1 ADAMS, ROBERT MARTIN. "Fiction Chronicle." HudR 8:627-32.
Includes a review of A Good Man Is Hard to Find. The stories are "Southern Gothic" or "Grand Guignol with hominy grits," which "is a bizarre and effective combination" but very limited in its range. The stories are too predictable.

2 ALDRIDGE, JOHN W. In Search of Heresy: American Literature in an Age of Conformity. New York: McGraw Hill, pp. 35-69.
In Chapter II, "The Writer in the University," attacks O'Connor as one of the new, conformist, academically trained novelists who are preferred by the literary establishment over writers such as Mailer and Styron, who are outside the academic in-group. Sees O'Connor as a southern writer whose subject is "rustic" enough to seem original and important to academic intellectuals: "she provides them with tone or chic, a little sprinkling of fake old magnolia blossoms." For a reply See 1958.B7.

3 ANON. Review of A Good Man Is Hard to Find. Grail (January), p. 59.
A brief review. O'Connor avoids "the pompous symbolism or greasy obesity of other contemporary writers." Her stories contain compassion, but she "neither pities nor condemns. She writes stories."

4 PRAZ, MARIO. "Racconti del Sud." SA 2:207-18.
Includes a review of A Good Man Is Hard to Find. O'Connor, McCullers, and Welty are the most faithful recorders of the modern South, avoiding the legend of the chivalric South found in Margaret Mitchell and Faulkner. If northern literature reflects the influence of the Puritans, southern literature seems to describe a tropical Ireland where nature is luxurious but sad, where closets have their skeletons, and where surrealism lives in the open. O'Connor's fiction suffers from a tendency towards

caricature and regional anecdote, but she and Welty have been unjustly ignored by Italian publishers.

1957 A BOOKS - NONE

1957 B SHORTER WRITINGS

1 ALPERT, HOLLIS. "Coterie Tales." SatR (19 January), p. 42.
A review of Prize Stories 1957, edited by Paul Engle with Constance Urdang. The stories selected are too intellectual and formal and represent an unwelcome, growing split between the mass audience and a "coterie audience." O'Connor's "Greenleaf," the winner of first prize, "is in the realm of Southern-type unfunny grotesque and culminates in a strained and garish climax." See 1957.B3.

2 ANON. "The Art of the Short Story: Principles and Practice in the United States." In American Writing Today: Its Independence and Vigor. Edited by Allan Angoff. New York: New York University Press, pp. 176-91.
A reprint of an undated article from the Times Literary Supplement. O'Connor is referred to as one of the best young southern short story writers.

3 ENGLE, PAUL. Introduction to Prize Stories 1957: The O. Henry Awards. Edited by Paul Engle and Constance Urdang. Garden City, N. Y.: Doubleday, pp. 8-12.
O'Connor's "Greenleaf," which won the first prize, is praised for its combination of "an authentic expression of character and society with a witty and ironic point of view." The details in the story are perfectly placed, and the story deals with "economic and social pressures on people." See 1957.B1.

1958 A BOOKS - NONE

1958 B SHORTER WRITINGS

1 ANON. "Motley Special: Interview with Flannery O'Connor." Motley (Spring Hill College, Mobile, Alabama), Spring, pp. 29-31.
Includes O'Connor's comments on the Catholic audience, on "pious" writers, and on Catholic censorship. She also discusses the question of what subject a writer should treat, the problem of a writer's prejudices, and the scope of the short story. She praises J. F. Powers and Graham Greene.

1958

2 COLBY, VINETA. "Flannery O'Connor." Wilson Library Bulletin 32:682.

A discussion of O'Connor's life and literary career. O'Connor's "fiction is stark, powerful, at times terrifying, but it is so not as Southern writing but as writing which reflects a stern moral judgment and a deep religious faith." This article is reprinted in the 1958 Current Biography, pp. 317-18.

3 ESTY, WILLIAM. "In America, Intellectual Bomb Shelters." Commonweal (7 March), pp. 586-88.

A hostile review of younger American writers and their inability to create art out of the political reality of the times. O'Connor is referred to as a member of the "Paul Bowles-Flannery O'Connor cult of the Gratuitous Grotesque." For replies See 1959.B5 and 1961.B5.

4 GORDON, CAROLINE. "Flannery O'Connor's Wise Blood." Crit 2, ii:3-10.

There are similarities between Wise Blood and the works of other southern writers, especially Capote's Other Voices, Other Rooms, but Capote's novel "reads like a case history" when compared with Wise Blood because O'Connor's novel has a theological basis. Unlike most modern writers, O'Connor knows theology and has Hazel concern himself with "the union of the divine with the human." O'Connor's characters "are victims of a rejection of the scheme of Redemption," and Haze in particular may be an Existentialist. O'Connor's vision is implicit and perhaps unconscious; it is "Blakean, not through symbol as such but through the actuality of human behavior."

5 HART, JANE. "Strange Earth, the Stories of Flannery O'Connor." GaR 12:215-22.

O'Connor "does definitely belong to the school of Southern Gothic writers," but she is a superior artist because her stories also contain a "rich red-clay reality." O'Connor "admits nothing light or beautiful" into her stories, but Time (See 1955.B7) is wrong in calling her sarcastic, since she treats her "maimed souls" with "mild compassion." O'Connor is indebted to Poe's dictums on the short story, but her characters, unlike Poe's, "seem unimpressed by the giant footsteps about to trample blindly over them"; they are victims of "blind Fate," of a "senseless evil brooding over people."

6 QUINN, SISTER M. BERNETTA, O.S.F. "View From A Rock: The Fiction of Flannery O'Connor and J. F. Powers." Crit 2, ii:19-27.

Both O'Connor and J. F. Powers are Catholic writers, but Powers "with somewhat less of spiritual poise, confidence, and reliance upon the assets that his faith offers him." O'Connor piles up horrors in her fiction, while Powers "writes of everyday incidents" that are also horrible "because they represent treason to an ideal." Powers's details are more obviously Catholic, but O'Connor's "whole world" is suffused with religious vision, and she tends to have more compassion for her characters. Both writers are honest recorders of what they see, but O'Connor has more depth.

7 RUBIN, LOUIS D., JR. "Flannery O'Connor: A Note on Literary Fashions." Crit 2, ii:11-18.

A reply to John Aldridge's attack on O'Connor (See 1956.B2). O'Connor's fiction is Catholic as well as southern, and it must be dealt with in itself, not merely as an example of some literary fashion. O'Connor "has never been known to deal in magnolia blossoms. The langugage is precise, bounded, direct, oddly masculine." Although her region and religion are important in her fiction, "The Displaced Person" shows that O'Connor's theme is the universal one of "men...coming to terms or failing to come to terms with the evil and tragedy of life."

8 WEDGE, GEORGE F. "Two Bibliographies: Flannery O'Connor and J. F. Powers." Crit 2, ii:59-70.

A bibliography of books and magazine fiction by O'Connor, of her articles and reviews, of biographical material on O'Connor, and of reviews and articles about her work.

1959 A BOOKS - NONE

1959 B SHORTER WRITINGS

1 ANON. Review of The Violent Bear It Away. Kirkus 27:931.

The novel "can be read as an allegory: a struggle for a soul, a conflict between evils." O'Connor specializes in "southern horror stories."

2 COINDREAU, MAURICE-EDGAR. Introduction to La Sagesse dans le Sang, by Flannery O'Connor. Translated by Maurice-Edgar Coindreau. Paris: Gallimard, pp. vii-xxiii.

An introduction to the French edition of Wise Blood that relates the lives of some of the more notorious American evangelists and briefly discusses treatments of this

(COINDREAU, MAURICE-EDGAR)
religious phenomenon in American fiction. O'Connor as a Catholic is able to see evangelism for the horror it is, and she has written more penetratingly about it than any other American writer. The characters in this novel are sacrilegious caricatures, and everything in the novel is grotesque. To describe this tragicomic world, O'Connor chose the only language possible, "un humour noir, allié à une brutalité qui n'a peur ni des mots ni des scènes."

3 FRAKES, JAMES R. and ISADORE TRASCHEN. Short Fiction: A Critical Collection. Englewood Cliffs, N. J.: Prentice-Hall, pp. 118-20.

A brief analysis of "The Artificial Nigger." Mr. Head "first suffered the irony of his tragic fall; he now is blessed with the irony of his resurrection and redemption." O'Connor uses subtle irony in her handling of black-white relations, since the statue of the black is "an analogue of Christ," and thus "the oppressed is the means of redeeming the oppressor." Also, she avoids sentimentality and false dichotomies in her treatment of race. See 1969.B16 for additional remarks.

4 LOCKRIDGE, BETSY. "An Afternoon With Flannery O'Connor." Atlanta Journal and Atlanta Constitution Magazine (1 November), pp. 38-40.

Recounts a visit with O'Connor in Milledgeville. O'Connor decries the mystique surrounding writers, describes her work as humorous, and states that her religion is valuable to her as a writer: "I can apply to a judgment higher than my own--I'm not limited to what I personally feel or think." She believes southern writing is the best in the nation. Conrad is O'Connor's favorite writer, and O'Connor discounts the importance of her illness.

5 McCOWN, ROBERT, S. J. "Flannery O'Connor and the Reality of Sin." CathW (January), pp. 285-91.

Reviewers of A Good Man Is Hard to Find have misread O'Connor, especially William Esty (See 1958.B3). O'Connor is interested in rendering reality as honestly as possible and in describing the same "palpable reality of sin" as European Catholic writers. O'Connor is a master of wit and satire, yet she has "compassion for those whom she satirizes." Her humor is reminiscent of Chaucer's, where the humorous and the serious is subtly combined. Her work "contains a delicately balanced, Christian humanism."

6 O'CONNOR, WILLIAM VAN. "The Grotesque in Modern American Fiction." CE 20:342-46.
Modern writers use the grotesque to protest against the cult of progress and to reveal the violent, irrational, and uncontrollable forces in human life. The grotesque has been prevalent in southern literature because of the "abnormality" caused by poverty and the persistence of "a code that was no longer applicable." O'Connor differs from Faulkner and Warren because she believes in Christianity, though "her dramatizations of these doctrines seem incongruous in the context of the society she is describing." O'Connor shares with many modern American writers a suspicion of the city, and in her use of the grotesque, "one finds Catholic orthodoxy erupting inside an amoral commercialism and an ill-defined and sometimes not very vigorous Protestantism." Writers of the grotesque disturb "our sense of established order," yet search for "the sublime" in "the anti-poetic and ugly" and try to give us a new, "more flexible ordering." See also 1962.B22.

1960 A BOOKS - NONE

1960 B SHORTER WRITINGS

1 ANON. "God - Intoxicated Hillbillies." Time (29 February), pp. 118, 121.
A review of The Violent Bear It Away. The novel is a "horror story of faith" where "the characters are for or against God with a kind of vindictiveness that...must make even Him uneasy." Although O'Connor's treatment of her characters "is based in religious seriousness, it seldom seems to rise above an ironic jape."

2 ANON. Review of The Violent Bear It Away. Booklist 56:478.
A capsule review. The novel will be admired for "its perfection of style," but some will be repelled by "many unpleasant and grotesque episodes."

3 ANON. Review of The Violent Bear It Away. Christian Century (1 June), p. 672.
A capsule review. O'Connor "can make the strange world of the Tennessee backcountry...frighteningly real." The novel is "genuinely funny...but like all great comedy it carries within it deep, haunting tragedy."

4 ANON. Review of The Violent Bear It Away. EJ 49:275.
A capsule review. The novel is "bizarre," and in it "arson and murder are scarcely reprehensible." The reader

(ANON.)
is "perplexed but not unaware of the originality and vigor of the author's prose."

5 ANON. Review of The Violent Bear It Away. Information (Paulist Fathers). (April), pp. 57-58.
Mentions O'Connor's sparsity of form, her nearly-grotesque characterizations, and her use of "violence and a somewhat macabre humor." The reviewer praises the novel, yet doubts that it will appeal to most readers.

6 ANON. Review of The Violent Bear It Away. NY (19 March), p. 179.
A capsule review. The novel is a "dark, ingrown, Gothic tale," and O'Connor's style, "which is packed with 'trembling' pink moons and people who have 'crushed' shadows, fits her material perfectly."

7 ANON. Review of The Violent Bear It Away. Punch (5 October), p. 505.
A capsule review. The novel is "more original than convincing, but not merely a curiosity."

8 ANON. Review of The Violent Bear It Away. VQR 36:lxxii, lxxiv.
A capsule review. In the novel the violent are the religious ones. O'Connor shows herself as "a major talent."

9 ANON. "Set Fair For Happiness?" TLS (14 October), p. 666.
A brief review of The Violent Bear It Away. The novel seems southern in its violence, but its "spiritual discords" remind the reader of The Turn of the Screw, though O'Connor writes without nuance. O'Connor has "extraordinary power and virtuosity, but her sophisticated pessimism creates a number of unrewarding moral culs-de-sac."

10 BALLIFF, ALGENE. "A Southern Allegory." Commentary (October), pp. 358-62.
A review of The Violent Bear It Away. The novel concerns young Tarwater's doomed quest to find an identity of his own. In the novel O'Connor is telling us "that the primitive Protestant experience is a breaking loose into consciousness and activity of fantasies which can be recognized as unconscious components of the modern experiences of alienation and self-creation." In this case the fantasy is primarily one of "homosexual incest," which is demonstrated by the references to seeds, by the numerous violations of the self, and by the literal rape near the

end of the novel. Despite the novel's "fantastic brilliance," the reader remains unconvinced because O'Connor presents these fantasies "too abruptly, too nakedly."

11 BERGER, YVES. Review of La Sagesse dans le Sang. L'Express (25 February), pp. 30-31.

A review of the French translation of Wise Blood. O'Connor is praised for showing the social reality of evangelistic fundamentalism and for demonstrating the psychological causes for the calling of prophecy. O'Connor has the talent to enlarge her fictional world and become another Faulkner.

12 CANFIELD, FRANCIS X. Review of The Violent Bear It Away. Critic 18 (April-May), 45.

The novel will seem "a gratuitous distortion" if the reader doesn't remember that a writer must be honest to reality. O'Connor is concerned with redemption, and in the novel "Christ's mission has been distorted by ignorance and idiocy." Nevertheless, "a compassion suffuses the whole."

13 CHARLES, GERDA. Review of The Violent Bear It Away. New Statesman (24 September), pp. 445-46.

A brief review. O'Connor is "a true and masterly novelist" whose "people live entirely on their own without her."

14 CREEKMORE, HUBERT. "A Southern Baptism." New Leader (30 May), pp. 20-21.

A review of The Violent Bear It Away that praises O'Connor's language, her accurate eye, and her wit, but finds the novel lacking in form, being more like a short story "expanded by repetitions and relatively unimportant diversions." The characters are narrow, and if the novel is supposed to be about redemption, no one in the novel presents redemption in a positive manner. The novel is a thesis novel without a clear thesis.

15 CRONIN, PAT SOMERS. Review of The Violent Bear It Away. Ave Maria (2 July), p. 25.

O'Connor has "obvious talent and clever humor" and her intent is religious, but the novel is not for "the average reader." O'Connor's manipulation of chronology is bothersome, and the homosexual rape is "unfortunate and unnecessary."

16 CZAPLEWSKI, BEN. "Sin and Salvation." Nexus (Mt. St. Mary's College, Winona, Minnesota). (October), p. 7.

1960

(CZAPLEWSKI, BEN)
A review of The Violent Bear It Away. Like Faulkner, O'Connor transcends "pure sensationalism" and creates characters who "are believable, if somewhat grotesque, human beings." Briefly discusses young Tarwater's decision to accept religious violence instead of Rayber's "sterility."

17 DANIEL, FRANK. "Good Writer Must Set His Book In a Region Which Is Familiar." Atlanta Journal (28 March), p. 27.
O'Connor's "prophet-freaks...are as indigenous to Georgia and Georgia literature as poverty." Includes comments by O'Connor on the importance of using a region, not to write regional literature but to write of the "realm of mystery."

18 DAVIDSON, DONALD. "A Prophet Went Forth." NYTBR (28 February), p. 4.
A review of The Violent Bear It Away. With this novel we know that O'Connor's fiction is "medicine...for the soul, and is not just Southern calomel and Epsom salts." This is O'Connor's best work, but the "meaning is muddled," probably because "the three main characters are so isolated from the general human context." They seem "irresponsible creatures belonging to some arbitrary world of fantasy."

19 DIDION, JOAN. "Two Up for America." NatR (9 April), pp. 240-41.
A review of The Violent Bear It Away. The novel is "difficult, perilously stylized...at every point controlled by Miss O'Connor's hard intelligence, by her coherent metaphysical view of experience, and by the fact that she is above all a writer, which is something different from a person who writes a book."

20 DOLLARHIDE, LOUIS. "Significant New Work by Flannery O'Connor." Jackson (Miss.) Daily News-Clarion Ledger (27 March), p. 6-D.
The Violent Bear It Away is praised for its characterization and style, its combination of tragedy and humor, and its compassion. O'Connor's artistry has led her to write "a tale of violence which is in itself not violent; a tale, containing all the elements of a decadent art, which is still not decadent; a story of religious experience which may be, not religion at all, but madness."

21 DRAKE, ROBERT Y., JR. "Miss O'Connor and the Scandal of Redemption." Modern Age 4:428-30.
A review of The Violent Bear It Away. O'Connor continues her "theologically orthodox" vision, contrasting her

"human grotesques," who often achieve salvation, with her "arch-fiends," the modern rationalists. Despite its achievement, the novel is "imperfectly realized," perhaps because O'Connor is primarily a short story writer or because she fails to develop "the 'tragic' potentialities inherent in the character of Rayber."

22 DUHAMEL, P. ALBERT. "Flannery O'Connor's Violent View of Reality." CathW (February), pp. 280-85.

Young Tarwater in The Violent Bear It Away progresses from seeing "only the part of reality that he wants to see" to a "prophetic or violent view of reality" that allows him to see beneath the surface of life. The novel treats the "encounter between a merely verbal, distorted and distorting view of things, and an intuitive, committed view of reality." In such a clash, the "violent bear all before them." O'Connor's work is not gratuitously grotesque or humorous; her directness, her use of only the essentials of characterization and setting, and her lack of sentimentality are all a result of her prophetic vision. Reprinted 1968.A1.

23 EMERSON, DONALD C. Review of The Violent Bear It Away. ArQ 16:284-86.

The novel is based on O'Connor's Christianity and contains a "sense of inescapable destiny." O'Connor is centrally concerned with the conflict of faith and "vacuous worldliness." She is a master of dialogue and employs a "mirthless humor" that does not preclude "compassionate understanding." She is not a writer like Tennessee Williams because her characters are not "pathetic." O'Connor's Christianity allows her a vision where each work "contributes to a total effect that is larger than the individual piece."

24 ENGLE, PAUL. "Insight, Richness, Humor, and Chills." Chicago Sunday Tribune Magazine of Books (6 March), p. 4.

The Violent Bear It Away is praised for its style and psychological insights. O'Connor's "humor, and her quiet and disenchanted view of people, everywhere shine in the book, lighting up the grave darkness in which the incidents take place."

25 FERRIS, SUMNER J. "The Outside and the Inside: Flannery O'Connor's The Violent Bear It Away." Crit 3, ii:11-19.

A review of the novel that notes the continuities with O'Connor's earlier fiction, but also notes that the novel has greater unity of structure than Wise Blood and "smoother and more flexible" rhythms. This novel is a study of souls,

1960

(FERRIS, SUMNER J.)
not personalities, and it derives its power from the clash of belief and unbelief. Although the baptism of Bishop is a result of Divine Providence, the characters have free will, and both Rayber and young Tarwater choose their own damnation. O'Connor "has shown that a Christian tragedy can be written; for in her novel fate and doom do not conspire against man."

26 FIEDLER, LESLIE A. Love and Death in the American Novel. New York: Criterion Books, pp. 449-51.
O'Connor and Elizabeth Spencer are described as second generation "distaff Faulknerians" whose fiction derives from the gothicism of early Faulkner.

27 FLINT, R. W. Review of The Violent Bear It Away. PR 27:378.
There are two sides to the novel: "a delightful, gothic mortuary comedy" and "a very serious and on the whole successful ethico-religio-mythical drama." The novel is O'Connor's best work.

28 FUGINA, KATHERINE, FAYE RIVARD and MARGARET STEIN. "An Interview with Flannery O'Connor." Censer (Fall), pp. 28-30.
O'Connor denies there is much brutality in her stories, says she has no talent for writing plays, and says that blacks aren't prominent in her fiction because "I don't understand them the way I do white people." She says that she emphasized uncle-nephew relations in The Violent Bear It Away because she wanted to avoid "the son searching for the father sort of thing." Also includes her comments on "The River," on symbolism, especially her use of the wooden leg in "Good Country People" and of the sun in much of her fiction, and on the importance of imagination and detail in writing fiction. "The Artificial Nigger" is O'Connor's favorite story.

29 GARDINER, HAROLD C. "A Tragic New Image of Man." America (5 March), pp. 682-83.
A review of The Violent Bear It Away. O'Connor leaves the interpretation of young Tarwater's final fate up to the reader, but it is clear that her theme is man's alienation from God. Some see the novel as humorous, but the humor is grotesque, and the novel is tragic.

30 GORDON, CAROLINE and ALLEN TATE, eds. The House of Fiction: An Anthology of the Short Story with Commentary. 2d rev. ed. New York: Charles Scribner's Sons, pp. 382-86.

A commentary on Capote's "The Headless Hawk" and O'Connor's "A Good Man Is Hard to Find." Although the fiction of these two writers has many similarities, O'Connor's implicit theology allows her a "direct gaze" at her characters, whereas Capote's work, for all its stylistic brilliance, is weakened by "a highly romantic style" that separates the reader from the action of the fiction. Also, Capote's "characters move through the same mists of despair and doom but we are not given to understand why they are so fated." O'Connor is sometimes inconsistent in her mode of narration, but her "prose...is...a subtle and powerful instrument with which she has achieved effects produced by no other writer of her generation."

31 GREENE, JAMES. "The Redemptive Tradition of Southern Rural Life." Commonweal (15 April), pp. 67-68.

A review of The Violent Bear It Away. O'Connor is "one of the country's most interesting creative talents." Her "style and concerns remind one of the best in French Catholic writing; yet she has found in her own native Georgia the sources and methods that mark her as uniquely American." The key character is old Tarwater, who reminds us of the biblical prophets.

32 H. B. H. "A Southern Tale by Flannery O'Connor." Springfield (Mass.) Republican (6 March), p. 50.

In The Violent Bear It Away O'Connor "introduces a deft blend of humor, pathos, satire, and grotesquerie, together with some vivid pictorial effects." The point of the novel is "that we are shaped by our environments and therefore should be charitable in our views of others, whose backgrounds and customs may be quite different from our own."

33 HICKS, GRANVILLE. "Southern Gothic With a Vengeance." SatR (27 February), p. 18.

A review of The Violent Bear It Away. This novel, better than Wise Blood, is "first-rate." The novel is filled with grotesqueries, but O'Connor forces us to believe in her characters, who are "not merely grotesque." Rayber and young Tarwater are torn between "fanaticism" and a sterile rationalism, but O'Connor shows compassion for them. Reprinted 1970.B24.

34 HOGAN, WILLIAM. "Flannery O'Connor's Tennessee Comedy." San Francisco Chronicle (25 February), p. 31.

A review of The Violent Bear It Away. The novel avoids the stock figures and settings of popular southern fiction, and it is not a typical southern "exercise in decadence and degeneracy." The novel "is in the Faulknerian tradition"

(HOGAN, WILLIAM)
and is "gay and stimulating" despite "its backwoods atmosphere and unwashed characters." The novel reminds the reviewer "of a concert by a superior hillbilly band."

35 HOY, CYRUS and WALTER SULLIVAN, eds. "An Interview with Flannery O'Connor and Robert Penn Warren." _Vagabond_ (Vanderbilt) 4 (February), 9-16.
Includes O'Connor's comments on the creation of "The Artificial Nigger" and "The Life You Save May Be Your Own." O'Connor and Warren attack the mystique of the writer, and O'Connor claims it is easier to write of the blemished than the cheerful. O'Connor believes in the compatibility of theology with literature "if you're a writer in the first place," has no interest in "fable or myth," and sees the South becoming more secular because "everybody wants the privilege of being as abstract as the next man." She contrasts her fiction with that of Capote and McCullers and admits the dangers of regional literature, but "if you're a real writer you can avoid that sort of thing." Reprinted 1966.B22.

36 HUNTER, ANNA C. Review of _The Violent Bear It Away_. _Savannah Morning News Magazine_ (21 February), p. 13.
Praises the novel for its "peculiar poignancy" and sees it as revealing the "canker" within fundamentalist fanaticism.

37 LAURAS, A. Review of _La Sagesse dans le Sang_. _Études_ 306:152.
A brief review of the French translation of _Wise Blood_. Haze's is the principle story in the novel, but the book's real subject is "toute cette moderne cour des miracles grouillant autour de lui." The reader may find the book difficult, but he should remember that O'Connor uses shock to communicate her Christian message to an unbelieving world.

38 LEVINE, PAUL. Review of _The Violent Bear It Away_. _Jubilee_ (May), p. 52.
O'Connor is basically a short story writer, but the novel is "a work of shattering power." The novel deals with "those who seek to be their own Salvation, only to lose it, and those who grapple with their Redemption, only to accept it."

39 LODGE, DAVID. Review of _The Violent Bear It Away_. _Tablet_ 214:1176.
A brief review. The novel contains "delicious comedy," but the end is "inevitably tragic." As with other southern

writers, the world created is "monstrous and mishapen [sic],"
yet O'Connor's style and power compel the reader's
attention.

40 MERCIER, VIVIAN. "Sex, Success and Salvation." HudR
13:449-56.

A review of The Violent Bear It Away and other works. The "characters are Faulknerian grotesques." The novel fails because "the realistic convention in which it is written jars too sharply against the basic improbability of the plot."

41 MILLER, NOLAN. "Of the Many, a Few: A Fiction Summary." AR 20:248-56.

A very brief mention of The Violent Bear It Away. O'Connor succeeds as well with this novel as she had previously with her short stories.

42 NYREN, DOROTHY. Review of The Violent Bear It Away. LJ 85:146.

A capsule review. The novel contains "too much argument, too little convincing action, to carry this rather macabre tale to a successful conclusion." O'Connor "writes...more as one driven by a moral need than as an artist."

43 PICKREL, PAUL. Review of The Violent Bear It Away. Harper's (April), p. 114.

The novel is "too schematic"; nevertheless, "if the hand of the manipulator is too evident in the book, it must be confessed that it is a very gifted hand."

44 PRESCOTT, ORVILLE. Review of The Violent Bear It Away. NYT (24 February), p. 35.

O'Connor claims that her "gruesome concoctions" have "the most exalted intentions," but in The Violent Bear It Away the reader faces "a grotesque and bizarre central situation that never seems real." O'Connor "is a sort of literary white witch." Reprinted 1964.B71.

45 QUINN, JOHN J., S.J. Review of The Violent Bear It Away. Best Sellers 19:414-15.

O'Connor uses shock, as in her converting the words of the title into "a shocking truth." The novel is "tragic-comic" and concerns young Tarwater's struggle with Rayber and with his mission. Although "Rayber is woefully wrong," O'Connor "cannot presume to offer any answer" to the question of whether he, as a representative modern man, is a sinner. Young Tarwater does not want to believe "that Christ is more than pure spirit," but the Devil teaches

1960

(QUINN, JOHN J., S. J.)
"Tarwater what it means to deny 'the bread of life.'" For an expanded version of this review see 1963.B18.

46 ROGERS, W. G. "Rich Material Used by Savannah Writer." Augusta Chronicle-Herald (13 March).
A review of The Violent Bear It Away that claims the novel's strength comes from O'Connor's use of "some of the most richly seasoned material available to a novelist."

47 ROSENBERGER, COLEMAN. "In a Bizarre Backcountry." New York Herald Tribune Book Review (28 February), p. 13.
A review of The Violent Bear It Away. O'Connor "writes in the well-worn tradition of Southern grotesques, but to the form she brings much individual vigor and imagery, occasional humor of sorts and some arresting theological symbols." The novel concerns prophecy and is "a fairly explicit parable of the twentieth century." The novel, however, demands careful reading.

48 RUTHERFORD, MARJORY. "Georgia Author Scores Again." Atlanta Journal and Atlanta Constitution (28 February), p. 2-E.
A review of The Violent Bear It Away. The novel is "harrowing and grim in theme and characterization" and contains "the blend of satire and compassion that are this writer's own." The novel is evidence of O'Connor's great ability and demonstrates her talent for using her region to write works of universal import.

49 SCHOTT, WEBSTER. "The Struggle of Ideals is Reality." Kansas City Star (5 March), p. 7.
The Violent Bear It Away is a "neo-Gothic tale" that can stand comparison with Faulkner's works. O'Connor is trying to show "a life in which idea and passion alternately rule action"; she is not interested in showing us the normal but rather the reality of madness. The weakness of the novel is O'Connor's lack of concern for "larger social responsibilities."

50 SULLIVAN, SISTER BEDE, O.S.B. "Flannery O'Connor and the Dialogue Decade." Catholic Library World 31:518, 521.
A review of The Violent Bear It Away. This novel "represents dialogue at the elite fiction level." O'Connor poses two choices for man, "God or nothing," and in doing so she is starting a dialogue with various kinds of Catholics: "the timid, the lazy, the critical." O'Connor "carries Catholic literature a pace beyond the achievements of Mauriac, Greene, and Waugh" and thus also helps the Catholic dialogue with the rest of the world.

51 _____. "Prophet in the Wilderness." Today (March), pp. 36-37.
A review of The Violent Bear It Away. O'Connor is praised for her religious vision, which is based on "sound theological dogma," her "stark and naked realism," her avoidance of sentimentality, and her uniqueness.

52 SULLIVAN, KATHLEEN E. Review of The Violent Bear It Away. Fonthill Dial (College of Mount Saint Vincent) 37 (May), 38.
Mentions the novel's "original, vigorous style" and its interest in psychology, especially the psychology of the abnormal. With young Tarwater, the novel presents us with a "'new' image of man [that] seems to be another in the list of victims of degeneracy and sin, common now in twentieth century literature, perhaps too common."

53 THORP, WILLARD. American Writing in the Twentieth Century. Cambridge, Mass.: Harvard University Press, p. 234.
Passing reference to O'Connor as one of the younger members of the "Southern Renaissance."

54 _____. "Suggs and Sut in Modern Dress: The Latest Chapter in Southern Humor." MissQ 13:169-75.
Although no direct link has yet been documented between the older southern humor tradition and such recent southern humorists as Faulkner, Caldwell, Capote, and O'Connor, there are several similarities between the old and the new. Both deal with unrespectable characters, and there is a conflict "between the untamable ones and the upholders of law and order." Both incidentally satirize the respectable, and both employ "a grim and outlandish fantasy."

55 TRAYNOR, JOHN J. Review of The Violent Bear It Away. Extension (July), p. 26.
The novel may be "more allegory...than fiction," but it "is enthralling and grotesque, and is of the sort that is appreciated more only by rereading." By the end of the novel young "Tarwater's catharsis is complete"; he has escaped both the "fiery brimstone patch" of his great-uncle's religion and the forces of evil.

56 TURNER, MARGARET. "Brenda Award and Missiles to Orbit at Theta Sig Fete." Atlanta Journal and Atlanta Constitution (24 April), p. 15-G.
An article on O'Connor's winning Theta Sigma Phi's award "for outstanding achievement in the literary field." Includes comments by O'Connor on the importance of region and on her belief that southern literature is currently the best in the country.

1960

57 TURNER, MARGARET. "Visit to Flannery O'Connor Proves a Novel Experience." Atlanta Journal and Atlanta Constitution (29 May).
Recounts a visit with O'Connor in Milledgeville. O'Connor claimed her characters were "at the same time drawn from life and entirely imaginary." She said that writers who do not agree with the majority's values must use shock in their writing.

58 WALTER, SARAH. "Strange Prophets of Flannery O'Connor." Censer (Spring), pp. 5-12.
O'Connor uses her region to write about all of America, and her Christianity allows her to see "the good in spite of and, in fact, through the bad." O'Connor has three major themes: the fight of good and evil, "the isolation of man," and "the theme of redemption...and belief in the goodness of man." Her characters show "the negative and the positive aspects of the Redemption" and are always involved in some quest. O'Connor's talent for description, dialogue, and humor, which relieves the horror, is also mentioned.

59 WARNKE, FRANK J. "A Vision Deep and Narrow." New Republic (14 March), pp. 18-19.
A review of The Violent Bear It Away. The novel is "a work of compelling power," yet "the final impression the book leaves is one of crankiness and provincialism." The work is very southern in its settings and characters, its combination of realism and allegory, and its reliance on theology. The tension between a sterile atheism and a "destructive and mad" religiousness is interesting, but Rayber is "a straw man," and O'Connor's favoring the mad "won't work."

1961 A BOOKS - NONE

1961 B SHORTER WRITINGS

1 BOWEN, ROBERT O. "Hope vs. Despair in the New Gothic Novel." Renascence 13:147-52.
A hostile review of The Violent Bear It Away. This "novel is distinctly anti-Catholic in being a thorough point-by-point dramatic argument against Free Will, Redemption, and Divine Justice." The style of the novel is self-conscious and artificial, and "a good deal of the stage paraphernalia is Southern Gothic." Like many modern writers, O'Connor is an enemy of hope and thus an enemy of literature itself. For replies See 1962.B21 and 1965.B23.

2 CUNLIFFE, MARCUS. The Literature of the United States. 2d rev. ed. Baltimore: Penguin Books, p. 341.

Brief reference to O'Connor in a chapter on contemporary writers. There have been good, new writers in America since 1945, but these writers find it difficult to escape the dominance of older writers. In the South, O'Connor and Peter Taylor have produced "excellent fiction," but "Faulkner and one or two older writers" still dominate the scene.

3 DONNER, ROBERT. "She Writes Powerful Fiction." Sign (March), pp. 46-48.

A recounting of a visit with O'Connor in Milledgeville. O'Connor does not live as a recluse, has no theory of literature, and reads few novels, with the exception of Dostoyevsky and Hawthorne. She is surprised that critics accuse her of a lack of compassion. Includes several details about the O'Connors' farm. O'Connor's mother "sold the timber rights to her trees to a lumber company," and "she employs a Polish refugee family and several Negro laborers to run the place." O'Connor's characters have an "earthiness and quality of permanence" that is very southern.

4 FANCHER, BETSY. "Authoress Flannery O'Connor is Evidence of Georgia's Bent to the Female Writer." Atlanta Constitution (21 April), p. 27.

An account of O'Connor's visit to the Agnes Scott College in Atlanta. When asked why Georgia's best writers have been women, O'Connor replied: "Women just have more time." She also said that she spent all her time working on her fiction and that a writer doesn't have to be topical or political.

5 FARNHAM, JAMES F. "The Grotesque in Flannery O'Connor." America (13 May), pp. 277-81.

A reply to William Esty's article (See 1958.B3). O'Connor uses the grotesque because she has a talent for it and "because she sees reality without grace as grotesque." Characters such as "Hazel Motes, the Bible salesman, The Misfit, Tom T. Shiftlet, and Marion Tarwater are so warped that she cannot conceive of their being saved." All of these pathetic characters find "redemption in evil." Reprinted 1964.B33.

6 GOSSETT, THOMAS F. "The Religious Quest." SWR 46:86-87.

In The Violent Bear It Away O'Connor is not involved "with the degeneracy theme developed by Caldwell and

1961

(GOSSETT, THOMAS F.)
Faulkner," and though she is a Catholic, she does not "inject dogmatic theology into her stories." Her fiction, however, is religious and concerns "off-center" characters. The novel is O'Connor's most ambitious work and "deals with the theme of the religious quest more imaginatively than any other contemporary American novel," but the characterization of old Tarwater is too extreme, so his religion often seems "mere bigotry."

7 HASSAN, IHAB. Radical Innocence: Studies in the Contemporary American Novel. Princeton: Princeton University Press, pp. 4, 79-80, 152, 332.

In the third chapter, on the hero as victim, claims that in Wise Blood Hazel Motes "gives up his very salvation"; nevertheless, "the victim of a grotesque nihilism remains the pinpoint of light in a society too smug both in its scepticism and belief." In Wise Blood and The Violent Bear It Away negation is one of God's weapons against "his [sic] Enemy." In the fifth chapter, on protagonists ruled by necessity, The Violent Bear It Away is mentioned as a novel with a "pattern of tragic irony."

8 HOFFMAN, FREDERICK J. "The Sense of Place." In South: Modern Southern Literature in Its Cultural Setting. Edited by Louis D. Rubin, Jr. and Robert D. Jacobs. Garden City, N. Y.: Doubleday.

See 1974.B13 for reprint of edition. Essay is described there.

9 HOOD, EDWARD M. "A Prose Altogether Alive." Kenyon Review 23:170-72.

In The Violent Bear It Away O'Connor's skillful prose and careful technique create "the full illusion of reality." Her talent suggests "the rendering and organizing powers of James, the satiric detachment of Flaubert, the close focus and economical progression d'ffet [sic] of Ford Madox Ford." The novel centers on the "Dostoevskian" problem of Bishop, and the problem is treated honestly and fairly. O'Connor turns the everyday world into "a living state of epiphany" and shows "the sudden penetration of grace, illuminating the natural order."

10 KILEY, FREDERICK S. Review of The Violent Bear It Away. Clearing House 36:188.

A prophet usually lies somewhere within a character of O'Connor's, but O'Connor does not make clear "the psychological necessities that provoke the action." Most of the characters "talk with the stunned wonder of men who have looked far into regions where men have no right to look."

11 LEVINE, PAUL. "The Violent Art." Jubilee (December), pp. 50-52.

O'Connor's comments on her use of violence and the grotesque apply to other modern American writers, since they use these materials to make us aware of the moral failings of our world. This emphasis on violence and the grotesque has its antecedents in earlier American literature and springs from the writers' perception of the "corruption of the perfect." These writers, however, do not despair, since "creation...must be an act of affirmation."

12 MIZENER, ARTHUR. "Some Kinds of Modern Novel." SR 69:154-64.

Includes a review of The Violent Bear It Away. The novel tells us Tarwater and his great-uncle "are saved, but all we are shown is their savage ignorance." O'Connor reverses Tobacco Road by turning a land of degradation into "a breeding ground for prophets," perhaps because she is too loyal to the South.

13 QUINN, JOHN J., S.J. Review of A Memoir of Mary Ann. Best Sellers 21:394.

O'Connor's introduction helps readers see "the meaning illuminating the picture."

14 RUBIN, LOUIS D., JR. and ROBERT D. JACOBS. "Introduction: Southern Writing and the Changing South." In South: Modern Southern Literature in Its Cultural Setting. Edited by Louis D. Rubin, Jr. and Robert D. Jacobs. Garden City, N. Y.: Doubleday.

See 1974.B19 for reprint. Essay is described there.

15 SULLIVAN, WALTER. "The Continuing Renascence: Southern Fiction in the Fifties." In South: Modern Southern Literature in Its Cultural Setting. Edited by Louis D. Rubin, Jr. and Robert D. Jacobs. Garden City, N. Y.: Doubleday.

See 1974.B20 for reprint. Essay is described there.

16 THOMAS, ESTHER. "Flannery O'Connor Helps Nuns Write Child's Story." Atlanta Journal (10 August).

An article on Mary Ann and on O'Connor's helping the Dominican Sisters with A Memoir of Mary Ann by writing the introduction and by sending the book to her publisher, who to her surprise accepted it for publication.

1961

17 WALDMEIR, JOSEPH J. "Quest Without Faith." Nation (18 November), pp. 390-96.

O'Connor is briefly mentioned as one of the novelists involved in a quest "to find a way to exist with dignity and self-respect within an enigmatic universe." These novelists do not explicitly reject society, but "the quest itself is implicitly a rejection of society's values." See 1963.B26 for reprint.

18 WRIGHT, AUSTIN M. The American Short Story in the Twenties. Chicago: University of Chicago Press, pp. 375-76.

O'Connor and Paul Bowles "have reacted against the episode of discovery, the Joycean epiphany...by constructing plots of violent action." O'Connor, Bowles, Eudora Welty, and Carson McCullers "carry the Faulknerian patterns of the grotesque to new extremes of bizarre horror and of caustic comedy and pathos."

1962 A BOOKS - NONE

1962 B SHORTER WRITINGS

1 ADLER, JOHANNA. "Author Flannery O'Connor...A Study in Contrast." Raleigh Times (12 April), p. 19.

Recounts O'Connor's delivering a lecture on "Aspects of the Grotesque in Southern Fiction" and the contrast between O'Connor's demure manner and appearance and O'Connor the "powerful author, provocative speaker."

2 COMAN, NOEL. Review of The Violent Bear It Away. Crux (29 May), p. 3.

The novel deals with "the inescapability of God and the fertility and tenacity of the mind." O'Connor "has tried to show that the inner conviction cannot be conquered by the outer will of convention." The novel affirms Christian belief.

3 DANIEL, FRANK. "Flannery O'Connor Shapes Own Capital." Atlanta Journal and Atlanta Constitution (22 July).

Recounts a visit to O'Connor and discusses her literary career and religious concerns. O'Connor dropped her contract with her British publisher after he retitled her first collection of stories "The Artificial Nigger." She said that The Humorous Stories of Edgar Allen Poe probably started her writing and that Gogol also was an influence.

4 FITZGERALD, ROBERT. "The Countryside and the True Country." SR 70:380-94.
A religious interpretation of "The Displaced Person." This story is something more than a story about race relations and xenophobia. Mrs. Shortley, the center of Part I of the story, and Mrs. McIntyre, the center of Part II, both end up "displaced." This displacement is not sectional; it is religious. O'Connor's stories "state again and again that estrangement from Christian plenitude is estrangement from the true country of man." Mrs. McIntyre's final condition is "tragic in the classic sense." Reprinted 1968.A1. For a reply See 1964.B52.

5 FREMANTLE, ANNE. "If a Seed Fall." Commonweal (16 February), pp. 545-46.
A review of A Memoir of Mary Ann. The "strange, almost causal, connection" between O'Connor's introduction and Nathanael Hawthorne's words and his daughter's deeds is mentioned. The book helps us to understand the problem of suffering.

6 FRIEDMAN, MELVIN J. "Flannery O'Connor: Another Legend in Southern Fiction." EJ 51:233-43.
O'Connor's works "abound in sordidness and poverty and yet maintain a delicate aesthetic balance on the side of gentility and religious affirmation." O'Connor has the ability to make even the impossible seem plausible in the context of her fiction, and she achieves this without using "new techniques or startling dislocations of structure." O'Connor is concerned with violence, redemption, and the grotesque; her work tends to follow the "transplantation-prophecy-return" pattern. O'Connor is compared and contrasted with Faulkner. Reprinted 1963.B7 and 1968.A1. For a considerably revised and expanded version See 1966.B13.

7 GARDINER, HAROLD C. "Recent and Most Readable." America (13 January), p. 474.
Includes a brief review of A Memoir of Mary Ann. O'Connor's introduction has "simplicity and depth" and O'Connor comprehends the meaning of suffering.

8 GRÖZINGER, WOLFGANG. "Der Roman der Gegenwart. Das Gefängnis Gesellschaft." Hochland 55 (December), 168-76.
Includes a review of Das brennende Wort, the German translation of The Violent Bear It Away. O'Connor is praised for her powers of presentation and characterization. The novel deals with the impossibility of escaping the religious illusions instilled in childhood, though one needs

(GRÖZINGER, WOLFGANG)
to be an American and have some experience of evangelism to see the novel as anything more than a curiosity.

9 GRUMBACH, DORIS. Review of Wise Blood. Critic 21 (October-November), 95.
A review of the reissue of the novel. Wise Blood is "a highly original, well-written novel whose tone is the dream world, the unreal ether of the psychotic mind, but which achieves, despite this, the moving reality of the human search for God."

10 HASSAN, IHAB. "The Character of Post-War Fiction in America." EJ 51:1-8.
O'Connor's southern setting is described as one of the many social worlds of the contemporary novel, all of them in their diversity signifying "the death of a coherent society." Wise Blood and The Violent Bear It Away are cited as containing the grotesque variant of the "rebel-victim," who is "the central and controlling image of recent fiction." Reprinted 1963.B9.

11 _____. "The Existential Novel." MR 3:795-97.
O'Connor, like Bellow, Mailer, Ellison, Styron, and others, writes "the existential novel," which has three characteristics: 1) a lack "of any presuppositions... about values, traditions, or beliefs," 2) a hero who creates "meaning out of meaninglessness," and 3) an "ironic catharsis" that entails "the recognition not only of irreconcilable conflicts but actually of absurdity."

12 HAWKES, JOHN. "Flannery O'Connor's Devil." SR 70:395-407.
O'Connor's use of images and symbols is "mildly perverse." She resembles Nathanael West in her "pure creation" and in her use of "the devil's voice" as a vehicle for satire. Although O'Connor claims to base her work on Christian belief, a look at her style and authorial attitude reveals that her art is at least partly dependent on "immoral impulse." Includes a close stylistic analysis of two passages from The Violent Bear It Away. Reprinted 1968.A1. For replies See 1963.B6, 1967.B7, 1973.B7, and 1973.B12.

13 _____. "Notes on the Wild Goose Chase." MR 3:784-88.
O'Connor, Djuna Barnes, and Nathanael West are the three American experimental novelists who explore "psychic materials" in the way that poetry often does, i.e., by "a formalizing of our deepest urgencies." They "come together in that rare climate of pure and immoral creation -

are very nearly alone in their uses of wit, their comic treatments of violence and their extreme detachment." This detachment is not inhumane, since "the product of extreme fictive detachment is extreme fictive sympathy." Reprinted 1969.B20.

14 HICKS, GRANVILLE. "A Writer at Home with Her Heritage." _SatR_ (12 May), pp. 22-23.

Recounts a visit to O'Connor in Milledgeville. O'Connor finds the southern belief in the Bible and in historical continuity useful for her fiction. She does not feel alienated from the South and claims that she agrees with old Tarwater of _The Violent Bear It Away_. She also claims that the grotesque "is more real than the real."

15 LEVINE, PAUL. Review of _Wise Blood_. _Jubilee_ (December), p. 47.

A capsule review of the reissued novel. The novel deals with religious themes and "is savagely comic and original, the product of intense imagination rather than accumulated experience." The novel is not as good as O'Connor's best stories or _The Violent Bear It Away_, but it is "disturbing"; O'Connor is "easily one of America's best writers."

16 LUDWIG, JACK. _Recent American Novelists_. University of Minnesota Pamphlets on American Writers No. 22. Minneapolis: University of Minnesota Press, pp. 36-37.

Wise Blood is indebted to the Bible for its passionate style; the novel is "grotesque to avoid being lukewarm." The novel contains no moral frame of reference, but the "ironic ending overcomes the grotesque: self-blinded and self-tortured Haze, dead, is transformed into 'back rent' and, in a mock-crucifixion (which doesn't eliminate serious application to the Crucifixion), is delivered to his worldly landlady." In _The Violent Bear It Away_ O'Connor "softens the grotesque with humor. To the familiar category of the _repulsively horrifying_ one adds the _amusingly absurd_."

17 McCOWN, ROBERT M., S.J. "The Education of a Prophet: A Study of Flannery O'Connor's _The Violent Bear It Away_." _Kansas Magazine_, no volume number, pp. 73-78.

The passage from Matthew on the title page of the novel refers not only to "those who win heaven for themselves by penance and self-denial" but to those who are called to be prophets. Many readers misunderstand the novel because they fail to see that the characters and settings, while intensely alive, also have symbolic significance. Old

1962

(McCOWN, ROBERT M., S. J.)
Tarwater represents belief and prophecy, while Rayber represents unbelief and naturalism. Powderhead symbolizes Edenic innocence and "the wilderness where prophets are forged; the city, on the other hand, is Babylon." The lake symbolizes both baptismal grace and death. Other symbols are also discussed, including the automobile crash, Tarwater's old clothes, the bottle opener, fire, and hunger. See 1962.B23.

18 MALIN, IRVING. New American Gothic. Carbondale: Southern Illinois University Press, pp. 7-10, passim.
O'Connor, along with Capote, Purdy, McCullers, Hawkes, and Salinger, is a practitioner of the "New American Gothic." This fiction is characterized by a dreamlike quality and by narcissistic protagonists. With such protagonists, love and family life are usually impossible. There are three central images in this type of fiction: rooms as psychological prisons, dangerous and/or circular journeys, and distorted reflections. O'Connor's works do have Christian elements, but occasionally, as in The Violent Bear It Away, the work is very ambiguous: "who is to say that Tarwater really sees the Light or simply the darkness of his own mind?" For a reply See 1972.B34. The third chapter of this study is reprinted in 1965.B51.

19 MEADERS, MARGARET INMAN. "Flannery O'Connor: 'literary witch.'" ColQ 10:377-86.
A biographical sketch by the faculty adviser to the student newspaper at Georgia College when O'Connor was a student there. The cartoons O'Connor submitted to the newspaper "were the most professional student work I have ever seen," and though no one knew O'Connor would become an important writer, "the economy of line and the swift, sure stabs were signposts of sorts, as were her small but telling rebellions against sacred systems and feminine foibles." Relates several such "rebellions" and quotes several of O'Connor's remarks on her art. As for her illness, "she bears it with equanimity and humor," and she is "disciplined, friendly, good-humored, hard-working, wise, fun."

20 (MEYERS), SISTER BERTRANDE. "Four Stories of Flannery O'Connor." Thought 37:410-26.
A discussion of "The Partridge Festival," "The Comforts of Home," "The Enduring Chill," and "A View of the Woods." O'Connor is a religious writer who uses shock to communicate her vision. There are three central aspects to these

stories and to O'Connor's work in general: "redemptive grace at work in the soul of man and his response to its influence; the choice of ordinary, often poor and deprived people with a defective sense of spiritual purpose as prototypes for this action of grace; and a sensitive, perhaps subconscious use of scriptural patterns of truth and experience."

21 NOLDE, SISTER SIMON M., O.S.B. "The Violent Bear It Away: A Study in Imagery." XUS 1:180-94.

A study of three kinds of imagery in the novel: "Eucharistic imagery, including images of bread, fish, and hunger," "images of silence," and "images describing the acceptance of the prophetic vocation." The images of silence suggest the supernatural, while the Eucharistic images suggest the Christian nature of vocation. The baptism of Bishop is a "compulsive act," but Tarwater's acceptance of his vocation is a free act. Contrary to Robert Bowen (See 1961.B1), the novel is neither deterministic nor pessimistic.

22 O'CONNOR, WILLIAM VAN. "The Grotesque: An American Genre." In The Grotesque: An American Genre and Other Essays. Carbondale: Southern Illinois University Press, pp. 3-19.

An expanded version of 1959.B6, with a discussion of the relation of the grotesque to tragedy and comedy added. Tragedy implies a moral order in the universe, comedy a rational social order. Modern writers, unable to believe in either, often write in the grotesque mode, which fuses tragedy and comedy. See 1959.B6 for other points. For a reply See 1972.B34.

23 WELLS, JOEL. "Off the Cuff." Critic 21 (August-September), 4, 5, 71, 72.

A reminiscence of a conversation with O'Connor. O'Connor defended her characters as faithful to the types of contemporary Southerners, predicted that Catholics would become more familiar with the Bible, and noted that her writing had to be drastic because of her audience's lack of religious belief. She disputed Evelyn Waugh's claim that a writer could not be a prophet; to her, "prophetic insight is a quality of the imagination." She also praised Robert McCown's article on The Violent Bear It Away (See 1962.B17).

1963

1963 A BOOKS - NONE

1963 B SHORTER WRITINGS

1 ANON. Review of Les braves gens ne courent pas les rues. Bulletin Critique du Livre Française 18:595-96.
A capsule review of the French translation of A Good Man Is Hard to Find. O'Connor draws her horrifying portraits, with all their cruel fantasy and dark humor, "avec un art extraordinaire du récit, un sens remarquable du trait incisif."

2 ANON. "Southern Writers Are Stuck With the South." Atlanta Magazine (August), pp. 26, 60, 63.
Recounts a visit with O'Connor at her farm and her comments on the changing nature of the South, the advantages of the South for the fiction writer, her use of shock in her fiction, the importance of the "sense of mystery" for the writer, and the necessity of transcending mere regionalism. She also downplays the importance of the racial crisis for writers and claims "the fiction writer is interested in individuals, not races."

3 BASSAN, MAURICE. "Flannery O'Connor's Way: Shock, With Moral Intent." Renascence 15:195-99, 211.
O'Connor is a "distinguished minor American writer" like "Sarah Orne Jewett or Elinor Wylie." She has often been misunderstood, but her intent is "to shock and startle an audience which is basically a Christian audience." In "A Temple of the Holy Ghost" O'Connor deals with "the terrible disparity between the divine potentialities of human beings and their depraved acts, conditioned by their secular environment." O'Connor, however, has a "cosmic optimism," since she shows "that in the imagination of a child, the mind of a freak, the sanctified actions of a priest, Grace is still operative in a universe basically hostile to it." This story lacks the "angriness" of some of her later work, where she puts more stress upon the dangers of secularism.

4 BAUMBACH, JONATHAN. "The Acid of God's Grace: The Fiction of Flannery O'Connor." GaR 17:334-46.
Unlike most of O'Connor's stories, where the religious content is merely implied, "Wise Blood is overtly, if unorthodoxly, Catholic." Hazel is the "fallen Adam" who journeys through the three possible spiritual conditions of man: "Adam, Satan, and Christ." Despite this theological framework, the novel is "claustrophobic," and the "gothic quality" of O'Connor's work "suggests that the nature of

her talent often distorts the theological concerns that inform her work." See 1974.B1 for a comment on this article. Reprinted 1965.B14.

5 BERGER, YVES. "Printemps noir." L'Express (8 August), p. 25.
A review of Les braves gens ne courent pas les rues, the French translation of A Good Man Is Hard to Find. O'Connor is one of the great contemporary writers, and she has brought a new spring, a black spring, to American literature. She writes of a sordid world not to denounce God, but rather to denounce the uses to which He is put by the corrupt.

6 CHENEY, BRAINARD. "Miss O'Connor Creates Unusual Humor Out of Ordinary Sin." SR 71:644-52.
An attack on John Hawkes's interpretation of O'Connor. (See 1962.B12). O'Connor does not closely resemble Nathanael West: she writes from a Christian viewpoint, while West is not especially concerned with either God or the devil. The key to O'Connor's humor is her ability to turn suddenly the apparently secular into the "metaphysical." Perhaps O'Connor can only be fully understood "by holding firmly to an unsentimentalized appreciation of the Sermon on the Mount." Reprinted 1968.A1. For a reply See 1969.B8.

7 FRIEDMAN, MELVIN J. "Flannery O'Connor: Another Legend in Southern Fiction." In Recent American Fiction: Some Critical Views. Edited by Joseph J. Waldmeir. Boston: Houghton-Mifflin, pp. 231-45.
A reprint of 1962.B6.

8 GRANDE, BROTHER LUKE M., O.S.B. "Gabriel Fielding, New Master of the Catholic Classic?" CathW (June), pp. 172-79.
In an article on the possibilities for a new Catholic writer of classic fiction, O'Connor is praised for doing what she does with such skill, but her work is harmed "by the shock of eccentric characters and situations. Her limited appeal, like a taste for caviar or escargots, is a measure of weakness."

9 HASSAN, IHAB. "The Character of Post-War Fiction in America." In Recent American Fiction: Some Critical Views. Edited by Joseph J. Waldmeir. Boston: Houghton-Mifflin, pp. 27-35.
A reprint of 1962.B10.

1963

10 HASSAN, IHAB. "The Way Down and Out: Spiritual Deflection in Recent American Fiction." VQR 39:81-93.
O'Connor is one of the many contemporary American writers who employ "the deflection of spirit from traditional forms or goals" in the hope that this deflection will lead us into and beyond nihilism as we search for "a new ground for transcendence." Hazel Motes as a "grotesque hero" stands between "the criminal or demonic hero" and "the saintly or sacrificial hero," and he is grotesque because "the grotesque...is a desperate attempt to express spirit." The grotesque and the picaresque share the middle ground between the criminal and the saint; both share a sense of absurdity, and "the awareness of absurdity or incongruity...is the controlling principle of the contemporary hero."

11 HILLS, L. RUST. "The Structure of the American Literary Establishment." Esquire (July), pp. 41-43.
O'Connor is placed in the "hot center" of the American literary establishment.

12 LAURAS, A. Review of Les braves gens ne courent pas les rues. Etudes 318:295-96.
A review of the French translation of A Good Man Is Hard to Find. The stories are filled with vain and unkind characters, but beneath O'Connor's detachment there is a pity for these characters. O'Connor is a Catholic yet avoids pious and uplifting stories; instead she writes of how a hopeless world "postule une Rédemption qui lui permette de vivre en se dépassant lui-même."

13 MAYHEW, LEONARD F. X. Review of Wise Blood. Commonweal (22 February), p. 576.
A capsule review. The reissue of the novel is "a literary event." O'Connor "has captured the grip that freedom and grace fasten upon conscience in a vivid, fully realized narrative."

14 MULLINS, C. ROSS, JR. "Flannery O'Connor/An Interview." Jubilee (June), pp. 33-35.
O'Connor discusses her "preoccupations with belief and with death and grace and the devil," the importance of manners and formality in southern racial relations, and the necessity of distortion in communicating her religious beliefs to a largely unbelieving audience. This distortion, however, doesn't obscure her work for believers, and some of her "best readers are Sisters." She believes that the writer's sensibility is improved by "wrestling with what

is higher than itself and outside it" and that in good fiction "judgement is not separated from vision." Also includes her comments on preferring to write short stories over novels, on the creation of stories, and on the danger of exhausting fictional materials.

15 MURRAY, JAMES G. "Southland a la Russe." Critic 21 (June-July), 26-28.

O'Connor is often labelled as a member of the "Southern Gothic School," but "her Southerness is an accident of geography." In O'Connor's writing we find ambiguity and opposition in mood, religious position, and even characterization, since her characters seem to be both individuals and types. What O'Connor's work contains is "enrichment," which means that she accepts chaos and allows into her work "a reality unhampered by art." As a writer O'Connor is closest to Gogol, Turgenev, and Dostoyevsky, all of whom "tended to allegorize their meanings" by making the particular symbolize the universal.

16 PEERMAN, DEAN. "Grotesquerie Plus." Christian Century (14 August), pp. 1008-09.

A review of the reissue of Wise Blood. O'Connor "is a master of Gothic grotesquerie," but her stories transcend the genre because of their complexity and their religious concern. Hazel demonstrates O'Connor's beliefs on free will that she describes in the note to the new edition.

17 POIRIER, RICHARD. Introduction to Prize Stories 1963: The O. Henry Awards. Edited by Richard Poirier. Garden City, N. Y.: Doubleday, pp. ix-xvi.

O'Connor's "Everything That Rises Must Converge," the winner of the first prize, and most of the stories in the collection exhibit "a delight in stylistically exploiting coterie behavior that verges on the theatrical, and a corresponding critical awareness of the necessary limitations or absurdities of such behavior." With O'Connor, "only violence...can break down false theories of relationship and expose the human mixtures of hate, guilt, and love that exist beneath the categories which her people mistake for reality."

18 QUINN, JOHN J., S.J. Review of The Violent Bear It Away. Esprit 7 (Winter), 28-31.

An expanded version of 1960.B45.

1963

19 ROSENFIELD, CLAIRE. "The Shadow Within: The Conscious and Unconscious Use of the Double." Daedalus 92:326-44.
The Violent Bear It Away employs both a demonic psychological double, young Tarwater's "stranger," and "realistic characters" who have demonic traits. The reader is torn "between sympathy and judgment" for the amoral irrational. At the end of the novel Tarwater has not really escaped the stranger, and O'Connor "is on the Devil's side without knowing it."

20 RUBIN, LOUIS D., JR. "The Difficulties of Being A Southern Writer Today: Or, Getting Out from Under William Faulkner." Journal of Southern History 29:486-94.
Brief mention of O'Connor. She is contrasted with the contemporary southern writer Madison Jones. Reprinted 1967.B16.

21 _____. The Faraway Country: Writers of the Modern South. Seattle: University of Washington Press, pp. 195-96, 238-40.
In a discussion of the climate of southern writing in the early fifties, O'Connor is described as a writer whose talent was "promising" but "limited in range and breadth" to the short story form. In a discussion of the changing nature of southern fiction, O'Connor is called "one of the best short story writers of our time." O'Connor's work reflects the changes in the South, since in "The Displaced Person" the outsider drastically changes the society, while in Faulkner strangers adjust to the society.

22 RUPP, RICHARD H. "Fact and Mystery: Flannery O'Connor." Commonweal (6 December), pp. 304-07.
Aside from O'Connor, America has few Catholic novelists, partly because the Catholic audience does not support them, but also because the Catholic writer must have a view that is "incarnational" and "redemptive." At the same time, he must be able to write of the secular world: "He must render both fact and mystery." O'Connor's stories begin in the quotidian and end in the visionary. She continually deals with the theme of sin and grace; her stories are like the "endless variations" of parables. They recall the Sermon on the Mount because "only the materially and spiritually destitute shall see God."

23 SHERRY, GERALD. "An Interview with Flannery O'Connor." Critic 21 (June-July), 29-31.
Includes O'Connor's comments on the superiority of the contemporary American novel to the contemporary British

novel, on her distaste for experimental fiction, on her belief that her fiction is not pessimistic, on regionalism, and on the teaching of literature in the high schools. Also includes her comments on the Catholic reading public and the Catholic press and on southern race relations.

24 STELZMANN, RAINULF. "Shock and Orthodoxy: An Interpretation of Flannery O'Connor's Novels and Stories." XUS 2:4-21.

O'Connor's fiction is based on Catholic orthodoxy and uses shock to attack the "smug complacency" of her readers. Her fiction has three basic themes: "Man's Conscious and Deliberate Aversion from God," "The Unstrained Quality of Mercy," and "Purification and Atonement," though this third theme is clearly present only in the novels. O'Connor's "attempt to represent Christian orthodoxy by 'unorthodox' means of expression" can result in misinterpretations, but does not lower the quality of her work.

25 WALDMEIR, JOSEPH J. "Bibliography." In Recent American Fiction: Some Critical Views. Edited by Joseph J. Waldmeir. Boston: Houghton-Mifflin, pp. 275-89.

A selected, annotated bibliography of books and articles on various aspects of contemporary American fiction, as well as selected, unannotated bibliographies on specific authors, including O'Connor.

26 _____. "Quest Without Faith." In Recent American Fiction: Some Critical Views. Edited by Joseph J. Waldmeir. Boston: Houghton-Mifflin, pp. 53-62.

A reprint of 1961.B17.

27 WEST, PAUL. The Modern Novel. Vol. 2: The United States and Other Countries. London: Hutchinson University Library, pp. 296-97.

Brief reference to O'Connor. O'Connor resembles Carson McCullers in her "sophisticated pessimism." The Violent Bear It Away is a novel "without nuance." Young Tarwater is a "warped boy," and his "futile dialogue" with Bishop "suggests the presence of devilish eavesdroppers."

1964 A BOOKS - NONE

1964 B SHORTER WRITINGS

1 ALICE, SISTER ROSE, S.S.J. "Flannery O'Connor: Poet to the Outcast." Renascence 16:126-32.

O'Connor sympathizes with her outcasts because her theme is "the warping evil of unaided human nature, the

1964

(ALICE, SISTER ROSE, S.S.J.)
ineluctable paradox of grace working through and within the humanly repulsive." O'Connor's fiction is not humorous - at times "the bizarre becomes almost banal" - but it is effective. The Violent Bear It Away, with its allegory of "the Christian Church, brooding over the death-agony of innocence in the world of materialism, sorrowing at the same time over the crudity of the human instruments of redemption," is O'Connor's key work. "The Lame Shall Enter First" is also powerful, indeed "bludgeoning." O'Connor is "a master of allegory and imagery."

2 ALLEN, WALTER. "Flannery O'Connor: A Tribute." Esprit 8 (Winter), 12.
O'Connor is the best southern writer since Carson McCullers. She was, however, not a regional but a religious writer. O'Connor was interested in "primitivism," and the "zest" of her fiction shows that "she was...something of a Primitive herself" in her preference for the broad stroke and the apparently crude. O'Connor's reputation should soon grow in England.

3 _____. The Modern Novel in Britain and the United States. New York: E. P. Dutton, pp. 307-09.
O'Connor demonstrates that "a new treatment of the South is possible in fiction." She sees the South from the viewpoint of a Roman Catholic and writes about "the spiritual distortions that are the consequence of Protestant primitivism."

4 ANON. "Baldwin Author Claimed by Death." Macon Telegraph (4 August), pp. 1-2.
An obituary. O'Connor "seemed least of anyone to be aware of fame that came to her."

5 ANON. "Flannery O'Connor." Milledgeville Union-Recorder (6 August), p. 2-A.
An editorial on O'Connor that lauds "the depth and strength of her character, the warmth and sincerity of her personality." O'Connor "attained the stature of greatness without taking notice or measure of it."

6 ANON. "Flannery O'Connor Dead." Georgia Bulletin (Archdiocese of Atlanta). (6 August), p. 1.
Calls O'Connor "one of America's foremost novelists and short story writers."

7 ANON. "Flannery O'Connor Dead at 39; Novelist and Short Story Writer." NYT (4 August), p. 29.

Briefly discusses O'Connor's life and fiction and calls O'Connor "one of the nation's most promising writers." Many of O'Connor's readers did not perceive her work as Christian "but enjoyed her nevertheless."

8 ANON. "Flannery O'Connor Leaves Inspiration." Atlanta Constitution (4 August), p. 4.
An editorial that praises O'Connor and describes her as "more understanding" about her characters than Caldwell or Faulkner were about theirs. She was influenced by her Roman Catholicism and by Poe and Gogol.

9 ANON. "Flannery O'Connor R.I.P." Georgia Bulletin (Archdiocese of Atlanta). (6 August).
O'Connor "epitomized the ideal wedding of the South with Catholicism." Her "writings concern freedom and integrity - and the violent turmoil at the heart of human affairs through which these gifts bear their fruit."

10 ANON. "Flannery O'Connor's Country." Esprit 8 (Winter), 4.
A tribute to O'Connor that stresses her similarity to the French theologian Pierre Teilhard de Chardin. O'Connor's characters are free to accept or reject "the divine, personal, transcendent Omega."

11 ANON. "Milestones." Time (14 August), p. 59.
A brief obituary. O'Connor was "an impassioned Roman Catholic" who found in the South "an appalling collection of lunatic prophets and murderous fanatics."

12 ANON. "Miss O'Connor." Atlanta Journal (4 August).
An editorial that mentions O'Connor's concern with rebellious prophets and claims that "her deep spirituality qualified her to speak with a forcefulness not often matched in American literature."

13 ANON. Obituary. Publishers' Weekly (17 August), p. 28.
A brief obituary. O'Connor is described as "a 'Southern' writer who was also very concerned with her own conception of the Christian faith."

14 BROTHER ANTONINUS. "Flannery O'Connor: A Tribute." Esprit 8 (Winter), 12-13.
O'Connor "was unique among American Catholic writers in that she did not deflect from the problem of violence that is the central preoccupation of our literature." O'Connor's "classicism" helped her get at essentials, and "her sharp intellectual dryness insured her situation in the twentieth century literary scene." O'Connor had "an

1964

(BROTHER ANTONINUS)
affinity to the humanity of her characters that could only have come from deep interior suffering."

15 BELLOW, SAUL. "Flannery O'Connor: A Tribute." Esprit 8 (Winter), 13.
Bellow admires O'Connor's books and "had the same feeling for the person who wrote them."

16 BISHOP, ELIZABETH. "Flannery O'Connor, 1925-1964." NYRB (8 October), p. 21.
A reminiscence of her correspondence with O'Connor, including the time she sent O'Connor "a cross in a bottle...crudely carved, with all the instruments of the Passion, the ladders, pliers, dice, etc., in wood, paper, and tinfoil, with the little rooster at the top of the cross." O'Connor's fiction "contains more real poetry than a dozen books of poems." Those who know the South will know that O'Connor did not exaggerate in her works. Reprinted in Esprit 8 (Winter 1964), 14, 16.

17 BOYLE, KAY. "Flannery O'Connor: A Tribute." Esprit 8 (Winter), 16.
O'Connor "was at the beginning of her career; but that beginning was filled with a wealth of achievement of which any American writer, no matter what his age, would be proud."

18 BRADBURY, JOHN M. Renaissance in the South: A Critical History of the Literature, 1920-1960. Chapel Hill: University of North Carolina Press, pp. 123-24.
O'Connor is a member of "the new Catholic wing" of the tradition of "symbolic naturalism" in twentieth century southern fiction: "For all her accent on the fantastic and on strange symbols of perverted religion, Miss O'Connor demonstrates...a mastery of the telling little naturalistic incident, and a sharp eye for the graphic detail of the environment. Her clean, neatly wrought prose succeeds in putting a convincing footing of realism under her often grotesque and frequently unpleasant inventions."

19 BRADY, CHARLES A. "Flannery O'Connor: A Tribute." Esprit 8 (Winter), 16-17.
Unlike Carson McCullers and Truman Capote, whose grotesques "were Dickensian," O'Connor's "were Dostoevskian with a classic sense of form." O'Connor was partly a disciple of Faulkner, though she was not interested in criticizing southern Calvinism. O'Connor's Christianity "always poises on the needle point of violent paradox."

20 BRASHERS, HOWARD C. An Introduction to American Literature for European Students. Stockholm: Svenska Bokförlaget, p. 209.

A brief mention of O'Connor in an introductory critical survey. O'Connor belongs with other writers of "Southern Gothicism"; her two novels treat "religious fanaticism," and A Good Man Is Hard to Find "is a shocking collection of a variety of grotesqueries."

21 BREIT, HARVEY. "Flannery O'Connor: A Tribute." Esprit 8 (Winter), 17.

A reprint of 1955.B10.

22 BRODIN, PIERRE. Écrivains américains d'aujourd'hui. Présences Contemporaines. Paris: Nouvelles Éditions Debresse, pp. 123-33, 217-18.

O'Connor is one of the few Catholic American writers with talent and an international reputation. O'Connor's style is direct, her view of the world is not comforting, and her method is often that of shock, but her work does not lack humor and tenderness. Although both Wise Blood and The Violent Bear It Away are meant to satirize southern fundamentalists, her characters are nevertheless human. O'Connor bears little resemblance to her fellow Catholic American writer, J. F. Powers; rather she resembles George Bernanos, Leon Bloy, and the film director Luis Buñuel. A very short bibliography of secondary works is found at the end of the book.

23 BROOKS, CLEANTH. "Flannery O'Connor: A Tribute." Esprit 8 (Winter), 17.

Mentions the "invincible integrity" of O'Connor's life and art.

24 CARGILL, OSCAR. "Flannery O'Connor: A Tribute." Esprit 8 (Winter), 17.

O'Connor is a victim of "facile labeling" when she is associated with the southern gothic novel. She was "a highly skilled craftsman with a passion for accurate reporting."

25 CHENEY, BRAINARD. "Flannery O'Connor's Campaign for Her Country." SR 72:555-58.

O'Connor "invented a new form of humor." Her stories begin with a seemingly secular action and tone but by means of a shocking action become "metaphysical." "The means is violent, but the end is Christian." O'Connor's works show a progression from the "Woe" of spiritual

(CHENEY, BRAINARD)
hunger in her early works to a more positive spiritual enlightenment in the later ones. Reprinted 1968.A1.

26 CLARKE, JOHN J. "The Achievement of Flannery O'Connor." Esprit 8 (Winter), 6-9.
A tribute to O'Connor and a brief discussion of her art. O'Connor did not write of pressing social issues, and she "eschewed most modern literary methods." The horrible events in her works must be seen from O'Connor's view that the modern, secular world is grotesque. In her works she sympathizes with "mistaken Truth Seekers," since they at least are concerned about God. O'Connor's "knack for the pithy simile," her ability to describe fully but briefly a character, and her irony are mentioned. O'Connor's fiction has resemblances to that of Stephen Crane, Hemingway, Nathanael West, and Hawthorne. O'Connor's "greatest accomplishment may have been to demonstrate that religion, far from being a barrier to art, should be its vital center."

27 COFFEY, WARREN. "Flannery O'Connor: A Tribute." Esprit 8 (Winter), 18.
O'Connor had "the satirist's ear and the visionary's eye." Two of her stories, "A Good Man Is Hard to Find" and "Good Country People," will endure, but the novels "suffer...from an excessive violence of conception."

28 CONNOLLY, FRANCIS X. "Flannery O'Connor: A Tribute." Esprit 8 (Winter), 18.
O'Connor's "world, especially in its violence, testifies to the importance of a heaven-seeking passion in the most unlikely characters." Wise Blood is "the supremely successful fictional treatment of the theme of original sin."

29 CONNOLLY, JOHN. "The Search: A Study in the Theme of Wise Blood." Esprit 8 (Winter), 66, 68.
A discussion of Hazel Motes's simultaneous search for and flight from Christ.

30 DRAKE, ROBERT. "The Harrowing Evangel of Flannery O'Connor." Christian Century (30 September), pp. 1200-02.
An orthodox Christian interpretation of O'Connor's attitudes toward "Laodiceans" and of her use of the grotesque. O'Connor's "style is often, one suspects, deliberately plain and graceless," and she was better at short stories than novels. Her later work shows greater "compassion." Her religion will create problems for many

readers. Reprinted in Esprit 8 (Winter 1964), 19-20, 22. See 1972.B7 for a reply.

31 DUHAMEL, P. ALBERT. "Flannery O'Connor: A Tribute." Esprit 8 (Winter), 22-23.
O'Connor was unusual among contemporary writers in her stress on ideas, especially "an emphasis upon the wisdom of the heart and the dangers of an isolated reason." She had little in common with southern literary critics except a humanism that allowed for emotion as well as reason. O'Connor's use of only essentials in characterization resembles the methods of William Golding and medieval morality plays.

32 ENRIGHT, ELIZABETH. "Flannery O'Connor: A Tribute." Esprit 8 (Winter), 23.
Praises O'Connor's "unsentimental tenderness" but feels that O'Connor's "preoccupation with mutilation, violence, and horror" occasionally made her work "comic in a way not intended."

33 FARNHAM, JAMES F. "Flannery O'Connor: A Tribute." Esprit 8 (Winter), 23-25.
A reprint of 1961.B5.

34 FIEDLER, LESLIE A. Waiting for the End. New York: Stein and Day, pp. 9-19.
In the first chapter, which discusses the deaths and influence of Hemingway and Faulkner, claims that O'Connor is one of the "Southern Lady Writers" who were influenced by Faulkner. This group, along with the southern "Effete Dandies" and Robert Penn Warren, learned from Faulkner "a fiction which takes the South as its background, terror as its subject, the grotesque as its mode, and which treats the relation of black men and white as the chief symbol of the problem of evil in our time."

35 FRIEDMAN, MELVIN J. "Les romans de Samuel Beckett et la tradition du grotesque." RLM, Nos. 94-99, pp. 31-50.
Compares Beckett with the contemporary southern fiction of O'Connor, Styron, and McCullers. Beckett's and O'Connor's characters are similar in their physical and psychological defects, their religious confusion, and their attachment to objects. Both authors write of futile quests.

36 GABLE, SISTER MARIELLA, O.S.B. "Ecumenic Core in Flannery O'Connor's Fiction." ABR 15:127-43.

(GABLE, SISTER MARIELLA, O.S.B.)
O'Connor has anticipated the Catholic ecumenical movement and its future directions in her fiction. She stresses the importance of Scripture and other widely-shared essentials of Christianity. Her work shares ecumenism's "apostolic urgency" to convert the unfaithful. Includes a discussion of Wise Blood, The Violent Bear It Away, and "The Lame Shall Enter First." O'Connor told the author that the devil rapes young Tarwater because young Tarwater's disgust will return him to God.

37 _____. "Flannery O'Connor: A Tribute." Esprit 8 (Winter), 25-27.
O'Connor was "the first great writer of ecumenical fiction anywhere in the world." Includes a reprint of a letter from O'Connor explaining why she writes about Protestants.

38 GAFFORD, CHARLOTTE. "The Fiction of Flannery O'Connor: A Mission of Gratuitous Grace." Catholic Week (Birmingham, Alabama). (October 9), p. 7; (October 16), p. 6; (October 23), p. 7; (October 30), p. 7; (November 6), p. 7; (November 13), p. 7.
O'Connor brought an undeserved revelation to her characters and readers. Includes excerpts from O'Connor's letters.

39 GARDINER, HAROLD, S.J. "Flannery O'Connor: A Tribute." Esprit 8 (Winter), 27-28.
Praise of O'Connor as a Catholic literary critic. O'Connor succeeded as a critic because her religion was not rigid and external but manifested "true inwardness."

40 GORDON, CAROLINE. "Flannery O'Connor: A Tribute." Esprit 8 (Winter), 28.
O'Connor was "almost alone...in wedding a revolutionary technique to its appropriate subject matter." This technique, rarely used since the Renaissance, is that of showing "the operations of supernatural grace in the lives of natural men and women."

41 GRESSET, MICHEL. "Le petit monde de Flannery O'Connor." Mercure de France 350:141-43.
A review of the French translation of A Good Man Is Hard to Find (Les braves gens ne courent pas les rues). O'Connor belongs in the school of southern literature, with its tradition of a humor that approaches the burlesque but does not exclude emotion. Her stories recall the horrors in Faulkner, and she also reminds the reader of Bosch, Poe, and Beckett. What makes O'Connor unique is the recurrence of certain almost obsessional images and themes: the sun, the sewer, the "ballet" of her abnormal characters

that leads to violence. Her work contains a macabre humor "qui porte parfois le lecteur aux limites de l'insupportable et à l'extrême point de l'ambiguïté tragi-comique." O'Connor sees through to nothing, but in its depth one finds the faint hope of mercy. O'Connor's Catholicism "est nu, tragique, et douloureux."

42 HALE, NANCY. "Flannery O'Connor: A Tribute." Esprit 8 (Winter), 28.

O'Connor was a conqueror of "unexplored literary territory," including "her solving of the problem of how a woman writer is to write about the most brutal and carnal facts of life without causing the reader embarrassment."

43 HALLINAN, PAUL J. "Archbishop's Notebook." Georgia Bulletin (Archdiocese of Atlanta). (6 August), p. 1.

O'Connor "served the cause of the supernatural by a working knowledge of the secular that an older generation would call 'uncanny.'" She wrote without "falsification," and she used the grotesque to show "God immediately present to his [sic] people."

44 HARDWICK, ELIZABETH. "Flannery O'Connor, 1925-1964." NYRB (8 October), pp. 21, 23.

O'Connor as a Catholic was "peculiarly sensitive to the incoherence" of Protestant fanatics, but her religion should not be overemphasized: "It has sometimes seemed to me that the author had something in her too of the girl with the wooden leg who suffered defeat at the hands of fools and frauds." Reprinted in Esprit 8 (Winter 1964), 28, 30.

45 HAWKES, JOHN. "Flannery O'Connor: A Tribute." Esprit 8 (Winter), 30.

Notes the "special quickness" and "wry, engaging, uninhibited humanity" of the same author "whose magical black humor and ruthless fictional stance kept her quite outside the circle of ordinary human response." O'Connor left us "the beauty of the paradox."

46 HICKS, GRANVILLE. "Flannery O'Connor: A Tribute." Esprit 8 (Winter), 30.

O'Connor "was one of the most richly gifted fiction writers of our time."

47 HOSKINS, FRANK L. "Editor's Comments." SSF 2, i:iii-iv.

On a visit to Milledgeville the author discovers that O'Connor's characters "actually live and breathe." The

(HOSKINS, FRANK L.)
visit to the town and O'Connor's grave recalls her "detached, sardonic rendering of the human condition between the lines of which we never fail to sense a deep compassion devoid of sentimentality." These remarks are reprinted in a slightly different form in Esprit 8 (Winter 1964), 31.

48 JACOBSEN, JOSEPHINE. "A Catholic Quartet." Christian Scholar 47:139-54.

O'Connor shares with her fellow Catholic writers, Graham Greene, Muriel Spark, and J. F. Powers, many common traits, including a rejection of the conventional, the parochial, and the superficial. All four join tragedy and comedy, stress the role of violence in our lives, and see mystery within the quotidian. They do not raise "the material into the realm of the spiritual which belongs to a day after life. In life their determination is to incorporate the spiritual into the body of humanity." They all emphasize "the inescapable necessity to be altered, to be otherwise." These four writers can be distinguished from each other by their "dominant approach": "Muriel Spark's implementation is that of style, Greene's that of paradox, Mr. Powers' that of discipline and Miss O'Connor's that of mystery."

49 SISTER JEREMY, C.S.J. "The Violent Bear It Away: A Linguistic Education." Renascence 17:11-16.

A stylistic analysis of the individual "voices" of the characters in the novel. The novel is patterned on the "communication of an oral tradition," and young Tarwater is taught by these different "voices." Mason Tarwater's speech is filled with biblical allusions and phrasings, uses concrete expressions, and is syntactically simple, whereas Rayber's speech is devoid of southern dialect but full of abstractions, and is often complex in syntax. Young Tarwater "puts the abstract, philosophical ideas that Rayber enshrines in vague and generalized language into the concrete idiom of the old uncle's dialect." The "voices" of many of the minor characters are also analyzed. Reprinted 1968.A1.

50 JONES, BARTLETT C. "Depth Psychology and Literary Study." Midcontinent American Studies Journal 5 (Fall), 50-56.

A psychoanalytical interpretation of "Good Country People." The stealing of the leg does not originate in American frontier humor, but stems from the common neurosis, photophobia, that Hulga and the Bible salesman share. In photophobia, a forbidden desire to view the parents' genitals leads to an avoidance of sunlight, which represents parental eyes, and to an obsession with other parts of the body, such as the eyes and feet. An awareness of this neurosis not only explains the two characters' behavior but also such details as Mrs. Freeman's gaze, which suggests "the strong parental eye." O'Connor's use of this perversion and our awareness of it neither support nor contradict the possibility of religious affirmation in the story.

51 JOSELYN, SISTER M., O.S.B. "Flannery O'Connor: A Tribute." Esprit 8 (Winter), 31-32.

The peacock, with its association with Christ, was O'Connor's "'objective correlative.'" The peacock is a good example of O'Connor's ability to write of the spiritual in terms of the concrete.

52 _____. "Thematic Centers in 'The Displaced Person.'" SSF 1: 85-92.

An extension of Robert Fitzgerald's analysis of "The Displaced Person" (See 1962.B4) that emphasizes the importance of symbols, not only as means but as ends in themselves. The story deals with two interrelated religious themes: Christian love and the Incarnation. Christ is an "analogue" for both the peacock and the Displaced Person. The characters' attitudes toward the peacock reflect their attitude toward Mr. Guizac and toward Christ Himself. In this story "it is the displacer who is truly displaced." Reprinted 1968.A1.

53 JUDGE, JOHN F., JR. "The Man Under the Microscope: A Look at 'The Displaced Person.'" Esprit 8 (Winter), 65.

"Mrs. Shortley and Mrs. McIntyre represent the world and the Pole represents Christ." Those who reject Christ "find themselves in a displaced state."

54 KERMODE, FRANK. "Flannery O'Connor: A Tribute." Esprit 8 (Winter), 33.

O'Connor "is not yet read in England," but she had "a powerful and interesting vision" and the ability to achieve "that complex union of reality and justice which tragedy affords."

55 KUNKEL, FRANCIS L. "Flannery O'Connor: A Tribute." Esprit 8 (Winter), 33.

O'Connor resembles Evelyn Waugh and J. F. Powers in her "ability to treat religious matters with humor." Most Catholic writers do not do this.

1964

56 LOWELL, ROBERT. "Flannery O'Connor: A Tribute." Esprit 8 (Winter), 33.
O'Connor's fiction had a unique "combination of humor and horror" and was "as surely and meticulously written as the best short poems."

57 LYTLE, ANDREW. "Flannery O'Connor: A Tribute." Esprit 8 (Winter), 33-34.
A reminiscence of reading aloud one of O'Connor's stories at the University of Iowa while she was a student there. O'Connor's fiction is similar to a "morality play" and shows "a society given over totally to the evil nature of man."

58 MACAULEY, ROBIE. "Flannery O'Connor: A Tribute." Esprit 8 (Winter), 34.
Much of O'Connor's life was a "torment" and thus "her great subject was the antiChrist [sic] - the fierce and bestial side of the human mind." O'Connor had a "confused and emotional hatred" for this side of man, but expressed this hatred "dryly, precisely, and penetratingly." Her precision comes from the certainty of "the Good" that her religion and humor gave her; the antichrist was one step on the road to Christ.

59 MAYHEW, LEONARD F. X. "Flannery O'Connor, 1925-1964." Commonweal (21 August), pp. 562-63.
O'Connor has been misinterpreted as "some neo-Gothic/neo-Virginia Woolf hybrid," but her real theme is free will. O'Connor had an "anagogical sense of Scripture" and was well-aware of contemporary Catholic thought. O'Connor sympathized with southern evangelism, yet as a Catholic felt a tension between her "loyalty to conviction and heritage" and her sense of alienation from her Protestant region. Reprinted in Esprit 8 (Winter 1964), 34, 36.

60 _____. "Flannery O'Connor's People: Authentic and Universal." Georgia Bulletin (Archdiocese of Atlanta). (6 August).
Mentions O'Connor's interest in the South and her belief in Christ, her blending of Catholicism with her sympathy for evangelism, and "her own fine sense of the ironic." O'Connor goes beneath the surface of her region to reveal its universal elements and beneath the surface of life to show that "the structure and relationships of daily experience are off-center and grotesque and violence-breeding."

61 MEEKER, RICHARD K. "The Youngest Generation of Southern Fiction Writers." In Southern Writers: Appraisals in our Time. Edited by R. C. Simonini, Jr. Charlottesville: University Press of Virginia, pp. 162-91. (Published 1964; last copyright date is 1961.)

O'Connor, along with Truman Capote, Carson McCullers, Shirley Ann Grau, William Styron and others, is one of a group of younger southern writers "whose themes are not essentially Southern." O'Connor writes an "inverted moral allegory," and her theme is "positive, Christian, and universal." In general, all the southern writers of this literary generation maintain the southern interest in style and rhetoric, but show less pride in their race, religion, or family and less awareness of the Civil War. Southern writers are becoming more like other American writers.

62 MERTON, THOMAS. "Flannery O'Connor." Jubilee (November), pp. 49-53.

O'Connor wrote of the false respect that her characters use to hide their contempt of themselves and others and God. O'Connor reveals this contempt yet does not pretend to understand or judge it, since to do so would make her one of "the demons practising contempt." O'Connor as a writer does not resemble any modern writer but "someone like Sophocles." See 1965.B28.

63 _____. "Flannery O'Connor: A Tribute." Esprit 8 (Winter), 36.

O'Connor's fiction was "completely disturbing and completely convincing." O'Connor's avoidance of overt judgement and direct authorial comment is "a delicate form of compassion." She will be most remembered for her "irony and compassion."

64 (MEYERS), SISTER BERTRANDE, D.C. "Flannery O'Connor: A Tribute." Esprit 8 (Winter), 13-14.

Critics of O'Connor, both admirers and detractors, were confused about her intent until she wrote "The Fiction Writer and His Country" for Granville Hicks's The Living Novel in 1957. Since then many critics have stressed O'Connor's religious intent, but at the expense of ignoring her "vocation," her ability to make a certain range of fictional events and characters "come alive." Includes a reminiscence of a discussion with O'Connor about The Violent Bear It Away.

1964

65 MURRAY, J. FRANKLIN, S.J. "Flannery O'Connor: A Tribute." Esprit 8 (Winter), 37.

O'Connor believed that "wicked men reflect their evil in their countenances and whole being." Her theme is that such wickedness is caused by the lack of grace. Her life, however, contradicted her fiction, "for she had a beautiful soul in an afflicted body."

66 O'CONNOR, WILLIAM VAN. "Flannery O'Connor: A Tribute." Esprit 8 (Winter), 37-39.

O'Connor is an orthodox Christian who writes of the perverse because of its association with original sin and because the modern, secular world adds to such perversity. O'Connor's "special vision" is a result of her confronting her Catholicism with this secularism and with southern fundamentalism. Unlike François Mauriac and Graham Greene, O'Connor's themes are "straight out of the Catechism."

67 PEDEN, WILLIAM. The American Short Story: Front Line in the National Defense of Literature. Boston: Houghton-Mifflin, pp. 29-30, 36, passim.

A Good Man Is Hard to Find "is perhaps the most memorable first book of short stories since Eudora Welty's A Curtain of Green," and since then O'Connor's talent has "deepened and widened." O'Connor's fiction, though "securely rooted in specific time and place," is Christian allegory or fantasy. Its bizarreness is compatible with its Christian themes. O'Connor "is in the highest sense a moralist working out of a preconceived dogma." A briefer version of these remarks can be found in Esprit 8 (Winter 1964), 39.

68 PERRINE, LAURENCE. "Flannery O'Connor: A Tribute." Esprit 8 (Winter), 39-40.

Recounts writing O'Connor to ask the significance of Mrs. May's name in "Greenleaf." O'Connor replied, "I must have named her that because I knew some English teacher would write and ask me why. I think you folks sometimes strain the soup too thin."

69 PORTER, KATHERINE ANNE. "Gracious Greatness." Esprit 8 (Winter), 50, 52, 54, 56, 58.

A reminiscence about O'Connor, with some photographs. O'Connor's work was probably finished. O'Connor's environment raises the question of where she learned all that she knew about life, but this is always a question about "genius." O'Connor's life in Milledgeville, Georgia was good for her because "nobody got in her way" as a writer. O'Connor's self-portrait may resemble the writer of "those blood-curdling stories," but it does not resemble "the living Flannery, whistling to her peacocks, showing off her delightfully freakish breed of chickens." Reprinted 1970.B34.

70 POWERS, J. F. "Flannery O'Connor: A Tribute." Esprit 8 (Winter), 40.
A brief tribute to O'Connor's talent for "striking fire and light."

71 PRESCOTT, ORVILLE. "Flannery O'Connor: A Tribute." Esprit 8 (Winter), 40-42.
A reprint of the 1955 review of A Good Man Is Hard to Find (1955.B22) and the 1960 review of The Violent Bear It Away (1960.B44).

72 QUINN, SR. M. BERNETTA, O.S.F. "Flannery O'Connor: A Tribute." Esprit 8 (Winter), 42-44.
A reminiscence of O'Connor's correspondence and O'Connor's visit to the College of St. Teresa in Winona, Minnesota.

73 RAGAN, SAM. "Southern Accent." News and Observer (Raleigh, N.C.) (16 August).
A reminiscence of O'Connor's lecturing.

74 RUBIN, LOUIS D., JR. "Flannery O'Connor: A Tribute." Esprit 8 (Winter), 44.
Mentions O'Connor's mild demeanor and her remark on the influence of Faulkner and briefly discusses some aspects of her fiction: her use of the grotesque, her religious intent, her ability to avoid mixing "fiction and homilectics," her "compassionate" humor, and the superiority of her short stories to her novels.

75 SCHARPER, PHILIP. "Flannery O'Connor: A Tribute." Esprit 8 (Winter), 45.
Praise of O'Connor's ability to make the eternal present in her fiction and of her "complexity" and "compassion."

76 SCOTT, NATHAN A. "Flannery O'Connor: A Tribute." Esprit 8 (Winter), 45-46.
Hopes that future criticism of O'Connor will be better than much of the previous criticism. O'Connor is a religious writer, not a writer of "'Southern Gothic.'"

77 SESSIONS, WILLIAM. "Flannery O'Connor: A Memoir." National Catholic Reporter (28 October), p. 9.
Recounts visiting O'Connor at Milledgeville and at Lourdes when O'Connor visited there in 1958. O'Connor "opened to the great Southern tradition of writing the hope of the center of Catholicism, and to Catholics, at least in

(SESSIONS, WILLIAM)
the United States, the values of a culture beyond the lonely crowd." O'Connor's "suffering gave her a landscape," that of her Georgia region and of the infinite.

78 SIBLEY, CELESTINE. "Death Was an Old Companion in Miss O'Connor's Brief Life." Atlanta Constitution (6 August), p. 5.
An obituary that describes O'Connor as "one of the country's outstanding short storyists and maybe the best writer Georgia has ever produced."

79 SPIVEY, TED R. "Flannery O'Connor: A Tribute." Esprit 8 (Winter), 46-47.
A reminiscence and a discussion of O'Connor's relevance to youth. Unlike J. D. Salinger and Carson McCullers, who write about misunderstood youth, O'Connor with her theology points to answers to youth's questions. O'Connor as a writer resembles Bernanos and Mauriac, as well as writers of "Existential theology" like Kafka and Dostoyevsky.

80 _____. "Flannery O'Connor's View of God and Man." SSF 1: 200-06.
O'Connor, who uses the "symbolic tale" of modern romance writers, is only now being fully understood. "The Lame Shall Enter First," which is partly a summation of The Violent Bear It Away, brings together many of her major themes. Rufus Johnson, the God-seeking criminal of much existential literature, has to fight not only the devil, but also "a decaying humanitarianism" and "a religious fanaticism that holds to truth but does no good." By the end of the story, Rufus realizes that salvation is only found in the acceptance of Christ, and Sheppard realizes his humanitarianism "stood in the way of love." Rufus differs from O'Connor's previous criminals because he at least sees the possibility of conversion to Christ. Reprinted 1968.A1.

81 STELZMANN, RAINULF. "Der Stein des Anstosses: Die Romane und Erzählungen Flannery O'Connors." SZ 174:286-96.
O'Connor differs from a Catholic confessional writer like Chesterton in her honesty to the concrete. She differs from most modern religious writers because she treats man's rejection of God as a conscious, spiritual act rather than the result of carnal weakness and because she refuses to treat the possibility of salvation from merely a human viewpoint and makes God a force in her works. O'Connor deals with three phases of the spiritual life: the

voluntary and knowing rejection of God, the superior strength of grace, and the obligation for purgation and penance. Her novels deal with these phases more fully than her stories. O'Connor is not didactic in the usual sense. Her exaggerated and grotesque characters recall the figures of Gothic art, and her characters, even after the revelation of grace, must still choose to follow God. There is no easy road to salvation.

82 TAILLEFER, ANNE. "A Memoir of Flannery O'Connor." Catholic Worker (December), pp. 2, 7.

A tribute that includes portions of a letter from O'Connor denying that her works satirize southern fundamentalism. O'Connor is an ecumenical writer whose novels show the collision of a "world preoccupied with God" with a totally materialistic world, whereas in her stories God is absent. In the stories, evil dominates, and "it is the writer who becomes the saint." O'Connor's loathing of sentimentality, her fusion of the tragic and comic, and her awareness of both the "glowing and hideous" sides of truth are mentioned.

83 TATE, ALLEN. "Flannery O'Connor: A Tribute." Esprit 8 (Winter), 48-49.

A reminiscence of the time he had to "'criticize'" the work of O'Connor when she was a student at the University of Iowa. He then thought O'Connor's style "dull" and her sentences "flat" and only later realized that they were a consequence of her temperamental Jansenism. In her stories "a principle of supernatural disorder" underlies the movement of the action. O'Connor's situation as a Catholic in the Protestant South and her "inexplicable genius" will probably make her unique in American writing.

84 TATE, MARY BARBARA. "Flannery O'Connor: A Reminiscence." Columns (Georgia College at Milledgeville). (Fall), pp. 8-9.

A reminiscence by a member of a group that met at O'Connor's every week to discuss literary works. Recounts some of O'Connor's views on southern fiction in general and on her own work. In O'Connor "there was no trace of the artist aloof or apart from everyday occurrences and interests."

85 TOWNEND, JOSEPH C. "The Inner Country: Design in 'The Lame Shall Enter First.'" Esprit 8 (Winter), 70.

O'Connor uses shock and the contrast of opposing values in this story to persuade us that "the spiritually well will ultimately outdistance the physically superior."

1964

86 VOSS, VICTOR. "A Study in Sin." Esprit 8 (Winter), 60-62.
A comparison of young Tarwater of The Violent Bear It Away with Raskolnikov of Dostoyevsky's Crime and Punishment. Both authors use other characters to demonstrate the various aspects of the protagonists' personalities, and both protagonists willfully and defiantly reject love, "although knowing beforehand that they could never really accomplish such a rejection." To each author, "rejection of love is sin in its essence."

87 WARREN, ROBERT PENN. "Flannery O'Connor: A Tribute." Esprit 8 (Winter), 49.
A reminiscence and praise of O'Connor's ability to make actuality turn into the fantastic and to make the fantastic seem "a form of truth."

88 WELLS, JOEL. "Flannery O'Connor: A Tribute." Esprit 8 (Winter), 49.
A brief reminiscence and a comment on O'Connor's art. O'Connor was "among the very best American short story writers of the last twenty-five years but everything she wanted to say was in her novel The Violent Bear It Away."

89 WELTY, EUDORA. "Flannery O'Connor: A Tribute." Esprit 8 (Winter), 49.
Writes of the "triumphant vitality" and "comic spirit" of O'Connor's works.

90 WEST, RAY B., JR. "Flannery O'Connor: A Tribute." Esprit 8 (Winter), 49.
O'Connor's view of the world would appear "distorted" to most people, but actually she had "a fresh vision."

91 WITHAM, W. TASKER. The Adolescent in the American Novel: 1920-1960. New York: Frederick Ungar, pp. 181, 188, 265.
Passing references to The Violent Bear It Away. The novel treats Protestant emotionalism and is an exception to the usually more idyllic portraits of adolescence in the rural South in novels published between 1950 and 1960.

1965 A BOOKS - NONE

1965 B SHORTER WRITINGS

1 ABRAHAMS, WILLIAM. Introduction to Prize Stories 1965: The O. Henry Awards. Edited by Richard Poirier and William Abrahams. Garden City, N. Y.: Doubleday, pp. ix-xii.

Contemporary short stories demonstrate a "high level of accomplishment" and "a more formidable claim" can be made for "Revelation," the winner of the first prize.

2 ALICE, SISTER MARY, O.P. "My Mentor, Flannery O'Connor." SatR (29 May), pp. 24-25.
A reminiscence about O'Connor that includes passages from several of O'Connor's letters to the author. O'Connor tells the author that her fiction will improve if she stresses observation and directness.

*3 ALVIS, JOHN. "Wise Blood: Hope in the City of the Profane." Kerygma 4 (Winter), 19-29.
See Abstracts of English Studies 9 (1966), No. 395.

4 ANON. "Flannery O'Connor." Current Biography, p. 307.
A brief obituary. O'Connor's "writings, set in the contemporary rural South, convey grotesque, sometimes terrifying images and stress stern moral judgment, deep Christian faith, and human alienation."

5 ANON. "God Breaks Through." America (5 June), pp. 821-22.
A review of Everything That Rises Must Converge and Hugh Nissenson's A Pile of Stones. In both writers "God keeps breaking through the web of pain, frustration, stiff-neckedness, and plain human meanness that mark [sic] the characters they create." The influence of Teilhard de Chardin on O'Connor is also discussed. Men may rise and converge, but only by humiliating themselves before God.

6 ANON. "Grace Through Nature." Newsweek (31 May), pp. 85-86.
A review of Everything That Rises Must Converge. O'Connor's sacramentalism and her sense of mystery are mentioned. Her stories start in "banalities" and move from them to a spiritual revelation. O'Connor wrote "some of the finest stories in the language."

7 ANON. "Of Ultimate Things." Time (4 June), p. 92.
A review of Everything That Rises Must Converge. The power of O'Connor's previous work is praised, and these new stories are also praised as some of the best "American Gothic." The stories are about the "violent dialogue of the demonic and divine." O'Connor is a "verbal magician" who is not interested in psychological or social verisimilitude but in everyday objects "charged with mysterious and terrible significance."

8 ANON. Review of Everything That Rises Must Converge. Booklist 61:1015.

1965

(ANON.)

A capsule review. O'Connor shows "her x-ray vision of human fallibility and self-deception, and of man's groping for and rejection of God."

9 ANON. Review of Everything That Rises Must Converge. Choice 2:387.

A capsule review. The "grotesque fables may manifest a surface sameness in setting, in characterization, even in incident, but they astonish the reader with their variety of insights into life - both natural and supernatural."

10 ANON. Review of Everything That Rises Must Converge. Kirkus 33:338.

The stories demonstrate O'Connor's "brilliance of style and intensity of statement." In the stories only the children have "freshness," but even they are "destroyed." The stories "reflect views of a unique social structure."

11 ANON. Review of Everything That Rises Must Converge. VQR 41: lxxxiv.

A brief review. O'Connor is praised for her "mastery of the realistic morality tale" and her "rendering of the shock of moral recognition."

12 ANON. "Year of the Fact." Newsweek (27 December), pp. 72-73.

A short review of Everything That Rises Must Converge in a year-end summary of books published in 1965. The review is essentially a summary of the earlier Newsweek review (See 1965.B6) but does add that this collection "is beyond doubt the finest work of fiction published during the past year."

13 BARRETT, WILLIAM. "Reader's Choice." Atlantic Monthly (July), pp. 139-40.

A review of Everything That Rises Must Converge. O'Connor was a faithful Catholic, but "she is never sentimentally pious." Her stories are southern but also universal. The moral "seems to be that the liberal mind, convinced of its own rationality and self-righteousness, cannot possibly understand the perverse depths of the human personality."

14 BAUMBACH, JONATHAN. "The Acid of God's Grace: Wise Blood by Flannery O'Connor." In The Landscape of Nightmare: Studies in the Contemporary American Novel. New York: New York University Press, pp. 87-100.

A slightly revised version of 1963.B4.

15 BERGAMO, RALPH. "Gallant Georgian's Legacy." Atlanta Journal and Atlanta Constitution (23 May), p. 2-B.

A review of Everything That Rises Must Converge. O'Connor "can match any American writer of the century" in her skill at the craft of fiction. O'Connor's theme is religious, and she belongs to no literary school. She writes "with a firm masculine hand" and "complete objectivity."

16 BLIVEN, NAOMI. Review of Everything That Rises Must Converge. NY (11 September), pp. 220-21.

Praises O'Connor's style, "an unmannered and exact translation of things into words," and her humor, which often arises from her characters' self-deception and which is at its best when it is combined with horror and natural beauty, as it is in the first two pages of "Greenleaf." O'Connor's grotesque characters are not as bad as her normal ones, who are petty, selfish, smug, and often self-deceived. O'Connor's stories are not ugly or provincial, but because of her isolated life, she had "a very young imagination." As a result, she continually emphasizes the conflict of generations and often makes the punishment greater than the crime. In her best stories, "Revelation" and "The Enduring Chill," she is more merciful.

17 BONE, LARRY EARL. Review of Everything That Rises Must Converge. LJ 90:2160-61.

A capsule review. The stories suffer from a sameness in plot and setting.

18 BORDWELL, HAROLD. "The Fiction of Flannery O'Connor." Today (October), pp. 29-31.

In O'Connor's work the "religious drive" is always "twisted," but the reader suspects that her crazy or nearly crazy prophets "may carry within themselves a bit of the truth." O'Connor's fiction "is characterized by a harsh honesty - often too harsh - toward the DPs who limp through her pages." None of her characters "seems to survive intact."

19 COFFEY, WARREN. "Flannery O'Connor." Commentary (November), pp. 93-99.

A review of Everything That Rises Must Converge and a general discussion of O'Connor's work. O'Connor wrote "tough and brilliant comic stories," but her novels suffer from an "excessive violence of conception." O'Connor was influenced by Faulkner, Ring Lardner, and Nathanael West, but the primary force behind her work was the Jansenism of

(COFFEY, WARREN)
American Catholicism. She was obsessed with intellectual pride and like European Catholic writers influenced by Jansenism, the "incommunicable pain arising from sex." This pain is transformed into art, which creates a comic view of the world, but the price of this avoidance of normal sexuality is a "loss of range and humanity." Within her range, however, "nobody could have gone deeper."

20 COPELAND, EDITH. Review of Everything That Rises Must Converge. Books Abroad 39:461.
A brief review. In the stories the "stubborn nature of unredeemed humanity explodes, violently, to evoke shock and an unsentimental pity."

21 CRUTTWELL, PATRICK. "Fiction Chronicle." HudR 18:442-50.
Includes a review of Everything That Rises Must Converge. Unlike many male writers today, O'Connor, Elizabeth Spencer, and Nadine Gordimer write complete works of art that do not need the outer world "for explanation or completion." O'Connor's "poetry is grotesque and neurotic," but it is powerful because "her writing is clearly the work of an authentically religious writer, Catholic but not obtrusively or aggressively so."

22 DAVENPORT, GUY. "The Top is a New Bottom." NatR (27 July), pp. 658-59.
A review of Everything That Rises Must Converge. Before her death O'Connor "had perfected an art of such integrity that she must be placed with Faulkner and Eudora Welty in the highest place among Southern writers." The South is a land "of moral emptiness," and the "title...is ironic." In the stories a character is "ensnared and obliterated by the sheer littleness of his own being." O'Connor is not "in the Gothic School"; the grotesque in her work "is but the visual equivalent of the outrage she feels before a world stupid with selfishness."

23 DAVIS, BARNABAS. "Flannery O'Connor: Christian Belief in Recent Fiction." Listening (Autumn), pp. 5-21.
Discusses O'Connor's use of "the perverse and unacceptable," her honesty to reality, her avoidance of the sentimental and the pornographic, and her hope that an increasing Catholic awareness of the Bible would help her Catholic readers with her fiction. Robert Bowen's charge (1961.B1) that The Violent Bear It Away is deterministic is misleading because O'Connor stresses "the complete gratuity of man's salvation," not the doctrine of free

will. O'Connor "emphasizes now one truth of the Christian faith, now another."

24 DEGNAN, JAMES P. Review of Everything That Rises Must Converge. Commonweal (9 July), pp. 510-11.
O'Connor is a master of details, a result of her "absolutely original vision. It is a vision that clearly sees the tragedy of a world in which people are hopelessly alienated from each other, but a vision which stresses the comedy of such a world."

25 DOWELL, BOB. "The Moment of Grace in the Fiction of Flannery O'Connor." CE 27:235-39.
O'Connor's fiction is not gothic but theological, and her use of the comic is "a necessary vehicle for carrying her unpopular theme." In O'Connor's fiction "without Christ one's actions only lead to evil"; grace comes when her characters realize this evil and the necessity for their submission to God.

26 DRAKE, ROBERT. "Hair-Curling Gospel." Christian Century (19 May), p. 656.
A review of Everything That Rises Must Converge. O'Connor shows that "the Christian gospel is enough to curl the hair of the genteel, the modern intellectual, the conventionally religious." In the stories "God is not to be mocked, neither is the devil to be ignored." Her stories are shocking in the same way the Gospels are.

*27 DUPREE, ROBERT. "The Fictional World of Flannery O'Connor." Kerygma 4 (Winter), 3-18.
See Abstracts of English Studies 9 (1966), No. 394.

28 DUPREY, RICHARD A. Review of Everything That Rises Must Converge. CathW (October), p. 54.
O'Connor "so believed in man's accountability to an omnipresent, omnipotent, and omniscient God that she seeks to paint that God terribly, frighteningly through his absence from the lives of her characters." Thomas Merton's comparison of O'Connor with Sophocles (1964.B62) is fitting.

29 FARNHAM, JAMES F. "The Essential Flannery O'Connor." Cross Currents 15:376-78.
A review of Everything That Rises Must Converge. Early misunderstandings of O'Connor's fiction as "Southern Gothic" seem to be passing. O'Connor was "one of the most compelling craftsmen in contemporary American fiction." Her basic situation is that of a fundamentalist or an

(FARNHAM, JAMES F.)
agnostic rationalist either being aided or destroyed by "a moment of revelation caused by the intrusion into his plotted world of the non-probable and the uncontrollable."

30 FITZGERALD, ROBERT. Introduction to Everything That Rises Must Converge, by Flannery O'Connor. New York: Farrar, Straus, and Giroux, pp. vii-xxxiv.

A biographical account by O'Connor's close friend, the noted poet and translator. Discusses O'Connor's life and literary career, and includes an account of the genesis of Wise Blood. O'Connor is compared with T. S. Eliot. As for this posthumous collection, the title is "taken in full respect and with profound and necessary irony." The stories have similarities with each other and with earlier stories and demonstrate O'Connor's artistic "ascesis" and her use of tragicomedy. See 1966.B5, 1968.B20, 1969.A1, 1970.B28, 1974.B8 for replies or remarks.

31 GABLE, SISTER MARIELLA, O.S.B. "But First It Must Rise." Critic 23 (June-July), 58-60.

A review of Everything That Rises Must Converge. The title is ironic because O'Connor writes of the present, not some possible utopian future. O'Connor used the grotesque to communicate with the non-Christian she wrote for, and she was best at short stories. Three of these stories, "The Lame Shall Enter First," "Greenleaf," and "A View of the Woods," are "classics of American literature."

32 GOSSETT, LOUISE Y. Violence in Recent Southern Fiction. Durham, N. C.: Duke University Press, pp. 75-97, 118, passim.

A discussion of O'Connor's use of physical and psychological violence in her handling of personal relationships, especially between parents and children, her use of "numerous metaphors and similes which suggest violence," her employment of sun images to symbolize the fury of her characters, and her attack on the various nostrums of our age, such as social engineering and "life-adjustment" philosophies. O'Connor "uses violence to stress the urgency of the problem which she explores, to recall to a complacent world the radical alternations which faith makes in man's life, and to illustrate the despair which its denial brings." Although O'Connor uses violence a great deal, she avoids the dehumanization of a writer like Erskine Caldwell because of her "firmly objective treatment of the characters" and her religious theme.

33 GRIFFITH, ALBERT. "Flannery O'Connor." America (27 November), pp. 674-75.
Only after her death is O'Connor getting recognition as a unique writer who is something more than a Southerner and a Roman Catholic. O'Connor was loyal to her region and her religion, but these categories must not blind us to her originality.

34 HASSAN, IHAB. "The Novel of Outrage: A Minority Voice in Postwar American Fiction." ASch 34:239-53.
The novel of outrage treats the threat to man's being from an ineluctable violence that is "not temporal but spatial" and "not historical but ontological." Some novels of outrage maintain a slight faith in man, some see the protagonist's victimization as serving "a sacrificial purpose", and some find no hope in this assault against man. Wise Blood belongs to the second category of the novel of outrage: "Motes responds to nihilism with fierce negation, reacts to spiritual death with murder and blasphemy; but he also ends by offering himself as a ritual sacrifice." Reprinted 1969.B19.

35 HAWKES, JOHN. "John Hawkes: An Interview." Wisconsin Studies in Contemporary Literature 6:141-55.
Mentions O'Connor as one of the writers who belong to what he considers the avant-garde. All of these writers have a "quality of coldness, detachment, ruthless determination to face up to the enormities of ugliness and potential failure within ourselves and in the world around us and to bring to this exposure a savage or saving comic spirit and the saving beauties of language." Compares O'Connor with Nathanael West and suggests again that O'Connor is "on the devil's side." See 1962.B12.

36 HICKS, GRANVILLE. "A Cold, Hard Look at Humankind." SatR (29 May), pp. 23-24.
A review of Everything That Rises Must Converge. O'Connor was not a saint; she was a devout Catholic, but "she refused to conform to the literary standards set up by many priests and laymen in the name of the Church." The best of these stories are O'Connor's best work, but they contain "almost no compassion." Although O'Connor seems to be a "simple, even casual sort of writer," her writing is very skillful. O'Connor "was one of the best writers of short stories this era has seen." Reprinted 1970.B24.

37 HIMY, ARMAND. "Dans la lignée de Swift." Preuves (January), pp. 88-89.

(HIMY, ARMAND)

A review of Les braves gens ne courent pas les rues, the French translation of A Good Man Is Hard to Find. The suffering in the stories arises from the characters' rejection of the other; in O'Connor "le massacre des innocents n'est pas le fait des seuls criminels, mais aussi celui d'un monde qui ne connait plus sa raison d'exister." O'Connor's dark humor springs from her region and from Swift, who also fought against metaphysical despair.

38 HOOBLER, THOMAS. Review of Everything That Rises Must Converge. Ave Maria (17 July), p. 18.

Two themes, "the conflict between young and old; and the relentless God embracing and crushing the mean, the weak, the petty," dominate the collection and give the stories a sameness. O'Connor uses epiphanies to communicate her vision, one that is "mystical" and concerned with the "essential man."

39 HOOD, EDWARD M. "Rural Georgia and the Starry Universe." Shenandoah 16, iv:109-114.

A review of Everything That Rises Must Converge that praises O'Connor for her "almost Dantean" use of every detail and mentions the movement in her stories "from a style of banal, monotonous constriction to a style of large, fluid release." Also discusses some of the recurring character-types in the collection.

40 HOWE, IRVING. "Flannery O'Connor's Stories." NYRB (30 September), pp. 16-17.

A review of Everything That Rises Must Converge. There is religion in the stories "but at so deep a level, as so much more than mere subject matter of fixed point of view, that the skeptical reader is spared the problem of an explicit confrontation with 'the Catholic sacramental view of life.'" The stories are very skillful and the "Gothic hi-jinks" of O'Connor's early work are avoided, but the stories lack "resonance," partly because O'Connor's irony turns to a smugness where only irony itself is free from attack and partly because the stories are too controlled, too lacking in surprise. In "Revelation" and "Parker's Back," however, O'Connor moved beyond this excessive control.

41 HUGHES, RILEY. Review of Everything That Rises Must Converge. Columbia (July), p. 34.

A laudatory review that cites O'Connor's use of "melodrama as a mode of contemplation" and her interest in mystery, including "our determined avoidance of mystery."

42 HYMAN, STANLEY EDGAR. "Flannery O'Connor's Tattooed Christ." New Leader (10 May), pp. 9-10.

A review of Everything That Rises Must Converge. "Parker's Back," "The Lame Shall Enter First," and "The Enduring Chill" are the best stories in the collection. Some of the other stories are "flawed," and in general O'Connor relies too much on death as a way to end the stories. O'Connor's themes are Christian, but her Christianity tends to be "dramatistic," dualistic, and extreme. O'Connor's work has connections with the symbolism of Melville, the dualism of Dostoyevsky, and the alienation of Nathanael West.

43 JACKSON, KATHERINE GAUSS. Review of Everything That Rises Must Converge. Harper's (July), p. 112.

The reviewer had "never read a short-story writer who had a surer sense of the evil in the human heart and who used so much humor in telling of it." The stories have "stunning directness and simplicity."

44 KANE, PATRICIA. "Flannery O'Connor's Everything That Rises Must Converge." Crit 8, i:85-91.

The stories have common elements, "but each story has its internal logic and special interest apart from the patterns in the total work." These individual stories should not be buried in generalizations about region and religion. Includes a brief discussion of three stories: "The Lame Shall Enter First," "A View of the Woods," and "Everything That Rises Must Converge."

45 KEVIN, SISTER MARY, O.S.B. "Flannery O'Connor: In Memory of a Vision Unlimited." Censer (Winter), pp. 37-42.

O'Connor creates characters who are aware of grace but reject it; the characters in her stories, except Bevel in "The River," show the beauty of grace by its absence from their lives. O'Connor's work does contain the grotesque, but her characters are grotesque because they have chosen to separate themselves from God.

46 KIELY, ROBERT. "The Art of Collision." Christian Science Monitor (17 June), p. 7.

The stories in Everything That Rises Must Converge benefit from being placed together. O'Connor has an advantage over many other modern writers in being "not mixed up." The "strange intensity and compelling seriousness" of her work come from "the evocation of a presence" of the divine. Her stories end in catastrophic collisions, but she was not "a young prophetess of doom," since "even prophecies of doom imply an alternative which chaos cannot provide."

47 LAWSON, LEWIS A. "Flannery O'Connor and the Grotesque: Wise Blood." Renascence 17:137-47, 156.
O'Connor's world resembles that of modern painting; her world is like a dream, "with characters who transpose themselves, with aimless actions endlessly performed, with bizarre mixtures of the known and the unfamiliar." Also discusses O'Connor's methods of characterization, including her constructing Haze as an "oxymoron," and her use of the theme of blindness versus sight. The "form" the novel is based on is the legend of St. Anthony. Wise Blood parallels and deviates from this legend, and we are able to understand Haze's behavior by these parallels and deviations. It is very likely that O'Connor created Haze in the manner of a parable: first came the abstract idea and the form of the legend, and then Haze was created to fit into this pattern. For a reply See 1970.B27. Reprinted 1968.A1.

48 LeCLEZIO, J. M. G. "L'Univers de Flannery O'Connor." NRF 13, No. 153:488-93.
A discussion of The Violent Bear It Away. In O'Connor's vision men and nature are bound together in a cursed universe where men are fanatics and where the adults, old Tarwater and Rayber, fight death by seeking to impose their systems on the young. Men seek peace but are unable to find it except in death or nothingness. All human relations are master-slave relations, and each man is both master and slave. Young Tarwater's initiation is an initiation into the hates, lies, and violence of adult life. Such a work, however, could only have been written by one who loves life and who understands that men are what they are because of the nature of life. The mystery of life is that men have a soul, which is valuable yet makes life tragic. This article is also the preface to the French translation of The Violent Bear It Away, Et ce sont les violents qui l'emportent, translated by Maurice Edgar Coindreau (Paris: Gallimard, 1965), pp. 7-13.

49 LEVINE, PAUL. "Flannery O'Connor's Genius." Jubilee (October), pp. 52-53.
A laudatory review of Everything That Rises Must Converge. The stories "reveal how splendid and austerely limited was her achievement." O'Connor's "vision was deep rather than wide and her development may be seen as a process of enriching a few themes and situations." She was influenced by Nathanael West and Faulkner but largely shunned Faulkner's rhetoric and turned "the vision of the absurd in West into a vision of the grotesque." "Revelation" is especially praised.

50 LLOYD, ERIC. Review of Everything That Rises Must Converge. Wall Street Journal (9 July), p. 8.
A brief review. O'Connor was "a pupil in the Southern school of fiction of Carson McCullers and Eudora Welty" and also a Roman Catholic. In her fiction "suffering made for strength and in the clash of spirit with material values, the vision of the poet won out with the prose writer."

51 MALIN, IRVING. "The Gothic Family." In Psychoanalysis and American Fiction. Edited by Irving Malin. New York: E. P. Dutton, Dutton Paperbacks, pp. 255-77.
A reprint of the third chapter, "The Family," of New American Gothic. See 1962.B18.

52 MALOFF, SAUL. Review of Everything That Rises Must Converge. Commonweal (3 December), p. 287.
A capsule review. The stories are "beautifully controlled and shaped and deeply reverberent [sic]."

53 MARTIN, SISTER M., O.P. "O'Connor's 'A Good Man Is Hard to Find.'" Expl 24: Item 19.
The grandmother in the story is "a good woman" at the end because her standard of goodness has changed from one of social decorum to "one of human responsibility and unity before God."

*54 SISTER MAURA. "Resurrection in August." Delta Epsilon Sigma Bulletin 10 (March), 17-19.

55 MAYHEW, ALICE. Review of Everything That Rises Must Converge. Commonweal (3 December), p. 289.
A capsule review. In these stories O'Connor's "theological structuring is less obtrusive," and "the sometimes jarring and constrictive neo-Gothicism was shattering under the impact of an increasing strength and gripping reality."

56 MERTON, THOMAS. "The Other Side of Despair: Notes on Christian Existentialism." Critic 24 (October-November), 12-23.
"A Good Man Is Hard to Find" and The Violent Bear It Away are referred to as examples of the Christian existentialist attack against "pragmatism and positivism," and other works by O'Connor are briefly discussed.

57 MONTGOMERY, MARION. "The Sense of Violation: Notes toward a Definition of 'Southern' Fiction." GaR 19:278-87.

(MONTGOMERY, MARION)

Distinguishes between a "Northern" writing that is "feminine" because the characters lack inner strength and a "Southern" writing that is "masculine" because the characters are capable of violating divine and human commandments but are also capable of assuming responsibility for their acts. This distinction is not so much geographical as philosophical, with Capote and McCullers being essentially "Northern" writers. O'Connor is a "Southern" writer, whose character young Tarwater recalls Agamemnon and his dilemma and whose writing does not satirize her characters but shows "the hard cold light of love, the salient quality of which I would call masculine." "Southern" writing avoids the "sickness" of "Northern" writing because it believes in community and mutual responsibility.

58 MORRIS, WRIGHT. "The Lunatic, the Lover, and the Poet." Kenyon Review 27:727-37.

In an essay on the reasons contemporary American writers use the grotesque claims that Sherwood Anderson freed the grotesque from merely humorous treatments and thus allowed such writers as Carson McCullers and O'Connor to be more than humorous. With O'Connor, the humor reinforces the horror.

59 MOYNAHAN, JULIAN. Review of Everything That Rises Must Converge. NYTBR (5 December), p. 4.

A brief review. O'Connor's characters "do actual or psychological violence to each other in situations charged, quite literally, with arrayed possibilities of damnation or salvation." Although many of these stories concern "fierce economic motivation" and death, O'Connor never lost "her fine sense of comedy" and never let religious themes destroy the individuality of her characters.

60 MUGGERIDGE, MALCOLM. Review of Everything That Rises Must Converge. Esquire (May), pp. 46, 48.

Like Mauriac, O'Connor "gets into her writing a shrinking horror of human behavior, whether in its fleshly or transcendental obsessions, which Jonathan Swift might have envied." The South may be as bad as O'Connor portrays, but the reviewer prefers the "cheerful" vision of the South in Huckleberry Finn.

61 OSTERMANN, ROBERT. "A World Without Love, as Seen by Miss O'Connor." National Observer (28 June), p. 19.

Everything That Rises Must Converge confirms O'Connor's position as a major American writer and follows "her austere, elliptical style and almost conversational tone" found in her previous work. O'Connor successfully integrated theology and fiction in these stories about "a world of all-but-total alienation of human beings from each other."

62 POIRIER, RICHARD. "If You Know Who You Are You Can Go Anywhere." NYTBR (30 May), pp. 6, 22.

A review of Everything That Rises Must Converge. The pride of O'Connor's characters is discussed, as well as her Catholic ability to see "Christian mysteries in things irreduceably [sic] banal." O'Connor has an "absolute sureness of timing," but her stories tend to be repetitious in the conclusions, often ending in the death of a parental figure. This repetitiousness indicates O'Connor's commitment; O'Connor "may be the only writer of English or American fiction in this century whose style, down to the very placing of a comma, is derived from a religious feeling for the simplest actualities." "Revelation" is a masterpiece.

63 POORE, CHARLES. "Books of the Times: The Wonderful World of Flannery O'Connor." NYT (27 May), p. 35.

A review of Everything That Rises Must Converge. O'Connor stands by herself as a writer and cannot be adequately categorized as a southern writer or a writer of the grotesque. Her stories always have a sense of the normal behind the grotesque, and in terms of the South she treats "war within families rather than the wars between symbolic brothers." "Greenleaf" is the best story in the book.

64 PRYCE-JONES, ALAN. "A Poignant Knowledge of the Dark." New York Herald Tribune (25 May), p. 23.

The stories in Everything That Rises Must Converge deal with "warring incomprehensions," but "never were stories of violence less crude, either in their statements or implications." Like her fellow invalid Kafka, O'Connor has "a poignant comprehension of the dark," but she does not exclude good from her vision.

65 QUINN, JOHN J., S.J. Review of Everything That Rises Must Converge. Best Sellers 25:124-25.

The "portraits of the characters" are similar to O'Connor's previous portraits, "yet each is distinctly itself." The stories are "illuminated with insight and with the spiritual dimension of religious significance." In one form or another, "Death is in each story."

1965

66 QUINN, SISTER M. BERNETTA, O.S.F. "A Gaze of Honesty Marks This Novel." Boston Sunday Herald (13 June), p. 8, Section 6.

A review of Everything That Rises Must Converge. Those who confuse art with life may misinterpret these stories, but the collection shows O'Connor's honesty, her treatment of each individual as unique, and her theme of Redemption. O'Connor "is master of image and its sister symbol, of humor and also a tragic quality controlled by her own impressive stability."

*67 RAGAN, MARJORIE. "Southern Accent." News and Observer (Raleigh, N. C.) (18 April), p. III-3.

68 RECHNITZ, ROBERT M. "Passionate Pilgrim: Flannery O'Connor's Wise Blood." GaR 19:310-16.

The novel is "a quest novel" where Haze devotes most of his time to "attempting to discover just what the goal should be." He experiences three threats to his ministry, Asa Hawks, Onnie Jay Holy, and Enoch Emery, that reveal to him the nature of his quest, and he ends in a mutilation which "is profoundly paradoxical: total commitment to his atheism becomes his highest affirmation of God's existence." His commitment gives him "tragic proportions" and leads him to the God of his grandfather, "a God merciless in his mercy."

69 SCHOTT, WEBSTER. "Flannery O'Connor, Faith's Stepchild." Nation (13 September), pp. 142-44.

A review of Everything That Rises Must Converge that places some emphasis on parallels between O'Connor's life and fiction, as in the stress on seeing, the family with only one parent, and the lack of eroticism. O'Connor's "Catholicism belongs...somewhere near the time of the Inquisition." Despite her claims to the contrary, her work has many similarities with that of John Hawkes and the existentialists. Her vision is very bleak, and her range is thus very small, but esthetically "her fiction is the most extraordinary thing to happen to the American short story since Ernest Hemingway."

70 SMITH, LILLIAN. "With a Wry Smile Hovering Over All." Chicago Sunday Tribune Book Section (6 June), p. 5.

A review of Everything That Rises Must Converge. O'Connor was a very skilled writer, yet her art ultimately fails because she saw social evil as personal evil and because she lacked compassion for her characters.

71 SNOW, OLLYE TINE. "The Functional Gothic of Flannery O'Connor." SWR 50:286-99.

O'Connor does employ various gothic devices, including the strange voice, the spirit, strange sounds, "the modernized evil religious figure," the tyrant, visions and dreams, mutilation, and several others, but unlike eighteenth century gothic writers she employs these devices not merely to shock but to further her "theme of man's ability to overcome perversity only if he becomes obedient to Divine Authority." Also discusses the gothic-influenced "circular structure" of The Violent Bear It Away and "horizontal structure" of "A Late Encounter with the Enemy," as well as the "'peaks' of spiritual revelation or Gothic-like visions" that pervade the stories.

72 SOLOTAROFF, THEODORE. "You Can Go Home Again." New York Herald Tribune Book Week (30 May), pp. 1, 13.

A review of Everything That Rises Must Converge that briefly discusses the problems of the southern writer, O'Connor's life, and her development as a writer. O'Connor "was not portraying Southern life so much as her own lurid sensations of the religious life." Her novels are harmed by an overabundance of bizarre melodrama, but her stories successfully treat the distance between the modern South and her sacramental view of life. The stories in Everything That Rises Must Converge demonstrate her skill as a writer and her newfound ability to avoid "merely being sardonic and bizarre." Reprinted 1970.B38.

73 STERN, RICHARD. "Flannery O'Connor: A Remembrance and Some Letters." Shenandoah 16 (Winter), 5-10.

An account of O'Connor's trip to Chicago in 1959 and several letters from O'Connor. In a discussion with the author, O'Connor denied that The Violent Bear It Away and some of her stories published at roughly the same time "showed the pressure of trying to get certain things said more directly than she'd said them before."

74 SULLIVAN, WALTER. "Flannery O'Connor, Sin and Grace: Everything That Rises Must Converge." HC 2 (September), 1-8, 10.

A review of Everything That Rises Must Converge that includes a general discussion of O'Connor. O'Connor was gifted, but her range was limited: she was solely interested in "the vulgarities of this world and the perfections of the other." Being a Southerner probably helped O'Connor, but the essentials of her fiction are religious, not regional. O'Connor is best at short stories. Her use

1965

(SULLIVAN, WALTER)
of exaggeration as a way of communicating her beliefs and her "fictional vision that discovery was all" mean that her novels lack the density and subtlety of fine novels. The conflict in O'Connor's works is not between characters who are good or evil but between those who believe in their own self-sufficiency and "those who are driven, in spite of their own failings, to do God's purpose." "The Lame Shall Enter First" is an excellent example of this conflict. Although O'Connor's vision may seem dark, she was a Christian optimist who saw life from the viewpoint of eternity and God's mercy. Reprinted 1971.B31 and 1972.B43.

75 TRACHTENBERG, STANLEY. "Black Humor, Pale Fiction." _YR_ N.S. 55:144-49.
Although she is a Catholic, O'Connor's humor in _Everything That Rises Must Converge_ has connections with "black humor" in the "disparity often manifest in the lack of proportion between the violence that occurs and that which may legitimately be anticipated" and in "the refusal... either to apologize for or explain an often incomprehensible fate."

76 WALSTON, ROSA LEE. "Flannery O'Connor: A Good Writer Is Hard to Find." _Columns_ (Georgia College at Milledgeville). (Fall), pp. 8-13.
A reprint of a lecture given by the head of the Department of English and Speech at O'Connor's alma mater. O'Connor is not a regional writer, but a religious one. She writes from a Catholic viewpoint, yet her work does not contradict orthodox Protestantism. O'Connor's "sparse" but graphic style, her flair for idiom, her emphasis on the sin of pride, and her "sense of commitment" are also discussed. O'Connor was best at short stories, and "The Lame Shall Enter First," perhaps her best story, shows that she does not lack compassion.

77 WELLS, JOEL. "Misfits in a Hung-Over Bible Land." _U. S. Catholic_ (July), pp. 62, 65.
A review of _Everything That Rises Must Converge_ that includes a general discussion of O'Connor's fiction and literary career. O'Connor was not "particularly disturbed" about the incomprehension of many critics or her lack of mass popularity. Her fictional region is the South, "but it seems more like some hung-over biblical land where nobody has gotten the word that the Old Testament ended a few thousand years ago." O'Connor is a religious writer who uses extreme means to get her point across and who relies

heavily on the Bible. The theme of her fiction is that true tragedy and grotesqueness lie in living without God and without even realizing His importance. "Revelation," "Greenleaf," and "Judgement Day" are highly praised.

78 WOODWARD, KENNETH L. Review of Everything That Rises Must Converge. Commonweal (3 December), p. 291.
A capsule review. O'Connor "had a grimly Gothic humor which at bottom resembled Blake more than Faulkner." For a Catholic, O'Connor was surprisingly biblical. She had great "narrative discipline."

1966 A BOOKS

1 DRAKE, ROBERT. Flannery O'Connor: A Critical Essay. Contemporary Writers in Christian Perspective. Grand Rapids: William B. Eerdmans.
A revised and expanded version of 1966.B9 that includes a brief account of O'Connor's life and a short, selected bibliography of criticism on O'Connor. O'Connor's use of "cartoons" to shock her nonreligious readers is also mentioned.

2 FRIEDMAN, MELVIN, J. and LEWIS A. LAWSON, eds. The Added Dimension: The Art and Mind of Flannery O'Connor. New York: Fordham University Press.
A collection of essays on O'Connor that includes some of her correspondence and some of her comments on her own and other fiction as well as a bibliography of works by and about O'Connor. The collection includes the following critical essays: Melvin J. Friedman, "Introduction," pp. 1-31; Frederick J. Hoffman, "The Search for Redemption: Flannery O'Connor's Fiction," pp. 32-48; Louis D. Rubin, Jr., "Flannery O'Connor and the Bible Belt," pp. 49-72; C. Hugh Holman, "Her Rue with a Difference: Flannery O'Connor and the Southern Literary Tradition," pp. 73-87; P. Albert Duhamel, "The Novelist as Prophet," pp. 88-107; Irving Malin, "Flannery O'Connor and the Grotesque," pp. 108-22; Caroline Gordon, "An American Girl," pp. 123-37; Nathan A. Scott, Jr., "Flannery O'Connor's Testimony: The Pressure of Glory," pp. 138-56; Sister M. Bernetta Quinn, O.S.F., "Flannery O'Connor, a Realist of Distances," pp. 157-83; Harold C. Gardiner, S.J., "Flannery O'Connor's Clarity of Vision," pp. 184-95; and Melvin J. Friedman, "Flannery O'Connor's Sacred Objects," pp. 196-206. The writings by O'Connor are the following: William Sessions, ed., "A Correspondence," pp. 209-25; Lewis A. Lawson, ed.,

(FRIEDMAN, MELVIN, J. and LEWIS A. LAWSON)
"A Collection of Statements," pp. 226-63; Flannery O'Connor, "Fiction Is a Subject with a History--It Should Be Taught That Way," pp. 264-68; and Norman Charles, ed., "A Lecture," pp. 269-79. The final portion of the book is the bibliography by Lewis A. Lawson, pp. 281-302. Descriptions of the critical articles about O'Connor and the bibliography are given below in the "B" section for this year.

3 HYMAN, STANLEY EDGAR. Flannery O'Connor. University of Minnesota Pamphlets on American Writers No. 54. Minneapolis: University of Minnesota Press.
Focuses on recurring images, symbols, character groupings, and themes in O'Connor's fiction. O'Connor's meanings are Christian, but "mainly in the mystic and ascetic tradition of St. John of the Cross," not in the "humanitarian tradition." O'Connor resembles Dostoyevsky in her constant use of "two of everything," the one divine and the other demonic, and in her use of art to purge herself of all she found repugnant. O'Connor's art is a personal catharsis that leaves her free to be "friendly and loving" and "devout and serene." Includes a selected bibliography of O'Connor's works and critical and biographical studies on O'Connor. For replies See 1968.B30, 1969.B12, and 1971.B22.

1966 B SHORTER WRITINGS

1 ANON. "Memento Mori." TLS (24 March), p. 242.
A review of Everything That Rises Must Converge and Fifty Best American Short Stories, 1915-1965, edited by Martha Foley. O'Connor was not a major but a "rare minor writer." Her imagination was limited by her inability to deal directly with the black experience in the South and by her Catholicism, though she manages to avoid too rigid dualisms. She was basically concerned with the family and its destruction by self-deception. O'Connor's work is preoccupied, as she herself was, with death, and this preoccupation makes her work stand above most of the too refined stories in the Foley collection, despite her own avoidance of direct treatment of social issues.

2 BANNON, BARBARA. Review of The Violent Bear It Away. Publishers' Weekly (27 June), p. 102.
The novel's style is called "fascinating" in this very brief review.

3 BRITTAIN, JOAN. "The Fictional Family of Flannery O'Connor." Renascence 19:48-52.

A discussion of the various recurring types of characters in O'Connor's fiction: "adolescents, young single males, widows, widowers, bachelors, old maids, whole families, and finally, children." Although there are differences, each group tends to have certain traits, and these common traits help to unify all of O'Connor's fiction. O'Connor's use of spectacles in her fiction emphasizes the "sameness of characters," since "the more complicated characters" wear these symbols of spiritual blindness. The only exception is Mr. Guizac, who wears spectacles, yet "among all the violently grotesque characters of Miss O'Connor, stands out as a pin point of light for all."

4 BURGESS, ANTHONY. Review of Everything That Rises Must Converge. Listener (7 April), p. 515.
The collection "breathes that not-so-sweet South which--after the large Faulkner concession--must be wholly hers. The range is astonishing."

5 BURKE, JOHN J., JR., S.J. "Convergence of Flannery O'Connor and Chardin." Renascence 19:41-47, 52.
Robert Fitzgerald's claim that the title, Everything That Rises Must Converge, should be taken with some irony (1965.B30) is true only if her stories are read on a naturalistic rather than a theological level. The end of the title story, with Julian's loss of pride, indicates that O'Connor took Teilhard de Chardin's ideas seriously and without irony. Also, the order of the stories in the collection shows that "we will converge with Christ, the Omega Point."

6 COLEMAN, JOHN. "Small-Town Miseries." Observer (27 March), p. 27.
A British review of Everything That Rises Must Converge that finds the stories having "narrow and overlapping interests," but praises O'Connor's "notable feats of impersonation," especially her family dialogues and her portraits of "the glassed-in ladies" of "Everything That Rises Must Converge" and "Revelation." Criticizes her characterizations of liberals and northern blacks, yet finds her "remarkable on the continuing matter of pretending, trying, and failing to be good."

7 COLEMAN, RICHARD. "Flannery O'Conner [sic]: A Scrutiny of Two Forms of Her Many-Levelled Art." Phoenix (College of Charleston) 1:30-66.
Compares O'Connor's self-portrait with her fiction, especially "The Artificial Nigger" and "The River." The

(COLEMAN, RICHARD)
portrait and the fiction reveal that O'Connor did not lack compassion; indeed, her central concern is love, and this she showed for her characters. In order to understand fully these characters we also have to love them. Claims that the self-portrait demands a medieval four-level analysis and gives an extended interpretation of the portrait's meaning.

8 DETWEILER, ROBERT. "The Curse of Christ in Flannery O'Connor's Fiction." CLS 3:235-45.

The language and images, the settings, the action, and the themes of O'Connor's fiction "are informed and determined by corresponding religious elements," and O'Connor "converts those elements into the structure and content of good literary art." Her language joins "revivalist term and phrase with 'normal' speech" and "Biblical and backwoods English." This joining indicates the "subjugation of the religious spirit to selfish modes of existence" and the gap between God and man, but the language is also incarnational in its fusion of such realms: it is "prophetic, kerygmatic, existential, and sacramental." The settings rely "upon the pervasion of spiritual moods," and they contain four types of characters: "Pentecostal fanatics," "militant atheists," "the religiously unconcerned," and "the conventionally religious." The action involves an inevitable encounter with Christ, a pattern "of redemptive and condemnatory action with a similar presence of an alter ego and the moment of grace." O'Connor's themes involve ambiguity: the ambiguity arising from fusing the tragic and the comic to create the grotesque and that deriving from "her merging of symbol and irony" to create paradox.

9 DRAKE, ROBERT. "'The Bleeding, Stinking Mad Shadow of Jesus' in the Fiction of Flannery O'Connor." CLS 3:183-96.

A "Christian" reading of O'Connor that stresses her uncompromising, though non-sectarian, theology, her unsentimental view of Christ, and her continual use of the theme of choosing or rejecting Christ. O'Connor's novels and some of her stories are briefly discussed, with emphasis on her suspicion of progress and modern intellectualism, her treatment of women and domestic life, and her belief that pride, either of will or intellect, is the worst of all sins. O'Connor's fiction is not like that of the "Southern Gothic School" because in her fiction "behind the grotesque lies the ultimate concept of straightness." Many will agree with O'Connor's "diagnosis of the human condition," but some tension is inevitable between O'Connor and those readers who cannot accept her beliefs. See 1966.A1.

10 DUHAMEL, P. ALBERT. "The Novelist as Prophet." In The Added Dimension, pp. 88-107.

See 1966.A2. The Violent Bear It Away resembles I'll Take My Stand, the 1930 collection of essays by the southern "Fugitives," in its rejection of scientism, its belief in the whole man and the importance of passion and conviction, and its call for leaders who will act, even to the point of violence. "The Fugitive essayists were calling upon the South to say NO to an all-engulfing Northern industrialism; Flannery O'Connor wrote to discipline her readers to a willingness to say NO to the forces denying God's place in reality." Also discusses O'Connor's theory of the novelist as prophet by comparing it with Tate's theory of metaphor and discusses O'Connor's "peculiar mimesis."

11 EMBLER, WELLER. Metaphor and Meaning. Deland, Florida: Everett/Edwards, pp. 98-99, 108-09.

Wise Blood is discussed as an example of the use of the rhetorical device of reversal, since O'Connor uses "the modern devices of reversal within reversal, image within contrary image, idea within contrary idea, paradox within paradox, the negation of the affirmed to the end that Hazel Motes' return to the faith must follow as the inescapable conclusion to a logical proposition." "Good Country People" displays the "irony of the absurd," since "the incident is not so much ironic as it is an objective correlative of the perverted inner lives of the characters."

12 FRIEDMAN, MELVIN J. "Flannery O'Connor's Sacred Objects." In The Added Dimension, pp. 196-206.

See 1966.A2. O'Connor's work is strikingly free of experimentation, except for her use of indirect interior monologue and her reliance on objects in her work. Her use of indirect interior monologue probably results from her association with the southern oral tradition, not from the early twentieth century revolutions in fictional technique. Her reliance on objects seems to be an application of Mircea Eliade's theory of "hierophany," i.e., the manifestation of the sacred in an ordinary object. This "clash" of the sacred and profane in her work should not be connected with the use of objects in the French "New Novel." Reprinted in a slightly revised version 1970.B18.

1966

13 FRIEDMAN, MELVIN J. Introduction to The Added Dimension, pp. 1-31.
See 1966.A2. A considerably revised and expanded version of 1962.B6. O'Connor's American reputation is assured, and her reputation should soon grow in Europe. For a reply See 1970.B12.

14 GARDINER, HAROLD C., S.J. "Flannery O'Connor's Clarity of Vision." In The Added Dimension, pp. 184-95.
See 1966.A2. Because of her Christian "clarity of vision," O'Connor eschews sentimentality in her portrayals of her characters, yet she makes us feel mercy for all of them. O'Connor's work is also one of mercy because she, like every genuine writer, implies "a universe of harmony and love" for which her grotesque characters yearn. Relates O'Connor's introduction to A Memoir of Mary Ann to O'Connor's fiction.

15 GORDON, CAROLINE. "An American Girl." In The Added Dimension, pp. 123-37.
See 1966.A2. O'Connor is "the American girl" whom Henry James predicted would be responsible for the future of American culture. O'Connor resembles James in her ability to unify a literary structure, and she was a pioneer in daring to write of religious conversion: "Miss O'Connor, almost alone among her contemporaries, adheres strictly to the great architectural principle (upon which James's three great later novels are based) that in the life of certain human beings supernatural grace operates as freely as natural grace - if only when being resisted."

16 GRIFFITH, ALBERT J. "Flannery O'Connor's Salvation Road." SSF 3:329-33.
Up until Shiftlet abandons Lucynell, "The Life You Save May Be Your Own" offers many parallels between Shiftlet and Christ, but with the abandonment the parallel breaks down. Shiftlet is not Christlike, nor is he an antichrist; he "seems to represent modern man called to follow the pattern of Christ, a pattern that is unfortunately often followed imperfectly and incompletely." The road signs and the boy's profanity force "Mr. Shiftlet to recognize his own flaw in the loveless boy. The shock of failure leads to his anguished prayer and to an answering shower from heaven."

17 HAMILTON, ALEX. Review of Everything That Rises Must Converge. Books and Bookmen (June), p. 45.
A British review. At the time of her death O'Connor "was reaching the peak of her skill," and she seemed

destined to be equal with the best of southern writers. Her characters are "comic and pathetic" because of "unconscious stubborness"; she achieved "some of the most whippy writing of our time."

18 HASSAN, IHAB. "The Dial and Recent American Fiction." CEA 29, i:1, 3.

Refers to O'Connor's two novels as examples of the "Gothic Novel," which "by refusing the comforts of irony, pushes negative transcendence towards its final goal, which is hell."

19 HOFFMAN, FREDERICK J. "The Search for Redemption: Flannery O'Connor's Fiction." In The Added Dimension, pp. 32-48.

See 1966.A2. Basically a discussion of Wise Blood and The Violent Bear It Away. O'Connor is for the most part describing two states of man: "the desperate need for redemption" and "the condition that exists in the absence (or the apparent absence) of redemption." Her work is written for readers who "need to be forced or shocked and/or amused into accepting the validity of religious states," and the violence in her work is the result of "the sparks caused by the clash of religious desire and disbelief."

20 HOLMAN, C. HUGH. "Her Rue with a Difference: Flannery O'Connor and the Southern Literary Tradition." In The Added Dimension, pp. 73-87.

See 1966.A2. O'Connor shared with other southern writers a passion for moral order, but her Roman Catholicism enabled her to see that southern Protestantism's emphasis on extreme individualism made a genuine spiritual community impossible. O'Connor's characters are "distorted" because they "seek with undeniable passion a meaning and order the Protestant South cannot give." Reprinted 1972.B21.

21 _____. Three Modes of Modern Southern Fiction. Mercer University Lamar Memorial Series No. 9. Athens, Ga.: University of Georgia Press, pp. 52-53.

Passing reference to O'Connor. Her work "may very well represent the best writing done by a Southerner during the past fifteen years."

22 HOY, CYRUS and WALTER SULLIVAN, eds. "An Interview with Flannery O'Connor and Robert Penn Warren." In Writer to Writer: Readings on the Craft of Fiction. Edited by Floyd C. Watkins and Karl F. Knight. Boston: Houghton-Mifflin, pp. 71-90.

Reprint of 1960.B35.

1966

23 JORDAN, RENE. "A Southern Drawl from Beyond the Grave." British Association for American Studies Bulletin N.S. 12/13:99-101.

A review of Everything That Rises Must Converge. O'Connor is "the easiest to put down" of all major modern American writers because her stories are unconvincing on a naturalistic level and have very heavy-handed plots. The collection was "conceived by a dying woman who is not afraid of going to hell: she's been in it too long and has begun to find it cosy and dull." "Revelation," with its yearning for a "holocaust," and "The Enduring Chill," with its bitterness over the failure of escape, are autobiographical. O'Connor "lived in death and achieved the compassionate irony of someone who truly writes from beyond the grave." Her work is "siren-singing to the suicidal."

24 KANN, JEAN MARIE, O.S.F. "Everything That Rises Must Converge." CathW (December), pp. 154-59.

A reminiscence of the author's friendship with O'Connor and a discussion of the influence of Teilhard de Chardin on O'Connor's later work. O'Connor's "letters, like her stories, show and especially advocate a relentless stripping, an inexorable purifying of sources." Her continual advice on writing was "dramatize more; report less." All of O'Connor's stories treat the explosion "upwards into God," and the violence in her works comes from the collision of illusion and reality, a reality that contains a spiritual dimension. Teilhard de Chardin's emphasis on an evolution towards God is found in O'Connor's stories.

25 LAWSON, LEWIS A. "Bibliography." In The Added Dimension, pp. 283-302.

See 1966.A2. A bibliography of "1) separate publication of stories and of chapters of novels; 2) chronology of editions of books; 3) book reviews; and 4) critical articles."

26 LENSING, GEORGE. "De Chardin's Ideas in Flannery O'Connor." Renascence 18:171-75.

O'Connor used allegory to close the gap between her use of shock and her Christian message. She also used comedy to increase the reader's awareness of her Christian themes and to point out human imperfection. In her vision "the world contains, not only the coexistence of imperfection and redemption, but the mutual dependence of each upon the other." O'Connor differs from southern gothic writers because she is not nostalgic for the old South and she is not interested in portraying social decay; she resembles Faulkner because "she uses her Southern setting allegorically."

27 McCARTHY, JOHN F. "Human Intelligence Versus Divine Truth: The Intellectual in Flannery O'Connor's Works." EJ 55: 1143-48.

O'Connor's intellectuals tend to deny God and try to put themselves in His place; they also tend to separate themselves from reality. They fail "because they cannot or will not recognize the involvement of divine grace and salvation with the human condition." Although her basic attitude towards her intellectual characters never changes, O'Connor's later work shows more sympathy and understanding for them.

28 MALIN, IRVING. "Flannery O'Connor and the Grotesque." In The Added Dimension, pp. 108-22.

See 1966.A2. O'Connor's Christianity and her psychological awareness of the grotesque are in conflict: "She must believe as a Christian in free will and spiritual design. But as a writer she reinforces the grotesquerie of existence." O'Connor's "great victory" is that she can see her flat, narcissistic characters for what they are and can thus "declare her sanity." For a reply See 1969.B14.

29 MARKS, W. S., III. "Advertisements for Grace: Flannery O'Connor's 'A Good Man Is Hard to Find.'" SSF 4:19-27.

O'Connor's literary affinities are with the "Pauline or Augustinian tradition" of Hawthorne and earlier allegorists. In religion she seems closest to Calvinistic evangelism, and in temperament she resembles Dostoyevsky and modern radical opponents of liberalism's faith in uniformity and rational progress. The story is filled with allegorical significance; for example, "the watermelon...symbolizes the sensual and specifically sexual gratifications allowed the Negro but denied the virtuous white man under the peculiar dispensations of the Protestant ethic," and the Misfit's disagreement with his psychiatrist represents "the intellectual quarrel between science and religion." O'Connor lacks "the psychological insight" of other major modern writers, and her characters are lifeless because of her lack of sympathy for them.

30 PRITCHETT, V. S. "Satan Comes to Georgia." New Statesman (1 April), pp. 469, 472.

A review of Everything That Rises Must Converge. O'Connor is a good example of the American superiority to England in the short story, a superiority perhaps arising from the loneliness, violence, and anxiety of American life, which allows writers to write of "the exposed character or the inner riot of the lonely man or woman."

1966

(PRITCHETT, V. S.)
O'Connor excells in her inobtrusive use of religious symbolism and her craftsmanship. Her stories deal with the abnormal, but "they are not case histories or indignation meetings." They treat "the violence which will purify but destroy." O'Connor has a profound awareness of the evil within man.

31 QUINN, SISTER M. BERNETTA, O.S.F. "Flannery O'Connor, a Realist of Distances." In The Added Dimension, pp. 157-83.
See 1966.A2. An examination of the role of prophecy in O'Connor's work that discusses the various characters' relation to prophecy and O'Connor's use of symbolism in connection with prophecy. Emphasizes the importance of the Bible to O'Connor. Also discusses O'Connor's use of the grotesque and contrasts her use of it with that of Sherwood Anderson.

32 REYNOLDS, HILARY. Review of Everything That Rises Must Converge. Dublin Magazine, Summer, pp. 89-90.
The collection is "a brilliant and profound meditation" on death and tragedy. The stories combine "violence and colour and the supernatural" with O'Connor's compassion for humans, especially mothers. O'Connor "is not morbid; she is preoccupied with salvation and man's search for redemption."

33 RUBIN, LOUIS D., JR. "Flannery O'Connor and the Bible Belt." In The Added Dimension, pp. 49-72.
See 1966.A2. Although O'Connor preferred southern fundamentalism to modern secularism, as a Roman Catholic writer she was aware of the limitations of fundamentalism. The protagonists of Wise Blood and The Violent Bear It Away are able to escape secularism, but they are grotesques because their God is the fundamentalist God of Wrath, not a God of Love. For a reply See 1969.B14. Reprinted 1967.B16.

34 _____. "Southerners and Jews." SoR N.S. 2:697-713.
Argues that most of the stories in Everything That Rises Must Converge are not as good as O'Connor's earlier stories because most of them lack any sympathy for human weakness. Only "Parker's Back" and "Judgement Day" are exceptions, probably because their protagonists are uneducated, non-middle class characters. Suggests that the southern renascence in literature, which gained strength from the clash of traditional and modern modes of life, may be disappearing and that O'Connor is so important in postwar southern literature because her Catholicism gave her an "impediment

to the general southern conversion to modern, secular experience." American Jews, who are midway in their own conversion, are in the midst of their own literary flowering. Reprinted 1967.B16.

35 SCOTT, NATHAN A., JR. "Flannery O'Connor's Testimony: The Pressure of Glory." In The Added Dimension, pp. 138-56.
See 1966.A2. Mainly discusses Wise Blood and The Violent Bear It Away. O'Connor is one of those modern writers who react against what Mircea Eliade calls "desacralization," the loss of a sense of mystery in life. O'Connor's strategy in confronting this "desacralization" is to push the secular to such an extreme that the spiritual once again becomes possible, "since negation, if it be profound enough, may itself, by reason of its very radicalism, begin to evoke sensibilities capable of a religious perception of reality." Reprinted 1968.B36.

36 SMITH, J. OATES. "Ritual and Violence in Flannery O'Connor." Thought 41:545-60.
O'Connor combines "Kierkegaardian anguish in the face of man's certitude and Kafkan anguish in the face of man's ignorance." She also resembles Freud in her preference for dualisms, but what is new for modern literature is her "commitment to the divine origin of the unconscious." Her work is not realistic or naturalistic; her theme "demands not only a surrealistic style but a surrealistic landscape." The work is filled with rituals and ceremonies because they offer a necessary counterpoise to her primitive extremism. This extremism leads her to neglect "human love." Despite her claims to be a Catholic, her work is Calvinistic in "the absolute denial of free will, the insistence upon the brutal, even bloody, and always catastrophic experience of faith, and the eclipsing of New Testament affirmation by Old Testament wrath." Emphasizes The Violent Bear It Away.

37 STEVENSON, JOHN W. "The Faces of Reynolds Price's Short Fiction." SSF 3:300-06.
O'Connor is briefly contrasted with Reynolds Price. Both use a setting of "rural Protestant fundamentalism," but "while Price underlines the simple virtues that give the character dignity and a name, Miss O'Connor, through distortion and violence, dramatizes the folly of smug ignorance." In O'Connor's world, "there is no sacramental ritual...only suspicious aloofness and a fear of death."

1966

38 STONE, EDWARD. Voices of Despair: Four Motifs in American Literature. Athens, Ohio: Ohio University Press, pp. 199-200, 214.

"Good Country People" is briefly discussed as one example of the modern writer's despair about and suspicion of science and its destruction of man's sense of the dignity and purpose of life.

39 STUCKEY, W. J. The Pulitzer Prize Novels: A Critical Backward Look. Norman: University of Oklahoma Press, pp. 166, 175, 181.

O'Connor is mentioned as a repeated victim of the obtuseness and preference for commercial favorites of the judges for the Pulitzer Prize in fiction.

40 WALSH, THOMAS F. "The Devils of Hawthorne and Flannery O'Connor." XUS 5:117-22.

Both writers "retell the story of the old Adam, and, in their versions, give considerable prominence to the antagonist of the original." Both "distrusted the self-sufficient, modern man," and both use devil-figures as "the objectifications of evil that each character must recognize in himself." In their works the devil can appear either as himself or in more human form, and the devil can, like Chillingworth in The Scarlet Letter, aid the cause of good. Despite these similarities, "Hawthorne's vision is more tragic than satiric. O'Connor's vision is more comic, and her characters are more susceptible to God's saving grace."

1967 A BOOKS - NONE

1967 B SHORTER WRITINGS

1 ANON. Review of Everything That Rises Must Converge. Publishers' Weekly (8 May), p. 63.

A capsule description of the paperback edition. The stories deal "with the individual needs of people and their frequent helplessness in the face of the pressures of their society."

2 ANON. Review of Wise Blood. Publishers' Weekly (1 May), p. 57.

The novel is called "extraordinary" in this very brief review.

3 BRITTAIN, JOAN T. "Flannery O'Connor: A Bibliography, Part 1." BB 25:98-100.

A bibliography that includes a chronological listing of O'Connor's fiction, a list of O'Connor's critical and nonfictional prose, a list of biographical articles on O'Connor, and a list of criticism and reviews of her work. See 1968.B7.

4 _____. "O'Connor's A Good Man Is Hard to Find." Expl 26: Item 1.

The collection has a greater unity than critics have realized. The first story begins with the problem of finding a good man, and the good man does not appear until Mr. Guizac appears in "The Displaced Person." The characters in the stories need "Christian living" but lack it. Mr. Guizac, with his gold-rimmed spectacles that suggest the ability to perceive beyond the material, represents the Christian way of life.

5 BURNS, STUART L. "'Torn By the Lord's Eye': Flannery O'Connor's Use of Sun Imagery." TCL 13:154-66.

The sun in O'Connor's fiction "functions as a visible manifestation of some Divine Agency, intervening in or judging the affairs of men." The sun shows "man's attitude toward God and, conversely, God's toward man." O'Connor also uses it in her "major recurrent pattern" of man's violently encountering God and achieving salvation despite human resistance.

6 DRISKELL, LEON. "'Parker's Back' vs. 'The Partridge Festival': Flannery O'Connor's Critical Choice." GaR 21:476-90.

O'Connor unified her collections of short stories with thematic connections. In A Good Man Is Hard to Find the beginning and ending stories reveal several parallels and contrasts, while in Everything That Rises Must Converge the collection is framed by "the deaths of representatives of the older order in the new changing South" and unified by the theme of redemption. O'Connor chose "Parker's Back" over "The Partridge Festival" for her second collection not for any esthetic reason but for a thematic one. "Parker's Back" suggests the hope of redemption, while "The Partridge Festival" emphasizes man's fall and "the predestined gracelessness of commercialism." Also, "Parker's Back" is far more dependent on biblical parallels.

7 FAHEY, WILLIAM A. "Out of the Eater: Flannery O'Connor's Appetite for Truth." Renascence 20:22-29.

A discussion of O'Connor's "structural interweaving" of "the hungry-fed dichotomy" throughout The Violent Bear It Away and a criticism of John Hawkes's interpretation of

1967

(FAHEY, WILLIAM A.)
O'Connor (1962.B12). In the novel the devil is "not a mere piercer of pretensions whose point of view is rather similar to O'Connor's." The early part of the novel makes this clear, but the homosexual rape should clear all possible doubts about the identity of the devil. O'Connor has many of her characters "share the devil's point of view," and she often does this humorously, as with the truck driver, but her viewpoint is a religious one.

8 GREEN, MARTIN. Yeats's Blessings on von Hugel: Essays on Literature and Religion. London: Longman's, Green, and Co., p. 116.
A passing reference to O'Connor. J. F. Powers and many other Catholic writers stress the "dullness and pettiness" of the environment, while O'Connor and Bernanos emphasize "its savagery and horror."

9 HOFFMAN, FREDERICK J. The Art of Southern Fiction: A Study of Some Modern Novelists. Carbondale: Southern Illinois University Press, pp. 74-95.
Discusses O'Connor and James Agee as two examples of the religious consciousness in southern fiction. O'Connor's fiction is filled with Christ-obsessed characters, but they may appear diabolic because she is mainly describing the need for redemption and the results of the lack of redemption. Although redemption is not always present in her fiction, O'Connor judges her characters by Christian standards: "The grotesqueries of her fiction are in effect a consequence of her seeing what she calls 'the Manichaean spirit of the times,' in which the religious metaphors retain their power but cannot be precisely delineated by persons driven by the necessities they see in them. Violence, in this setting, assumes a religious meaning; it is, in effect, the sparks caused by the clash of religious desire and disbelief."

10 SISTER JEREMY. "The Comic Ritual of Flannery O'Connor." Catholic Library World 39:195-200.
O'Connor's comedy springs from her awareness "that man is a comic figure in his alienation from God; that God Himself has turned the tragedy of sin into a joke by means of the redemption." Also discusses O'Connor's intellectuals as partly self-parodies, her stress on original sin, and her two main categories of sinners: the proud intellectual and the materialistic woman.

11 KIRKLAND, WILLIAM. "Flannery O'Connor, The Person and the Writer." East-West Review 3 (Summer), 159-63.

A reminiscence by the rector of the Episcopal church in Milledgeville. O'Connor "felt called" to battle godless humanism and knew her region very well. The God in her stories may "sometimes act like the devil," but she felt that exaggeration was necessary. O'Connor's illness might have had the effect of turning her against godlessness, but her later works, probably because of the influence of Teilhard de Chardin and the changes in the Catholic Church, "seem to indicate a wider range of compassion and sympathy." Visitors might find O'Connor distant, but those who knew her knew "her compassion and her liking for people."

12 LAWSON, LEWIS A. "The Grotesque in Recent Southern Fiction." In Patterns of Commitment in American Literature. Edited by Marston LaFrance. Toronto: University of Toronto Press, pp. 165-79.

The grotesque is a "mode of illusion" created by the tension in the reader's mind resulting "from the clash of real and unreal, from the bisociation of physical and psychic reality, of the concrete and symbolically indirect." Practitioners of the grotesque stress ambiguity and distortion by combining "photographic accuracy of description" with "manneristic tropes." The grotesque has been so prevalent in modern southern literature because the grotesque flourishes in periods of cultural confusion and because Southerners believe in a "dualistic philosophy" of man that gives them a wider conception of reality than that of most modern American writers. Like other southern writers, O'Connor uses the grotesque, as in her use of mechanical images to describe humans, to reflect the changing nature of society and to make "a call to order." O'Connor's novels are "pure chaos and absurdity" because she wrote in a time when the southern tradition had completely disintegrated. More recent southern fiction has an existential viewpoint, where writers "embrace a philosophy of the absurd." For a reply See 1972.B34.

13 LEVINE, PAUL. "The Intemperate Zone: The Climate of Contemporary American Fiction." MR 8:505-23.

Relates O'Connor's stated reasons for using distortion in her fiction to the use of distortion by other contemporary American writers: contemporary reality is distorted, and the writer must make the reader see this reality for what it is. Also discusses the blending of reality and nightmare in contemporary society, which leads to such forms as the "non-fiction novel," where the real and the fantastic are inseparable.

14 MILLER, JAMES E., JR. "The Quest Absurd: The New American Novel." In Quests Surd and Absurd: Essays in American Literature. Chicago: University of Chicago Press, pp. 3-30.

Discusses the five chief characteristics of the American novel since World War II - "The Nightmare World," "Alienation and Nausea," "Quest for Identity," "The Humor in the Horror," and "A Thin, Frail Line of Hope" - and then evaluates contemporary novelists. O'Connor, J. D. Salinger, Saul Bellow, and Wright Morris are the four contemporary novelists who "have made serious claims for some kind of permanent recognition." All four novelists describe a surreal and violent landscape, but "none of these novelists is a novelist of despair."

15 QUINN, THOMAS. "Lewis and O'Connor: Prophets of the Added Dimension." Report (January), pp. 32-33.

A review of Melvin J. Friedman and Lewis A. Lawson, eds. The Added Dimension: The Art and Mind of Flannery O'Connor and W. H. Lewis, ed., Letters of C. S. Lewis that compares and contrasts O'Connor and C. S. Lewis. Both authors used the spiritual dimension in their writing, and both were "teachers of Christianity." Lewis, however, was better educated, wrote out of "a long cultural tradition," and was much involved in the religious thought of contemporary Anglo-Catholics, whereas O'Connor's reading and tradition were primarily American, and she got nothing from contemporary American Catholic thinkers. Paradoxically, Lewis, the Protestant, was a rational Thomist while O'Connor, the Catholic, was the writer indebted to "explosive" Augustinianism. O'Connor has had greater critical success because she spoke for no cultural tradition and thus was free from being an apologist; her readers can admire her "intensely dramatic art" without having to accept "a set of values and traditions."

16 RUBIN, LOUIS D., JR. The Curious Death of the Novel: Essays in American Literature. Baton Rouge: Louisiana State University Press, pp. 239-61, 263, passim.

A collection of essays that includes reprints of 1963.B20, 1966.B33, and 1966.B34.

17 SCHOLES, ROBERT. The Fabulators. New York: Oxford University Press, pp. 59, 67.

Passing references to O'Connor as one of the novelists John Hawkes admires. Scholes's theory of "fabulation" - of the importance in modern literature of the artist as shaper who puts a high premium on art itself and on form and style instead of documentary realism - is useful for understanding the climate of fiction in which O'Connor wrote.

1968 A BOOKS

1 REITER, ROBERT E., ed. Flannery O'Connor. The Christian Critic Series. St. Louis: B. Herder.
A collection of previously published essays. Includes Brainard Cheney, "Flannery O'Connor's Campaign for Her Country," pp. 1-4 (1964.B25); Melvin J. Friedman, "Flannery O'Connor: Another Legend in Southern Fiction," pp. 5-24 (1962.B6); John Hawkes, "Flannery O'Connor's Devil," pp. 25-37 (1962.B12); Brainard Cheney, "Miss O'Connor Creates Unusual Humor Out of Ordinary Sin," pp. 39-49 (1963.B6); Lewis A. Lawson, "Flannery O'Connor and the Grotesque: Wise Blood," pp. 51-67 (1965.B47); Robert Fitzgerald, "The Countryside and the True Country," pp. 69-82 (1962.B4); Sister M. Joselyn, "Thematic Centers in 'The Displaced Person,'" pp. 83-92 (1964.B52); P. Albert Duhamel, "Flannery O'Connor's Violent View of Reality," pp. 93-101 (1960.B22); Sister Jeremy, "The Violent Bear It Away: A Linguistic Education," pp. 103-110 (1964.B49); and Ted R. Spivey, "Flannery O'Connor's View of God and Man," pp. 111-18 (1964.B80).

1968 B SHORTER WRITINGS

1 ANON. "Displaced Persons." TLS (12 September), p. 975.
A review of a British reissue of A Good Man Is Hard to Find. O'Connor was no more provincial than Thomas Hardy, and unlike Faulkner, her horrors "are always evoked with a luminous precision." Her work is a "divine comedy" and "all her best stories are parables." O'Connor sided with outsiders, but she was best at turning the "scheming gossip" of her female characters into "comic and terrifying paradoxes." "The Displaced Person" is a masterpiece.

2 ANON. "Long Day's Preaching." TLS (1 February), p. 101.
A review of a British reissue of Wise Blood. The novel's "curiously haunting allegorical quality" is a result not only of O'Connor's Christianity, but of her indebtedness to Hawthorne and Melville. O'Connor describes the "same sad landscape depicted by Carson McCullers, but now charged with religious mania and the comedy of religious exploitation."

3 ASALS, FREDERICK. "The Mythic Dimensions of Flannery O'Connor's 'Greenleaf.'" SSF 5:317-30.

Despite her protestations to the contrary, O'Connor did sometimes write with non-Christian fables or myths in mind. The bull suggests a fertility god like Dionysus, the Beloved of the Song of Songs, or Christ, while Mrs. May's name suggests the spiritual and natural fertility she is unwilling to accept. Her sons are "grotesque reflections of her own values." The Greenleafs, though crude and "anarchic," believe "the time can be redeemed through the renewals of nature itself and through the healing power of the Word." The story contains numerous oppositions, but these are reconciled by the cycle of natural renewal and the related Christian paradoxes. Mrs. May resembles "the Pentheus figure," and her death is also a marriage with the divine, a reconciliation that suggests the Crucifixion. O'Connor's fusion of Christianity and classical myth displays "the syncretic catholicity of the early Church."

4 BAILEY, PAUL. "Maimed Souls." Observer (11 February), p. 27.

A British review of Wise Blood that notes O'Connor's preoccupation with "tormented innocents" and finds the novel "full of paradox, grimly comic, written with charitable irony in a fastidious, spare prose." The story occasionally suffers from arbitrary twists of plot, as with Solace Layfield, but it is "totally original," the complete opposite of the sentimentality of Tennessee Williams. O'Connor "invested her human relics with a ferocious dignity."

5 BLEIKASTEN, ANDRÉ. "Aveugles et Voyants: Le thème du regard dans Wise Blood." Bulletin de la faculté des lettres de Strasbourgh 47:291-301.

O'Connor, a "'Cartoonist' manquée," is an enemy of poetic vagueness. The novel concerns an unsuccessful rebellion against God, but it also concerns seeing. In the novel seeing is not a passive but an active desire for possession, and blindness and seeing are both ambiguous. Blindness suggests both the blindness of sin and the ability to see the supernatural, while seeing suggests both the natural powers of seeing and a blindness to the supernatural. Haze's impatience to see leads first to voyeurism, which leads to guilt and a fear of being seen, since being seen equals being culpable in the eyes of others, including God. Ultimately, the novel is not concerned with sight as such but vision, and despite Haze's impatience to find the light, the light finally finds him.

6 BRADBURY, MALCOLM. Review of A Good Man Is Hard to Find. Guardian Weekly (12 September), p. 14.
O'Connor adds her Catholicism to the "Southern grotesque tradition" to achieve "a special element of damnation and moral probing."

7 BRITTAIN, JOAN T. "Flannery O'Connor: A Bibliography, Part 2." BB 25:123-24.
A continuation of 1967.B3. For a list of errata in the two parts of this bibliography see Joan T. Brittain, "Flannery O'Connor: A Bibliography, Addenda," BB 25 (1968): 142. See also 1971.A1.

8 BROWN, ASHLEY. "Grotesque Occasions." Spectator (6 September), pp. 330, 332.
A review of A Good Man Is Hard to Find. O'Connor's work is so concentrated that she is best at the short story. Despite differences in their works, she was most influenced by Hawthorne, and she is "the heir to Hawthorne and Poe." Theology is crucial to O'Connor's work, and her use of the grotesque is "deliberate." "The Displaced Person" is one of "the small classics of American fiction."

9 BROWNING, PRESTON M., JR. "Flannery O'Connor and the Grotesque Recovery of the Holy." In Adversity and Grace: Studies in Recent American Literature. Edited by Nathan A. Scott, Jr. Essays in Divinity, vol. 4. Chicago: University of Chicago Press, pp. 133-61.
In part, O'Connor wrote to attack the complacency of Americans in the nineteen fifties. O'Connor uses three kinds of characters: the positivist intellectual, the positive-thinking nonintellectual, and the "criminal compulsive." The first two types of characters confront a reality they had previously ignored, because O'Connor, like Dostoyevsky, believes that man is more mysterious than the modern world realizes. The Misfit, with his interest in ultimate questions and his belief that anything is allowed if God does not exist, closely resembles some of Dostoyevsky's heroes. The Violent Bear It Away treats a clash between "two different views of the world" and "two radically divergent concepts of freedom." The rationalist Rayber achieves a sterile freedom from emotional commitment. Tarwater may seem to be "the victim of a neurotic compulsion," but he is really freer than Rayber because his is a committed freedom. Despite O'Connor's claims to orthodoxy, her interest in the grotesque and profane is similar to Thomas Mann's and Dostoyevsky's belief that the spiritual is often achieved through disease or evil.

1968

10 BURNS, STUART L. "Flannery O'Connor's The Violent Bear It Away: Apotheosis in Failure." SR 76:319-36.

The "structural pattern" of the novel is that of the journey, as in St. Cyril's allegory of the dragon or Joseph Campbell's formula of "separation-initiation-return." Many critics see the novel as ironic; the novel, however, treats the inevitable failure of Tarwater to achieve independence because "self-realization or psychic wholeness follows complete self-abnegation or psychic disintegration." The irony in the novel is not that Tarwater has failed to come to terms with God, since he has, but that his "mission is so obviously destined to fail." In the modern world "madness (if one wishes so to call the prophetic vision) is a necessary adjunct to salvation."

11 BURROWS, MILES. "Little Monsters." New Statesman (2 February), pp. 146-47.

Wise Blood "is a work of delightfully controlled irony in the Irish manner, of accurate somewhat pedantic description. It recalls Samuel Beckett, but is smoother, more humorous and effervescent, less controlled."

12 BYRD, TURNER F. "Ironic Dimension in Flannery O'Connor's 'The Artificial Nigger.'" MissQ 21:243-51.

Critics of this story fail to see O'Connor's "ironic mode" and "accept Mr. Head's judgment of his condition in the denouement as a true moment of grace, rather than as an extension of his stubborn, misguided, self-proclaimed omniscience." The beginning and end of the story take place in the "weakened and deceptive" light of the moon. Vergil is O'Connor's "inspiring guide," not Mr. Head's, and Mr. Head's association of himself with Raphael is misleading, for he is really like the blind Tobit. Mr. Head's and Nelson's failure to bring the lunch means that "the help of God is not available to Tobias/Nelson." Mr. Head's comments on the statue merely indicate racial arrogance, and unlike the journey through Hell in Dante, where the journey leads out of sin, Mr. Head and Nelson end up where they began.

13 CARTER, THOMAS H. "Rhetoric and Southern Landscapes." In Essays and Reviews, by Thomas H. Carter. Edited by James Boatwright. Lexington, Va.: Shenandoah Quarterly, pp. 54-59.

A reprint of 1955.B12.

14 DRAKE, ROBERT. "The Paradigm of Flannery O'Connor's True Country." SSF 6:433-42.

O'Connor is an example to the aspiring writer of "what a writer can achieve who seeks only to tell the truth about his true country, no matter how limited it may appear to be, whether geographically, ideologically, or otherwise." O'Connor stuck with "her one story" of man's confrontation with Christ and with her region of rural Georgia, though she was not a "regional" writer, and "she did not believe fiction to be either argument or news." In her work the grotesque is never arbitrary; it is "an outward and visible sign of an inward and spiritual dis-grace [sic]."

15 FAHEY, WILLIAM A. "Flannery O'Connor's 'Parker's Back.'" Renascence 20:162-64, 166.

Parker is drawn to Sarah Ruth, "with the ice pick eyes," and to tattooing because "masochistic practices...have often provided an escape from the uncertainty of the doubter before the absolute." Parker's last tattoo, his "alternative to 'straight Gospel' religion," may seem "merely grotesque," but his "tattooed Christ brings completion and renewal." Even his "tears signal a return" to Christ.

16 FEELEY, SISTER M. KATHLEEN, S.S.N.D. "Thematic Imagery in the Fiction of Flannery O'Connor." SHR 3:14-32.

O'Connor uses thematic imagery primarily to show "the epiphanies of her characters" and spiritual struggle. In The Violent Bear It Away she uses hunger, thirst, silence, and fire images, while in her work in general she also uses images suggesting the conflict of wills within the self, images suggesting hierophany as well as balancing images of evil, and eye and biblical imagery. O'Connor's "thematic imagery both makes her fiction realistic and illuminates the themes which undergird it."

17 FRAMPTON, MARALEE. "Religion and the Modern Novel: A Selected Bibliography." In The Shapeless God: Essays on Modern Fiction. Edited by Harry J. Mooney, Jr. and Thomas F. Staley. Pittsburgh: University of Pittsburgh Press, pp. 207-17.

A selected bibliography of critical work on literature and religion, including some works by or about O'Connor.

18 FREESE, PETER, DIETRICH JÄGER, and HORST KRUSE. "Erzählende Kurzprosa in Amerika: Ein Überblick." In Amerikanische Erzählungen von Hawthorne bis Salinger. Edited by Paul G. Buchloh. Neumünster: Karl Wachholtz Verlag, pp. 9-88.

O'Connor resembles other southern writers in various ways, including her use of physical and mental cripples and her stress on life in the family and society, but she does

1968

(FREESE, PETER, DIETRICH JÄGER, and HORST KRUSE)
not idealize the past, and unlike other major southern writers, her work has a clearly religious meaning. The baldness of her religious themes, however, weakens her work; compared with Faulkner or Porter she is more narrow, bloodless, and less mysterious. Southern literature may have reached its peak with the writers preceding O'Connor.

19 GEHER, ISTVAN. "Flannery O'Connor." Minden Összefut, by Flannery O'Connor. Translated by Istvan Geher, Bálazs László, László B. Nagy, and Levente Osztovits. Budapest: Európa Könyvkiadó, pp. 255-67.

A critical and biographical postscript to the Hungarian translation of Everything That Rises Must Converge that describes O'Connor as a writer of modern tragedy and perhaps the greatest postwar American writer. O'Connor eschews the myths of Faulkner and describes the South in all its horror, yet her work draws us because of the tension within its atmosphere. Her protagonists often struggle against another person, and a third person, an outsider, precipitates the tragedy, a tragedy brought on by the contradictions in the protagonist's life, especially his holding to the illusion of his personality while in reality his corrupt society totally controls him. O'Connor's stories merely examine and question theology; they do not ask us to accept it.

20 GORDON, CAROLINE. "Heresy in Dixie." SR 76:263-97.

A discussion of O'Connor's life and a comparison of her work, especially "Parker's Back," with Flaubert's The Temptation of St. Anthony. Comparisons of O'Connor with contemporaries like Faulkner, Welty, and Capote are "profitless"; O'Connor is one of the mystics that Flaubert predicted would arise in the dark age of the modern world. Flaubert too was a mystic, but unlike O'Connor he lacked "a sound theological foundation." Whereas his Temptation deals unsuccessfully with numerous heresies, O'Connor in "Parker's Back" successfully treats the heresy of "Docetism, which denied that Our Lord possessed corporeal substance, and made Him, in consequence, a phantasm." Flaubert's St. Anthony ends believing in a doctrine close to the evolutionary mysticism of Teilhard de Chardin; O'Connor, as Robert Fitzgerald notes (1965.B30), is more aware of the earthly suffering that precedes salvation.

21 GRAHAM, KENNETH. "Ruined Raj." Listener (5 September), p. 313.

Includes a brief review of a British reissue of A Good Man Is Hard to Find. The collection "still impresses with its bitter comedy, its laconic horror, and the brilliance of its dramatic effects." In O'Connor's fiction "Jesus and the Devil loom up in the most unlikely places, usually with their values inverted, but opening the door to hell, if nowhere else."

22 HAMBLEN, ABIGAIL A. "Flannery O'Connor's Study of Innocence and Evil." UR 34:295-97.

In "A Good Man Is Hard to Find" O'Connor shows us "that reason does not guide events, that victimizers and victims alike are shuffled unwittingly into strange patterns as broken and casual as those of a kaleidoscope. Further, though Evil is stronger than Innocence, it is no less foolish and no more artful." Both the evil and the innocent implicitly share the belief that anything may be done if Christ is rejected.

23 HAYS, PETER L. "Dante, Tobit, and 'The Artificial Nigger.'" SSF 5:263-68.

In the story there are parallels with Dante's descent into hell and Raphael's restoring the vision of the elder Tobias, though there is no one-for-one correspondence between the story and the two narratives. The city, however, "is a counterpart of Dante's shade-inhabited Hell," and "the statue must represent Satan, and through him the sin of pride." As with Dante and Tobias, the journey is "a journey of enlightenment."

24 HILLS, PENNY CHAPIN and L. RUST, eds. How We Live: Contemporary Life in Contemporary Fiction. New York: MacMillan, pp. 787-89.

A collection of short stories and excerpts from novels with the theme of contemporary life in America. At the end of "Everything That Rises Must Converge" the editors discuss the story in terms of its treatment of the race problems of the South. Julian's mother, who identifies with the past, maintains a false innocence by refusing to recognize present reality. The black woman strikes Julian's mother because she totally rejects the past. Julian is the southern intellectual, who must overcome his lack of ability to gain strength from the past, who must aid racial understanding by more than mere tokenism, and who "must somehow take action to prevent the collision of converging, rising forces."

25 LIPPER, MARK. "Blessed Are the Destitute in Flannery O'Connor." Shippensburg (Pennsylvania) State College Review (October), pp. 20-23.

(LIPPER, MARK)
O'Connor's emphasis on the Bible and her avoidance of "spiritual isolationism" demonstrate that the major influence on her work was not Roman Catholicism but southern Christianity. Perhaps Catholicism contributed to "her defensive attitude" towards her audience and her major themes of sin and grace, and perhaps her illness contributed to the "morbid attitude in her writing."

26 LORCH, THOMAS M. "Flannery O'Connor: Christian Allegorist." _Crit_ 10, ii:69-80.
O'Connor's religious beliefs led her to use allegory in her fiction. In _Wise Blood_ she employs a traditional Christian allegory along the lines of Bunyan's _Pilgrim's Progress_, whereas in _The Violent Bear It Away_ and in some of the stories in _Everything That Rises Must Converge_ she uses an allegory "in which individual characters represent distinct inner forces and the conflicts between these characters on the literal level portray inner conflicts." The two "fully developed Christian allegories" among her later work are _The Violent Bear It Away_ and "The Lame Shall Enter First." The novel can be read as "an allegorical portrait" of the conflict within young Tarwater's mind between religion and secularism. O'Connor's religion, however, does limit her work, since she never questions her religious assumptions and allows her characters only the "specious" freedom of accepting God. Also, her work is often too schematic.

27 LYNSKEY, WINIFRED. _Reading Modern Fiction: 31 Stories with Critical Aids_. 4th rev. ed. New York: Charles Scribner's Sons, pp. 413-16.
In a commentary on "A Good Man Is Hard to Find" discusses the story in terms of existentialism: O'Connor's declared differences with the existentialists, the Misfit as a symbol of existentialism, the family's existential confrontation "with terrifying, inexplicable evil," and the existential setting.

28 MONTGOMERY, MARION. "Beyond Symbol and Surface: The Fiction of Flannery O'Connor." _GaR_ 22:188-93.
An essay review of Melvin J. Friedman's and Lewis A. Lawson's _The Added Dimension: The Art and Mind of Flannery O'Connor_, Stanley Edgar Hyman's _Flannery O'Connor_ and Robert Drake's _Flannery O'Connor_ that pleads for less haste in publishing criticism on O'Connor and for more emphasis on her vision, less on "the arithmetic of word-measure or the geometry of symbolic configurations."

29 _____. "Flannery O'Connor and the Natural Man." MissQ 21: 235-42.

O'Connor "keeps pulling artificial legs out from under modern shorings of the natural, self-made man as object of worship, whether supplied by Nietzsche, Sartre, Freud, or the variety of Artists as Young Men." She has the larger view of a Dante or Chaucer that allows her to see "the prospect of Hell from a position beyond terror and pity." This view allows for her humor and her ability to "affirm human nature transformed by the blessings of the Incarnation."

30 _____. "Flannery O'Connor's 'Leaden Tract Against Complacency and Contraception.'" ArQ 24:132-46.

Stanley Edgar Hyman's characterization of "A Stroke of Good Fortune" as a "leaden tract" (1966.A3) is misleading because the story is not naturalistic. The story treats Ruby's rejection of love, her attempt to escape responsibility, and the reality of death. In the story "Mystery" is present because of O'Connor's loose parallels or ironic contrasts with St. Luke, St. Augustine, and St. John of the Cross.

31 _____. "Miss Flannery's 'A Good Man.'" Denver Quarterly 3 (Autumn), 1-19.

A discussion of "A Good Man Is Hard to Find." Unlike Dante, O'Connor places her demonic figures in the real world. These figures are endowed with what Jacque Maritain calls "the pre-philosophy of common sense" that helps them succeed in the world, though they unintentionally serve good. The Misfit resembles his victims because "the grandmother's whole family is devoted to meanness," but he also teaches the grandmother that the devil is real. O'Connor does not use "strict allegory," yet she is "constantly hinting at analogue." The grandmother suggests Eve in Eden while the Misfit suggests Satan and Cain. The dialogue between the two suggests "a black confessional" with the Misfit confessing to the priest-grandmother. The grandmother's recognition of the Misfit and the description of her after her death imply her free act of awareness and her triumph over evil. The ending is tragic in the tragic irony of the Misfit's triumph, the sense of waste in the lives of the characters, and the role of the Misfit as precipitator of the tragedy, since in Christianity Satan "is the cause of all tragedy."

32 _____. "Miss O'Connor and the Christ-Haunted." SoR N.S. 4: 665-72.

(MONTGOMERY, MARION)
O'Connor's fiction deals primarily with the "Christ-haunted" rather than the "Christ-centered" or the "oblivious," since "they reflect as drama the struggle between health and illness in the spirit." She has an unsentimental compassion for her characters, and in her work "Grace is the necessary agent to the soul's existence ex nihilo." She cannot be placed in the "romantic myth of revolt" in modern literature, and she had no sympathy for Freudians or Existentialists. The Christ that "shadows her work" is not like Odysseus in Joyce's Ulysses, because this Christ tells us "why life is not finally illusion." O'Connor "was fundamentally unmoved by pity and terror, and could consequently view our worldly struggle against pity and terror with humorous, rather than sardonic, irony." The gap between her larger view of life and most men's concern with the mere surface creates "a comedy in Dante's sense of the term."

33 MOONEY, HARRY J. "Moments of Eternity: A Study of the Short Stories of Flannery O'Connor." In The Shapeless God: Essays on Modern Fiction. Edited by Harry J. Mooney, Jr. and Thomas F. Staley. Pittsburgh: University of Pittsburgh Press, pp. 117-38.
O'Connor is best with short stories, since "her art to some extent depended upon its preternatural intensity." Because of O'Connor's interest in eschatology, "the confrontation between good and evil...is usually stark, yet it is also subtle and capable of all sorts of ironic reversals." O'Connor's characters suffer from various weaknesses: a philosophical self-sufficiency that denies God, a belief in the power of property, or an overwhelming righteousness. These characters' "lives are often shattered by revelations of an order beyond their grasp," and O'Connor frequently uses a journey to achieve this revelation. O'Connor also uses, as in "The Lame Shall Enter First," ironic reversal, and her landscapes, especially her sun images, "assert their Creator."

34 NYE, ROBERT. "A Peculiar Flavour." Manchester Guardian (8 February), p. 12.
A review of Wise Blood. O'Connor's reputation in Great Britain is greater among writers than the general reading public. Her work is not gothic since "she is too delicate in her probing of chaos, too sensuous-spinsterish, too exact." As for the novel, her "theological argument about the evasiveness of integrity is not to everyone's taste--but no one should miss the comedy that informs this author's passion for ravaging a few souls."

35 PRICE, R. G. C. Review of A Good Man Is Hard to Find. Punch (4 September), p. 346.
A brief review. The stories "have an extra bite and originality." Aside from Faulkner's, they may be the best southern stories.

36 SCOTT, NATHAN A., JR. "Flannery O'Connor's Testimony: The Pressure of Glory." In Craters of the Spirit: Studies in the Modern Novel. Washington: Corpus Books, pp. 267-85.
A reprint of 1966.B35.

37 SHEAR, WALTER. "Flannery O'Connor...Character and Characterization." Renascence 20:140-46.
O'Connor's characters are limited by their background and their "nearly willful ignorance," and O'Connor's main interest is in the confrontations of these characters with "a premonition of the infinite." Using vision as a "key metaphor," she writes of the "blindness to self" of many of her characters. O'Connor also matches characters of good intent with "extreme figures of evil" and sometimes reverses this technique by having interchangeable characters. O'Connor values the individual, yet she is always stressing the limitations of her characters before "some kind of divine force." This force, however, "is composed of equal parts of good and evil."

38 SHINN, THELMA J. "Flannery O'Connor and the Violence of Grace." ConL 9:58-73.
O'Connor "knew that the violence of rejection...demands an equal violence of redemption," and both as a Catholic and a Southerner she believed in "redemption achieved through suffering." She resembles Carson McCullers in her use of grotesques, of which she used three types: physical, spiritual, and secular. She and Graham Greene feel that sinners are more likely to be saved than the indifferent "because they are in the spiritual realm." Her fiction at the end of her life was complete because in "The Lame Shall Enter First" she shows the secular man, Sheppard, being "saved from emptiness." Also discusses O'Connor's humor, her avoidance of allegory, and her theme of displacement.

39 SPIVEY, TED R. "Flannery O'Connor: Georgia's Theological Storyteller." In The Humanities in the Contemporary South. School of Arts and Sciences Research Paper No. 17. Atlanta: Georgia State College, pp. 19-28.
"Existential theology," to which she adds the modern concern with violence, is the key to O'Connor's work. She is concerned with four character types: "the criminal seeking God, the fanatic, the secular humanitarian, the

(SPIVEY, TED R.)
traditionalist." She is an orthodox Christian who rejects fanaticism, secular humanitarianism, and sterile traditionalism, and who achieves her best work in her portraits of criminals seeking God.

40 STEPHENS, MARTHA. "Flannery O'Connor and the Sanctified-Sinner Tradition." ArQ 24:223-39.

Much of O'Connor's work, her theology especially, can be better understood by reference to the essays and fiction of European Christian writers than to those of other southern writers. O'Connor belongs with the "extremely traditionalist and conservative" group of Christian writers, and she believes, as Eliot said in his essay on Baudelaire, that "it is better, in a paradoxical way, to do evil than to do nothing." She thus writes in the "sanctified-sinner tradition," with Hazel Motes, the Misfit, Johnson, and young Tarwater being sanctified sinners. Hazel bears a strong resemblance to Pinkie of Greene's Brighton Rock, a novel that may have influenced Wise Blood, and to Harry of Eliot's The Family Reunion, a play she was reading when she wrote the novel. Eliot's play also has the divine erupt into the normal, "a distinguishing feature" of O'Connor's work. Mauriac's Thérèse Desqueyroux is also similar to O'Connor's sanctified sinners, but with the difference that O'Connor in her two novels shows redemption for these sinners.

41 SULLIVAN, WALTER. "The Achievement of Flannery O'Connor." SHR 2:303-09.

O'Connor's novels are inferior to her short stories. As a writer she resembles Stephen Crane because both had an "inflexible" style and a talent for writing of "only one human posture, one metaphysical relationship," in O'Connor's case, "that of the gnostic, believing in himself and asserting the myth of his own independence." "The Displaced Person" demonstrates O'Connor's skill in "sharp reversal" and her "subtle exploitation of symbolism." O'Connor's combination of "the Christian and the Agrarian" made her "the only truly original voice among all her Southern contemporaries. And she is the only Southern writer of any generation who has yet made the old images viable for our immediate time."

42 ______. "In Time of the Breaking of Nations: The Decline of Southern Fiction." SoR N.S. 4:299-305.

Southern literature declined in quality after 1945 because the older, agrarian, religious South has been replaced by a secular South much like the rest of America.

Only O'Connor escaped this decline because the primary source of her fiction was her Roman Catholicism, not the South. Future southern writers will have to look to something other than the South itself for the "prime mover" of their fiction. Reprinted 1972.B43.

43 TAYLOR, HENRY. "The Halt Shall Be Gathered Together: Physical Deformity in the Fiction of Flannery O'Connor." WHR 22:325-38.

In O'Connor's fiction those who are deformed or somehow peculiar often have greater self-awareness than others "because they are led to brood on their peculiarities." Such characters "may often bring others to some sort of self-awareness." They may even, as Hazel Motes and young Tarwater do, "stand as a symbol of the possibility that the deformed, grotesque inhabitants of the dark city may awaken to an awareness that they are the children of God."

44 TINDALL, GILLIAN. "Doldrums." New Statesman (6 September), p. 292.

A brief review of A Good Man Is Hard to Find. O'Connor "wrote about the poor whites of America with knowledge, style, and an ear for random speech." Some of the stories, however, are "too gratuitously brutal for significance," and there is a question about how seriously O'Connor took them. The stories leave us with a sense "of indomitable ignorance which keeps everyone going."

45 TROWBRIDGE, CLINTON W. "The Symbolic Vision of Flannery O'Connor: Patterns of Imagery in The Violent Bear It Away." SR 76:298-318.

The key images in the novel are loaves and fishes because O'Connor "takes the idea of man's spiritual hunger literally and makes the parable of the loaves and the fishes serve as the major...image of the novel." Fish symbolize the soul and bread the soul's nourishment, and the other images, such as water, thirst, struggle, seed, and fire, tend to "cluster around" one of these two key images. O'Connor wants us to take her symbols and figures of speech literally; she uses them "to make a work not more suggestive but more explicit." Other images, such as the road, the sun, and silence, are also discussed.

46 VANDE KIEFT, RUTH M. "Judgment in the Fiction of Flannery O'Connor." SR 76:337-56.

Many readers of O'Connor find "the task of unearthing judgments sunk in the work...uncommonly difficult" because O'Connor's rebel-prophet protagonists are given over to

(VANDEKIEFT, RUTH M.)
anger, whereas "every virtue and merit" of her "liberal" or "respectable" antagonists "is shown to be totally useless." Much in the stories is comic, but the often horrible endings, where awareness is achieved at a terrible price, are not. O'Connor is not, however, "sadistic," yet neither is she a Christian humanist. Her vision emphasizes death because in her work usually only death brings awareness. Parts of O'Connor's work, such as the baptism-drowning of Bishop, are morally disturbing, and the question of O'Connor's moral stance "remains endlessly debatable." Includes fairly extensive commentary on "Greenleaf."

47 WAGER, WILLIS. American Literature: A World View. New York: New York University Press, p. 266.
In a passing reference O'Connor's work is referred to as "more solid" than Capote's and her stories described as "almost like Maupassant in their sharpness, each focused on a cataclysmic moment of moral or spiritual awareness."

1969 A BOOKS

1 MARTIN, CARTER W. The True Country: Themes in the Fiction of Flannery O'Connor. Nashville: Vanderbilt University Press.
An "orthodox Christian" reading of O'Connor which relies to some extent on O'Connor's comments on her own work. O'Connor, however, "grinds no theological ax," and not all her characters are "conceived of in terms of religious meaning." Chapters on O'Connor's sacramentalism, on her spiritually deficient characters, on her characters who embody grace, on her characters who move toward spiritual illumination, on her use of symbolism, on her "gothic impulse" and her use of the grotesque, on her humor, and on her use of satire and irony. O'Connor's satire and irony often lead the casual reader to misunderstand her fiction: her fiction is not a satire on the South or on intellectuals, but on human folly. O'Connor may share the "gothic impulse" with such writers as Capote and McCullers, but the presence of spiritual reality in her work makes her closer to such writers as Faulkner, Warren, and Welty. The genre of her work, as Robert Fitzgerald claims (See 1965.B30), is Christian tragicomedy. Includes a selected bibliography of works by and about O'Connor. For a reply See 1973.B7.

1969 B SHORTER WRITINGS

1 ANON. "Dust for Art's Sake." Time (30 May), p. 70.
A review of Mystery and Manners. The essays "can do little to enhance her already considerable reputation. Nonetheless, they do further illuminate its foundations and the problem of being a true Southerner, a devout Catholic and a practicing creative artist at the same time."

2 ANON. Review of Mystery and Manners. Choice 6:1398.
A capsule review. The book is useful, but it is unfortunate that the editors did not identify the editorial changes they made and the sources of the material.

3 ANON. Review of Mystery and Manners. NY (19 July), p. 84.
"The essays...are repetitious, studded with homely family anecdotes, equally scathing toward the secularist and the Catholic pietistic worlds," yet they are also "truer and sounder and wiser about the nature of fiction and the responsibilities of reader and writer than anything published since James's 'The Art of the Novel.'"

4 ANON. Review of Mystery and Manners. VQR 45:cxxxvii.
"These essays reveal once again a distinctly personal idiom combining devout Catholicism with practical wisdom." The Fitzgeralds are praised for making O'Connor's thoughts available.

5 ANON. "Roots." TLS (24 July), p. 829.
A British review of Carter Martin's The True Country: Themes in the Fiction of Flannery O'Connor that mainly discusses how O'Connor has been unfairly ignored.

6 ASALS, FREDERICK. "The Road to Wise Blood." Renascence 21: 181-94.
A discussion of "The Geranium," "The Capture," "Woman on the Stairs," and "The Train" as predecessors of Wise Blood. The stories show some of the achievement of Wise Blood in "the fumbling at the religious theme, the uncertain beginnings of the detachment of the authorial voice from the central consciousness, the gradual discovery of the possibilities of irony, the flashes of grotesque perception, the greater imagistic rendering of the material in the later of the stories." The stories do not, however, prepare us for the humor or "control and assurance" of the novel, which came from O'Connor's reading of West's Miss Lonelyhearts. O'Connor found in West's novel "the conjunction of the ironic voice, grotesque perception, and the theme of the religious quest."

7 BRITTAIN, JOAN T. and LEON V. DRISKELL. "O'Connor and the Eternal Crossroads." Renascence 22:49-55.

O'Connor's "characters embody her search for a location at which the exigencies of time and place will have relevance to the larger scope of eternity." O'Connor did not satirize the South; she used biblical and southern history as "the means of interpreting the Fall." O'Connor's religious purposes were not clear to critics until the appearance of her "The Fiction Writer and His Country" in Granville Hicks's The Living Novel (1957). O'Connor was not a polemicist but used the facts of her region, including the racial ones, for her religious and artistic purposes.

8 BROWNING, PRESTON, JR. "'Parker's Back': Flannery O'Connor's Iconography of Salvation by Profanity." SSF 6:525-35.

Brainard Cheney's comment (1963.B6) that O'Connor's stories move from the natural to the metaphysical should be changed to state that the two blend together, with the metaphysical "gradually manifesting itself through the secular and natural." Parker's quest for identity draws him to the strangeness of tattooing and Sarah Ruth. The burning tree suggests Moses,and the tattoo of Christ, Parker's acceptance of God. At the end Parker is "Moses and Jonah and Obadiah and O. E. Parker." Both Sarah Ruth and the story itself are ambiguous, Sarah because she is both a fanatic and an aid to Parker's conversion and the story because it implies a God both "'all-demanding'" and unappeasable.

9 BURCH, FRANCIS F. Review of Mystery and Manners. America (5 July), p. 16.

These essays of O'Connor "reveal the incisiveness, if not the range, of her critical ability." Her "remarks on writing are not highly original, but they are expressed with her typical wit and form a coherent esthetic." Her basic argument is that we must "accept the writer and his story for what they are," and her remarks on the relation of literature and religious belief are especially worthwhile.

10 BURNS, STUART L. "Flannery O'Connor's Literary Apprenticeship." Renascence 22:3-16.

A discussion of O'Connor's stories before Wise Blood: "The Geranium," "Wildcat," "The Barber," "The Crop," "The Capture," and "Woman on the Stairs," retitled "A Stroke of Good Fortune." The "four major ingredients" of O'Connor's work - "violence, supraliteral characterization, symbolic duplication, and functional metaphor" - are found in these stories "but often in nonfunctional form." The stories are "valuable...in a limited way" as hints of O'Connor's future achievement.

11 _____. "Structural Patterns in Wise Blood." XUS 8, ii:32-43.
A discussion of O'Connor's "use of water, sex, and coffin symbolism," with the water symbolism suggesting Haze's futile denial of Christ and his eventual salvation, the sex symbolism, the origins of his guilt, and the coffin symbolism, "the absolute quality of his dilemma." O'Connor often transforms the literal into the symbolic and makes her symbols interact, as in Haze's association of sex, sin, and death, and his incestuous association of other women with his mother. Haze finally learns that "redemption results from a successful encounter with sin, not from an avoidance of it." The novel "re-creates [sic] the age-old cycle of the Fall, Death, and Re-birth [sic]."

12 CARLSON, THOMAS M. "Flannery O'Connor: The Manichaean Dilemma." SR 77:254-76.
A discussion of several of the stories in Everything That Rises Must Converge. Stanley Edgar Hyman (1966.A3) is wrong in labelling O'Connor a dualist; as a writer she opposes all Manichaean attempts to separate flesh and spirit, whether they take the form of puritanism or humanitarianism. "Greenleaf" uses the "typological symbolism" of Zeus and Europa to show the key "enveloping action" in O'Connor's work: "the fall of the divine man into the natural world and his subsequent struggle with the conflicting multiplicities of that world." O'Connor's "art, like that of the great tragedians, also dealt with and became an instrument for the union (not identity) of spirit and substance," and her characters' limited awareness "gives them some limited dimension of tragic stature." Their relative ignorance creates the comedy in her work, but she does not emphasize deformity or ignorance. Her emphasis is on "the perception of resemblances, man's relationship to man, to nature, and to God."

13 DRISKELL, LEON V. "Flannery O'Connor: Property of Specialists?" Louisville Courier Journal and Times (15 June), p. 5-G.
A review of Mystery and Manners and Carter Martin's The True Country: Themes in the Fiction of Flannery O'Connor. In Mystery and Manners the essay "The Teaching of Literature" is "among those few admittedly great summations of the art and reach of fiction," and the collection as a whole should help critics understand how O'Connor uses her orthodox Christianity in her fiction. Martin's book is

1969

(DRISKELL, LEON V.)
"helpful," but he misses the "most evocative elements" in the stories, and his claim that only serious readers can fully appreciate O'Connor's fiction is a "real disservice to Miss O'Connor."

14 EGGENSCHWILER, DAVID. "Flannery O'Connor's True and False Prophets." Renascence 21:151-61, 167.
Various critics, including Irving Malin (1966.B28) and Louis Rubin (1966.B33), have failed to understand old Tarwater in The Violent Bear It Away because they failed to understand that the novel is based on "the opposition of pride (to which narcissism, hatred, and a vengeful God of Wrath are variously related) and self-abnegation (of which love is one form)." O'Connor backs old Tarwater because "she is backing him in a struggle with himself as well as with unbelievers." Young Tarwater and Rayber are also torn by this conflict of values, but young Tarwater achieves self-abnegation while Rayber is left with his pride. The same opposition operates in Wise Blood, where Hazel "associated salvation with death" and fought self-abnegation until near the end of the novel.

15 ESCH, ROBERT M. "O'Connor's 'Everything That Rises Must Converge.'" Expl 27: Item 58.
At the end of the story the mother may already be dead, but her eye's looking on Julian and then closing "reflects the mother's final rejection of the son she had wanted to believe in throughout her life."

16 FRAKES, JAMES R. and ISADORE TRASCHEN, eds. Short Fiction: A Critical Collection. 2nd rev. ed. Englewood Cliffs, N. J.: Prentice-Hall, pp. 126-29.
Essentially the same remarks on "The Artificial Nigger" as in the 1959 edition (1959.B3) but with some additions. The story is called "a theological drama." Nelson's confrontation with blacks, for him the unknown, creates "a crisis in identity," and the racial conflict "ironically reveals Nelson's conflict within himself, caused in part by his pride as a white."

17 FRIEDMAN, MELVIN J. "Flannery O'Connor." In A Bibliographical Guide to the Study of Southern Literature. Edited by Louis D. Rubin, Jr. Baton Rouge: Louisiana State University Press, pp. 250-53.
A bibliography of critical articles on O'Connor along with a brief review of the criticism written so far and some possible future directions for criticism.

18 GILMAN, RICHARD. "On Flannery O'Connor." NYRB (21 August), pp. 24-26.

A review of Mystery and Manners that includes a recounting of a visit with O'Connor in 1960. Includes the following description of O'Connor: "Tough-minded, laconic, with a marvelous wit and an absolute absence of self-pity, she made me understand, as never before or since, what spiritual heroism and beauty can be." Gives an unflattering portrayal of O'Connor's mother and claims she is important in many stories "as the fulcrum of their violent moral action." Several of O'Connor's views on her art, region, and religion are recounted, as well as her admitting that her characterization of Rayber was not fully successful. O'Connor "possessed nothing of what we like to call an 'inquiring' mind," but she was able to use this narrowness to her artistic advantage.

19 HASSAN, IHAB. "The Novel of Outrage: A Minority Voice in Postwar American Fiction." In The American Novel Since World War II. Edited by Marcus Klein. Greenwich, Conn.: Fawcett Publications, pp. 196-209.

A reprint of 1965.B34.

20 HAWKES, JOHN. "Notes on the Wild Goose Chase." In The American Novel Since World War II. Edited by Marcus Klein. Greenwich, Conn.: Fawcett Publications, pp. 247-51.

A reprint of 1962.B13.

21 HICKS, GRANVILLE. "Literary Horizons." SatR (10 May), p. 30.

A review of Mystery and Manners. Hicks also recounts his 1962 visit with O'Connor and his impression that O'Connor "was a young woman who had come to terms with herself and her life" after making three important decisions: to become a writer, to reaffirm her Catholic faith, and to live in Milledgeville. Her introduction to A Memoir of Mary Ann "has a tenderness that must be remembered when we think of her toughness." Reprinted 1970.B24.

22 HOLMAN, C. HUGH. "The View From the Regency-Hyatt: Southern Social Issues and the Outer World." In Southern Fiction Today: Renascence and Beyond. Edited by George Core. Athens, Ga.: University of Georgia Press, pp. 16-32.

O'Connor shares with three other writers, T. S. Stribling, Thomas Wolfe, and Erskine Caldwell, an interest in the twentieth century Piedmont and Mountain South. All four of these writers will sometimes focus on the social world, all four tend to write in a personal and consistent style, and all describe grotesque characters inhabiting a

1969

(HOLMAN, C. HUGH)
region of unrealized potential. One indication of the changing nature of this region is that O'Connor, the most contemporary of these writers, saw her characters as spiritually deprived, whereas the earlier writers saw the deprivation as mainly social and economic. Reprinted 1972.B21.

23 HUELSBECK, CHARLES J. "Of Fiction, Integrity, and Peacocks." CathW (December), p. 128.
Highly praises Mystery and Manners and claims "'The Nature and Aim of Fiction' is a statement of universal literary theory almost equalling Aristotle's Poetics, Pope's Essay on Criticism or The Art of the Novel by Henry James."

24 JACKSON, KATHERINE GAUSS. Review of Mystery and Manners. Harper's (June), p. 94.
Although most of the material has been published before, "the collection is a pleasant mixture; the very light mixed with the very serious."

25 KELLOGG, JEAN. "'We Have Had Our Fall.'" Christian Century (9 July), p. 927.
A review of Mystery and Manners. The book helps the reader understand O'Connor's underlying spiritual purpose and her use of her region. The Fitzgeralds are praised for their editing.

26 KUEHL, LINDA. "An Interview with Joyce Carol Oates." Commonweal (5 December), pp. 307-10.
Oates doubts that O'Connor influenced her because O'Connor was religious in the usual sense while Oates is not.

27 MALOFF, SAUL. "On Flannery O'Connor." Commonweal (8 August), pp. 490-91.
The essays in Mystery and Manners contain "a steady expansion of implication and statement to the point where the ideas essential to her life and art gathered toward the makings of something like a system." O'Connor "does not court the reader," but she is "never high-flown." Her comments on the relations of mystery and manners in literature and her strictures against "pious trash" are especially good.

28 MANO, D. KEITH. Review of Mystery and Manners. NYTBR (25 May), pp. 6-7, 20.
The reviewer "had never read more sensible and significant reflections on the business of writing." Discusses

O'Connor's "anti-Manichean" world-view, the positive role of her faith, and her belief in a coherent culture. "The Nature and Aim of Fiction" and "Writing Short Stories" amount to "a veritable purgative of all the romantic fallacies that are encrusted on the story-teller's art," and "The King of the Birds" reveals the most about O'Connor -- "You are judged, she seems to say, by what you are willing to endure for beauty's sake."

29 MONTGOMERY, MARION. "Flannery O'Connor's Territorial Center." Crit 11, iii:5-10.

O'Connor's fiction "has a territorial center to its spiritual geography in the regions of the Inferno rather than in Purgatorio or Paradiso" because ours is an age that needs to be shocked out of its unbelief. To O'Connor, the "historical analogy" to our times "is that hiatus between the Old and New Testaments, between Malachi and the appearance of John out of the desert." O'Connor uses the South and its idiom as her characters "attempt to fulfill an unfamiliar mission in familiar surroundings." Her work is often full of horrors, but her characters are not defeated because O'Connor grounds the transcendent in the concrete.

30 _____. "A Note on Flannery O'Connor's Terrible and Violent Prophecy of Mercy." Forum (Houston), 7 (Summer), 4-7.

O'Connor, like Hawthorne, was opposed to the "gnostic invasion of Christianity" that separated matter from spirit. Teilhard de Chardin appealed to O'Connor because he opposed such a separation and because he was "primarily concerned for human significance in the evolutionary processes," but O'Connor differs from Teilhard because she as a writer sees evil as active and thus dramatic, not as passive.

31 _____. "O'Connor and Teilhard de Chardin: The Problem of Evil." Renascence 22:34-42.

O'Connor agrees with Teilhard de Chardin that nature is sacred, but she rejects his "cosmic determinism," his view "that evil is the necessary wastage of energy" in the universe's evolution toward perfection. O'Connor believes in free will and the reality of the devil; her theology is thus more orthodox than Teilhard's. She does, however, have a conception of evil similar to Teilhard's belief in evil as ill fortune, but only in the spectacle, the physical action, in her work. In the spectacle of her fiction we have a sense of good and evil both bound up with progress, as at the end of "Everything That Rises Must Converge."

1969

32 MONTGOMERY, MARION. "The Prophet's Eye." Triumph (October), pp. 35-36.

Although O'Connor had the "prophet's eye" for seeing the operations of grace in nature, her Christian beliefs created two problems: alienation from a secular audience and the temptation of didacticism. O'Connor seems to contradict herself by claiming that her audience should be concerned with her Christian message, yet also inveighing against art as moral uplift. There is no contradiction here, however, since the Christian artist teaches by developing his artistic gift and by purifying himself, not by preaching to others. O'Connor's fictional tactics derive less from modern fictional techniques and the New Criticism than from "consciously pursued orthodoxy."

33 MORRISSET, HENRI. Preface to Mon mal vient de plus loin, by Flannery O'Connor. Translated by Henri Morrisset. Paris: Gallimard, pp. 7-15.

A preface to the French edition of Everything That Rises Must Converge that emphasizes the bleakness of O'Connor's fictional world: the drab landscape, the poor racial relations, the nasty characters, and the shocking use of religion, including the fraud of evangelism. Nevertheless, O'Connor's fiction is not so violent that her characters are reduced to puppets; she does allow a certain mystery to each being. Her humor also attenuates this bleakness. O'Connor was both dramatic and classical in technique, and she was best at the short story, the form that allowed her the fullest release of the violence that ravaged her body.

34 MULLER, GILBERT H. "The City of Woe: Flannery O'Connor's Dantean Vision." GaR 23:206-13.

"The Artificial Nigger" was consciously designed with Dante's Inferno in mind. Mr. Head suggests Vergil; the city, Hell; the Negro section, Dis; the Negro woman, Medusa; etc. As in Dante, O'Connor uses the dangerous quest as her basic metaphor for spiritual development, while adding her own realism and humor. This story, O'Connor's "finest treatment" of this dangerous quest, also recalls aspects of Hawthorne's "Young Goodman Brown" and Melville's "Benito Cereno."

35 ______. "The Violent Bear It Away: Moral and Dramatic Sense." Renascence 22:17-25.

O'Connor follows "James's distinction between morality and moralism" and like James uses "the dramatic sense" to reinforce meaning. The novel's three sections are "dramatically arranged to form a beginning, middle, and end," and the "convoluted and fugue-like" first section involves the reader in young Tarwater's struggle. The novel is also unified by "a dialectic of violence" and by "the fact that its twelve chapters correspond closely to verses one through twelve in Matthew 11 [Eleven]." In the novel O'Connor attacks men like Rayber "and those who, like old Tarwater, try to rush the introduction of the heavenly kingdom and only do violence to it and themselves." Young Tarwater, "however, is neither heretical nor premature."

36 NANCE, WILLIAM L. "Flannery O'Connor: The Trouble With Being a Prophet." UR (University of Missouri at Kansas City) 36: 101-08.

O'Connor's "subject, her problem, is superior knowledge - that endowment which is hers necessarily as author, hers in an acutely self-conscious way in virtue of her satirical bent, hers in a pre-eminent and especially problematical way in her role as Christian prophet." Her "theme is Intellect in Search of Salvation," and she herself was torn "between pride-of-intellect and the need to exorcise it." This tension led her to create self-caricatures like Hulga and some of the other characters. The tension also reveals itself in the violence of the stories, with their "jagged immediacy, driving to conclusions that are less resolutions than admissions of insolubility, of desperation." In "The Artificial Nigger" O'Connor achieves the distance necessary to avoid violence and to present "the redemptive experience whole and self-contained." O'Connor belongs with those modern American writers who reject the city and seek an individual solution to the problems of life.

37 NELSON, ELIZABETH R. Review of Mystery and Manners. LJ 94: 1994.

The book is valuable whether the reader reads just the parts he finds interesting or the entire book.

38 PRAMPOLINI, GAETANO. "Poetica di Flannery O'Connor." SA 15: 321-39.

A discussion of O'Connor's fiction that relies heavily on her own comments about fiction, especially those in Mystery and Manners. O'Connor wrote from a Catholic viewpoint; she tried to show the role of grace in human life. Her use of the grotesque and violence follows from her attempt to communicate with modern unbelievers. Like Conrad, she stressed the importance of seeing; she did not separate her theology from the demands of fiction. Her fiction balances distortion on the one hand and realism on the other. Her theological concerns separate her from other

(PRAMPOLINI, GAETANO)
southern writers, but the role of the South in her fiction must not be ignored.

39 QUINN, JOHN J., S.J. Review of Mystery and Manners. Best Sellers 29:76.
Praises O'Connor's essays and the Fitzgeralds' editing. This book "will rank with the precious few classical critical studies on the art of fiction ever to be published."

40 RISO, DON, S.J. "Blood and Land in 'A View of the Woods.'" New Orleans Review 1:255-57.
O'Connor employs the archetype of land as mother, sky as father in this story, as well as the ancient association of blood and land. Mr. Fortune rejects both blood and land, and Mary Fortune Pitts, as her name indicates, suggests the tension between innocence and materialism. By the end of the story she rejects Mr. Fortune for blood and land, and Mr. Fortune finds that the land is inescapable.

41 SAMUELS, CHARLES THOMAS. "Flannery O'Connor: From Theology to Fable." Book World (Washington Post). (4 May), pp. 1, 3.
A review of Mystery and Manners. The essays are repetitious, but this repetitiousness evinces "the depth of the author's convictions." O'Connor's fiction is based in "a contempt hardened by a sense of divine alternatives and a rage that such alternatives are no longer recalled," and this attitude explains the power of her work and its occasional lapses into "screeching." O'Connor's description of the peacock's song is "the perfect metaphor for her own art."

42 SCHULZ, MAX F. Radical Sophistication: Studies in Contemporary Jewish-American Novelists. Athens, Ohio: Ohio University Press, p. 12.
Modern Jewish-American writers do not see "the situation...as so desperate that man must opt for a modern vision of religious violence, such as one finds in the stories of Flannery O'Connor."

43 SULLIVAN, WALTER. "The New Faustus: The Southern Renascence and the Joycean Esthetic." In Southern Fiction Today: Renascence and Beyond. Edited by George Core. Athens, Ga.: University of Georgia Press, pp. 1-16.
Joyce is a modern Faust who has led writers, including southern writers, to the dead end of an amoral estheticism.

This estheticism, combined with a decline in the southern respect for order and tradition, has caused the decline of southern literature. O'Connor's Roman Catholicism enabled her to avoid this decline. Reprinted 1972.B43.

44 TISCHLER, NANCY M. Black Masks: Negro Characters in Modern Southern Fiction. University Park, Pa.: Pennsylvania State University Press, p. 38.

The old yardman in "The Displaced Person" is mentioned as an example of what sociologists call "accomodation behavior," where southern blacks indirectly express their displeasure with whites.

45 TRUE, MICHAEL D. "Flannery O'Connor: Backwoods Prophet in the Secular City." PLL 5:209-23.

O'Connor succeeds in communicating with nonbelievers because of her comic irony; like many comic writers, "she combines a radically conservative religious position with a great distrust of detached intellectualism." She resembles Isaiah in the beauty of her prose and in her emphasis on the sinfulness of the city. In her work the "backwoods anti-prophets," such as the Misfit, Rufus Johnson, and Manley Pointer, become heroes because they are closer to God than those who merely claim to believe. Her work does not tell us if good is stronger than evil, and her genuine prophets, like young Tarwater, are very similar to her anti-prophets in their backwoods origin and their "singlemindedness." Includes a discussion of some previous criticism on O'Connor.

1969-1970

46 RUBIN, LOUIS D., JR. "Southern Literature: A Piedmont Art." MissQ 23:1-16.

O'Connor, who although born in Savannah lived most of her life in the Piedmont South, is another example of the superiority of Piedmont writers over their counterparts from the coastal South. This superiority primarily arose from the Piedmont's lack of a traditional, genteel literary culture that the writer felt bound to and from the greater social change that occurred in the Piedmont from the end of the Civil War to World War II.

47 WALDMEIER, JOSEPH J. "Only an Occasional Rutabaga: American Fiction Since 1945." MFS 15:467-81.

O'Connor is placed in the category of the "quest novelists," who reject social criticism or accomodation as well

(WALDMEIER, JOSEPH J.)
as "Beatism" and "absurdity of either the black humor or existential variety." The quest in the novels of these writers is for "love and its concomitant, responsibility."

1970 A BOOKS

1 HENDIN, JOSEPHINE. The World of Flannery O'Connor. Bloomington: Indiana University Press.

There were two O'Connors, the good Catholic daughter and the rebellious writer, and this tension is reflected in her work. O'Connor's characters are projections of her fantasies of rebellion. What makes O'Connor's work new is the "affectless grotesque." O'Connor's soulless characters and her flat style create a one-dimensional world, and her protagonists, who are estranged from other humans, use violence to get back at the world. Unlike Faulkner or Styron, who expand the dimensions of reality, O'Connor is similar to Capote in her reduction or reflection of these dimensions. O'Connor is not a symbolist or a Christian humanist. Her art is a cartoon, and as such has affinities with the French "new novel" and with the American "demythologizing" tradition of W. C. Williams and Wallace Stevens. Includes a selected bibliography of work by and about O'Connor. For replies See 1973.B7 and 1975.B8.

1970 B SHORTER WRITINGS

1 ABBOT, LOUISE HARDEMAN. "Remembering Flannery O'Connor." SLJ 2 (Spring), 3-25.

A remembrance of the author's friendship with O'Connor. O'Connor's surroundings, her relations with her townspeople, her attitude toward her illness, and some of her favorite books are recounted. O'Connor is presented as a devout Christian who had a "terrifying" quality in her - not a lack of compassion, but an "utter seriousness" about this author's own religious problems and about men in general. The "terrifying" quality is also a result of confronting O'Connor's "humility and charity" and her "fierce and faithful holding on to the truth."

2 ABRAHAMS, WILLIAM, ed. Fifty Years of the American Short Story: From the O. Henry Awards, 1919-1970. Garden City, N. Y.: Doubleday. Vol. 2, p. 510.

O'Connor's stories that won the O. Henry Award are listed in an index of the authors and stories that won such awards from 1919 to 1970.

3 ASALS, FREDERICK. "Flannery O'Connor's 'The Lame Shall Enter First.'" MissQ 23:103-20.

A New Critical close reading of the story. O'Connor herself must have been influenced by the New Criticism, and this story contains a "richness and coherence of language and imagery." The language and imagery in the story concerning nature, food, sex, biblical parallels, and lameness are discussed. The story is "metaphysical or theological rather than moral," since both Johnson and Sheppard are morally wrong, but Johnson accepts nature with its imperfections and also recognizes a spiritual order. He is both "demonic and divine," but Sheppard, who denies the spiritual and whose altruism is a cover for his own pride and egoism, is the worse off of the two. The end of the story, however, "leaves a gleam of sober hope" that Sheppard's guilt will "be the basis for new life."

4 _____. "Flannery Row." Novel (Brown University) 4:92-96.

A review of Mystery and Manners and Carter Martin's The True Country: Themes in the Fiction of Flannery O'Connor. The essays by O'Connor show she was "no critical theorist," but they are valuable because the near-contradictions among some of her ideas and the tensions she describes point to "her ability to project her own conflicting 'wills' into the action of the fiction while holding with tense poise to a single vision that transcends all of them." Martin is criticized for relying too much on O'Connor's own pronouncements, for having an oversimplified view of O'Connor's religion, and for overemphasizing classification.

5 BERGUP, SISTER BERNICE, O.S.B. "Themes of Redemptive Grace in the Works of Flannery O'Connor." ABR 21:169-91.

O'Connor's works treat the sin of man's directly or indirectly rejecting God and the redemptive grace which comes to aid him. O'Connor always treats this grace as an aspect of "the experiential dimension"; it does not come "extraneously like a deus ex machina." In O'Connor, man is free to accept or reject either grace or evil, but as The Violent Bear It Away makes clear, true freedom lies only in redemption. O'Connor uses the grotesque to tell us "that men without Christ are grotesque." In her fiction "the obviously abnormal ones understand the spiritual basis of abnormality while the 'normal' ones do not or will not recognize their abnormality." Includes discussions of Wise Blood, The Violent Bear It Away, and several of the stories.

1970

6 BLEIKASTEN, ANDRÉ. "Théologie et dérision chez Flannery O'Connor." LanM 64 (March-April), 28-38.
O'Connor's works contradict her proclaimed religious beliefs. In her works her satire is so bitter the reader feels that to O'Connor everything is abhorrent. The Christianity in her works is dark and unorthodox: the humanity of Christ is ignored; man's fall, not his redemption, is exclusively emphasized; and grace, when it comes, is no more comforting than evil. Places most emphasis on O'Connor's two novels and also discusses O'Connor's use of sun, fire, eye and peacock imagery. See 1973.B5.

7 BRYANT, JERRY H. The Open Decision: The Contemporary American Novel and Its Intellectual Background. New York: The Free Press, pp. 258-64, 267-68, 281.
A study of the contemporary American novel that stresses the scientific and philosophical background of modern literature, especially the idea of the "open decision." Modern man must choose his actions and values in a world lacking traditional guideposts and transcendental sanctions. O'Connor is one of the modern novelists who affirm the irrational as a way of affirming the value of the individual as the center of his world. Although O'Connor openly rejects modern relativism, "she cannot escape the atmosphere of her time." In Wise Blood Hazel Motes becomes an example of how "the real and the valuable" is "found in the indeterminate authenticity of the experiencing subject, whose value is confirmed by the act of faith which is the choice of its being, and not the being conferred, supposedly, by some transcendent agent." Haze's affirmation is made "for no objectively valid reason."

8 BRYER, JACKSON R. and NANNESKA N. MAGEE. "The Modern Catholic Novel: A Selected Checklist of Criticism." In The Vision Obscured: Perceptions of Some Twentieth Century Catholic Novelists. Edited by Melvin J. Friedman. New York: Fordham University Press, pp. 241-68.
Includes a selected bibliography of criticism on O'Connor and other Catholic writers, as well as a general bibliography of books and articles treating Catholic literature.

9 BURNS, STUART L. "The Evolution of Wise Blood." MFS 16: 147-62.
An analysis of Wise Blood based on a study of the five previous stories that in various ways contributed to the novel: "The Train," "The Heart of the Park," "Woman on the Stairs," "The Peeler," and "Enoch and the Gorilla." The

novel lacks unity because O'Connor failed to integrate the elements of the stories into the novel. For example, Hazel's religious obsession is confused with O'Connor's original conception of Hazel as suffering from Oedipal guilt, and many of the chapters on Enoch should have been omitted from the novel.

10 CASPER, LEONARD. "The Unspeakable Peacock: Apocalypse in Flannery O'Connor." In _The Shaken Realist: Essays in Modern Literature in Honor of Frederick J. Hoffman_. Edited by Melvin J. Friedman and John B. Vickery. Baton Rouge: Louisiana State University Press, pp. 287-99.

O'Connor's works are laden with the occurrence of death and with images implying death, but her fiction is "remarkably free of morbidity" because she is not concerned with death itself but with "the apocalyptic vision of possibility." O'Connor's "private emblem" is the peacock, "traditional symbol of the Second Coming." O'Connor is essentially a short story writer because of "her recognition of the 'terrible speed of mercy,' the traumatic convergence of time and eternity." Her interest in the grotesque and in the paradox of the intermingling of sacred and profane is a result of her interest in the mysterious workings of grace. O'Connor's system of values is close to that of Teilhard de Chardin, who equates "being with being one." Unlike most modern writers, who stress the self as ultimate value, O'Connor has "retained respect for and responsibility to history as fable of epic possibility; to social order as ceremony of hope; to place and person as concrete precedent for universals." For O'Connor and other southern writers, "there can never fully be an I unless there is an I-Thou."

11 COLES, ROBERT. Review of _Mystery and Manners_. _Harvard Educational Review_ 40:130-35.

Discusses O'Connor's book and two nonfiction works on the South. O'Connor's world view "finds the presence of such consuming and fearful and scarring illnesses [as hers] quite unsurprising," and her central concern is mystery "as _us_, the whole lot of us, here for what must be a few seconds in eternity's scheme of things, and so very full and certain of ourselves." Her essays reveal her understanding of the art of fiction and "cut away at dreary sentimentality and simple-minded optimism and showy 'art' and vulgar literary opportunism and, yes, cut away at the kind of cheapened, degraded faith that has become American political moralism." O'Connor was able to create for herself a unique and important place in American letters.

12 DAVIS, JACK and JUNE. "Tarwater and Jonah: Two Reluctant Prophets." XUS 9, i:19-27.

O'Connor and the writer of the biblical tale of Jonah use violence "as a dramatic device to resolve the conflict between their alienated prophets and a wrathful God" and "as a communicative device to shock their readers into realizing the enormity of their own alienation from God." Melvin J. Friedman is wrong in seeing young Tarwater as a "defeated prophet" and in arguing that the novel follows a pattern of "'transplantation-prophecy-return'" (1966.B13). The novel follows the biblical tale in being "structured around an initiation motif involving commandment, resistance, punishment, and capitulation." Also, Mason Tarwater is paralleled with the prophet Elisha, whose corpse could give life to others.

13 DRAKE, ROBERT. "Miss O'Connor: The Shadow and The Substance." CEA 32, vii:13.

A review of Mystery and Manners with a brief mention of Carter Martin's The True Country: Themes in the Fiction of Flannery O'Connor. Martin is "on the right track in many of his observations and assessments." O'Connor is concerned with mystery, which "seems to represent some ultimate shape or form, inscrutable to the boldest interpreter," and manners, "those concrete furnishings within this inscrutable universe." Like Conrad, she saw her duty as an artist "was almost entirely to do nothing but tell the truth," and she believed "that, if the writer will simply take care of the truth, then the religion, the Church, the Faith will take care of itself."

14 FARNHAM, JAMES F. "Flannery O'Connor and the Incarnation of Mystery." Cross Currents 20:252-56.

A review of Mystery and Manners. In this collection O'Connor reveals herself as one of the few writers who is also a good critic. The collection treats four major topics: "the modern romance tradition in literature, the aesthetics of narrative fiction, the function or purpose of fiction, and the relationship of an artist's religious beliefs to his art." In O'Connor's case, her theory and her fiction are consistent.

15 FRENCH, WARREN. "The Age of Salinger." In The Fifties: Fiction, Poetry, Drama. Edited by Warren French. Deland, Florida: Everett/Edwards, pp. 1-39.

Passing reference to O'Connor in an essay on Salinger as the dominant and representative writer of the fifties. O'Connor can be categorized as either a member of the southern "religious school" of the fifties or as a forerunner of the "black humorists."

16 _____. "Bibliography." In The Fifties: Fiction, Poetry, Drama. Edited by Warren French. Deland, Florida: Everett/Edwards, pp. 291-304.
A selected bibliography of criticism on writers of the fifties. Contains a brief summary of books, either full-length treatments or collections of essays, on O'Connor.

17 FRIEDMAN, MELVIN J. "By and About Flannery O'Connor." JML 1: 288-92.
A review of Mystery and Manners and Carter Martin's The True Country: Themes in the Fiction of Flannery O'Connor that praises O'Connor for her "useful judgments about technique and narrative focus" and "her fine sense of the epigrammatic." Despite some flaws, Martin's book is "impressive."

18 _____. "Flannery O'Connor's Sacred Objects." In The Vision Obscured: Perceptions of Some Twentieth Century Catholic Novelists. Edited by Melvin J. Friedman. New York: Fordham University Press, pp. 67-77.
A slightly revised version of 1966.B12.

19 FRIELING, KENNETH. "Flannery O'Connor's Vision: The Violence of Revelation." In The Fifties: Fiction, Poetry, Drama. Edited by Warren French. Deland, Florida: Everett/Edward, pp. 111-20.
Discusses the stories in A Good Man Is Hard to Find. O'Connor uses "violent revelation" to make her characters see the true nature of the grotesque and the potential for grace. O'Connor presents this revelation through four techniques that are often fused in her stories: "(1) the recognition of an emblem's full significance, (2) the realization of a cliché's true implications, (3) the emerging epiphanic gesture indicating the recognition of humanity and the acceptance of grace, and (4) the violently catalytic effect of the presence of a prophet figure, typically an anti-prophet." The "concentrated revelatory illumination" of these stories is probably more palatable to contemporary readers and more artistically successful than a novel-length treatment of these illuminations would be.

20 GAFFORD, CHARLOTTE K. "Chaucer's Pardoner and Haze Motes of Georgia." In Essays in Honor of Richebourg Gaillard McWilliams. Edited by Howard Creed. Birmingham-Southern College Bulletin 63, ii:9-12.

(GAFFORD, CHARLOTTE K.)

Suggests that Chaucer's Pardoner and Hazel Motes resemble each other in being unrespectable and thus apparently damned, yet still capable of spiritual perception and thus of redemption. "When Haze reaches a spiritual state which may be likened to the Pardoner's pronouncement of the efficacy of Christ in the sacrament of penance, he has entered that interior area where questions and answers, credentials, doctrines do not matter, and where recognition of failure is the only requisite for redemption."

21 GRAS, GABRIELLE. "Flannery O'Connor." Europe 48 (January), 236-38.

A review of Mon mal vient de plus loin, the French translation of Everything That Rises Must Converge. The world of the stories is a bleak one, but the "grandeur" of O'Connor's art overcomes the reader.

22 GRESSET, MICHEL. "L'audace de Flannery O'Connor." NRF 18 (December), 61-71.

The most striking feature of O'Connor's work is its audacity, audacity not in a sociological sense, but an audacity of form. Like Conrad and the best of the Anglo-Saxon symbolists, O'Connor writes a pure fiction which is still loyal to the concrete. The center of her works is revelation, with death serving as a dramatic metaphor and fire as a symbolic metaphor for this revelation. These revelations are shown, not told about, and they cannot be transported out of the fiction as a message. O'Connor was not interested in preaching; her faith was the motor of her work, but it is external to the fiction. In the work we find revelation, not grace. O'Connor's faith gave her a coherence of vision that permitted her audacity, but her audacity reaches a second level in her refusal to put this faith in the work. O'Connor resembles Beckett because his lack of faith has given him this same artistic boldness.

23 HENDIN, JOSEPHINE. "In Search of Flannery O'Connor." Columbia Forum 13, i:38-41.

Discusses a visit to Milledgeville and the near impossibility of getting beyond the image of O'Connor as "Southern Gentlewoman": "for the most patrician ladies in town, Flannery O'Connor is about as human as a Hepplewhite chest. She is displayed to advantage and said to contain the most neatly folded Southern virtues." In reality, O'Connor's life and art were centered around the tensions between "an eternal cheeriness and suffering, graciousness and fear of human contact, acquiescence and enduring fury." O'Connor "became more and more the pure poet of the Misfit, the oppressed, the psychic cripple, the freak--of all of those who are martyred by silent fury and redeemed through violence."

24 HICKS, GRANVILLE. Literary Horizons: A Quarter Century of American Fiction. New York: New York University Press, pp. 135-49.

A reprint of some previous reviews of O'Connor's works, with a brief foreword. See 1955.B18, 1960.B33, 1965.B36 and 1969.B21.

25 KELLOGG, GENE. The Vital Tradition: The Catholic Novel in a Period of Convergence. Chicago: Loyola University Press, pp. 2, 26, passim.

A study of Catholic novels in France, England, and America that emphasizes historical background. Catholic novelists achieved artistic maturity only when the Catholic community was "in the condition of tension between separation and convergence" with the outside society and when the Catholic artist opposed not only the secular world but also his own tradition. J. F. Powers and O'Connor are discussed as American Catholic novelists. Powers writes in the tradition of American Catholic "pragmatism," though he often satirizes its despiritualization, whereas O'Connor's imagination is largely formed by Jansenism and its close relative, "Irish American Puritanism." Both of O'Connor's novels treat two opposing types, "the rebellious God-haunted soul and the frustrated man-oriented soul," but The Violent Bear It Away does so more clearly and successfully. O'Connor's characters have a very limited freedom, and her Jansenism may create "a bit of uneasiness" in many orthodox Catholics. She was, however, "not only a great artist but a Catholic typical of her time and place." A briefer version of this argument can be found in "The Catholic Novel in Convergence," Thought 45 (1970), 265-96.

26 LEVINE, PAUL. "Flannery O'Connor: The Soul of the Grotesque." In Minor American Novelists. Edited by Charles Alva Hoyt. Carbondale: Southern Illinois University Press, pp. 95-117.

Relates O'Connor to Sherwood Anderson and Nathanael West and claims that Miss Lonelyhearts, with its confrontation of secularism and "the fundamentalist religious vision" is the "model" for O'Connor's fiction. O'Connor is similar to many contemporary novelists in her use of extremes to communicate her vision, her use of the grotesque to attack "bourgeois complacency," and in Wise Blood, her use of the "search for experience." In her stories, her middle class

(LEVINE, PAUL)
protagonists often "achieve a glimpse of salvation" when the demonic intrudes into the ordinary; in the novels, on the other hand, the protagonists more closely resemble the "demonic antagonists" of the stories. Their "lives are not tales of sudden epiphany but of the struggle for revelation." Both novels deal with the dehumanization resulting from materialism and with the ultimately unsuccessful struggle of the protagonists against their own salvation. Tarwater, however, is a more positive character than Haze, since he moves beyond atonement. Haze resembles Miss Lonelyhearts, but young Tarwater reminds us of David Schearl, the young hero of Henry Roth's mystical Call It Sleep.

27 LITTLEFIELD, DANIEL F. "Flannery O'Connor's Wise Blood: 'Unparalleled Prosperity and Spiritual Chaos.'" MissQ 23: 121-33.

In O'Connor the "grotesqueness of characters - this distortion of spiritual purpose - is a product of our 'unparalleled prosperity.'" Lewis A. Lawson (1965.B47) is wrong in calling the world of the novel unreal because the minor characters embody "the 'normal' objective world" and wrong in seeing the novel lacking in plot and character development because the characters are motivated by their quest for material prosperity. The sincere characters, Hazel and Enoch, use prosperity "as a means to an end," while the hypocrites, Asa Hawks, Hoover Shoats, and Mrs. Flood, "pursue it as an end." O'Connor describes all these characters as bestial. Only Hazel escapes the bestial and finds redemption.

28 MAIDA, PATRICIA DINNEEN. "'Convergence' in Flannery O'Connor's 'Everything That Rises Must Converge.'" SSF 7:549-55.

An examination of the significance of the title and its relation to Teilhard de Chardin's The Phenomenon of Man. The identical hats and "the convergence of the two women" raise the questions of identity and responsibility. O'Connor and Teilhard de Chardin resemble each other because "she attempts to penetrate matter until spirit is reached," particularly in the violent scene in the story, but O'Connor is less optimistic than Teilhard de Chardin. He takes the cosmic view while she focuses on the present. The irony that Robert Fitzgerald notes (1965.B30) is not, however, directed at Teilhard de Chardin but at the contrast between the real and the ideal. Nevertheless, the ending is somewhat optimistic, since Julian may change after his illumination.

29 MALE, ROY R. "The Two Versions of 'The Displaced Person.'" SSF 7:450-57.

Aside from the addition of Part Two of the story, the revised version of "The Displaced Person" that appeared in A Good Man Is Hard to Find incorporates several changes from the original Sewanee Review version. In the revised version, O'Connor is closer to Mrs. Shortley and more accurately captures her idiom. Mr. Guizac is drawn more precisely, and his plan for marrying his cousin is revealed. The story is made more organic and by adding ten years to Mrs. Shortley's age, more plausible. The peacock was also added, but it fits in well in the revised version. It is as crucial to the story and as mysterious as O'Connor wanted it to be.

30 MAY, JOHN R., S.J. "Language - Event as Promise: Reflections on Theology and Literature." Canadian Journal of Theology 16:129-39.

"Revelation" is briefly discussed as "an excellent illustration of the hermeneutical function of language and of a literary text" because Mary Grace's words to Mrs. Turpin judge the latter and "the story itself speaks this word of judgment to the reader."

31 _____. "The Pruning Word: Flannery O'Connor's Judgment of Intellectuals." SHR 4:325-38.

O'Connor's treatment of intellectuals can be understood by applying "the eschatological language of apocalypse or revelation" to her stories. In the stories "the action of grace...is...the 'pruning word' of revelation spoken by the antagonist" that either simply condemms the intellectual for his arrogance and narrow vision or converts him from his error. In O'Connor's stories, "the mind is impotent, of itself, to save the world or any portion of it."

32 ORVELL, MILES. "Flannery O'Connor." SR 78:184-92.

A review of Mystery and Manners; The Added Dimension: The Art and Mind of Flannery O'Connor, edited by Melvin J. Friedman and Lewis A. Lawson; and The True Country: Themes in the Fiction of Flannery O'Connor, by Carter W. Martin. O'Connor is her own best critic. Criticism of O'Connor needs to place less stress on themes and more on "the unique formal integrity of the individual work." There is also a need for more study of O'Connor's literary relations with other writers.

33 PEARCE, RICHARD. Stages of the Clown: Perspectives on Modern Fiction from Dostoyevsky to Beckett. Carbondale: Southern Illinois University Press, pp. 2, 4, passim.

Emphasizes Wise Blood and The Violent Bear It Away, since these two novels show O'Connor's world most fully. O'Connor, "in the tradition of Plato's foolish Socrates and Erasmus's Christian Fool, affirms what conventional rationality denies." In her fiction, "the world is turned upside down by a comic surprise, and in each case, with the apocalypse, human value is unexpectedly asserted in a world without meaning." O'Connor belongs with those modern writers, from Dostoyevsky to Beckett, who use the clown figure in one of its various manifestations to demonstrate the absurdity of the world. This demonstration, however, is not pessimistic, since man is "most alive and free when confronted with the maximum possibility of surprise."

34 PORTER, KATHERINE ANNE. "Flannery O'Connor at Home." In The Collected Essays and Occasional Writings of Katherine Anne Porter. New York: Delacorte Press, pp. 295-97.

A reprint of 1964.B69.

35 PRAMPOLINI, GAETANO. "Flannery O'Connor: Una Scrittrice Cattolica della Georgia." RLMC 28:85-110.

An overview of O'Connor's life and literary career. Her fiction can only be understood if the reader realizes the importance of her Catholicism, of her region, and of her sense of herself as a writer. Her writing does show the reality of the South.

36 RUPP, RICHARD H. Celebration in Postwar American Fiction: 1945-1967. Coral Gables, Florida: University of Miami Press, pp. 10, 11, passim.

Our times are unable to "celebrate reality," to praise reality and God who created it. Writers like O'Connor respond to this dearth of celebration by stressing festivity and a joyous assent to reality. O'Connor writes of "hidden feast" and "public famine," what O'Connor herself describes as "mystery and fact." In O'Connor, the "feasts are guerilla raids on the unfestive society overhead - a society that refuses to acknowledge the divine mystery of existence." O'Connor is more closely related to French Catholic literature than to southern literature.

37 SMITH, FRANCIS J., S.J. "O'Connor's Religious Viewpoint in The Violent Bear It Away." Renascence 22:108-12.

Although O'Connor's attitude towards physical violence is unclear, "it is a scandal to suppose that O'Connor would understand the gospels in this revolting sense, approving violent means to an evangelical end." What O'Connor wants is "an active Christian," and in this sense she supports old Tarwater, though she probably finds his type of faith "uncongenial." The novel "is a kind of southern Everyman," with Part One being "Tarwater's Vocation," Part Two his "Ministry," and Part Three "'The Little Death.'" Finally, however, the novel is boring because of "the prolix relation of her characters' thoughts and actions, the repetitiousness, and the unsavory characters themselves."

38 SOLOTAROFF, THEODORE. The Red Hot Vacuum and Other Pieces on the Writing of the Sixties. New York: Atheneum, pp. 156, 171-76.

A slightly revised version of the 1965 review (See 1965.B72). Also, in an essay on James Purdy, O'Connor is mentioned as one of those modern writers who react against modern society and "move farther and farther back into their sensibility to get their bearings."

39 WYLDER, JEAN. "Flannery O'Connor: A Reminiscence and Some Letters." North American Review 255 (Spring), 58-65.

Recounts her friendship with O'Connor when they were both students at the University of Iowa and their correspondence up to the time of O'Connor's death.

1971 A BOOKS

1 DRISKELL, LEON V. and JOAN T. BRITTAIN. The Eternal Crossroads: The Art of Flannery O'Connor. Lexington, Ky.: University Press of Kentucky.

A chronological analysis of O'Connor's works, with emphasis on the literary and theological influences on O'Connor. Although there are traces of Nathanael West in Wise Blood, the important influences on O'Connor's early work were Hawthorne and Mauriac, who influenced her in her situations, symbols, and themes. As O'Connor progressed, however, she came to accept the "optimistic and idealistic Christology" of Teilhard de Chardin. Her early work follows Mauriac in showing the steps leading up to grace, but her later work more often shows the operation of grace in her characters. This study also stresses the biblical parallels and symbols in the fiction and the unity of each of the two collections of stories. O'Connor's work is not grotesque: she was interested in showing life in a particular time and place as well as the "crossroads" where this earthly life meets eternity. Includes an extensive bibliography of

(DRISKELL, LEON V. and JOAN T. BRITTAIN)
material by and about O'Connor, largely based on 1967.B3 and 1968.B7. Secondary material includes biographical articles.

1971 B SHORTER WRITINGS

1 ANON. Review of Flannery O'Connor: The Complete Stories. New Republic (20 November), p. 34.
A noncommital review that mentions O'Connor's dislike of liberals: "Her conviction that some of the truest voices are the most brutal has led some readers to call her fiction exaggerated. Others just say it's powerful."

2 ANON. Review of Flannery O'Connor: The Complete Stories. NYTBR (5 December), p. 83.
The collection is recommended as one of the year's best works of fiction.

3 BLACKWELL, LOUISE. "Humor and Irony in the Work of Flannery O'Connor." RANAM 4:61-68.
O'Connor's humor is more traditional than most critics have realized. Traditional humor, especially primitive humor, often has a cruel streak, and in O'Connor's works the "hostile" humor shows through in her portrayals of the middle class. She uses irony in her treatment of middle-aged women, and the sources of her humor are the staples of traditional comedy: folk wit, child-adult relationships, sex, dialogue, and primitivism. O'Connor's use of misfits is traditional, but the difference is that in O'Connor's fiction the misfits "stare back at the audience," challenging us to see ourselves in them.

4 CLEMONS, WALTER. "Acts of Grace." Newsweek (8 November), pp. 115-17.
A review of Flannery O'Connor: The Complete Stories. O'Connor's early, uncollected stories already show her artistic power, and the collection as a whole shows her humor and the growth of "her profound moral vision." Some of her stories are melodramatic, but many are excellent. "Revelation" is O'Connor's "masterpiece."

5 DAVENPORT, GUY. "Even As the Heathen Rage." NatR (31 December), pp. 1473-74.
Includes a review of The Complete Stories. Discusses O'Connor's Christianity, which "had that purity of the first centuries when to be civilized was the opposite of to be a Christian," and her skill as a comic writer and

argues that the stories "have been read too long as grotesqueries from the midden of the late Confederacy. Their appeal is universal."

6 DUFFY, MARTHA. "At Gunpoint." Time (29 November), pp. 87-88.
A review of Flannery O'Connor: The Complete Stories. O'Connor places little faith in commonsensical virtues, and she often laughs at the South. She is "seldom compassionate," feeling that people "cannot or will not see the wonder and terror of their existence." O'Connor's "best are among the best American short stories ever written."

7 FLORES-DEL PRADO, WILMA. "Flannery O'Connor's Gallery of Freaks." SLRJ 2 (September-December), 463-514.
Examines the various kinds of religious, mental, moral, and physical "freaks" in O'Connor and argues that O'Connor reveals charity for these characters because she believes in a transcendent realm and because she shows characters as free in their choice of good or evil and aware of the consequences of such a choice. Her compassion is also demonstrated by her ecumenical approval of non-Catholic prophets and her emphasis on social causes as partly explaining the characters' behavior. O'Connor's belief that evil can serve good and her stress on "the acquisition of insight" result from the influence of Teilhard de Chardin. Also discusses O'Connor's life.

8 GIROUX, ROBERT. Introduction to Flannery O'Connor: The Complete Stories. New York: Farrar, Straus, and Giroux, pp. vii-xvii.
A biographical account of this publisher's long relationship with O'Connor, including portions of a letter from Paul Engle, her instructor at Iowa. O'Connor is compared with her admirer, Thomas Merton.

9 GROSS, THEODORE L. The Heroic Ideal in American Literature. New York: The Free Press, p. 120.
O'Connor's "gothic stories," like much modern southern literature, "struggle...with the breakdown of nineteenth-century values; and their special brilliance lies in their challenge to one set of beliefs by another."

10 GULLASON, THOMAS A. Review of Flannery O'Connor: The Complete Stories. SatR (13 November), pp. 57, 63-64.
The inclusion of the early uncollected stories shows O'Connor's later artistic development. Although readers may be troubled by the oddity of her characters and situations, O'Connor was "mainly a writer of morality plays" who

(GULLASON, THOMAS A.)
used the grotesque for purposes of revelation. O'Connor's work joins the tragic and comic and "translates moral and religious abstractions into living presences."

11 HARRISON, MARGARET. "Hazel Motes in Transit: A Comparison of Two Versions of Flannery O'Connor's 'The Train' with Chapter 1 of Wise Blood." SSF 8:287-93.

Between the thesis version of the story and the later Sewanee Review version, O'Connor improved the story by separating narrative style from the style of the characters, by shifting Haze's interest from the porter himself to the porter as suggesting his home town, and by being less consciously poetic. Between the Sewanee Review version and the first chapter of Wise Blood, O'Connor improved the story and made it fit the novel by stressing the sight versus blindness motif and by increasing the importance of the woman on the train, the flexibility of the point of view, and the visual detail. The essential change lies in O'Connor's moving from the story's "psychological insight" to the novel's more forceful Haze and a concern for "the mystery of redemption."

12 HAYS, PETER L. The Limping Hero: Grotesques in Literature. New York: New York University Press, pp. 95-98, 122.

In a chapter on "sterility figures" some of O'Connor's characters with maimed or otherwise disabled legs are discussed. In O'Connor's fiction, "a leg wound...does testify to human inability and weakness, the impotence of man to achieve salvation by himself." With O'Connor, however, the leg wound does not suggest sterility; rather, it prepares a character for grace.

13 INGE, M. THOMAS. "Contemporary American Literature in Spain." TSL 16:155-67.

Translations of some of O'Connor's work are mentioned in this article on translations of and critical interest in contemporary American authors. O'Connor was one of the writers two Spanish publishing firms thought should have greater recognition in Spain.

14 INGRAM, FORREST L. Representative Short Story Cycles of the Twentieth Century: Studies in a Literary Genre. The Hague: Mouton, pp. 18, 139.

Everything That Rises Must Converge is mentioned as an example of a collection of short stories that are arranged by theme into a "story cycle," which "is a set of stories so linked to one another that the reader's experience of each one is modified by his experience of the others." In a footnote the author briefly mentions his argument that the first seven stories constitute the true cycle, an argument that is developed at greater length in 1972.B23.

15 KAZIN, ALFRED. "Heroines." NYRB (11 February), pp. 28-34.
In an article on women as writers discusses O'Connor's fierce religion, her repetitiveness, her sense of human limitation, and her ability to fuse orthodoxy and artistic freedom. O'Connor "as a woman even more reduced to inaction than most women...links power (as ownership) to violence." Perhaps O'Connor's religious fierceness is a result of her being a woman.

16 ______. Review of Flannery O'Connor: The Complete Stories. NYTBR (28 November), pp. 1, 22.
O'Connor was essentially a short story writer because of her talent for finding "people 'complete' in the smallest gesture." Her sentences are "exact...the way different parts of a body fit each other." She had "an unyielding sense of our limits, and the limits could only be raised by death." Too much emphasis has been placed on her theology, not enough on her environment and her illness.

17 LASK, THOMAS. "Death Never Takes a Holiday." NYT (3 December), p. 37.
A review of Flannery O'Connor: The Complete Stories. Readers who do not share O'Connor's philosophical viewpoint or fully understand every aspect of her work can still enjoy her fiction. Although she seems obsessed by death, death in her fiction functions as "a reminder of our mortality" and as a warning against pride. O'Connor's "religious concerns add a density to her texts that is at once both an obstacle and a challenge."

18 LINDBERG-SEYERSTED, BRITA. "American Fiction Since 1950." Edda 71:193-203.
O'Connor is briefly discussed as a southern writer who follows Faulkner in her characters and settings and in her use of the grotesque, but who "differs most radically from Faulkner in her passionate emphasis on religious themes."

19 LORENTZEN, MELVIN E. "A Good Writer Is Hard to Find." In Imagination and the Spirit: Essays in Literature and the Christian Faith presented to Clyde S. Kilby. Edited by Charles A. Huttar. Grand Rapids: William B. Eerdmans, pp. 417-35.
Although O'Connor has often been misunderstood, she proves that Christianity can be central to works of fiction.

(LORENTZEN, MELVIN E.)
Her craft saved her from "the pitfall of preaching." As "A Good Man Is Hard to Find" demonstrates, she had for her characters a "Christian compassion" that is the opposite of "mushy sentimentality," and she was concerned with two mysteries: "the mystery of iniquity and the mystery of redemption." In the story "divine grace is at work in the Grandmother, and it culminates in her triumph over the Misfit because she accepts it." Contemporary Catholic writers are superior to contemporary Protestant ones because "the sacramental view of life may be inherently more conducive to artistic expression than the propositional stance of nonliturgical traditions." Recounts remarks by O'Connor that Mauriac "was the greatest single influence on her as a writer."

20 MALOFF, SAUL and ELIOT WRIGHT. "Critics' Choices for Christmas." Commonweal (3 December), pp. 232, 239.
Both critics mention Flannery O'Connor: The Complete Stories. Maloff claims that O'Connor "is a writer who is as likely to become 'permanent' as any of her generation."

21 MARTIN, CARTER. "Flannery O'Connor and Fundamental Poverty." EJ 60:458-61.
O'Connor portrayed the poor in her fiction not for sociological reasons but because she believed all men are spiritually impoverished by original sin and because her poor, with their emphasis on formality, are "people in whom mystery and manners are not dissociated."

22 MONTGOMERY, MARION. "Flannery O'Connor: Realist of Distances." RANAM 4:69-78.
A Christian reading of O'Connor that finds her opposing the belief that consciousness is an "accident," using the regional to write of the universal, and struggling against "Manicheanism," a struggle that associates her with T. S. Eliot and "the Vanderbilt Fugitive Agrarians." The author takes aim at two kinds of critics: the "geographical provincial," who see O'Connor as a recorder of southern decadence, and the "spiritual provincial," especially Stanley Edgar Hyman (See 1966.A3), who read O'Connor according to their own secular frameworks. O'Connor uses distortion because of the disparity between her beliefs and those of her audience. Includes brief biographical remarks: O'Connor seemed "somehow miraculous."

23 _____. "In Defense of Flannery O'Connor's Dragon." GaR 25: 302-16.

Today's young radicals, with their rejection of American materialism and the modern "doctrine of man as an accident of nature," may be attracted to O'Connor's work. She rejects modern hypocrisy and our equation of good with material progress, as she shows in her portrayal of Shiftlet in "The Life You Save May Be Your Own," and she suggests, with young Tarwater, that the young must move beyond their own failings, including their lack of a belief in "objective or transcendent grounds to truth." Modern readers find O'Connor disturbing because she insists upon our "personal involvement in evil" and will not allow us the palliatives of environmental determinism and "social adjustment."

24 ______. "On Flannery O'Connor's 'Everything That Rises Must Converge.'" Crit 13, ii:15-29.

The protagonist is Julian, not his mother, and he has "two presences": the "detached" Julian and the destroyer of his mother. Julian is a "pseudo-existentialist" who, like the Misfit, takes pleasure in hurting others, namely his mother, but "his meanness is paralysed force, gesture without motions." Julian lives in a world of abstract principles without a basis in reality. He resembles the black woman because both deny love and because both are more concerned with surface appearance than underlying value. Julian learns from his mother's death "the necessity of putting aside childishness to become a little child." Although the "spectacle" of the end is violent, "the most violent collision is within Julian, with effects Aristotle declared necessary to complex tragedy."

25 OATES, JOYCE CAROL. "Realism of Distance and Realism of Immediacy." SoR 7:295-313.

Includes a laudatory review of Mystery and Manners, with emphasis on O'Connor's belief that fiction should concern itself with mystery. O'Connor's "writing is incarnational--a celebration of the distant in terms of the immediate."

26 O'BRIEN, JOHN T. "The Un-Christianity of Flannery O'Connor." Listening 6:71-82.

As "Greenleaf," "Revelation" and "Parker's Back" reveal, O'Connor's theology is not orthodox Christian because she denies free will. The Violent Bear It Away demonstrates that O'Connor's religion "is Christ-centered but without love," love being "replaced at times by mercy, by patience, by obedience, by humility." The key to her theology "is the recognition of and faithful adherence to the divine will." The theology is not orthodox, nor is it Platonist,

(O'BRIEN, JOHN T.)
and it will probably be some time before critics really understand it.

27 PRESCOTT, PETER S. "The Year in Books: A Personal Report." Newsweek (27 December), pp. 57-61.
Flannery O'Connor: The Complete Stories is included in a list of books published in 1971 that the reviewer found "particularly good for one reason or another."

28 QUINN, JOHN J., S.J. Review of Flannery O'Connor: The Complete Stories. America (11 December), pp. 518-20.
This collection shows O'Connor's growth into the finest short story writer of our time. She belongs in the "Conrad-James tradition of literature as 'the art of making (the reader) see.'" O'Connor has a grotesque vision of "the essential man" and her stories climax in an epiphany or "some minor revelation."

29 ______. Review of Flannery O'Connor: The Complete Stories. Best Sellers 31:383.
O'Connor is a "supreme artist of integrity" whose "Christ-intoxicated people represent the essential man in an existential milieu."

30 SESSIONS, WILLIAM A. Review of Mystery and Manners. SSF 8: 491-94.
O'Connor and Blake had "that element of faith" that led to "their repetitions of a few cosmic themes that seem almost simple-minded at times." Her essays treat one or the other of "two great simplicities," the South and Catholicism. Her esthetic principles, however, demand the "subtle shading" that her fiction gives us. Her essays dealing primarily with esthetics are more successful than the more theological ones, because the latter will create problems for the skeptical reader. The comments on Catholic censorship in "The Church and the Fiction Writer" are of doubtful authenticity, since O'Connor "complained about the editorial handling of this piece in America and specifically about the rewriting of passages in it." See 1972.B19 for a reply.

31 SULLIVAN, WALTER. "Flannery O'Connor, Sin, and Grace: Everything That Rises Must Converge." In The Sounder Few: Essays from the Hollins Critic. Edited by R. H. W. Dillard, George Garrett, and John Rees Moore. Athens, Ga.: University of Georgia Press, pp. 101-19.
A reprint of 1965.B74. Includes a listing of American, British, and Canadian editions of O'Connor's books.

32 TANNER, TONY. City of Words: American Fiction 1950-1970. New York: Harper and Row, p. 204.

Passing reference to O'Connor as one of the writers in John Hawkes's "literary lineage" (See 1965.B35). Although Tanner does not discuss O'Connor, his book may help to place her work, since it discusses many of the philosophical and literary concerns of contemporary writers. Contemporary writers seek a balance between individual freedom and order, a balance that is tenuous but necessary because too much freedom would lead to chaos and too much order would lead to the loss of freedom. Also, contemporary American writers, like many previous American writers, are obsessed with "foregrounding," i.e., playing with language in a way that draws attention to language as the medium of the work. For American writers, this "City of Words" is a space of freedom from the restrictions of the environment, but it is also dangerous, since "there is the suspicion that by living too much in language you may cut yourself off from direct contact with reality."

33 TRUCHLAR, LEO. "Flannery O'Connors 'The Artificial Nigger.'" Die Sprachkunst 2:265-71.

O'Connor's use of epiphany differs from that of Joyce and Rilke because she does not use epiphany as a modern stylistic device the way Joyce does, and her epiphanies are used to illuminate communication between human beings, not to reveal the state of the soul of the isolated individual.

34 VALENSISE, RACHELE. "Tre Scrittrici del Sud: Flannery O'Connor, Caroline Gordon, Carson McCullers." SA 17:251-89.

These three writers are involved in a quest for a new mythology to replace that of the traditional South, and all affirm a sacramental view of art and life and the necessity for spiritual coherence in the face of the chaos of reality. McCullers differs from the other two because she sees this coherence and the promise of love only as hypothetical possibilities against which the chaos and estrangement of her characters' lives can be measured. While all three combine symbolism and realism and thus employ biblical and classical motifs, McCullers does so not to reinforce the religious but to demythologize it. O'Connor as a Catholic gives us a theological interpretation of reality where the central issue is man's choice of good or evil, and where true freedom lies in total submission to God. O'Connor's language, with its use of the backwoods combination of the mythical and profane, demonstrates her desire for a language tied to reality, while her repeated use of certain key gestures tends to reduce some of her characters

(VALENSISE, RACHELE)
to automata. Her continual emphasis on sight and the sun stresses her theme of illumination.

1971-1972

35 MONTGOMERY, MARION. "Flannery O'Connor's Transformation of the Sentimental." MissQ 25:1-18.

O'Connor is against both sentimentality and obscenity because they divorce "larger aspects of reality from the immediate emotional response to nature itself." She is also against "pretended goodness," and she felt that many of her Catholic and non-Catholic readers were liable to all three of these errors. Given our age of sentimentality, "in which distinctions of words are abandoned, she resorts to a 'wildly' comic mode." She uses two forms of the grotesque, one where nature is distorted and one where it is "sharply heightened," and she often fuses the two at a story's climax. She also attacks our sentimental attempts to remove violence from our lives and uses violence "to underline the preciousness of life." In her works we must come to terms with spiritual violence, since her "remedy for recovery from spiritual decay is nothing less than an acceptance of grace which destroys the old self."

1972 A BOOKS

1 EGGENSCHWILER, DAVID. The Christian Humanism of Flannery O'Connor. Detroit: Wayne State University Press.

A study of O'Connor's Christian humanism that analyzes her similarities with modern theologians, sociologists, and psychologists. O'Connor's main themes are wholeness and incompleteness. She agrees with modern theologians like Tillich and Niebuhr in defining sinfulness as estrangement from oneself, from others, and from God. Many of the central characters in her work suffer from some form of neurosis, which theists see as the psychological result of the attempt to escape insecurity or dread by sin. Many of these characters eventually accept grace and achieve a spiritual revelation that the story has prepared us for and that is more complex and realistic than many critics admit. Far from being provincial or eccentric, O'Connor is in the tradition of Christian humanism, and her work displays "a balanced attitude that produced her finest literary qualities: satirical tough-mindedness combined with compassion, concern for transcendence tempered by delight in human gestures, and stylistic exuberance controlled by sureness of structure."

2 FEELEY, SISTER KATHLEEN, S.S.N.D. Flannery O'Connor: Voice of the Peacock. New Brunswick, N. J.: Rutgers University Press.

A study of O'Connor's fiction based on reading the books in her library. Since many of the books are not dated, it is hard to tell if they were sources or merely confirmations of O'Connor's own ideas, but it is clear that O'Connor had affinities with writers such as Hawthorne and with religious thinkers such as St. Augustine, Newman, Eliade, Teilhard de Chardin, and Voegelin. Theology is the key to O'Connor's work and the reason for her success, though she is not a Catholic apologist or a satirizer of modern Protestants. Her approach was ecumenical, and she had a "total apprehension of reality," where both faith and reason are necessary for spiritual wholeness. Chapters on O'Connor's vision, on her characters' pursuit of false gods, on her alienated modern men, on her use of death and biblical paradigms to create a sense of history, on "the numinous quality of reality," and on the importance of prophecy in her work. Includes a selected bibliography of material by and about O'Connor, as well as a listing of the books in O'Connor's library that were used in this study.

3 MULLER, GILBERT H. Nightmares and Visions: Flannery O'Connor and the Catholic Grotesque. Athens, Ga.: University of Georgia Press.

O'Connor follows Hieronymous Bosch in her use of the grotesque for spiritual ends. She places her characters in an absurd and meaningless world and then seeks to balance or overcome this grotesque world with grace. She employs exaggeration, deformity, caricature, melodramatic plots, and the fusion of the animate and inanimate and the human and nonhuman to achieve the grotesque union of horror and ludicrousness - where the horror is released through humor. Her obsessed characters usually undertake a quest for spiritual illumination, though most of them never fully succeed in escaping the demonic world of the grotesque. O'Connor's strength as a writer lies in her ability to use objects that symbolize the spiritual; the effect of her use of such objects is to produce "disengagement from the finite world of the story with a prolongation of the theological...consequences produced."

4 ORVELL, MILES. Invisible Parade: The Fiction of Flannery O'Connor. Philadelphia: Temple University Press.

(ORVELL, MILES)

The two main influences on O'Connor's fiction were the nineteenth century American romance tradition of Poe, Melville, and Hawthorne and native American humor, though she was also influenced by such various sources as Nathanael West, Faulkner, the cinema, and cartoons. O'Connor's work embodies the Christian paradox that the flesh is a place of spirit yet must be mortified, but the religious depth of her work is not always apparent to her readers, and sometimes the religious depth does not fit the surface of her stories. The tension in O'Connor's viewpoint "between the austerely Christian and the failingly human" is a key to her success as a writer, but many readers will be unable to accept all of the implications of her fiction, especially when she seems to deny completely the value of secular humanism. At her best, though, she achieves the balance between plausibility and mystery that has characterized the American romance tradition. Includes a selected bibliography of material by and about O'Connor.

1972 B SHORTER WRITINGS

1 ANON. "Paradox of the Peacock." TLS (25 February), p. 213.

A review of Mystery and Manners. Discusses O'Connor's critical treatment of regionalism, the grotesque, and her Catholicism, as well as her emphasis on the "transcendent paradox of the peacock" and her "aesthetic independence." O'Connor "has come to seem the saintly, secular nun of twentieth-century American literature."

2 ANON. Review of Flannery O'Connor: The Complete Stories. Review for Religious 31 (January), 158-59.

A capsule review stating that O'Connor's "corpus is small but precious."

3 ANON. Review of Flannery O'Connor: The Complete Stories. VQR 48:ci.

A capsule review. The first story, "Geranium," and the last, "Judgement Day," show the development of O'Connor's art.

4 AVANT, JOHN ALFRED. Review of Flannery O'Connor: The Complete Stories. LJ 97:85.

The collection shows not only O'Connor's ability to create masterpieces, but also her weaknesses: her lack of variety in her themes, her occasionally too blatant allegories and "too accessible" use of irony.

5 BARCUS, NANCY B. "Psychological Determinism and Freedom in Flannery O'Connor." Cithara 12, i:26-33.
Up to and including the point of the baptism-drowning of Bishop, The Violent Bear It Away seems to exemplify Freudian determinism, since neither Rayber nor young Tarwater is able to find the freedom they seek. With Tarwater's blurting out the obscenity to the woman at the grocery store and the subsequent homosexual rape, he realizes that he is not "self-motivated" and that evil exists within him and the world. With this revelation he finds the freedom to accept his vocation. Thus, the novel employs "dramatic reversal" to assert O'Connor's Christian beliefs.

6 BECHAM, GERALD. "Flannery O'Connor Collection." FOB 1:66-71.
A description of the manuscript collection at Georgia College. The manuscripts of the fiction are listed separately. The rest of the material--manuscripts of lectures by O'Connor, introductions and book reviews by O'Connor, as well as "a file of clippings, representative editions of all of Miss O'Connor's published works, translations of her works, criticisms, and anthologies in which her works are reprinted"--is not listed separately.

7 BLACKWELL, LOUISE. "Flannery O'Connor's Literary Style." AntigR 10:57-66.
Robert Drake's (1964.B30) description of O'Connor's style as "ugly" is misleading. Her "direct style" arises from her "placing of stress upon the behavior of characters rather than upon qualities which have to be described." Her style is characterized by a "rich" texture, with frequent use of metaphors relating inanimate objects to men or animals to inanimate objects and of traditional Christian symbols. Wise Blood is emphasized.

8 BOYD, GEORGE N. "Parables of Costly Grace: Flannery O'Connor and Ken Kesey." Theology Today 29:161-71.
A contrast of "The Artificial Nigger" and One Flew Over the Cuckoo's Nest that sees O'Connor holding a "traditional" and Kesey a "radical" theology. The essential difference is that in Kesey "redemptive self-sacrifice is heroic, through the inspirational power of heroism to elicit imitation," while in O'Connor "grace is primarily the experiencing of forgiveness, and the humbling of self is both its preparation and its effect." With Kesey, the basic sin is apathy, with O'Connor, pride, and O'Connor has more sympathy for the bad. Both writers, however, are similar in showing that "redemption comes through ordinary experience... and when it is authentic, it means a real and painful transformation."

1972

9 BURNS, STUART. "Freaks in a Circus Tent: Flannery O'Connor's Christ-Haunted Characters." FOB 1:1-23.

A discussion of O'Connor's "Christ-haunted" characters, including Rayber, Asa Hawks, Shiftlet, the Misfit, Rufus Johnson, O. E. Parker, and the twelve year old girl in "A Temple of the Holy Ghost." These characters share "their common commitment for or against Christ," but are very different in most respects. The stories in which they appear, however, "are those in which their author demonstrates the most sympathy for the frailities of human nature." Also, O'Connor's "absolutist view" prevented her from presenting those who deny grace, like Rayber, as tragic, though it "led her to admire commitment in any form." O'Connor believed that if Christ lived in our society, "he would be considered a circus freak...or, at least, a Displaced Person."

10 CATTANI, RICHARD J. "The Consequences of Airing a Potted Geranium." Christian Science Monitor (Eastern Edition). (20 January), p. 7.

A review of Flannery O'Connor: The Complete Stories that praises O'Connor's art but questions the stories' ultimate value because "the tragedy of Flannery O'Connor's stories fails to rise above itself. Her writings are an endless expiation of her mordant Irish, Southern, and Catholic tendencies."

11 COLES, ROBERT. Review of Flannery O'Connor: The Complete Stories. ASch 41:480.

The Complete Stories are recommended for summer reading, along with the novels of Walker Percy. O'Connor is "more unnerving and at times more hilarious than Percy."

12 COSGRAVE, MARY SILVA. Review of Flannery O'Connor: The Complete Stories. Horn Book 48:171.

The stories are "original, strong, sparse, and shattering." The characters are broken and unhappy, with children being "the most pitiable victims of all."

13 DESMOND, JOHN F. "The Lessons of History: Flannery O'Connor's 'Everything That Rises Must Converge.'" FOB 1:34-45.

O'Connor was influenced by Teilhard de Chardin's The Phenomenon of Man, and in "Everything That Rises Must Converge" all three main characters try to isolate themselves from human history and its evolutionary convergence of mankind through love toward "Omega" or God. With such characters, "it takes an apocalyptic-like violence to penetrate their shell." The two women are linked by their identical hats and by "the child Carver - whose name suggests the difficult process by which suffering is transformed through Christ-like love." His mother's death ends Julian's pseudo-liberalism and nostalgia for the past and forces him to confront "the reality of history...- and unprepared in his innocence, he wishes to retreat from this terrible knowledge."

14 DETWEILER, ROBERT. "The Moment of Death in Modern Fiction." ConL 13:269-94.

The moment of death in "A Late Encounter with the Enemy" is discussed along with several other modern works in an analysis of the nature and effects of the moment of death in modern fiction. The analysis is indebted to phenomenological and structuralist criticism and to the criticism of Georges Poulet. It establishes a "lexicon" and "grammar" of the death moment, relates this moment to the narrative structure, and finally extends to "extra-fictive meaning." These moments "bring home to the imagination the reality of individual death," force us "to consider a new mode of thinking that can function in the proximity of death" and urge us "to consider bricolage, improvisation, as the mode of thought and the life style that helps one most valuably to confront nothingness and transform death from the ultimate terror into the supreme possibility."

15 DRAKE, ROBERT. Review of Flannery O'Connor: The Complete Stories. Modern Age 16:322-24.

O'Connor is enormously popular because the reader "either loves...or loathes" her work. Her controversial central concern was "the Jesus question," and "she was never false to her vision, her story." The early stories "are unsure and defective, compared with her later and her best work."

16 DULA, MARTHA A. "Evidences of the Prelapsarian in Flannery O'Connor's Wise Blood." XUS 11, iii:1-12.

The novel "suggests at least a symbolic re-enactment of the original Fall" with the proud Haze trying to deny his own participation in our fallen nature. Enoch Emery partly "is a kind of inverted savior," a parody of Christ who achieves false innocence, though his overall significance is ambiguous--a weakness in the novel. Haze's self-blinding represents "his acceptance of the human condition," and his "hunger" for salvation is satisfied in his death.

1972

17 FREEDMAN, RICHARD. Review of Flannery O'Connor: The Complete Stories. Book World (Washington Post). (30 January), p. 11.
O'Connor was probably the finest short story writer since Faulkner. Although her Catholicism was of "the gloomy François Mauriac-Graham Greene sort," her stories are lightened by her "gallows humor" and "at least the possibility of grace in her characters." O'Connor's alienation as a Southerner, a Catholic, and an invalid gave her "ultimate objectivity and clarity of vision."

18 HEGARTY, CHARLES M., S.J. "A Man Though Not Yet a Whole One: Mr. Shiftlet's Genesis." FOB 1:24-38.
A discussion of the three versions of "The Life You Save May Be Your Own" based on a reading of the manuscripts at Georgia College. In the first version, the mother is the central character, and the story is a farce about "a con-man out-conned by a country woman." In the second version, Shiftlet is the main character, and he finally returns to his family in Mobile after abandoning Lucynell, only to discover that home is no solace to him. The second version is overwritten and melodramatic. The third and final version is "a profound parable of the mystery of redemption" where Shiftlet is "a man unwittingly in the process of being saved." Shiftlet's speech on his mother to the boy in the car refers to both his mother and Lucynell and shows that "he could be a victim of both his high rhetoric and his self-realization."

19 _____. "A Note on Flannery O'Connor." SSF 9:409-10.
A reply to William Sessions's review of Mystery and Manners (1971.B30). The version of "The Church and the Fiction Writer" that appears in Mystery and Manners is based on O'Connor's original typescript. The version of the essay in America shows "drastic editorial rewriting." O'Connor's original passage shows her habitual concern that the artist be free to concern himself with his art; it is not an atypical passage. The America version, by contrast, shows "the studied logic of the original versions."

20 HIGGINS, GEORGE C. "Critics' Choices." Commonweal (25 February), p. 500.
Flannery O'Connor: The Complete Stories is "one of the five best books of the year in any category."

21 HOLMAN, C. HUGH. The Roots of Southern Writing: Essays on the Literature of the American South. Athens, Ga.: University of Georgia Press, pp. 1, 96-108, 177-86, 194, 200.
Includes reprints of 1966.B20 and 1969.B22.

22 HOWELL, ELMO. "Flannery O'Connor and the Home Country." Renascence 24:171-76.

O'Connor's development from "A Late Encounter With the Enemy" to the later "Judgement Day" is one "of making the regional material not merely a prop to a message but giving it an interest in its own right." "Judgement Day" also displays her increased compassion, especially for the southern middle class, and her newfound ability to avoid overt allegory. Her use of region is not "reportorial," but her attachment to her region led her "to turn more closely to the local scene in and for itself."

23 INGRAM, FORREST L. "American Short Story Cycles: Foreign Influences and Parallels." In Proceedings of the Comparative Literature Symposium, Vol. V: Modern American Fiction. Insights and Foreign Lights. Edited by Wolodymyr T. Zyla and Wendell M. Aycock. Lubbock: Texas Tech Press, pp. 19-37.

O'Connor dropped "The Partridge Festival" from her planned collection, and Robert Fitzgerald added "Parker's Back" and "Judgement Day." The first seven stories of Everything That Rises Must Converge, that is, the collection minus Fitzgerald's additions, form a genuine "short story cycle," which is "any set of linked units, or any set of stories so linked that the reader's experience of each one is modified by his experience of all the others." Although O'Connor was far more conservative in theology than Teilhard de Chardin, his influence is present in the collection because both writers believed that spirit is in matter and both emphasized "seeing and showing." Also, "each of the seven stories...advances, through the slow and painful process of opening a character's eyes, the cosmic convergence of the human race toward point Omega." See 1973.B18.

24 IVĂNESCU, MIRCEA. "Flannery O'Connor." România Literară (10 August), p. 28.

Relates O'Connor and other southern writers to the literature stemming from Puritanism and claims that the work of these writers is not depressing, but rather an honest cry against degrading conditions. O'Connor opposes the often brutal and inhuman world of the South depicted in her fiction with her vision of a humane existence. It is her humanism, not her theology, that is the key to her work. Sees O'Connor as a major writer whose work deserves quick translation into Romanian.

1972

25 KELLER, JANE C. "The Figures of the Empiricist and the Rationalist in the Fiction of Flannery O'Connor." ArQ 28: 263-73.

O'Connor's Christianity and her desire to shock her secular audience led her to satirize two modern types of secularist: the "empiricist" and the "rationalist." The "empiricist," like Hazel Motes and young Tarwater, believes only in empirical evidence and stresses, as do existentialists, the will and freedom. The "rationalist," for example, Rayber, believes in systems, reason, and caution and values freedom less than the "empiricist." The empiricist is "closer to salvation" because "the empirical man can lower his own barriers and can see God's hand at work in the universe," while the rationalist can be saved only by God's intervention. Rayber "is doomed in life and in death," but with her other rationalists, Julian of "Everything That Rises Must Converge," Asbury of "The Enduring Chill," and Sheppard of "The Lame Shall Enter First," O'Connor seems to have learned from Teilhard de Chardin's concept of "hominisation" that rationalists can learn through suffering. O'Connor's religion is "fierce" because secularization "is so great that God's tender mercy is no longer called for."

26 KROPF, C. R. "Theme and Setting in 'A Good Man Is Hard to Find.'" Renascence 24:177-80, 206.

Critics underestimate the importance of the southern setting in the story. The turning off the main road represents an "attempt to live in an idealized past," while Red Sammy's, which brings together crucial details of the story, is "a metaphorical hell." Both the Misfit and the Grandmother have false conceptions of the past, he of the Christian past and she of the southern, and both err morally. In symbolic terms, "the Misfit is Grandmother's son, and her salvation lies in her recognition of that fact immediately before her death."

27 LEVIDOVA, INNA M. "Carson McCullers and her Last Book." In Soviet Criticism of American Literature in the Sixties. Edited and translated by Carl R. Proffer. Ann Arbor: Ardis Publishers, pp. 89-95.

In a review of Carson McCullers's Clock Without Hands O'Connor is mentioned as a writer "already known to the Russian reader."

28 McCULLAGH, JAMES C. "Aspects of Jansenism in Flannery O'Connor's Wise Blood." Studies in the Humanities 3, i: 12-16.

O'Connor's treatment of sex in Wise Blood reveals her Irish inheritance of some aspects of Jansenism, since in the novel "sex is demoniac; sexual sin is the only sin; ... images of suffering and death are grouped around a central maternal figure." Despite Haze's attempts to escape his mother, the presence of the maternal figure Mrs. Flood at his death "makes it speculative whether Hazel reaches Christ through either blasphemy or extreme penance."

29 MAY, JOHN R., S.J. "Of Huckleberry Bushes and the New Hermeneutic." Renascence 24:85-95.

O'Connor's criticism in Mystery and Manners is referred to as an example of "Old Criticism" because O'Connor believed in art as communication and because she saw fiction treating reality, both that of the world of fact and that of "the realm of grace." The New Criticism in literature and the New Hermeneutic in theology fail because of a lack of emphasis on historical reality and a belief in an impossible, ahistorical objectivity.

30 _____. Toward a New Earth: Apocalypse in the American Novel. Notre Dame: University of Notre Dame Press, pp. 40, 92, 126-44, passim.

The Violent Bear It Away is related to Faulkner's As I Lay Dying and West's Miss Lonelyhearts. O'Connor's novel not only shows the influence of these two novels in its symbolism, characters, and themes; it also belongs with them as representatives of the early and early middle twentieth century apocalyptic strain in American literature, which emphasizes the individual. The Violent Bear It Away is analyzed in terms of its "symbolism of judgment," which involves "a pattern of contrasted words and deeds, supported by certain specific and recurring symbols related to hunger, purification, and time." The novel employs the Judaeo-Christian apocalyptic pattern and therefore ends on a promise of rebirth.

31 MAYER, DAVID R. "The Violent Bear It Away: Flannery O'Connor's Shaman." SLJ 4, ii:41-54.

Aspects of Tarwater's initiation into prophecy, including his seclusion from the world at Powderhead, his trances, and his "two mystical deaths," parallel various aspects of initiations into shamanism throughout the world. He is not, however, "an exact copy of any one tribal shaman," and "the jumble of characteristics" indicates that while O'Connor favors the spiritual, she is against "the purely mystical view of reality." O'Connor favors a balance of reason and mystery and stresses mystery because

(MAYER, DAVID R.)
of the power of reason in our age; therefore, both Rayber and young Tarwater are parodied. Also, the baptism-drowning indicates that her work cannot be interpreted theologically because in Catholic theology "an intention to baptize is required for a valid baptism."

32 NELIGAN, DORRIS P. "A Room for Flannery." Columns (Georgia College at Milledgeville), Fall, pp. 3-6.
An article on the drive to raise funds for a room to hold the O'Connor collection at Georgia College.

33 NELSON, GERALD B. Ten Versions of America. New York: Alfred A. Knopf, pp. xiii, 111-25.
A study of the protagonists of ten twentieth century American novels that focuses on these novels as reflections of American society and on the failure of the "American Dream." Hazel Motes of Wise Blood is compared and contrasted with Miss Lonelyhearts of Nathanael West's novel and Dr. O'Connor of Djuna Barnes's Nightwood. All three suffer in one way or another because they are among the few in our world who take Christ seriously. In Wise Blood Enoch looks for love and Haze for truth, but neither have any effect on the indifferent world, even when they murder. Haze finally blinds himself because he cannot bear the world or himself and because the act of blinding is an apology to Christ for the failure of Haze's spiritual vision.

34 PRESLEY, DELMA EUGENE. "The Moral Function of Distortion in Southern Grotesque." SAB 37, ii:37-46.
The theories of William Van O'Connor (1962.B22), Lewis A. Lawson (1967.B12), and Irving Malin (1962.B18) about southern writers' use of the grotesque are all misleading because these theorists forget what O'Connor made clear in her criticism and fiction: "the function of distortion in Southern grotesque is essentially moral in nature; this mode presents simultaneously an image of man's incompleteness and an understanding of what he ought to be." Carson McCullers, Tennessee Williams, and William Faulkner all use the grotesque for this moral purpose.

35 ROWSE, A. L. "Flannery O'Connor--Genius of the South." Books and Bookmen (May), pp. 38-39.
A review of Mystery and Manners that places O'Connor "in a comparable class with Emily Bronte," and calls her "probably the greatest short-story writer of our time." As a "tragic ironist" O'Connor is not understood by Americans, who "think of her as a humorous writer." O'Connor's

essays, while not as important as her fiction, are extremely perceptive about the nature of writing.

36 RUBIN, LOUIS D., JR. The Writer in the South: Studies in a Literary Community. Mercer University Lamar Memorial Lectures No. 15. Athens, Ga.: University of Georgia Press, p. 65.

Passing reference to O'Connor in a chapter on Twain. Claims O'Connor's prose style was influenced by Twain.

37 SIMPSON, LEWIS P. "Introduction. The South and the Poetry of Community." In The Poetry of Community: Essays on the Southern Sensibility of History and Literature. Edited by Lewis P. Simpson. Spectrum: Monograph Series in the Arts and Sciences (Georgia State) 2:xi-xxvi.

O'Connor's and Percy's "definition of the South...expresses an attenuated relationship between the life of the South in the past and the drama of the quest for salvational community in modern times," yet their Christian vision is part of the southern consciousness.

38 SKAGGS, MERRILL MAGUIRE. The Folk of Southern Fiction. Athens, Ga.: University of Georgia Press, pp. 6, 20, 219, passim.

O'Connor uses the nineteenth-century southern "plain folk tradition" in her work to show that this tradition is false. O'Connor ironically treats such varying elements of this tradition as pride, a democratic unwillingness to evaluate others, a belief in hard work and common sense, and a belief in the Old South and southern racial harmony. Although O'Connor inverts this tradition, her humor is close to that of nineteenth-century southern humor, since "it springs from a sense of the vulgar and grotesque."

39 SONNENFELD, ALBERT. "Flannery O'Connor: The Catholic Writer as Baptist." ConL 13:445-57.

O'Connor's "relation to her work is identical to John the Baptist's incendiary assault on the kingdom of Heaven. Her fiction marks the culmination of John's way...in anticipation of the hoped for, eventual transition to the way of Jesus, the way of the victim." The endings of both novels indicate the protagonists' passage from violence to Christ. In The Violent Bear It Away "Mason Tarwater's violence was the necessary final station of the old order of John the Baptist," and Rayber is more than "a lukewarm Pharisee"; he is "a double, a mirror, of young Tarwater... who has rejected violence and by this abdication failed." In O'Connor, "the essential violence of salvation" is "a

1972

(SONNENFELD, ALBERT)
movement from the figurative to the literal and back to a renewed and heightened figuration." In her work, "the Word always leads to the Act" because "she leads away from intention and back to action."

40 SPIEGEL, ALAN. "A Theory of the Grotesque in Southern Fiction." GaR 26:426-37.

The grotesque character in southern fiction stems from the collapse of the old social and moral order, and he embodies either "the death of the old order or the aberrations of the new," thus becoming a means of attacking society's complacency. We never forget this character's humanity, and we sympathize with him. Northern fiction, with its use of "nightmare fantasy" rather than the depiction of society, its employment of "Promethean" characters, its strategy of having a normal character survey a chaotic world, and its contempt for its characters, is gothic, not grotesque. Because of the greater viability of society in the South, the southern grotesque employs a passive, grotesque, yet sympathetic character who is "the one abnormal character in a normal world."

41 SPIVEY, TED R. "Flannery O'Connor's South: Don Quixote Rides Again." FOB 1:46-53.

O'Connor and southern culture in general were influenced by Spanish culture, especially Cervantes. Don Quixote and O'Connor's prophets resemble each other in their search for community, their "literalism," and their "madness." Cervantes and O'Connor "see life essentially as comedy, and both are aware of the deep tragic nature of existence. But whereas Cervantes' comedy is always discovering underlying tragedy, O'Connor's is always merging with horror." The author also discusses his meetings with O'Connor. O'Connor was a Christian writer, influenced by such Catholic theologians as Romano Guardini and Karl Adams, and very much aware of the intellectual and literary trends of her time. She was not a "Sibyl," nor was she either alienated or politically conservative.

42 _____. "Religion and the Reintegration of Man in Flannery O'Connor and Walker Percy." In The Poetry of Community: Essays on the Southern Sensibility of History and Literature. Edited by Lewis P. Simpson. Spectrum: Monograph Series in the Arts and Sciences (Georgia State) 2:67-79.

Percy and O'Connor treat the theme of man's quest "both in terms of his own soul and in terms of his relationship to the cosmos." The quest starts in the disintegration of death and hell, but the full quest ends in man's spiritual reintegration with the cosmos. The Misfit in "A Good Man Is Hard to Find" and Bolling in The Moviegoer only begin the quest, whereas Mrs. Turpin of "Revelation" and Barrett in The Last Gentleman achieve this reintegration.

43 SULLIVAN, WALTER. Death by Melancholy: Essays on Modern Southern Fiction. Baton Rouge: Louisiana State University Press, pp. ix, 17, 22-35, passim.

Includes reprints of 1965.B74, 1968.B42, and 1969.B43.

44 TUTTLETON, JAMES W. The Novel of Manners in America. Chapel Hill: University of North Carolina Press, pp. xiii, 271-72.

O'Connor, along with other modern southern, black, and Jewish writers, treats "issues that transcend the question of manners." Her "fundamentalist territory" is mentioned as one of the "isolated milieux" that have replaced the broader social territory of the novel of manners.

45 WALSTON, ROSA LEE. "Flannery: An Affectionate Recollection." FOB 1:55-60.

A recollection by the former head of the English and Speech Department at Georgia College, O'Connor's alma mater. O'Connor's illness, in the author's opinion, had no influence on her work. The author "suspect[s] that Flannery was like the iceberg in exposing but one-ninth of itself. That part which we were privileged to know was gallant and gay and compassionate and unassuming." O'Connor was very well-read.

1973 A BOOKS

1 STEPHENS, MARTHA. The Question of Flannery O'Connor. Baton Rouge: Louisiana State University Press.

O'Connor's fiction is often difficult for the reader to accept because her "Christian faith was as grim and literalistic, as joyless and loveless a faith, at least as we confront it in her fiction, as we have ever seen in American letters." O'Connor's strength as an artist is "the peculiar tension between high comedy and high religious seriousness," but often her contempt for ordinary humanity creates a "tonal problem" in her work. In "A Good Man Is Hard to Find," for example, the comic tone of the first half of the story does not fit in with the contempt O'Connor shows for the grandmother's family in the second half. O'Connor resembles Lawrence in maintaining beliefs

(STEPHENS, MARTHA)
that are unacceptable to many readers, and like Lawrence she fails most when her own beliefs are most clearly expressed. Her narrow beliefs and life led her to create a "highly static" art, one that employed only "the negative, grotesque, comical features of her character, her domestic situation, and her relationship with her mother." Her novels often have problems with tone; her stories are "too closely knit and overlapping," but occasionally, as in the description of Hazel's self-blinding and the first part of The Violent Bear It Away, as well as several of the stories, she achieved full artistic success. Includes a selected bibliography of works by and about O'Connor, with some annotations.

2 WALTERS, DOROTHY. Flannery O'Connor. Twayne's United States Authors Series No. 216. New York: Twayne Publishers.

O'Connor uses irony, conflict, satire, and the grotesque to achieve a tragicomic vision of life. Her characters are "Jonsonian 'humours,'" but at their moment of catastrophe the "esthetic distance is abruptly shortened," and the mood in the work changes from "the essentially comic to the overwhelmingly serious." Although O'Connor's vision is a Christian one, there is an unconscious demonic element in her work that creates tension in the meaning and thus leads to varying critical interpretations. O'Connor has affinities with American frontier humor, with major southern writers, and with the Absurdists and Surrealists, but her true affinity is with the medieval world view. Her fiction, though it skillfully uses particulars, moves toward allegory, since reality is ultimately in "abstract mysteries of being." Chapters on influences on O'Connor, on her tragicomic mode, and on O'Connor's place in contemporary literature and the objections raised to her work. Specific works are discussed in chapters on specific themes, such as prophecy, the methods of receiving grace, the sacraments, the relations of blacks and whites, and social change. Includes a chronology of O'Connor's life and a selected bibliography of works by and about O'Connor, with brief annotations of the secondary material.

1973 B SHORTER WRITINGS

1 ANON. "Models for Our Time." Sign (March), pp. 9-10.

O'Connor is described as one of the modern Catholic women who can serve as an example for others.

2 ANON. Review of Flannery O'Connor: The Complete Stories. Catholic Library World 44:425.
A brief review that finds "many of the stories...riotously funny, some...at first reading, depressing."

3 ASALS, FREDERICK. "Hawthorne, Mary Ann, and 'The Lame Shall Enter First.'" FOB 2:3-18.
O'Connor's introduction to A Memoir of Mary Ann indicates her indebtedness to Hawthorne and suggests the influence of Hawthorne's "The Birthmark" as well as the story of Mary Ann on "The Lame Shall Enter First." Although the story has its origins in early versions of The Violent Bear It Away, the focus of the final story and "the two central symbols of the story--the club foot and the telescope" are probably a result of O'Connor's knowledge of Mary Ann and the Hawthorne story. O'Connor adds to Hawthorne's story her own use of shock and her greater naturalistic ability. O'Connor also differs in treating Sheppard as comic and in distributing the "imaginative tensions" throughout the story, whereas Hawthorne sees Aylmer of "The Birthmark" as "a tragic idealist" and centers the tensions of the story within him. Hawthorne's story is full of his ambivalence toward Aylmer's ideals, but in O'Connor "any doubt or denial is exorcised in fictional projection, flayed by an irony that deepens into astringent satire on the one hand and merges with terror on the other." The character of Rufus Johnson shows the influence of Hawthorne's Georgiana and her imperfection, Mary Ann and her illness and piety, and the "demonic child monster" that O'Connor recounts in her discussion of Rose Hawthorne in the introduction.

4 BELLMAN, SAMUEL. "The Apocalypse in Literature." Costerus 7: 13-25.
A genuine apocalypse in a work of literature must be largely unanticipated and not too obvious if it is to have the necessary "prophetic and shockingly unfamiliar quality." For this reason, apocalypses in the theological sense are not necessarily literary apocalypses. There is no apocalypse in O'Connor's "Revelation," but instead "straightforward theological instruction."

5 BLEIKASTEN, ANDRÉ. "Flannery O'Connor." In Amerikanische Literatur der Gegenwart. Edited by Martin Christadler. Stuttgart: Alfred Kröner, pp. 352-70.
Basically the same article as 1970.B6 but adds praise for O'Connor because she had the artistic integrity to avoid interposing her proclaimed beliefs between her readers and her fiction.

1973

6 BOYD, GEORGE N. and LOIS A. Religion in Contemporary Fiction: Criticism from 1945 to the Present. San Antonio: Trinity University Press, pp. 40-43.

An unannotated selected bibliography of criticism on O'Connor. The book also contains selected bibliographies on topics dealing with the relation of literature and religion, as well as a list of earlier bibliographies on religion and literature.

7 BROWNING, PRESTON M., JR. "Flannery O'Connor and the Demonic." MFS 19:29-41.

Carter Martin's The True Country: Themes in the Fiction of Flannery O'Connor (1969.A1) overstresses O'Connor's religion, and Josephine Hendin's The World of Flannery O'Connor (1970.A1) unjustly ignores it. John Hawkes's interpretation of O'Connor (1962.B12), though finally "untenable," is very useful because both writers reveal the subconscious, and O'Connor does use terror and the demonic to shock both her characters and readers out of their complacency. With characters like Singleton in "The Partridge Festival" and Rufus Johnson in "The Lame Shall Enter First," she "seems to say that in a time so well adjusted to itself that reflection becomes superfluous, the only way to the Holy is through the demonic." She is on the side of the demonic in the sense that the demonic and holy are inextricably connected.

8 DESMOND, JOHN F. "The Mystery of the Word and the Act: The Violent Bear It Away." ABR 24:342-47.

The novel concerns young Tarwater's rejection and final acceptance of his prophecy, which entails "the mysterious union of word and act." Young Tarwater moves from his early Manichean sense of prophecy, which resembles Rayber's divorce of word and action, to an attempt to silence "the 'Word' of his great-uncle's legacy" by "a kind of pure existentialism of action" that denies the past and dependence upon God. The baptism-drowning shows that he cannot escape the Word. His later cursing reveals that "like Rayber, he has 'lost' the moment to act, for Tarwater is now 'possessed' demonically by words he cannot control." He accepts his calling only "when his illusion of personal inviolability is destroyed."

9 DOXEY, WILLIAM S. "A Dissenting Opinion of Flannery O'Connor's 'A Good Man Is Hard to Find.'" SSF 10:199-204.

The story is flawed because "the point-of-view shifts from the grandmother to the Misfit and the reader is suddenly left holding the bag." There is also a "lack of proportion between the Misfit's large character and his slight foreshadowing." The explanation for these flaws lies in O'Connor's Catholic emphasis on grace, since the evil encountered must be "strongly characterized." The explanation, however, does not excuse the esthetic flaws.

10 EVANS, ELIZABETH. "Three Notes on Flannery O'Connor." NConL 3, iii:11-15.

Brief discussions of a paragraph in "A Good Man Is Hard to Find" that describes the family's trip, of Mrs. May's reliance on insurance in "Greenleaf," and of the association of the bull with Christ in the first three paragraphs of the same story.

11 FRIEDMAN, MELVIN J. "Flannery O'Connor: The Canon Completed, the Commentary Continuing." SLJ 5, ii:116-23.

A review of Flannery O'Connor: The Complete Stories and Josephine Hendin's The World of Flannery O'Connor. The collection of O'Connor's stories reveals that "the Flaubertian way in which Flannery O'Connor went about her work apparently prevented these startling and rather terrifying leaps from apprenticeship to early prime to full maturity to latter manner--which so many writers go through." Hendin's biographical conjectures are dubious, but her interpretation of the fiction is "a necessary corrective to the insistently religious interpretations."

12 ______. "John Hawkes and Flannery O'Connor: The French Background." BUJ 21, iii:34-44.

Hawkes's preference for a luxuriant style, first person narration, and West's Day of the Locust instead of Miss Lonelyhearts separates him from O'Connor, but both writers often see the victims of violence in complicity with their assailants, and both write of what Frederick J. Hoffman in The Mortal No calls "the landscape of violence," a dehumanized landscape which is, in Hoffman's words, "full of spatial images, whose qualities are repetitious and lifeless." Neither O'Connor nor Hawkes is a chosiste in the manner of Sarraute, Robbe-Grillet, and Beckett, yet "both reveal a fascination with the surface of objects and acknowledge the importance of 'things.'" Both "have in common a modified form of picaresque," and both are willing to show the darker side of life. Hawkes's essay on O'Connor (1962.B12) is praised for illuminating Hawkes's own practice and a side of O'Connor most critics ignore.

13 GREEN, JAMES L. "Enoch Emery and his Biblical Namesakes in Wise Blood." SSF 10:417-19.

(GREEN, JAMES L.)
O'Connor uses both of the biblical Enochs in her delineation of the novel's Enoch. Enoch in Wise Blood parallels Enoch the son of Cain because his father "carries the mark of Cain." When Hazel hits Enoch with a rock, "the scene is an inverted analogue of the murder of Abel by Cain." There is an ironic parallel between the novel's Enoch and Enoch the father of Methuselah. This biblical Enoch is carried to heaven by God, while the novel's Enoch disappears by becoming nonhuman. This ironic parallel explains Enoch's disappearance from the novel.

14 HASSAN, IHAB. Contemporary American Literature: 1945-1972. An Introduction. New York: Frederick Ungar, pp. 52, 64, 67, 69-70.
An introductory survey that briefly discusses O'Connor's works in terms of her stress on alienation and decay, her belief that self-love or pride is "invariably demonic," her treatment of the flight from salvation in the novels, and her use of horror in her stories. A shortened version of these remarks can be found in World Literature Since 1945: Critical Surveys of the Contemporary Literature of Europe and the Americas, edited by Ivar Ivask and Gero von Wilpert (New York: Frederick Ungar, 1973), pp. 18, 19, 21.

15 HELLER, ARNO. Odyssee zum Selbst: Zur Gestaltung jugendlicher Identitätssuche im neueren amerikanischen Roman. Innsbrucker Beiträge zur Kulturwissenschaft. Sonderheft 32. Innsbruck, pp. 14, 48, 119, passim.
Emphasizes The Violent Bear It Away, which O'Connor wrote to seek her own salvation in the act of writing. The novel can be read as a religious novel, with O'Connor's rejection of rationality and her use of violence being understood in a religious context, but a closer look at the novel shows us that it is a novel about a failed initiation, since at the end young Tarwater regresses into the one-dimensional world of his childhood, a world of a loveless and grotesque religious fanaticism.

16 HOWELL, ELMO. "The Developing Art of Flannery O'Connor." ArQ 29:266-76.
A discussion of Everything That Rises Must Converge. As O'Connor's art developed, "she gave up the flights of allegory and settled on the surface of life" and increasingly centered her attention on the arrogance of modern liberalism, at the same time becoming more sympathetic with the southern middle class. In "Revelation" she brings together her spiritual concerns and her attitudes towards liberalism and the South. She was not alienated from her community.

17 IDOL, JOHN. Review of Flannery O'Connor: The Complete Stories. SSF 10:103-05.
The arrangement of the collection in chronological order weakens the "dramatic impact and emotional counterpointing" that the stories had in the original collections, but this collection does show O'Connor's development as an artist. It also reveals O'Connor's weakness: her overreliance upon death.

18 INGRAM, FORREST L. "O'Connor's Seven Story Cycle." FOB 2: 19-28.
See 1972.B23. The seven first stories of Everything That Rises Must Converge are united by "a static and a dynamic structure." The "static structure consists in geometric relationships" among the seven stories, and "the major dynamic structure...is the progressively revealed pattern, on all levels, of rising and converging." The last story, "Revelation," sums up the cycle by bringing in "themes, character-types, and central conflicts of the first six stories" and by rounding out "a community of the self-righteous" who try to teach others but who end up with a moment of self-revelation.

19 KAZIN, ALFRED. Bright Book of Life: American Novelists and Storytellers from Hemingway to Mailer. Atlantic Monthly Press Book. Boston: Little, Brown, pp. 24, 34, passim.
O'Connor, along with Peter Taylor, Walker Percy, and Carson McCullers, is a member of the nonrhetorical school of southern writers, where "the overpowering Southern voice is absorbed into the logic of the story itself." O'Connor believed that "human beings are absolutely limited" and that all human action and power are vain: "What people do is always grotesque." O'Connor is one of the few Catholic writers "who managed to fuse a thorough orthodoxy with the greatest possible independence and sophistication as an artist." O'Connor's short stories are better than her novels, but suffer from being too alike - a result of "the South's intellectual moralism."

20 LACKEY, ALLEN D. "Flannery O'Connor: A Supplemental Bibliography of Secondary Sources." BB 30:170-75.
Corrects and expands previous bibliographies and brings the bibliography of secondary work on O'Connor through 1972. This bibliography is intended to supplement those of Lewis Lawson (1966.B25) and Leon Driskell and Joan Brittain (1971.A1).

1973

21 McCULLAGH, JAMES C. "Symbolism and the Religious Aesthetic: Flannery O'Connor's Wise Blood." FOB 2:43-58.

The Catholic novel from Mauriac through Greene to O'Connor has become increasingly "existential" and "psychological," and in Wise Blood O'Connor uses psychology to demonstrate the nature of Hazel's quest. Hazel's struggle to escape "his Oedipal entrapment" with his mother and "his attempt to blaspheme his way to Christ" are inextricably bound together. Only when he destroys the mummy and throws away his mother's glasses does he escape the Oedipal trap and begin to free himself from blasphemy. Nevertheless, his mother's glasses help him avoid sin in the Army and later help him to see "how much he is tied to her. The mother who has haunted him becomes, in some respects, the instrument of his redemption."

22 McDOWELL, FREDERICK P. "Toward the Luminous and the Numinous: The Art of Flannery O'Connor." SoR N.S. 9:998-1013.

A review of Mystery and Manners and Flannery O'Connor: The Complete Stories as well as several book-length studies of O'Connor. Mystery and Manners makes clear O'Connor's religious intentions, while The Complete Stories reveals the superiority of her stories to her novels and her continual growth in artistry as "her firmness of vision and her increased sympathy are translated outwardly into an increased aesthetic control." Future criticism of O'Connor should be more concerned with O'Connor's "total artistry."

23 MARTIN, CARTER W. "Flannery O'Connor's Early Fiction." SHR 7:210-14.

A discussion of O'Connor's Iowa thesis stories: "The Geranium," "The Barber," "Wildcat," "The Crop," and "The Turkey." These early stories contain "the wit, outrageousness, ambiguity, and moral insight" of O'Connor's later fiction, though they are not as well-crafted and generally lack the religious dimension of her later work. They are not likely to change any critic's overall view of O'Connor, but they "demonstrate clearly that Flannery O'Connor improved as an artist in rough proportion to her movement toward a violent expression of her Christian themes."

24 MAY, JOHN R., S.J. "Flannery O'Connor and the New Hermeneutic." FOB 2:29-42.

In her theoretical writings in Mystery and Manners, O'Connor stressed "theological realism," with its indebtedness to traditional hermeneutics and its belief that language should express both material and spiritual reality. O'Connor's fiction, however, shows that she also used the techniques of the New Criticism and the New Hermeneutic, the first of which emphasizes the "relationship of form to meaning" and the second, "the ultimate power to interpret in the Word itself."

25 _____. "The Violent Bear It Away: The Meaning of the Title." FOB 2:83-86.
The passage from Matthew is very ambiguous and difficult to translate, and the only way to ascertain what O'Connor meant by the passage is to study the novel itself. The "interpretation...that seems most in accord with the exegetical possibilities and the demands of Flannery O'Connor's fictional world is this: The kingdom of heaven manifests itself violently, and men in violence take hold of it." O'Connor uses violence because it reveals the essential self and because "violence has been a mark of the prophet."

26 MINTZ, EDWARD N. "Celebrity Spotlight." Travel (22 January), p. 12.
A brief reference to Flannery O'Connor: The Complete Stories, which shows O'Connor "off for the fine regional writer she was."

27 OATES, JOYCE CAROL. "The Visionary Art of Flannery O'Connor." SHR 7:235-46.
A discussion of Everything That Rises Must Converge. O'Connor did not use the phrase from Teilhard de Chardin ironically, and "there is no ultimate irony in her work, no ultimate despair or pessimism or tragedy, and certainly not a paradoxical sympathy for the devil." Her work is Augustinian in its separation of the City of Man and the City of God, and she resembles Dostoyevsky in being "politically reactionary, but spiritually fierce, combative, revolutionary." While she rejects secular existentialism, "her perverted saints are Kierkegaardian knights of the 'absurd.'" Her disease led her to a fatalism and a belief in "disease-as-revelation"; her religion led her to see the divinity in such suffering. The spiritual realm she explores is beyond ethics, philosophical systems, and dogma. "Her world is that surreal primitive landscape in which the Unconscious is a determining quantity that the Consciousness cannot defeat, because it cannot recognize. In fact, there is nothing to be recognized--there is only an experience to be suffered."

28 OPPEGAARD, SUSAN HILL. "Flannery O'Connor and the Backwoods Prophet." In Americana Norvegica, IV: Norwegian Contributions to American Studies Dedicated to Sigmund Skard.

(OPPEGAARD, SUSAN HILL)
Edited by Brita Seyersted. Oslo: Universitetsforlaget, pp. 305-25.

O'Connor's prophets are neither "saints" nor "pathological fanatics"; they are grudging "witnesses for their Lord." They bear many resemblances to Old Testament prophets, in their being called by God, their hostility to the morality of their times, their rejection of pride and false gods, and their belief in commitment through faith rather than intellectualism or ambivalence. They also share the same kind of commitment: "a sense of sin shared with all men; an awareness of the Lord's grace in spite of one's sins; a face hardened towards the world's disbelief; a violence that the world terms madness." The essential difference is that the God of O'Connor's prophets is a God of mercy. Critics take various approaches to O'Connor's prophets, including the "psychoanalytic," the "social humanist," the "biographical," and the "polemical." Only those critics who accept O'Connor's "dogmatic presuppositions" are able to distinguish the prophets from such lost sinners as the Misfit.

29 PEARCE, HOWARD D. "Flannery O'Connor's Ineffable Recognitions." Genre 6:298-312.

Some readers have difficulty with the recognitions in O'Connor's fiction, partially because they do not realize that she is heavily indebted to drama and "that she is attempting a spirit both tragic and comic." Her concern with the themes and elements of tragedy, especially with mystery, fits her themes of "faith and rationality, pride and humility." Her recognitions are often mysterious because her characters make a "leap into faith" which is beyond rational comprehension. In "Everything That Rises Must Converge" and "The Lame Shall Enter First" the recognitions are fairly explicit because the theme is "an understanding and acceptance of...human frailty," but in the two novels and "A Good Man Is Hard to Find" the basic theme is that of faith, and thus the recognitions are more "ineffable." The "novels turn on recognitions that, though explicable, cannot be quite verbalized except in symbolic terms."

30 QUINN, JOHN J., S.J. "A Reading of Flannery O'Connor." Thought 48:520-31.

A reading of "A Good Man Is Hard to Find" that applies the medieval four-level exegesis. The literal level concerns "the age-old theme of appearances vs. reality," and the allegorical level concerns "the relationship of sin to redemption within human experience," with emphasis on the

Misfit's rebellion from God. The moral level deals with "Christian conduct" and "the presence or absence of grace," in this case, the grandmother's finally seeing herself for what she is. The anagogical level treats "the four last things: death, judgment, heaven, and hell," though O'Connor expands this level to include the entire sense of the divine. Since O'Connor herself labels all three levels beyond the literal as "anagogical," these distinctions should not be applied too rigidly.

31 SCHULZ, MAX F. Black Humor Fiction of the Sixties: A Pluralistic Definition of Man and His World. Athens, Ohio: Ohio University Press, p. ix.

In the preface claims that labeling writers such as O'Connor and Laurence Sterne "Black Humorists" is an unnecessarily vague and indiscriminate use of the term.

32 SCOUTEN, KENNETH. "The Mythological Dimensions of Five of Flannery O'Connor's Works." FOB 2:59-72.

A discussion of parallels with Sophocles's Oedipus plays and Antigone in Wise Blood, "A Good Man Is Hard to Find," The Violent Bear It Away, and "Good Country People" and of the parallels with "Greek dramatic festivals" in "The Partridge Festival." O'Connor used these parallels "because she felt the need for 'common beliefs' to supply allegorical backgrounds for her works" and because "myths usually demonstrate that man cannot go against the gods without fear of punishment."

33 SULLIVAN, WALTER. "Southerners in the City: Flannery O'Connor and Walker Percy." In The Comic Imagination in American Literature. Edited by Louis D. Rubin, Jr. New Brunswick, N. J.: Rutgers University Press, pp. 339-48.

A comparison of two southern Catholics, O'Connor and Walker Percy. Much of Percy's humor springs from his characters' playing a role they do not fit, while in O'Connor the humor "comes from dialogue and characterization." Percy is a city writer who comforts us despite our problems. O'Connor's portrayals of the country give us "fresh images"; her "genius for comedy and reconciliation was unique in her time." O'Connor's religious vision allowed her to see "sanctity" issuing from violence. Discusses "A Good Man Is Hard to Find" and The Violent Bear It Away.

34 THORNTON-SMITH, C. B. Review of Mystery and Manners. AUMLA (November), p. 301.

Criticizes the lack of biographical information and of critical discussions by other critics, as well as the

1973

(THORNTON-SMITH, C. B.)
inclusion of noncritical pieces like "The King of the Birds" and "Introduction to A Memoir of Mary Ann." O'Connor's essays on the art of fiction are most useful for illuminating her position as a southern Catholic writer in America and for justifying her "mysterious, grotesque highly personal vision."

35 VOSS, ARTHUR. The American Short Story: A Critical Survey. Norman: University of Oklahoma Press, pp. 302, 333-42, 347, 350.
A discussion of several of O'Connor's short stories. O'Connor's work creates problems in interpretation and evaluation because of her combining the gothic and the religious, but even those who cannot accept O'Connor's theology must admire her craft and psychological insight.

36 WILSON, JAMES D. "Luis Buñuel, Flannery O'Connor, and the Failure of Charity." MinnR NRP4 (Spring), 158-62.
A comparison of "The Lame Shall Enter First" and Luis Buñuel's film, "Viridiana." O'Connor "like Buñuel, portrays a world where evil is omnipresent; and those who engage in the seemingly praiseworthy task of 'saving' other men frequently discover that the darkest sins of all lurk within themselves."

37 WOODWARD, ROBERT H. "A Good Route is Hard to Find: Place Names and Setting in O'Connor's 'A Good Man Is Hard to Find.'" NConL 3, v:2-6.
The route of the family in the story does not correspond to any real geography but does contain foreshadowings of death and a reference to Paul's epistles to Timothy. The main characters in the story violate Paul's advice in the epistles.

38 YARDLEY, JONATHAN. "The New Old Southern Novel." PR 40: 286-93.
Flannery O'Connor: The Complete Stories is reviewed along with several southern novels and short story collections. O'Connor's "consciousness of violence, pain, endurance and redemption places her squarely in the center of the Southern tradition," and only Faulkner was a better writer.

1974 A BOOKS

1 BROWNING, PRESTON M., JR. Flannery O'Connor. Carbondale: Southern Illinois University Press.

An interpretation of O'Connor that stresses her use of psychology because her religion is both a system of beliefs and what Tillich calls "ultimate concern," which means that her "religious meaning emerges via human behavior and psychology." O'Connor combines Christian orthodoxy and "a traditional though qualified Southern view of human nature" with "an attraction for the extreme, the perverse, the violent, and for the grotesque for its own sake and not merely as a fictional technique." This combination results partly from her belief in "'spiritual crime'" and partly from her desire to attack "the ethos of the 1950's." In Wise Blood O'Connor "must have felt the inadequacy of Haze's salvation," yet she "appears to say that obsession, with its concomitant violence and crime, is perhaps a necessary instrument in man's quest for meaning and salvation." The Violent Bear It Away treats not only the struggle with vocation but also the clash between two visions of reality and freedom. A Good Man Is Hard to Find centers on the themes of deception and self-deception and often uses three types of characters, "the positivist, the positive thinker, and the criminal compulsive," while Everything That Rises Must Converge stresses the individual character and his neurosis. Although O'Connor and Teilhard de Chardin disagree about evil, his influence is clear in this collection. Includes a selected bibliography of material by and about O'Connor.

1974 B SHORTER WRITINGS

1 ASALS, FREDERICK. "Flannery O'Connor as Novelist: A Defense." FOB 3:23-39.

The novels are usually underrated; they belong with such "short intense, symbolic works" as The Narrative of Arthur Gordon Pym, The Scarlet Letter, The Red Badge of Courage, The Great Gatsby, and Miss Lonelyhearts, though they "lack finally the range of those books." Jonathan Baumbach (1963.B4) has demonstrated the unity of Wise Blood, but he fails to see the novel's "creative playfulness." Wise Blood is indebted to "the astringent comic perception, the episodic action, and the non-mimetic techniques of Miss Lonelyhearts," whereas the "more traditional" The Violent Bear It Away is indebted to The Scarlet Letter for "the dense concentration, exquisite sense of form and structure, and intense interior examination of moral struggle." The charge

1974

(ASALS, FREDERICK)
that the novels merely repeat the short stories is pointless and also untrue: the stories concern "ordinary folk" while the novels deal with "Christian heroes."

2 BASS, EBEN. "Flannery O'Connor and Henry James: The Vision of Grace." Studies in the Twentieth Century, No. 14 (Fall), pp. 43-68.

O'Connor resembles Henry James in her use of restricted point of view, her emphasis on such character-types as the child, the "inept male intellectual," and the "matriarch," her stress on sight as a part of point of view, her characters' visions, which "are akin to the flash of insight" in James's characters, and her concern with grace. She also employs "the Hawthorne-James mirror and portrait motif, the reaction of horror when the ego confronts its own image."

3 BOOTH, WAYNE C. A Rhetoric of Irony. Chicago: University of Chicago Press, pp. 152-69, 171, 175, passim.

Discusses how we as readers discover the values of the "implied author" in "Everything That Rises Must Converge." It is easy to notice the ironies directed at Julian, but careful attention to the meaning of the title and the portion of the story after the catastrophe reveals the "traditional, conventional values we share with the author." Those who are aware of O'Connor's religion may find the story more profound than readers who perceive only a secular meaning, but such readers can still get the essential experience of the story. With O'Connor's works, unlike those of many other writers, the values of the "implied author" are fairly clear to the reader.

4 BURNS, STUART L. "O'Connor and the Critics: An Overview." MissQ 27:483-95.

A review of several of the book-length studies of O'Connor that finds "the criticism, like its subject...both rich and redundant." Explications of individual works tend to be repetitive, and works that stress a thesis rather than individual readings are more rewarding once the reader has read some of these explications. Future criticism of O'Connor should address the question "of whether O'Connor is consistent in her absolutist premises, or whether she manipulates the concept of paradox so that her philosophy appears consistent" and the question of why secular readers are drawn to her fiction. Future criticism should avoid "servile adulation."

5 CUNNINGHAM, JOHN. "Recent Works on Flannery O'Connor: A Review Essay." SHR 8:375-88.
A rather critical review of recent book-length studies of O'Connor, with praise by and large limited to Carter Martin's The True Country: Themes in the Fiction of Flannery O'Connor and Sister Kathleen Feeley's Flannery O'Connor: Voice of the Peacock. Points out possible areas for future "good essays."

6 DRAKE, ROBERT. "Flannery O'Connor and American Literature." FOB 3:1-22.
In the conflict in American literature between the "Gung-Ho or Happiness Boys," Emerson, Whitman, Wolfe, and Sandburg, and the "Loyal Opposition," which includes Hawthorne, Melville, Poe, James, Eliot, Faulkner, Hemingway, and perhaps Thoreau, O'Connor stands with the latter group. By whatever terms they use, the members of this latter group believe in life's "inscrutable mystery," man's fall, and in God's or some superior force's ultimate control of the Earth. What makes O'Connor unique is her completely explicit Christian message, perhaps a result of her having to address "the post-Christian world." O'Connor shares with southern writers her respect for particulars and her "sense of rightness or 'oughtness,'" but she was not influenced by contemporary southern writers. She is "a kind of major-minor figure in our literature - perhaps...like Donne or Hopkins in English poetry."

7 FARNHAM, JAMES F. "Disintegration of Myth in the Writings of Flannery O'Connor." ConnR 8, i:11-19.
O'Connor's fiction treats the necessity for men to have some myth, some general explanation of life, to live by. When one of her characters loses his own myth and the identity connected with it and cannot accept the author's Christian myth, then he becomes "a freak, a displaced person."

8 GORDON, CAROLINE. "Rebels and Revolutionaries: The New American Scene." FOB 3:40-56.
Gives brief comments on several of the articles that have appeared in The Flannery O'Connor Bulletin and claims that O'Connor "has a greater affinity with James than with Hawthorne." Both were "masters of illusionism"; both were revolutionaries in literary technique. Both employed visionary protagonists, and both were expert in creating literary structures. O'Connor "was the first American author, possessed of a first-rate talent, to look at the rural South through the eyes of a Roman Catholic." Robert

1974

(GORDON, CAROLINE)
Fitzgerald (1965.B30) is correct in stating that O'Connor used the title of Everything That Rises Must Converge with a certain amount of irony.

9 GORDON, CAROLINE, ROBERT DRAKE, FREDERICK ASALS, ROSA LEE WALSTON, and MARION MONTGOMERY. "Panel Discussion." FOB 3:57-78.

A panel discussion of several facets of O'Connor's work, including her supposed anti-intellectualism, the nature of her world view, which is not "chilling and repulsive," her use of the grotesque as opposed to the gothic, and her rank among contemporary writers. The panel was hesitant to rank O'Connor, but did suggest that there was a need for more emphasis on esthetics in criticism of her work and that various critics should stop confusing the views of O'Connor's characters with her own.

10 GOSSETT, THOMAS F. "Flannery O'Connor on Her Fiction." SWR 59:34-42.

Paraphrases O'Connor's comments on her fiction from some of her unpublished letters. The letters "show...a writer extraordinarily sure of the effects she strove to achieve."

11 _____. "Flannery O'Connor's Opinions of Other Writers." SLJ 6 (Spring), 70-82.

O'Connor's comments on many writers of her time, based on paraphrases of her still unpublished letters. Includes some other biographical materials, including O'Connor's recounting of a dinner with Mr. and Mrs. Robert Lowell and Mary McCarthy, her account of the weekly group discussions of literature and theology at Andalusia, and some of her comments on the blacks of rural Georgia.

12 GREISCH, JANET ROHLER. "The Refiner's Fire." Christianity Today (26 July), pp. 19-20.

A general article on O'Connor as a Christian writer that relies heavily on O'Connor's statements about her fiction.

13 HOFFMAN, FREDERICK J. "The Sense of Place." In South: Modern Southern Literature in Its Cultural Setting. Edited by Louis D. Rubin, Jr. and Robert D. Jacobs. 1961. Reprint. Westport, Conn.: Greenwood Press, pp. 60-75.

A reprint of 1961.B8. O'Connor as a southern writer concerned with place belongs in that class of writers "which reveals the genuinely native particulars of a scene, while at the same time communicating their existence in time and commenting on it."

14 KATZ, CLAIRE. "Flannery O'Connor's Rage of Vision." AL 46: 54-67.

A psychological reading of O'Connor that challenges the usual religious interpretations of her fiction. O'Connor's fictional world is one where the narrator, "by wit as well as by plot structure," functions as a violent superego and expresses the same "demonic impulses" for which the characters are punished. O'Connor especially humiliates rebellious children, women, and intellectuals--those characters who are partly O'Connor herself. Her fiction is both an expression and chastisement of her own infantile fantasies. In the fiction, "the environment becomes a projection of sadistic impulses and fears so strong that the dissolution of the ego's power, ultimately death, is the only path to safety." O'Connor's work appeals to us because of our modern need, like that of the characters, to assert ourselves, though in O'Connor power is finally achieved only "in the power of the parent God." The fiction is limited by its failure to portray adult relationships, but it is so powerful that "we identify with freaks, equate human with grotesque, and renounce our humanistic heritage and the desire to grow up."

15 MAYER, DAVID R. "Apologia for the Imagination: Flannery O'Connor's 'A Temple of the Holy Ghost.'" SSF 11:147-52.

The story demonstrates O'Connor's "incarnational" method because the young girl in the story takes what she hears and elements of her Catholic background to create an imaginative version of the hermaphrodite's appearance at the circus. Her imagination allows her to develop an awareness of the potential holiness within all men and the "interconnectedness of the sacred and the profane achieved in the Incarnation."

16 MELLARD, JAMES M. "Violence and Belief in Mauriac and O'Connor." Renascence 26:158-68.

O'Connor and François Mauriac resemble each other in their sense of region, in the initial incomprehension of their readers, and in the Protestant Jansenist overtones of their Catholicism. Both writers also "share a religion and a style characterized by violence," but O'Connor's work contains far more "overt, physical violence." O'Connor's works move "toward a union of the violence of event and the violence of visionary language," which constitutes a nonintellectual, irrational revelation, as opposed to the "intellectual apprehension" in Mauriac. Both these writers and other modern writers, religious or not, use violence to communicate their visions to a complacent audience.

1974

17 MILLICHAP, JOSEPH R. "The Pauline 'Old Man' in Flannery O'Connor's 'The Comforts of Home.'" SSF 11:96-99.
Like many other southern writers, O'Connor is Calvinist in her conception of man, and Thomas's dead father is "a figure analogous to the Pauline 'old man.'" Up until the end of the story, Thomas denies the evil within himself, though at the end he may have come to an awareness that will eventually save him.

18 MONTGOMERY, MARION. "Flannery O'Connor: Prophetic Poet." FOB 3:79-94.
O'Connor's fiction resembles poetry in its careful use of imagery, metaphors, and symbols, but unlike the symbolists or the New Critics, O'Connor never intends her fiction to be a closed system, referring only to itself. She is similar to Dante in desiring "her symbols to open upon larger spiritual concerns," though she is more flexible in her use of symbols. There are many parallels in technique and theme between Wise Blood and T. S. Eliot's poetry.

19 RUBIN, LOUIS D., JR. and ROBERT D. JACOBS. "Introduction: Southern Writing and the Changing South." In South: Modern Southern Literature in Its Cultural Setting. Edited by Louis D. Rubin, Jr. and Robert D. Jacobs. 1961. Reprint. Westport, Conn.: Greenwood Press, pp. 11-25.
A reprint of 1961.B14. Despite the collapse of the older community in the South, O'Connor is one of the southern writers whose works "remain 'Southern' by virtue of their attitude toward language, their conception of man as a limited, dependent being."

20 SULLIVAN, WALTER. "The Continuing Renascence: Southern Fiction in the Fifties." In South: Modern Southern Literature in Its Cultural Setting. Edited by Louis D. Rubin, Jr. and Robert D. Jacobs. 1961. Reprint. Westport, Conn.: Greenwood Press, pp. 376-91.
A reprint of 1961.B15. O'Connor, one of the younger southern writers, uses Christianity in her fiction now that an agreed-upon code of ethics for the South has disappeared. Although the reader does not identify with her characters, O'Connor succeeds because of her "consummate technical skill" and her "strict Christian point of view."

*21 _____. "The World of Flannery O'Connor." WDCN, Nashville.
A film for educational television on O'Connor's life and fiction that emphasizes her Milledgeville environment. The film is available to educational television stations in the Southeast. [Source: Gerald C. Becham, "The Flannery O'Connor Collection: GC's Vital Legacy. Columns, Fall, pp. 3-5. See 1975.B1.]

1974-1975

22 DESMOND, JOHN F. "The Shifting of Mr. Shiftlet: Flannery O'Connor's 'The Life You Save May Be Your Own.'" MissQ 28: 55-59.

At the beginning of the story Mr. Shiftlet perceives a spiritual reality, but he is infected with the false innocence of Manicheanism, just as Mrs. Crater is infected with the false innocence of materialism. Later in the story he realizes that his spirit cannot be free of the world, and he switches from being a "potential redemptive agent" to a "satanic figure." Shiftlet saves himself by fleeing life, "but the self he saves is a false and sterile parody of the redeemed creature."

1975 A BOOKS - NONE

1975 B SHORTER WRITINGS

1 BECHAM, GERALD C. "The Flannery O'Connor Collection: GC's Vital Legacy." Columns (Georgia College at Milledgeville), (Fall), pp. 3-5.

A history of the founding of the Flannery O'Connor Room at Georgia College and a description of the O'Connor Collection. Mentions that in 1976 a special issue of The Flannery O'Connor Bulletin will be a catalog of the manuscripts in the collection. This work is being done by Professor Robert Dunn of Indiana University. Also mentions the educational film on O'Connor (See 1974.B21).

2 BURNS, STUART L. "How Wide Did 'The Heathen' Range?" FOB 4: 25-41.

An examination of the manuscript of O'Connor's unfinished novel, "Why Do the Heathen Rage?" indicates that there is "no novel there at all." The manuscript demonstrates that O'Connor was best at the short story, that it was extremely difficult for her to write novels, and that "Why Do the Heathen Rage?" shows no new direction in O'Connor's work; indeed, "almost all the manuscript's usable parts were incorporated into various stories in Everything That Rises." O'Connor's "materials of plot, narrative detail and characterization were sufficiently similar so as to be interchangeable from one piece of fiction to another," and it is her symbols that distinguish her stories and tended to make her a writer of "epiphanic fiction, a type much more adaptable to the short story genre."

3 DENHAM, ROBERT D. "The World of Guilt and Sorrow: Flannery O'Connor's 'Everything That Rises Must Converge.'" FOB 4: 42-51.

An analysis of the story indebted to R. S. Crane's argument that in analyzing a story we should move from a story's moral and emotional effect upon us to its "'essential cause.'" In this story our expectations are reversed as we experience at the end of the story an "agreeable astonishment" because we are glad Julian is being transformed into a better person and because we are surprised that he is capable of such a transformation. The "'essential cause'" of this story is Julian's moral growth. The bus scene in the story is discussed in terms of O'Connor's "making Julian into a morally unsympathetic character and providing a means for the story's climax."

4 DORSEY, JAMES E. "Carson McCullers and Flannery O'Connor: A Checklist of Graduate Research." BB 32:162-67.

A list of theses and dissertations on O'Connor and McCullers up to February, 1975.

5 GREGORY, DONALD. "Enoch Emery: Ironic Doubling in Wise Blood." FOB 4:52-64.

An article detailing the ways in which the unthinking Enoch is an ironic double of the always conscious and troubled Haze. O'Connor uses Enoch as a double to show "that the isolation which moves both characters to violence and murder is not unique, even if their reactions to it may be" and to have "a comic counterpoint which heightens the reader's awareness of the tragic dimensions of Haze's quest." Similarities in character, experiences, obsessions with objects, and O'Connor's descriptions of their experiences are discussed.

6 McKENZIE, BARBARA. "Flannery O'Connor Country: A Photo Essay." GaR 29:328-62.

Photographs of rural Georgia that show the spiritual and physical aspects of O'Connor's "country." The photographs "substantiate through visual rather than literary evidence the primacy of vision as fiction's base." A considerably revised and expanded version of this essay and series of photographs, entitled Flannery O'Connor's Georgia, is scheduled to be published by the University of Georgia Press in the fall of 1976. See 1976.A3.

7 MARTIN, CARTER. "Comedy and Humor in Flannery O'Connor's Fiction." FOB 4:1-12.

Like Faulkner's As I Lay Dying, O'Connor's comedy is related to traditional comedy, which often stresses the grotesque. Her comedy has a "social signification," and she follows Bergson's dictum of using only aberrations that the reader can imitate or identify with, though in her case, as with Tarwater in The Violent Bear It Away, we first laugh at the aberration and then recognize that "he is the norm and the world becomes the aberration." With "A Good Man Is Hard to Find" we can only recognize the "organic" nature of O'Connor's comedy if we understand that we could become the Misfit and if we are "capable of extreme comic detachment," a detachment O'Connor creates in the story. In this story O'Connor avoids the usual comic ending and uses "a form of comedy more primitive than that of Aristophanes." The story "is a reversion to the original action of propitiatory sacrifice in which the victim is lost to the world but saved spiritually."

8 MAY, JOHN R. "Flannery O'Connor: Critical Consensus and the 'Objective' Interpretation." Renascence 27:179-92.

Argues against E. D. H. Hirsch's contention that the valid interpretation of a work lies in the work itself: "'objectivity' is relative to the historical period and... it lies in the direction of consensus within the community of literary critics and theologians." With any important writer, there are three stages in the development of criticism: the first stage, characterized by "a mixture of judgment and interpretation," the second stage, where the criticism is evaluated by its relation to the works, and the third stage, where the passage of time leads to "the emergence of a new language tradition" and genuine reevaluations of the work appear. Criticism of O'Connor in the first stage was marked by much facile labeling and "subjectivity." The criticism is now moving into the second stage, with a growing sense of consensus emerging among the critics. Only Josephine Hendin (See 1970.A1) has attempted a "'reevaluation,'" but hers did not succeed. Points out areas of substantial agreement in criticism of O'Connor and areas where there is still disagreement or much more work to be done and also notes that criticism of O'Connor shows the "tension" between the formal and semantic aspects of literary interpretation. See 1976.A4.

9 MAYER, DAVID R. "The Blazing Sun and the Relentless Shutter: The Kindred Arts of Flannery O'Connor and Diane Arbus." Christian Century (30 April), pp. 435-40.

O'Connor and the photographer Diane Arbus resemble each other in their treatment of shocking or disturbing subjects, their hostility to vanity, and their refusal to satisfy our demands for facile, happy situations. Arbus, however,

1975

(MAYER, DAVID R.)
lacks O'Connor's religious faith. O'Connor's fiction allows us hope; Arbus's photographs "record merely our incompleteness."

10 NELSON, ED. "Flannery O'Connor: A Religious Experience: She Kept Going Deeper." Columns (Georgia College at Milledgeville). (Fall), pp. 6-8.

A reprint of a sermon at Georgia College that highlights the shocking quality of O'Connor's fiction, as well as her stress on "absolute Faith and dependence on Christ" and on our fallen nature. Emphasizes "The Lame Shall Enter First."

11 TATE, J. O. "The Uses of Banality." FOB 4:13-24.

O'Connor resembles Flaubert and Joyce because they too were "banality collectors" and because all three wrote anatomies, the ideal form "for dealing with 'Ideas' and especially for rendering them absurd." On the other hand, she does not resemble a user of banality like Ring Lardner because her stories "contain a higher end than the enumeration of banalities...in her work the vulgar is always set off by the sublime or the numinous." O'Connor's characters use banality to deny temporality. She should not be blamed for describing the world as she does because she did not create this world; it was given to her by the modern world itself. O'Connor is not a southern writer in the sense of usually being specifically concerned with southern history, but she is southern in her "concentration on the authority of time." Emphasizes Wise Blood.

12 WALKER, ALICE. "The Reconstruction of Flannery O'Connor." Ms. Magazine (December), pp. 77-79, 102, 104-06.

This black poet and novelist spent part of her childhood in poverty near O'Connor's farm and has an ambivalent attitude toward O'Connor, admiring O'Connor's unsentimental portraits of white women, her increasingly honest and respectful attitude toward blacks in her later fiction, and her ability to transcend race in her basic religious concerns, yet at the same time unable to accept some of O'Connor's comments on blacks and their position in the South, and the gap between O'Connor's social position and that of poor southern blacks. In her later fiction, O'Connor limited herself to describing only the outward behavior of her black characters, thus allowing "them...in the reader's imagination, to inhabit another landscape, another life, than the one she creates for them."

13 WYNNE, JUDITH F. "The Sacramental Irony of Flannery O'Connor." SLJ 7 (Spring), 33-49.

Critics who stress O'Connor's theology and her own commentary on her works "limit the ironic by reducing it to the allegorical." Her "irony can be seen as sacramental, not because it works with the stuff of religious belief and non-belief, which it does, but because it itself operates as a vehicle of revelation." O'Connor disrupts the usual categories by presenting both the fantastic and the moral as grotesque and both the absurd and the normal as comic. She joins the grotesque and the comic to create her satiric irony, an irony the reader, caught between his sympathy for the moral and normal as well as for what disrupts them, often finds directed at himself. Discusses "Revelation," "A Good Man Is Hard to Find," "Good Country People," and "A View of the Woods."

1976 A BOOKS

*1 FARMER, DAVID. A Descriptive Bibliography of the Works of Flannery O'Connor. Scheduled for publication fall 1976. New York: Burt Franklin/Lenox Hill.

A bibliography of O'Connor's books, contributions to books, contributions to periodicals, miscellaneous writings, and early published art work, as well as translations, adaptations, films, and parodies of her work. [Information supplied by Professor Farmer.]

2 McFARLAND, DOROTHY TUCK. Flannery O'Connor. Modern Literature Monographs. New York: Frederick Ungar.

An introduction to O'Connor's work and life for students and general readers that includes a fair amount of plot summary as well as brief discussions of some of the central issues in criticism of O'Connor. O'Connor's illness was important because "it brought home to her the experience of human limitation." Her use of the grotesque and irony and the tension in her work between a usually "flat" style and an often somber tone on the one hand and her religious content on the other are aspects of her religious vision. O'Connor did not detest nature or beauty; she was against sentimentalism and often seems harsh because she wants to present the religious experience as truthfully as possible. She rejected Manicheanism and "insisted that transcendence is to be found not through escaping from the limitations of the body, but, paradoxically, through embracing physical realities that the human mind tends to find repellent." Includes a selected bibliography of works by and about O'Connor.

1976

*3 McKENZIE, BARBARA. Flannery O'Connor's Georgia. Athens, Ga.: University of Georgia Press. Scheduled for publication fall 1976.
See 1975.B6. [Information supplied by Professor McKenzie.]

4 MAY, JOHN R. The Pruning Word: The Parables of Flannery O'Connor. Notre Dame: Notre Dame University Press.
A series of close readings of all of O'Connor's fiction, including the stories not in the first two collections, that sees the major works employing "the pruning word" of revelation to communicate with both the characters and the reader. Although O'Connor in her criticism stressed "theological realism," her fiction is close to the "New Hermeneutic" since we do not interpret the text; rather, "man is to be interpreted by the text--the possibilities of his situation to be illumined by it." Our awareness of the closeness of the fiction to the principles of the "New Hermeneutic" resolves the question of art versus belief so common in criticism of O'Connor, since "word in the New Hermeneutic is radically human--and therefore possibly religious rather than specifically Christian" and since the language of her fiction "cannot demand [the reader's] assent." Her works are parables in the narrow sense that Dan Otto Via uses the term: they stress man's "radical poverty in the face of reality. They startle him with the suddenness of the sacred in the midst of the ordinary." They are like the parables of Jesus because "the parables of Jesus are not allegories but dramatic narratives involving conflicts between human beings that symbolize rather than describe man's relationship to ultimate reality." Includes a critical introduction that is a revised version of 1975.B8, and a selected critical bibliography that lists by titles of O'Connor's works criticism of particular works. O'Connor's manuscripts are discussed in several of the analyses in this book.

1976 B SHORTER WRITINGS - NONE

Ph.D. Dissertations on Flannery O'Connor

1961 BAUMBACH, JONATHAN. "The Theme of Guilt and Redemption in the Post-Second-World-War American Novel." Stanford University. (Discusses Wise Blood)

1966 BLACKWELL, ANNIE LOUISE. "The Artistry of Flannery O'Connor." Florida State University.

CONNOLLY, JANET M. "The Fiction of Flannery O'Connor." Columbia University.

DUNN, SISTER FRANCIS MARY. "Functions and Implications of Setting in the Fiction of Flannery O'Connor." Catholic University of America.

1967 ASALS, FREDERICK J. "Flannery O'Connor: An Interpretive Study." Brown University.

DINNEEN, PATRICIA M. "Flannery O'Connor: Realist of Distances." Pennsylvania State University.

GREGORY, DONALD L. "An Internal Analysis of the Fiction of Flannery O'Connor." Ohio State University.

MARTIN, CARTER W. "The Convergence of Actualities: Themes in the Fiction of Flannery O'Connor." Vanderbilt University.

MULLER, GILBERT H. "Flannery O'Connor and the Catholic Grotesque." Stanford University.

RECHNITZ, ROBERT M. "Perception, Identity, and the Grotesque: A Study of Three Southern Writers." University of Colorado. (Discusses O'Connor, McCullers, and Welty)

SMITH, PATRICK J. "Typology and Peripety in Four Catholic Novels." University of California, Davis. (Discusses The Violent Bear It Away)

1968 BREWSTER, RUDOLPH A. "The Literary Devices in the Writings of Flannery O'Connor." East Texas State University.

GATTUSO, JOSEPHINE F. "The Fictive World of Flannery O'Connor." Columbia University.

RACKY, DONALD J. "The Achievement of Flannery O'Connor: Her System of Thought, Her Fictional Techniques, and an Explication of Her Thought and Techniques in The Violent Bear It Away." Loyola University, Chicago.

STEPHENS, MARTHA T. "An Introduction to the Work of Flannery O'Connor." Indiana University.

1969 BROWNING, PRESTON M. "Flannery O'Connor and the Grotesque Recovery of the Holy." University of Chicago.

SHORT, DONALD A. "The Concrete Is Her Medium: The Fiction of Flannery O'Connor." University of Pittsburgh.

1970 COALE, SAMUEL C. "The Role of the South in the Fiction of William Faulkner, Carson McCullers, Flannery O'Connor, and William Styron." Brown University.

CRUSER, PAUL A. "The Fiction of Flannery O'Connor." University of Pennsylvania.

FEELEY, SISTER MARY K. "Splendor of Reality: The Fiction of Flannery O'Connor." Rutgers University.

GOSS, JAMES. "The Assembling of the Meaning of God in the Short Stories of Flannery O'Connor, Bernard Malamud, and John Updike." Claremont Graduate School and University Center.

HOFFMAN, ARNOLD R. "The Sense of Place: Peter deVries, J. F. Powers, and Flannery O'Connor." Michigan State University.

KEANE, MELINDA. "Structural Irony in Flannery O'Connor: Instrument of the Writer's Vision." Loyola University, Chicago.

KELLER, JANE C. "The Comic Spirit in the Works of Flannery O'Connor." Tulane University.

KLEVAR, HARVEY. "The Sacredly Profane and the Profanely Sacred: Flannery O'Connor and Erskine Caldwell as Interpreters of Southern Cultural and Religious Traditions." University of Minnesota.

ORVELL, MILES D. "An Incarnational Art: The Fiction of Flannery O'Connor." Harvard University.

QUINN, J. J. "The Tragicomic Vision in the Writings of Flannery O'Connor: A Study of Her Analogical Imagination." University of London.

1971 BUNTING, CHARLES T. "The Christian Elements in the Writings of Flannery O'Connor." University of Southern Mississippi.

DESMOND, JOHN F. "Christian Historical Analogues in the Fiction of William Faulkner and Flannery O'Connor." University of Oklahoma.

DIBBLE, TERRY J. "The Epiphanal Vision in the Short Fiction of Flannery O'Connor." University of Nebraska.

DUNN, ROBERT J. "A Mode of Good: Form and Philosophy in the Fiction of Flannery O'Connor." University of Michigan.

HAND, JOHN T. "Letters to the Laodiceans: The Romantic Quest in Flannery O'Connor." Kent State University.

PALMS, ROSEMARY. "The Double Motif in Literature: From Origins to an Examination of Three Modern American Novels." University of Texas, Austin. (Discusses The Violent Bear It Away)

STRASSBERG, MILDRED P. "Religious Commitment in Recent American Fiction: Flannery O'Connor, Bernard Malamud, John Updike." State University of New York, Stony Brook.

THOMAS, LEROY. "An Analysis of the Theme of Alienation in the Fictional Works of Five Contemporary Southern Writers." Oklahoma State University. (Discusses Wolfe, Warren, Welty, McCullers, and O'Connor)

1972 BAUMBACH, GEORGIA A. "The Psychology of Flannery O'Connor's Fictive World." Ohio State University.

DARRETTA, JOHN L. "The Idea and Image of Retribution in the Fiction of Flannery O'Connor." Fordham University.

FINGER, LARRY L. "Elements of the Grotesque in Selected Works of Welty, Capote, McCullers, and O'Connor." George Peabody College for Teachers. (Discusses Wise Blood and The Violent Bear It Away)

GOLDEN, ROBERT E. "Violence and Art in Postwar American Literature: A Study of O'Connor, Kosinski, Hawkes, and Pynchon." University of Rochester. (Discusses The Violent Bear It Away)

HOFFMAN, ELEANOR M. "A Study of the Major Structures Intrinsic to the Fiction of Flannery O'Connor." University of Texas, Austin.

LACKEY, ALLEN D. "Flannery O'Connor and Her Critics: A Survey and Evaluation of the Critical Response to the Fiction of Flannery O'Connor." University of Tennessee.

MacDONALD, SARA J. "The Aesthetics of Grace in Flannery O'Connor and Graham Greene." University of Illinois, Urbana-Champaign.

PADGETT, THOMAS E. "The Irony in Flannery O'Connor's Fiction." University of Missouri, Columbia.

1973 BORGMAN, PAUL C. "The Symbolic City and Christian Existentialism in Fiction by Flannery O'Connor, Walker Percy, and John Updike." University of Chicago.

CARLSON, THOMAS M. "Flannery O'Connor: The Manichaean Dilemma." University of North Carolina, Chapel Hill.

CLEVELAND, CAROL L. "Psychological Violence: The World of Flannery O'Connor." Saint Louis University.

HAUSER, JAMES D. "The Broken Cosmos of Flannery O'Connor: The Design of Her Fiction." University of Pennsylvania.

HEGARTY, CHARLES M. "Vision and Revision: The Art of Flannery O'Connor." University of Chicago.

JOHNSON, RHONDA E. "A Translation of Silence: The Fiction of Flannery O'Connor." State University of New York, Buffalo.

LUBIN, SISTER ALICE M. "I. Southwell's Religious Complaint Lyric. II. Becky Sharp's Role Playing in Vanity Fair. III. Grotesques in the Fiction of Flannery O'Connor." Rutgers University.

MAYER, DAVID R. "The Hermaphrodite and the Host: Incarnation as Vision and Method in the Fiction of Flannery O'Connor." University of Maryland.

MUTKOSKI, BARBARA E. "The Teilhard Milieu: Pierre Teilhard de Chardin's Influence on Flannery O'Connor's Fiction." Fordham University.

Ph.D. Dissertations on Flannery O'Connor

1974 LANGFORD, ROBERTA B. "The Comic Sense of Flannery O'Connor." Duke University.

MATCHIE, THOMAS F. "The Mythical Flannery O'Connor: A Psychomythic Study of 'A Good Man Is Hard to Find.'" University of Wisconsin, Madison.

MEHL, DUANE P. "Spiritual Reality in the Works of Flannery O'Connor." Saint Louis University.

NISLY, PAUL W. "Flannery O'Connor and the Gothic Impulse." University of Kansas.

SHLOSS, CAROL. "The Limits of Inference: Flannery O'Connor and the Representation of 'Mystery.'" Brandeis University.

SMITH, JOHN C. "'Written with Zest': The Comic Art of Flannery O'Connor." Harvard University.

1975 CHARNIGO, RICHARD J. "A Structural Analysis of the Short Fiction of Flannery O'Connor." Bowling Green State University.

EMERICK, RONALD R. "Romance, Allegory, Vision: The Influence of Hawthorne on Flannery O'Connor." University of Pittsburgh.

KATZ, CLAIRE R. "Flannery O'Connor: A Rage of Vision." University of California, Berkeley.

KISSEL, SUSAN S. "For a 'Hostile Audience': A Study of the Fiction of Flannery O'Connor, Walker Percy, and J. F. Powers." University of Cincinnati.

McCULLAGH, JAMES C. "Aesthetics and the Religious Mind: François Mauriac, Graham Greene, and Flannery O'Connor." Lehigh University. (Discusses _Wise Blood_ and _The Violent Bear It Away_)

OLSON, CHARLES J. "The Dragon by the Road: An Archetypal Approach to the Fiction of Flannery O'Connor." University of New Mexico.

TATE, JAMES O. "Flannery O'Connor and _Wise Blood_: The Significance of the Early Drafts." Columbia University.

Caroline Gordon: *A Reference Guide*

Mary C. Sullivan

Introduction

Caroline Gordon (1895-   ) began publishing short stories in the late 1920's and is now working on the novel which she intends to be her last: A Narrow Heart: The Portrait of a Woman. Her reputation illustrates a familiar but distressing phenomenon. Though her published work and the published criticism of her work reveal a writer of finely crafted stories and novels highly esteemed by people whose critical judgment is commonly respected, Caroline Gordon - perhaps for substantial reasons, perhaps for only accidental ones - has not been a popular writer. Of her nine novels and two volumes of short stories, eight titles have been recently reprinted. However, none of these is available in a paperbound edition. Thus her fiction has not become broadly known and appreciated, studied and criticized - especially in those forums where the literary reputations of writers are most vigorously generated and cultivated when their work is accessible for study: namely, the graduate schools of universities, from which chiefly come the editors and contributors to the literary journals where literary worth is first acknowledged and memorialized.

In 1956 Joan Griscom, presenting her "Bibliography of Caroline Gordon" (Critique, Winter 1956), found that the writings about Caroline Gordon's work which she reviewed were generally "surprising and disappointing" and the majority of the reviews "either negligible or inadequate as criticism." Although the picture has changed considerably since that time, one could not yet say that Caroline Gordon's work has been fully and adequately examined or judged.

Caroline Gordon published her first short story, "Summer Dust," in Gyroscope, No. 1 in November 1929. Since that year her short stories, novels, and critical works have received serious critical attention in the form of substantial articles, a few books, and significant portions of books from such writers and critics as Ford Madox Ford, Robert Penn Warren, Katherine Anne Porter, Andrew Nelson Lytle, Vivienne Koch, Robert D. Jacobs, Louis D. Rubin, Jr., Robert B. Heilman, William Van O'Connor, Frederick J. Hoffman, Willard Thorp, Louise Cowan, Ashley Brown, John M. Bradbury, Brainard Cheney, Chester E. Eisenger, Frederick P. W. McDowell, James E. Rocks, Thomas H. Landess, Donald E. Stanford, William J. Stuckey, Melvin E. Bradford, and Howard Baker. These critics have contributed significantly to the breadth of our understanding and evaluation of Caroline Gordon's works.

During the 1950's and 1960's a large number of perceptive scholarly articles on her work appeared, augmenting the handful of such articles that had been published prior to 1953, the year in which Louis D. Rubin, Jr. and Robert D. Jacobs published the *Hopkins Review* symposium entitled *Southern Renascence*. In the 1970's scholarly interest in Caroline Gordon's work has continued to grow, stimulated by the re-issue in 1971 of eight of her volumes which had been out of print, by the publication in 1972 of her ninth novel, *The Glory of Hera*, and by Miss Gordon's own disciplined dedication to the completion of its companion volume: her tenth novel, *A Narrow Heart: The Portrait of a Woman*, now in progress.

Two numbers of major journals have been devoted to analysis and evaluation of Caroline Gordon's fiction: *Critique: Studies in Modern Fiction* (Winter 1956) and *The Southern Review* (Spring 1971). To date, only one monograph and two hardbound volumes on her work have been published: Frederick P. W. McDowell's *Caroline Gordon* (University of Minnesota Pamphlet, 1966), William J. Stuckey's *Caroline Gordon* (Twayne, 1972), and Thomas H. Landess' edition of a critical symposium on *The Short Fiction of Caroline Gordon* (1972).

Consequently, to a large extent, the most insightful and detailed criticism of Caroline Gordon's novels and short stories remains in journal articles and in certain book reviews which have appeared over the last four decades.

As one peruses the whole body of this critical material, encompassing well over two hundred pieces, one encounters the full range of critical sophistication from simple claims that *Green Centuries* is a "robust story" and *The Forest of the South* a "charming" collection to seminal critical analyses such as Andrew Lytle's "Caroline Gordon and the Historic Image" (1949), Robert B. Heilman's "The Southern Temper" (1953), and Howard Baker's recent brilliant and probing analysis (1973) of the mythic consciousness in *Penhally* and *The Glory of Hera*. It is now necessary to assemble in one place the full body of public reaction to Caroline Gordon's work in order to establish the quality and manner of her work and its reception.

The most significant critical efforts devoted to Caroline Gordon's work have usually focused on the nature of her vision, on her achievement in conveying this vision, and, increasingly, on the significance of the total corpus: the development, consistency, and unity of the ontological statement or myth which she projects in her fiction as a whole. While many have seen a more explicitly Christian, even Roman Catholic, dimension in her writing after her entrance into the Roman Catholic Church in 1947, many other critics have demonstrated the internal consistency of her vision from the beginning:

the logical development from southern Agrarianism to a more formal religious perspective and the mythic tension between nature and salvific presence or gift ("grace") which have informed all her work.

Many scholars who have studied the southern literary movement that centered on the Fugitives and the Agrarians in the 1920's and 1930's have attested to Caroline Gordon's solid place in this renascence of Southern Literature--a place earned by the durable quality of her fiction. At first her vision was labeled "Southern" but increasingly its more universal and mythic intentions were recognized. Like so many writers with whom she is compared, she is now seen to have found the universal in the local.

Much of the published writing on Caroline Gordon's work acknowledges the classically conservative quality of her ontological vision. She is viewed as predominantly an essentialist, respectful of an inherent and ancient order in nature. She has in her fiction become increasingly explicit about the incompleteness of nature and of man and woman in it.

Only one critic has actually said that Caroline Gordon is "second rank." Whether or not assigning numerical order in the history of literature is useful, critics of Caroline Gordon's fiction have cited certain weaknesses which they have perceived in particular works: apparent fear of or avoidance of the genuinely tragic potentialities implicit in the action of her fiction; an emotional reticence that militates against the creation of memorable characters; an undesirable ambiguity of tone; a preference for technique over engagement. Each of these complaints has led to re-examination of such fundamental matters as Caroline Gordon's theory of fiction, her structural use of the epical mode, and her concept of human tragedy, although none of these issues has been conclusively settled. Since the publication of _The Glory of Hera_, her novel of Heracles as a man-made-into-a-god in a Greek mythological setting, the repeated earlier claim that all Caroline Gordon's fiction tells but "one story" now seems to need further investigation.

In 1935, Robert Penn Warren wrote of Caroline Gordon's "_intensive_ talent, a talent exhaustively aware of the immediate richness and implication of the single scene," the kind of talent that triumphs "in its sudden and illuminating perception." Over the years critics have more and more voiced their admiration of the ways by which Caroline Gordon indirectly suggests such perceptions in her fiction. This suggestiveness, this strategem of the slowly revealed "underground water" has been celebrated especially in two recent essays by Radcliffe Squires (1971.B9) and Howard Baker (1973.B1).

Fruitful critical approaches to the fiction of Caroline Gordon have focused on the historic images that inform her work, the natural symbols by which the meaning of past time is rendered contemporaneous for modern man, and the mythic structure of her works. Her fiction has also been interpreted within the pattern of Dante's Commedia, especially the conversion experience of the Purgatorio.

Discussion continues whether Caroline Gordon's best genre is the short story or the novel. Miss Gordon sees herself primarily as a novelist, as do some critics who name various of her novels as masterpieces. Other scholars point to a half dozen or so of her short stories as among the most remarkable stories written in this century and think that Caroline Gordon's chief talents and successes are in this shorter form.

This guide will, it is hoped, provide scholars and others interested in the work of Caroline Gordon with helpful references to books, articles, and reviews about her and her work. The Guide is intended to be a complete annotated listing of all published writings about Caroline Gordon and her work, for the period 1931-1973, though undoubtedly some items may have been missed. The absence of entries for 1974, and the single one for 1975, may in part reflect the lapse of time before certain annual bibliographies are available and in part an unfortunate dry period in Gordon studies.

All items here listed have been seen and read by the author except for one which has not been located; this is asterisked, and the source of the bibliographical information cited in brackets.

In preparing this Reference Guide on Caroline Gordon, the author adhered to two principles of selection: to include works in which Caroline Gordon is mentioned only in passing because such works often indicate, even if briefly, her place and importance in American letters; and to write fairly long annotations where such annotations might better serve to display an individual author's argument. The annotations are descriptive, not evaluative. Wherever possible the author's own words are quoted in order to be more faithful to the exact tone and argument of each writing.

It should be noted that material on Caroline Gordon in standard reference works and reviews of Gordon criticism have been excluded as have remarks in short story anthologies except where these remarks seem to make a significant contribution to the criticism of a particular short story. Reprints of articles are cited and cross-referenced in the Guide.

The Reference Guide is organized chronologically by date of publication of writings about Caroline Gordon. Each year has two sections: "A" numbers and lists in alphabetical order monographs, books exclusively about Caroline Gordon, and books in which several essays deal with Caroline Gordon or her work; "B" numbers and lists in alphabetical order reviews, articles, and books in which only a chapter or a few pages are devoted to Caroline Gordon. The "A" and "B" entries are numbered anew and separately for each year and this coding is used in cross-references, for reprints, and in the index at the back of the Guide. Thus "1968.B5" indicates the fifth article in the "B" section for 1968.

The titles of some periodicals and journals are abbreviated. Most of the abbreviations are taken from those found in the Modern Language Association International Bibliography. A few additional abbreviations for widely-known journals or for periodicals cited frequently in this Reference Guide have been added. In the case of certain newspapers where confusion as to source may easily arise, no abbreviations have been used. A table of these abbreviations appears on page 201.

At the end of the Guide there is a chronological listing of Ph.D. dissertations about Caroline Gordon.

I am indebted to the bibliographical work on Caroline Gordon done by various scholars, especially that of Joan Griscom, Frederick P. W. McDowell, William J. Stuckey, and Melvin E. Bradford. I have in a few instances made corrections in items from previous bibliographies. I have not attempted complete coverage of articles dealing generally with Southern literature or with modern American fiction, even though references to Caroline Gordon may be discovered.

Many persons and institutions have helped in the preparation of this Reference Guide. I would like to thank Sister Mary Borromeo Povero for translating Rachele Valensise's article from the Italian. For assistance in locating and obtaining material I would especially like to thank the following persons and libraries: Mary Ann Young and the Wallace Memorial Library, Rochester Institute of Technology; the Rochester Regional Research Library Council and the Inter-Library Loan systems with which it cooperates; the Chicago Public Library; the Library of the State University of New York at Oswego; the Library of Saint Bernard Seminary, Rochester; Rush Rhees Library of the University of Rochester; the Library of the University of Notre Dame; Ernan McMullin, University of Notre Dame; and Robert E. Golden, Rochester Institute of Technology. Mary Ann Young was an especially faithful guide throughout this research, making nearly all the arrangements for inter-library loan. For financial assistance I am deeply indebted to Paul Bernstein, Dean of the College of General Studies, Rochester Institute of Technology, and to the Sisters of Mercy of Rochester, New York, of which I am a member. For help in preparing the Index and for other material assistance I wish to thank Sister Marilyn Williams. I wish also to thank those who typed: Joan Smith and Karen Velasco. It is hard to know exactly how to limit the definition of "material assistance": may many others know that they are deeply thanked.

Finally, I wish to express my deep gratitude to Caroline Gordon herself, for assistance in locating some articles and for her letters to me.

Table of Abbreviations

CathW	Catholic World
Crit	Critique: Studies in Modern Fiction
HudR	Hudson Review
LJ	Library Journal
MissQ	Mississippi Quarterly
NatR	National Review
NYTBR	New York Times Book Review
SA	Studi Americani (Roma)
SatR	Saturday Review
SHR	Southern Humanities Review
SoR	Southern Review
SR	Sewanee Review
SSF	Studies in Short Fiction
TLS	(London) Times Literary Supplement
VQR	Virginia Quarterly Review
WHR	Western Humanities Review
WR	Western Review: A Journal of the Humanities
YR	Yale Review

Works by Caroline Gordon

The following are the novels, collections of short stories, and full-length critical works published by Caroline Gordon. Her uncollected short stories and essays may be located through the bibliographies noted in this Reference Guide supplemented by the usual reference works.

NOVELS

Penhally. New York: Scribner, 1931. Reprinted: New York: Cooper Square Publishers, 1971.

Aleck Maury, Sportsman. New York: Scribner, 1934; as The Pastimes of Aleck Maury: The Life of a True Sportsman. London: Dickson, 1935. Reprinted: New York: Cooper Square Publishers, 1971.

None Shall Look Back. New York: Scribner, 1937; as None Shall Look Back: A Story of the American Civil War. London: Constable, 1937. Reprinted: New York: Cooper Square Publishers, 1971.

The Garden of Adonis. New York: Scribner, 1937. Reprinted: New York: Cooper Square Publishers, 1971.

Green Centuries. New York: Scribner, 1941. Reprinted: New York: Cooper Square Publishers, 1971.

The Women on the Porch. New York: Scribner, 1944. Reprinted: New York: Cooper Square Publishers, 1971.

The Strange Children. New York: Scribner, 1951; London: Routledge, 1952. Reprinted: New York: Cooper Square Publishers, 1971.

The Malefactors. New York: Harcourt Brace, 1956.

The Glory of Hera. New York: Doubleday, 1972.

SHORT STORIES

The Forest of the South. New York: Scribner, 1945.

Old Red and Other Stories. New York: Scribner, 1963. Reprinted: New York: Cooper Square Publishers, 1971.

OTHER

How to Read a Novel. New York: Viking Press, 1957.

A Good Soldier: A Key to the Novels of Ford Madox Ford. Davis: University of California Library, 1963.

Editor, with Allen Tate. The House of Fiction: An Anthology of the Short Story, with Commentary. New York: Scribner, 1950; revised edition, 1960.

NOVEL-IN-PROGRESS

A Narrow Heart: The Portrait of a Woman.

Published Writings about Caroline Gordon, 1931 — 1975

1931 A BOOKS - NONE

1931 B SHORTER WRITINGS

1 ANON. Review of Penhally. Booklist 28:151.
Very brief mention. The story "is told in episodes, in an impressionistic style, and is uneven in interest."

2 ANON. Review of Penhally. Boston Transcript (18 November), p. 2.
"After a mild career of short stories," Gordon has "tried her hand at a long chronicle." Hers is "the curious experiment of telling a necessarily slow and languid tale in quick modern staccato-short sentences, brief feverish references to this and that, so that one's feeling is of haste and confusion, rather than of beauty and the long shadows of peace." She has rushed "a multitude of persons...before our eyes, like a motion picture." There is "much fine feeling in this, but very little judgment. One cannot do detailed justice to a century in less than three times that many pages."

3 ANON. Review of Penhally. Springfield (Mass.) Republican (4 October), p. 7e.
Very brief mention. Discusses "what Walter H. Page used to call a 'shirt-tail,' in which the history of the family is brought through the rise of the New South and down to the present." In narrative method "the story diverges somewhat from the Old South conventions, introducing more reporting and a less sentimental attitude."

4 ANON. Review of Penhally. Wisconsin Library Bulletin 27:256.
Brief notice. "The early chapters, up to the Civil War, are the best. In its later half the story weakens."

5 ANON. "A Southern Mansion." NYTBR (20 September), pp. 6-7.
Reviews Penhally. If the philosophy of the Agrarian Movement "is sincerely believed in, it is a blessing to the

1931

(ANON.)
novelist," whatever else it is or isn't. Penhally has a "certain internal consistency" though one might object to Gordon's "ancestor religion." Yet "her story is credible at all points, her single scenes are good, even when her situations involve working in the trite and melodramatic stuff of many a novel of the Confederacy." All in all, Penhally is "good fiction," but "the defect of the novel lies in that it tries to encompass too much; it focuses on a house and on a family connection, and individual troubles and joys are thereby subordinated to a total effect that mutes tragedy and turns it into something nearer pathos." Therefore, "the book is never more than mildly moving," lacking the "fire of more personal tragedy, seen from close up" as found, for example, in Stark Young's River House.

6 BRICKELL, HERSCHEL. "Land and the Love of It." New York Herald Tribune Books (27 September), p. 7.
Reviews Penhally, a "skillfully fictionized chapter of American cultural history," based on "a genuinely significant theme": the "ownership of land and its influence upon the lives of people." Though this is a "complicated story, covering a full century and touching upon the lives of so many people in different generations," Gordon has "the pattern always quite clear in her mind." She naturally sympathizes with her characters but "she does no pleading for them, preserving her objectivity quite successfully. Her prose is polished and rhythmic, a good instrument."

7 DANIELS, JONATHAN. "Love of Earth." SatR (21 November), p. 309.
Reviews Penhally. "Though 'Penhally,' the plantation is the true protagonist..., the novel is a genealogy of hard-bitten commonsense and quixotic passions in the vivid and diverse Llewellyns from the first bitterness at the breaking of the patriarchial ideal to a final desperation when at last and forever the land is lost to the blood." Hence, there is "something almost Biblical" about this novel. Against the background of a sort of "Southern exodus" Gordon "has built her story firmly out of patterns like the dramas of Isaac and Jacob, and Abel and Cain," using the following Biblical elements: the diverse tribe, the intermixed blood, the passionate determination to hold the land, the half brother, and finally, the fratricide. "The ultimate tragedy comes, not because of this hardbitten commonsense [the decision to sell the land] but because of a love of earth, fine and beautiful but, in a world of material standards and farming impotence, quixotic." The

novel is "the best American treatment...in that field of modern fiction associated commonly with Mr. Galsworthy's Forsytes." Gordon points human weakness "by a penetrating native comedy." Perhaps the best scene is that in which Nicholas, who accepts slaves as property, "kills a Yankee soldier who is tormenting a Negro hag." Yet Gordon is "not quite so successful in writing the modern portions of her story as she is in recreating the past. Old Nicholas dead possesses more reality than his heirs living, but old Nicholas Llewellyn is a supreme character for any book."

8 FORD, FORD MADOX. "A Stage in American Literature." Bookman 74:371-76; portrait, 384.

Reviews Penhally in a larger context. France has always had a literary tradition; England has "no movement" in literature now and "above all there is no Movement" there; but in the United States there is "something like a literary movement" today, and it is "being reinforced by the South." The publication of Penhally marks "a very definite stage in the evolution of American literature" and Gordon is one of the five American writers who interest Ford most. "As befits the work of a woman who has served a long apprenticeship to her art Penhally, though dealing with the tragedy of a race and the disappearance of a deeply in-bitten civilization, is a work of great composure and tranquility." It deserves the label "novel" and "is the best American novel that I know," though this statement "need not be taken as appraising." Penhally "curiously unites attributes" of The Spoils of Poynton, The Red Badge of Courage, and The House of the Seven Gables, and is "an achievement at once of erudition and of sombre and smouldering passion." It is "the epic of a house and its fugitive generations of inhabitants" and "the doom is pronounced in the first few words." It "differs from other historical works" in that Gordon has "lived herself into the past of her race and region"; hence, the novel "is a piece of autobiography," a "chronicle of reality," a "great literary achievement."

9 MOORE, VIRGINIA. "The Changing South." Nation (7 October), pp. 367-68.

Reviews Penhally. Gordon "produces in the reader by cumulative effect a sad and powerful sense of changing time and interrupted destiny" in the old South where the unit "was the family and not the individual." The novel is neither sentimental nor disparaging. Gordon has "taken the middle way of implicit praise and censure, of divination by sympathy, of sensitive observation and honest reporting." The truth about the South "is a question of relation and

1931

(MOORE, VIRGINIA)
proportion," as Gordon has realized. "Her characters are not saints and villains." John Llewellyn is "the finest single study in a complex book." Chance has "no call" to murder his brother and, "indeed, that final violence leaves me not entirely convinced. Like the last third of the book it is not quite so clearly and solidly motivated as the rest of the story." One would prefer "the quiet rehearsal of quiet events...to carry the quiet meaning to its modern, tragic, and humiliating conclusion," but nonetheless, Penhally is "a novel far above the ordinary" and important "because it condemns by worthier example" novels of the South which are "too saccharine or too brutal." It "approaches in excellence" Elizabeth Madox Roberts' novels of Kentucky and is similar to Stark Young's River House. Gordon's mind "is in quality distinguished and lovely."

10 SCOTT, EVELYN. Review of Penhally. New Republic (4 November), pp. 332-33.

Penhally is a "slightly mazy" account. "This is an intricate group history; and to cram, within the 282 pages of the book, the suggestive happenings which will chronicle it, has been a problem in rigorous selection of matter." Joan Parrish "from abroad" plays an important role in the end of the novel. Told in "impressionistic flashes, episodically," Penhally gives "an illusion of contemporaneity to nineteenth and twentieth-century happenings." Gordon's method "demands close-ups and dwarfs perspective, which becomes as difficult for the reader as for a person in the midst of events." Only in the end does "the continuity of Penhally emerge through the confusion of the existences that have been bound to it." There are some "quite perfect scenes" but the pattern of relations is "of a somewhat conventionalized kind, so that the effect of the whole book, despite pictorial realism, is not quite actual enough to move deeply." One wishes the emotions were not "so tightened" by the design, and that Gordon would describe human feelings as freely as she interprets the exterior world.

1932 A BOOKS - NONE

1932 B SHORTER WRITINGS

1 ANON. Review of Penhally. American Mercury 25 (April), xxiv.

Briefly reviews Penhally, "a good piece of work until the last scene." Gordon "has not prepared the ground for the easy-going Chance's desperate defiance of his elder brother." Yet this is a "small matter in a book that depicts so faithfully and so effectively the changing South."

2 ANON. Review of Penhally. Pittsburgh Morning Bulletin (January), p. 4.
"The house always holds the center of the stage."

1934 A BOOKS - NONE

1934 B SHORTER WRITINGS

1 ANON. "Portrait of Sportsman." NYTBR (2 December), p. 7.
Reviews Aleck Maury, Sportsman. "This novel in autobiographical form might be labeled an action story, but only on the most superficial consideration. Actually it is a novel of character, and an exceptionally good one, with portraiture of the same high level of excellence" as in Penhally.

2 ANON. Review of Alec Maury, Sportsman. Springfield (Mass.) Republican (16 December), p. 7.
Brief mention. Discusses Aleck Maury as "a man portrayed by a woman as a man would see him and as men are." The novel is "a man's book by a woman." "A sporting novel is one thing, a novel of outdoor sport is another, and a novel which is the biography of a sportsman is yet another": Gordon's is the latter. There is integral unity in this "chronicle of 70 years of a man's human and spiritual existence." This is "a good book at any time for a man to whom sport and the life of the outdoors call."

3 GRUENING, MARTHA. "The Vanishing Individual." Hound and Horn 7:317-35.
Reviews fourteen novels by younger American novelists, among them Penhally. Gordon is one of "the most propagandist regionalists whose work is definitely tied up with the Southern Agrarian movement." Penhally, "the outstanding novel of this group," is a "pageant" which "fails to be moving except as this convention of glamor over the chivalrous South and filial piety in regard to it make it so." There is in Penhally "a surprising lack of human forms and human faces," though there is "skill in marshalling the forces of the pageant." One accepts the hurried pace hoping to "come upon a meaning," but only to arrive at "the unsufficiently motivated and unconvincing violence of the final murder." Gordon returns here to the Edwardian

1934

(GRUENING, MARTHA)
tools of fiction though uses them more skillfully than the Edwardians. Penhally gives us the house, but inadequately helps us to deduce the human beings who lived there. The novel is a "brilliant apologia for the life of the Southern ruling class." Only one memorable character [Lucy] is drawn in the round, "in slight episodes." Though her double betrayal by love "is never made quite clear," in her implacable refusal to view the body of her dead son, "we see her most clearly."

4 HANSEN, HARRY. Introduction to O. Henry Memorial Award: Prize Stories of 1934. Edited by Harry Hansen. Garden City, N. Y.: Doubleday, Doran and Co., pp. vii-xi.
Caroline Gordon is awarded Second Prize for "Old Red"; First Prize goes to Louis Paul for "No More Trouble for Jedwick"; and "third place" to William Faulkner for "Wash." One judge found "Old Red" superior to Paul's story. "This is an excellent character study, well written in spite of dots and dashes. The old good-for-nothing knew pretty well what things of this earth were worthwhile. The author has imagination and sensitiveness." Another judge regarded "Old Red" as "in some respects finer" than Paul's story, but "less well done in detail."

5 PATERSON, ISABEL. Review of Aleck Maury, Sportsman. New York Herald Tribune Books (4 November), p. 6.
Summarizes much of the plot. Aleck is "Early American, just sufficiently adapted to the nineteenth century to earn a fair wage in a routine occupation." The novel is "serene, unpretentious, but accomplished."

1935 A BOOKS - NONE

1935 B SHORTER WRITINGS

1 ANON. Review of Aleck Maury, Sportsman. Booklist 31 (January), 167.
Very brief mention. This "autobiographical novel" is "entirely lacking in nature sentimentality."

2 ANON. Review of Aleck Maury, Sportsman. Nation (9 January), p. 55.
A brief note. The novel is "more than a technical achievement to be admired for the manner in which it makes use of a thousand details pertaining to the angler's art." It is, "more interestingly, an account of one man's wise

and quiet way of life," though Gordon does not insist on Aleck's "secret" about how to live with dignity, serenity, and form: namely, with moderation--not the spleen, petulance or passions "which flap in the pages of many a contemporary Georgia or Mississippi fable." This is "one of the most distinguished and beautiful novels to come out of the South in recent years, and as a document supporting the Southern Idea--if it is that at all--it is worth tons of polemic literature, agrarian, libertarian, unreconstructivist, or what not."

3 LYTLE, ANDREW. "The Passion of Alex [sic] Maury." _New Republic_ (2 January), pp. 227-28.

Reviews _Aleck Maury, Sportsman_. About the events of the society represented in this novel there is "the magnitude of a great wake" at which this society "foregathered to bid farewell to itself." _Aleck Maury_ "is the history of a passion. But it is on no small sentimental scale." Rather it is "a prose Aeneid" written with economy and constraint so that the reader is aware only at the end that Aleck is a "hero." Further explores the epic parallels. "In his own way [Aleck] lives a complete life that no dilettante of field and stream and no professional sportsman ever knows." The novel is a "difficult technical feat." "After sociological and propaganda novels, here is a purer type of fiction."

4 WARREN, ROBERT PENN. "The Fiction of Caroline Gordon." _Southwest Review_ 20 (January), 5-10.

Reviews _Aleck Maury, Sportsman_ within a larger discussion of Gordon's talent which "may be termed _intensive_ rather than _extensive_." The extensive talent "works by accumulating illustration" and "primarily depends for its success on the degree of structural sense the writer possesses and the degree to which the writer is committed to a single vigorous leading conception by which situations can be defined." An intensive talent is "exhaustively aware of the immediate richness and implication of the single scene." Whereas "the _extensive_ treatment triumphs in its logic, its exposition," the _intensive_ treatment "triumphs in its poetry, that is, in its sudden and illuminating perception, which can re-order a body of experience." The special power of _Aleck Maury, Sportsman_ "inheres in the development of this treatment." His passion for fishing "dominates his life and sustains him." It is "the constant, rich, and abiding factor" in his chronicle. "The real force of the novel derives from something other than the overt objective ["a simple chronicle"]: there is the sense of a full and intense emotional life, which is never

(WARREN, ROBERT PENN)
insisted upon, rarely stated, but implied, somehow, on almost every page. The birth of the first child, the drowning of the son, and the death of the wife are scenes unsurpassed in contemporary fiction for discipline of execution or fullness of effect." Gordon's fiction is never "personal in a bad sense, that is, mannered and trademarked." The success of Aleck Maury, Sportsman "is that it is not Caroline Gordon's novel, but, after all, the autobiography of Aleck Maury."

1937 A BOOKS - NONE

1937 B SHORTER WRITINGS

1 ANON. "After the Big Wind." Time (1 March), pp. 70, 72, portrait.
Reviews None Shall Look Back, which "came out in the wake of that typhoon of best-sellers, Gone With the Wind." It "blew a nearer, straighter course than its circling predecessor" but "could not be rated a first-class gale." The "domestic pictures" are much more successful than the war episodes which involve "real but rarely actualized figures...marred by many a lampy smudge." The "real hero" is Forrest. To "rescue him from the half-oblivion in which he lurks," the author "pens many a panegyric page," and "sometimes lets her feminine enthusiasm get the better of military idiom, as when she speaks of Forrest's horse as being 'shot out from under him.'"

2 ANON. "Caroline Gordon." Wilson Bulletin for Librarians 12 (September), 10.
This very brief biographical sketch, with portrait by Rose Chavanne, describes Gordon's physical appearance, background, and life on the farm near Clarksville, Tennessee. "Charades are a favorite recreation and she is clever at organizing really amusing ones, as she never discards an article that might be used for a costume and is ever ready to produce exciting words." Gordon is "intolerant toward social decadence and passionately upholds the traditions of the South." She has "extensive knowledge of Southern history and during the writing of None Shall Look Back documented the historical references with...inexhaustible patience."

3 ANON. "Civil War Again Theme of Novel." Springfield (Mass.) Republican (28 March), p. 7.

Reviews None Shall Look Back. Though "not quite epic in scope," the novel is "entirely dispassionate in its attitude" toward the Civil War, "indicating in more than an incidental way the issues fundamentally in dispute." Forrest is "the outstanding figure of the narrative as a whole, though not improbably some of the lesser persons will fix themselves more lastingly in the reader's sympathies and memory." Military matters are "discriminatingly and skillfully handled"; they are pertinent and "contribute interpretation." Simultaneously, life among "the noncombatants back home" goes on, "touched by the war, sometimes directly."

4 ANON. "Literary Guerrilla." Time (1 November), pp. 86-87.
Reviews The Garden of Adonis. Gordon "belongs to that well-educated guerrilla band of Southern regionalists who about a decade ago took up where the Confederate Army left off in its fight against the Yankee cultural and economic invasion." In her earlier work Gordon followed "the approved regionalist tactics of firing from the safely concealed ambush of the South's past." In The Garden of Adonis she "opens up at close contemporary range to kill off the Yankee opinion which attributes the evils of sharecropping to Southern landlords." The narrative "is as involved as the writing is simple," employing shifts of setting and consciousness. The "chaotic literary result of these shifts" is not comparable, one presumes Gordon would say, to the "living chaos of Southern life since the invasion of the North." The implication of the novel is that "if plantation life still offered its pre-Civil War social opportunities," the events of the novel would not have occurred.

5 ANON. "The New Novels: American Civil War Tales." TLS (7 August), p. 575.
None Shall Look Back and Royce Brier's Boy in Blue are briefly reviewed. Treatment of the Civil War in fiction "has become so conventionalized that it demands an especial act of the imagination to break out of the rut and achieve originality." None Shall Look Back is "a clear case of the way in which even a highly gifted writer, failing such liberation, may find the effect of her evident abilities qualified if not nullified." The novel is "above the average in its kind, yet never quite comes creatively to life." Characters and incidents derive from other stories of the Confederacy. "The whole is very well written with what one accepts as broad historical accuracy," and "the characters have within their limits, that individual life which a capable actor can always give to a

1937

(ANON.)
conventional part." Yet every emotion and almost "each incident save in its local variation, is known beforehand." "One seeks in vain in these pages" for imagination, authentic newness. The characters are not "impelling enough to dominate the war" nor are the issues and the outline of the war ever "stated with sufficient clarity" to order the whole "into something like adequate form."

6 ANON. Notice of None Shall Look Back. The Open Shelf (Cleveland). (March), p. 8.
A one-sentence précis.

7 ANON. "Owners and Tenants in Southern States." Springfield (Mass.) Republican (26 December), p. 7.
Reviews The Garden of Adonis. Gordon's purpose is not to critique the tenant-farmer system but to "depict a set of persons all in the same 'mess'" and this, "as much through individual character and temperament as through the effects of any 'system.'" Perhaps the "word 'sordid' serves as well as any to characterize roughly the 'atmosphere' created by the attitudes and doings" of the four groups associated in the tale. "There is valid human nature in the behavior of the persons in the story and an understanding of it in the author," especially in the "sound psychology that motivates the unexpected tragedy" which engulfs Allard and Ote Mortimer.

8 ANON. Review of None Shall Look Back. Booklist 33:243.
Brief review. The novel is "not another Gone With the Wind," though it offers "some episodes of definite power"--the eulogistic portrait of Forrest and the military action around Donelson and Chickamauga. "A traditional Southern romance" with "an element of noble tragedy," the novel is "smooth flowing, sincere, and readable, but lacking in unity."

9 ANON. Review of None Shall Look Back. CathW 145 (July), 508.
Gordon's "vital" and "masterly new novel" in which Rives Allard, on whom the "plot hinges" and his "sad and lovely" wife Lucy are surrounded by "the clearly drawn figures of a blasted family and a disintegrated society." "The outstanding achievement of this book is in its power, through sheer truthfulness, to enable us to live another life in another era, and thus to enter into a new understanding of our country and a greater sympathy with our neighbor."

10 ANON. Review of None Shall Look Back. Nation (20 March), p. 332.

Brief review. The novel is "shorter, less verbose, less spectacular" than Gone With the Wind by which Civil War novels "seem destined to be measured." "The narrative flows less freely, the details are not so lavish; and there is more intelligence," of a "distinguished and excellent sort." The climax is the Battle of Chickamauga. The battle scenes "have a power and passion lacking and perhaps necessary in other sections of the book." For example, the beginning of the romance between Rives and Lucy is muted; hence, "there is not sufficient contrast at the end when the war is lost and the old life is ended and Rives is dead." Gordon may have been more interested in Forrest than in Rives. Forrest is a satisfying heroic figure, who will cause "an admirable novel to be remembered" despite its faults of "understatement and restraint but never of sentimentality or cheap melodrama."

11 ANON. Review of None Shall Look Back. Newsweek (20 February), p. 39.

The novel is "inevitably compared" with Gone With the Wind which sells "at the rate of 10,000 a day," yet there "should be satisfactory profits in None Shall Look Back." "Like Margaret Mitchell, Caroline Gordon writes of places and people she knows," from the vantage point of her home overlooking the Cumberland Valley. Forrest is "the giant of this story." He is "only one of many historic officers revealed in the magnificent battle scenes." In addition, the chief characters are Fontaine Allard, Lucy Churchill, and Rives Allard. "Through them and a confusion of relations, Miss Gordon shows the terror, suffering, and ruin which the invading Northern armies brought to the South." The reader may toward the end "find the din of battle too continuous" or regret that Gordon "didn't cut her cast and develop a few individuals more thoroughly." Parts are "memorable" yet "even the thunder of guns doesn't explain the absence of someone like Scarlett O'Hara." Photograph of Gordon.

12 ANON. Review of None Shall Look Back. Wisconsin Library Bulletin 33 (April), 86-87.

Very brief mention. "Now and then the continuity of the book is marred by alternate chapters treating different groups," but the reader is never released from "the feeling of the horror of war and what it does to countries and individuals."

1937

13 BENÉT, STEPHEN VINCENT. "The Long Shadow of Bedford Forrest." New York Herald Tribune Books (21 February), p. 3.

Reviews None Shall Look Back. The Western war, the subject of Gordon's book, "has been relatively neglected in Civil War fiction." The action of the novel centers around Donelson and Chickamauga, and the fascinating "shadow of Forrest is long across the book": a general considered by Sherman "'the most remarkable man the Civil War produced on either side.'" Yet Gordon's "fictional plot is neither as alive nor as unusual as Forrest's own story." The canvas is "overcrowded with minor figures" and "the main fictional characters seem faint." The obligatory scenes of war, love, and family, though often well handled and honestly described, "remain individual sketches rather than part of a whole." The Rives-Lucy love affair "seems more of a convenience than a necessity," the characters "more vivid apart than together," and neither as vivid as Forrest, Ben Bigstaff, or the spy, James Paul. The book lacks unity and "the drive and march of successful narrative." The story "really never gets going," except in spots and flashes: Rowan's death, Rives' capture, the battle of Chickamauga. "Too many characters who have no importance to the narrative are introduced for brief appearances, where they speak a line or so and then leave the stage." The final impression is that of a series of "interesting but separate scenes, selected almost at random." When Forrest appears he overpowers the book and the other fictional characters as well. However, in individual passages Gordon's "ability as a writer is obvious": e.g., Spencer Rowe's characterization, the last view of Forrest, and "half a dozen other bits of description." Moreover, there is "a moving sense of inevitable ruin in the last section of the book." Yet the shifts of point of vision and of focus of importance are disturbing. In this Gordon is not so successful as Evelyn Scott in The Wave where "the hero was the war itself"; or as Margaret Mitchell whose "heroine was never out of sight." In None Shall Look Back the background and the foreground "war against each other and neither quite attains a resolution." Portrait of Gordon.

14 BOUGHTON, JAMES. Review of The Garden of Adonis. New York Herald Tribune Books (31 October), p. 10, portrait.

"The book oddly interrupts itself in the middle with a totally different story." Gordon has in the past proved that she can control the design of her novels, but here "she has two novels in one, not integrated successfully nor either of them separately as rich in development and depth as they might be."

*15 BRIGHOUSE, HAROLD. Review of None Shall Look Back. Manchester (England) Guardian (7 July), p. 7.
[Cited in Book Review Digest, 1937.]

16 BUTCHER, FANNY. Review of None Shall Look Back. Chicago Daily Tribune (20 February), p. 8.
The novel is not "a new 'Gone With the Wind'"; "the treatment is wholly different." Whereas Gone With the Wind was "primarily the story of one woman's surcharged and fate filled life, and through her eyes the reader saw the historic panorama," Gordon's novel "is the panorama itself... essentially a great, and terrible force going its own inevitable way." The novel has "memorable historic scenes" of the escape from Fort Donelson, of women's tragedy. None Shall Look Back is "like a print of the civil war with every minute figure, every cannon, every shattered tree brought to life."

17 CARSWELL, CATHERINE. Review of None Shall Look Back. The Spectator (2 July), p. 32.
A one-page review of six novels including None Shall Look Back. In presenting her picture of the Civil War, Gordon "has elected to introduce its famous figures rather as points and landmarks than as individuals with whom we can become intimate." Instead, the Allards "are supplied as our mirror, and they are so well supplied that they have a reality impossible to historical figures not shaped by a poet who is also a dramatist." The novelist's first interest is a ramified family. "Here is one way of writing historical fiction."

18 CLARK, WILLIAM H. "None Shall Look Back." Boston Transcript (27 February), p. 3.
The South has become a "popular subject." None Shall Look Back is "as excellent a novel of its kind as has appeared in many years." To her familiarity with the South, the author "adds the polish of newspaper experience." The novel is "both superbly descriptive and magnificently moving while her characters are entirely adequate to sustain the burden of recreating" the Civil War. Forrest is "the giant of the piece." Rives and Lucy are the most important Allards. "However, while the war is the major motif, mass murder is not the whole plot." Through the love romances and scenes of the "vanished life of the period," Gordon creates a "complete canvas" with the final ironic emphasis of Jim's entry into "the industrialism which is now coming of age."

1937

19 COLLINS, DOROTHEA BRANDE. "None Shall Look Back." American Review 8:497-501.

Reviews None Shall Look Back, which "truly demands praise." It is shapely, vital, and illuminating, and "written in a style so perfectly suited to its matter that it goes straight to that heaven of all true lovers of style." Rives' "emergence from adolescence" surpasses other such narratives. The novel though evidently well documented does not convey "the feeling that it was written with works of reference open at her elbow." For the Northern reader the illumination of the novel in part dispels the notion of the "unimaginative ignorance of the South" without "descending into the raucousness and implausibility of most propaganda." Yet the novel "does not suffer because it carries this 'social' effect." Here is "prose beyond praise," in which the past is re-presented "by some enchantment." "It is undoubtedly that suitability of every sentence to what it is meant to convey that is the secret of Miss Gordon's effect."

20 FORD, FORD MADOX. "None Shall Look Back." [Scribner's Bookbuyer (?): an in-house review published by Charles Scribner's Sons], March, pp. 5-6.

Gordon is "for me the most mysterious of writers." Though her "outside-the-study activities" are vivid, brilliant, even clamorous, "her calm self...gets itself into her writings." To have a permanent effect the Southern Literary Movement "must be based on solid, on convincing, on erudite groundings. It must have its classical side. And that is what is mysterious about Mrs. Tate. Her Southern mansions are burned by unimpassioned men from Michigan with no more outcry than will attend upon a Westchester public funeral." Only when you have finished reading None Shall Look Back do you realize that "you have been present at a very horrid affair." The novel "is most of all a landscape," as is The Iliad. "You are suspended above a great territory.... Below you run men in grey or blue, goring the gentle bosom of the earth...and beside you, as if herself watching, Mrs. Tate remains mysterious, unimpassioned, almost impartial as the tragic destiny unrolls itself beneath you both." In its method of attack, the novel resembles War and Peace, but "lacking Tolstoi's moral point of view and his rather transparent military solecisms it is really a better book against War." It "has a peculiar quality of tranquility" with "no single harrowing scene," and embodies the "great lesson that all artists must learn before they can write tragedies--that if your approach to horror is not that of the quiet and collected observer and renderer you will fail in attaining to the real height of tragedy."

21 J., H. M. Review of The Garden of Adonis. SatR (6 November), pp. 19-20.

The novel "derives its title from a quotation out of 'The Golden Bough' describing the baskets or pots filled with earth which were tended chiefly by women, and whose plants, fostered by the sun's heat, sprang up rapidly but, being rootless, soon withered away." The "moral of the story is here implied: the transitory satisfactions which come to the personages of the novel who have various love affairs are spiritual gardens of Adonis." The theme is not new, but the characters are vivid, the setting gives significance, and the lower class Southern speech rhythms are accurate. However, there are two major difficulties: the structural discontinuity in the treatment of Ote Mortimer while Jim Carter is introduced and followed; and the novel's final failure to reach tragic depths of passion and defeat [as, for example, Paul Green's work does]. The Garden of Adonis is "thoughtful, intelligent, restrained; but it is never quite good enough to be memorable....technical excellence in the details is made an unconscious substitute for the organic demands of art of the first order."

22 NEVINS, ALLAN. "War in Tennessee." SatR (20 February), p. 6, portrait.

Reviews None Shall Look Back. Forrest comes late into the novel but dominates it through the impression he makes on "its hero," Rives. "One of Miss Gordon's real achievements is a vivid and arresting, if incomplete, presentation" of Forrest. In the last chapter, "the invented hero of the book, Rives, lies dead on the field" but "the real hero, the great cavalry leader [is] still in the field, still pushing on." Yet "of plot the book has little; a few scenes of ante-bellum Kentucky, a few love-passages, a marriage, and then the war swallows all private lives." Characterization "is not elaborate or convincing." Few readers are likely to feel that Rives, Lucy, or Fontaine "ever really existed." Moreover, the "action is too episodic, and the point of view is changed too frequently and abruptly." The novel "never achieves unity of effect, never crystallizes." Its chief merits are patches of admirable writing and the portrait of Forrest. While "eminently readable," None Shall Look Back does not earn "a place among the better pieces of Civil War fiction."

23 PORTER, KATHERINE ANNE. "Dulce et Decorum Est." New Republic (31 March), pp. 244-45.

Reviews None Shall Look Back. Miss Porter begins by comparing and contrasting the beginning and the ending of

(PORTER, KATHERINE ANNE)
the novel. Jim Allard is represented as the "truly defeated man," the opportunist, whereas Gordon's "story is a legend in praise of heroes, of those who fought well and lost their battle, and their lives." Miss Porter celebrates heroism and the need for it, as well as Gordon's pride in such devotion. "All-seeing as an ancient chronicler, she has created a panorama of a society engaged in a battle for its life," and she "moves about, a disembodied spectator timing her presence expertly." Gordon has chosen to "observe from all points of view" and so the scenes "move rapidly"; "the effect could easily have become diffuse without firm handling, and the central unalterable sympathies of the chronicler herself." Gordon did not do the "neat conventional thing" of telling the story through the adventures of the young lovers, Lucy and Rives. Their tragedy is only a part of the larger tragedy; "the book is not theirs, nor was it meant to be." "There is no accounting for Forrest and Miss Gordon does not attempt the impossible. He remains what he was, a hero and a genius." In the novel, "the Allard family is a center,...a point of departure and return." The end of each member of the family is "symbolically exact": imbecility, grief, death, dry rot, numbness--in contrast to what Kentucky planters and their families were "born to be" [as the reader has seen in the novel]. The Kentucky tone is "here, properly." None Shall Look Back is "in a great many ways a better book" than Penhally or Aleck Maury; here, Gordon's "style" is at its best.

24 R., W. K. Review of None Shall Look Back. Christian Science Monitor (8 March), p. 16.
The story centers "most of all in Lucy" and Rives Allard. They, and "the large family and local groups with which their lives were interlocked, are soundly imagined and portrayed." The "emphasis is on actual fighting and military strategy." The story "of these imagined characters, well composed and reasonably presented, appeals to the intelligence of the reader, but it does not stir his emotions as much as does the actual history of General Forrest." Three times Forrest stands out "in dramatic contrast to his fellow-generals": at Donelson when he leads his cavalry to safety; when he pleads with Bragg to let him "attack Burnside before Rosecrans [can] get his troops out of Chattanooga"; and the reader's last vision of him, when he gallops across the plain straight to the Federal fortifications. The novel has a "transparent, quietly effective but not lively style."

25 TUCKER, AUGUSTA. "Southern Conflicts." NYTBR (7 November), p. 7, portrait.
Reviews The Gardon of Adonis. "As a sociological document" the novel is "a provocative study." Gordon's intention is "to show the Southern share-cropper, the plantation owner, and the industrialist in conflict and in character; to explore their strata in relation to economic dependence and emotional outlook." In terms of the conflict, Gordon has succeeded, but "in creating character to display it she has, for me, failed. I do not see her people." The only two characters of consequence are Ote Mortimer and Ben Allard. Ote's murder of Ben is "a Faulknerian twist, but without the Faulknerian wrist." Other characters come to life only "for the flicker of a paragraph" which fades in the spreading of the scenes. "Numerous and unnecessary" characters not "hinged into the plot" should have been eliminated. For example, "there is a long description and scene involving a farmer turned preacher which seems unrelated to the plot, and...there comes to visit at the plantation house an amusing enough Southern windbag who has no part in the general scheme of the novel." If Gordon believes, as perhaps her epigraph indicates, that Southern society is "an unstable conglomeration of boring and irresponsible people, this book fulfills her purpose." Her characters have "none of the clarity" of Elizabeth Madox Roberts' or of "Ellen Glasgow's finished portraits." The flashback device on which Gordon leans should not be turned to "until her character is completely alive." Gordon is "best at old men, but she can only tell you what happened to them, and never, with that indefinable insight, permit you to know them as they once were"--which Ellen Glasgow does. Yet Gordon has attempted a "desperately difficult task" in trying to write of the contemporary scene.

26 VAN DOREN, MARK. "Fiction of the Quarter." SoR 3:159-82.
Reviews seventeen current novels by different authors, among them None Shall Look Back [two pages], in terms of whether or not each has exercised "its primary function": the telling of "a story about certain persons who, as the action advances, become known to us as individuals"; in other words, whether the novel has "substantiality." None Shall Look Back has "still greater excellence": "every detail is life-like," which is perhaps why some persons "find it difficult to read," since Gordon has not "led them by the nose." Her characters "go about their own business in a fashion rare to fiction," and the author "refrains from intruding a style." She has done here "what every novelist would do if he could, and what perhaps one in a hundred does. She has been real."

1937

27 WALTON, EDITH H. "Miss Gordon's Civil War Novel." NYTBR (21 February), p. 6.

Reviews None Shall Look Back, "a distinguished addition to the fiction dealing with that theme," and the "most ambitious" of Gordon's novels. Her style is "vastly superior" to Margaret Mitchell's, and her battle scenes are equal in clarity and brilliance to MacKinlay Kantor's. Gordon is seldom "unduly sentimental," and plantation life here is neither cloying nor prettified. Yet the novel "is not quite the book it should be," failing to move and excite "as much as one might expect." Gordon does not focus interest sufficiently on any character or group of characters. The "real hero" is Forrest, and the Kentucky Allards are only "dim, inadequate symbols of the South's suffering and doom." Chickamauga is "the high point, the climax of the novel. The rest is tragedy." Gordon has chosen to "dwell on the slow collapse of the Confederacy rather than on the fortunes of private individuals," but "sacrifices a good deal in doing so." Such a story needs a pivot for sympathies, and "neither Rives nor Lucy will serve." Both "become more and more shadowy" as the novel progresses: in the end, Rives is "merely a convenient medium" for the portrayal of Forrest, while Forrest himself is "too remote a figure." Any novel "must have as its center a compelling drama of individual fortunes as well as a larger theme." A "good story is essential," as Gone With the Wind has "abundantly proved." Moreover, having chosen the panoramic view, Gordon "might have dealt more explicitly with the issues at stake": "why they fought, and for what." Yet, "there is always a danger of being unfair to a book of superior caliber." None Shall Look Back is disappointing largely because it promised so well, "and essayed a much more significant theme" than Aleck Maury. It "belongs with the half-dozen really good novels of the Civil War which have appeared during the last decade." Portrait of Gordon.

1938 A BOOKS - NONE

1938 B SHORTER WRITINGS

1 GLASGOW, ELLEN. A Certain Measure: An Interpretation of Prose Fiction. New York: Harcourt, Brace, and Co., p. 147.

Gordon is one of "an impressive group of Southern writers" who "after breaking away from a petrified past overgrown by a funereal tradition...recoiled from the uniform concrete surface of an industrialized South"; and "it is significant that, for the first time in its history, the

South is producing, by some subtle process of aversion, a literature of revolt."

1941 A BOOKS - NONE

1941 B SHORTER WRITINGS

1 ANON. Notice of Green Centuries. The Open Shelf (Cleveland). (December), p. 24.
A nine-word précis.

2 ANON. Review of Green Centuries. Booklist 38 (December), 113.
Brief mention. "It is a robust story, with real characters."

3 ANON. Review of Green Centuries. Springfield (Mass.) Republican (21 December), p. 7.
Brief mention. Discusses Gordon's "usual capacity for detail," her "flowingly pictorial" prose, and her familiarity with the terrain. "Her characters have body--of mind, purpose, and imagination as well as three dimensions." The "action is slow gathering and never inspires that can't-leave-it-alone state," yet Gordon "takes firm and honest hold of her reader."

4 ANON. Review of Green Centuries. Wisconsin Library Bulletin 37 (December), 201.
Brief notice. The novel is "very detailed and gives a good picture of frontier life, although horrors are piled on rather thick toward the end." Rion "carries the burden of the story."

5 BENÉT, STEPHEN VINCENT. "Land Beyond the Mountains." New York Herald Tribune Books (2 November), p. 4.
Reviews Green Centuries, an "excellent, sensitive and thorough historical novel" that "deals with a period that presents peculiar difficulties for the writer of fiction." We have a stereotyped image of the frontiersman but "the truth about him is a good deal harder to get at." Gordon renders "the Indians as human beings, not merely as painted adversaries or speechifying Noble Savages," and gets "into the skin of her period to an unusual degree." Actual historical characters "are naturally introduced and walk on their own feet." The novel is weakest "in its final section. Too many catastrophes fall upon the main characters too suddenly." When it comes to "the almost accidental

(BENÉT, STEPHEN VINCENT)
unfaithfulness of Rion and its consequences," the reader "is bound to feel that Miss Gordon is merely putting the big pot on the little one. It is a failure of construction, not a failure of fact," but it is her "only failure of construction" in an otherwise "distinguished, vivid and continuously readable novel."

6 FADIMAN, CLIFTON. Review of Green Centuries. New Yorker (1 November), p. 70.

Brief review. Gordon "doesn't belong either to the curtsy [to our ancestors] or to the skeptical school. Her historical novels don't have much pace, but they do have reality, an interior reality rather than that which comes merely from flawless research." The story "is not exciting nor are the characters complex. What counts is the realness of the scene...the sense Miss Gordon conveys of what Flaubert...meant when he spoke of 'the melancholy of barbarian tribes, with their migratory instincts and their innate loathing of life which compelled them to abandon their country as if they were abandoning themselves.'"

7 WALTON, EDITH H. "The Frontier South." NYTBR (2 November), pp. 4-5.

Reviews Green Centuries. The novel is written with "a gravity, dignity and authority which are wholly characteristic." Increasingly, Gordon "seems to have abandoned the vein of [her] two early books [Penhally and Aleck Maury, Sportsman] and to be adopting the themes and approach of a major novelist." Though a novel of real stature, Green Centuries sometimes seems to lack "human warmth." Despite all its action, it has the same weakness as None Shall Look Back: Gordon's failure "to interest one crucially in any of her characters." They are portrayed "perfunctorily and without real warmth"; only Casey and Rion, and then only in the latter sections of the novel, "suddenly come to life vividly as they have never done before." Otherwise, there is something about the novel that is "a little chill and austere." Yet, on its own terms, Green Centuries is "a superbly rich and authentic picture of life on the frontier, and the kind of men who made it what it was." Gordon knows the Cherokees, and draws them as deftly as she does her white characters.

1942 A BOOKS - NONE

1942 B SHORTER WRITINGS

1 GISSEN, MAX. "Two With Indians, One Without." New Republic (5 January), p. 27.
Reviews three novels, including Green Centuries. "The plain truth" about Gordon's novel "is that it's mighty slow going but pays off in sincerity and page-for-page clear writing," though "the story isn't much or new." "Whole sections of the book are first rate" [e.g., the chapter on the fear and loneliness of a child alone in the wilderness], and the characters are well developed, but Gordon "seems to have been blind to faults that any first novelist wouldn't have been guilty of in his first draft." [Except for references to "conventional situations" that make the last seventy pages "dead weight," these faults are not specified.] "And after 400 pages of going her own quiet way, Miss Gordon recklessly pulls all the stops, as if she had suddenly decided to run to formula. The book is dedicated to Maxwell Perkins, but why wasn't he around?"

1944 A BOOKS - NONE

1944 B SHORTER WRITINGS

1 ANON. "Come, Die Along With Me." Time (22 May), pp. 99-100, 102.
Reviews The Women on the Porch. "Catherine is chief of a dozen characters who move through [the novel] like shrouded figures on their way to the graveyard." The novel is a "desolate, often poignant, hypersensitive study of life in death." Its theme is this: "in the world of today the dead are more alive than the living, memories more tangible than reality." The chief quality of the novel is "a sustained mood of doom that pervades every walk of life," and lives on hopes for and recollections of death. "The cold rage of Author Gordon's mood and prose gives The Women on the Porch literary distinction."

2 ANON. Review of The Women on the Porch. Booklist 40:355.
Brief mention. "Introspective writing for limited audience."

3 ANON. Review of The Women on the Porch. New Yorker (3 June), pp. 73-74.
"The pasts of these three aging women are sketched with great delicacy and sound a ghostly note throughout the

1944

(ANON.)
book," and "it is in her talent for creating by suggestion that Miss Gordon's distinction lies," making the reader feel more than the author tells. It is hard to say why "Miss Gordon has not turned out a wholly satisfactory novel. Perhaps it is because, although a sense of tragedy pervades the book, she seems in the end afraid of tragedy."

4 BULLOCK, FLORENCE HAXTON. "Full of Beauty and Naturalness." New York Herald Tribune Weekly Book Review (7 May), p. 3.
Reviews The Women on the Porch. Misnames Catherine Chapman, "Caroline Chapman." The atmosphere of the novel "is produced in part by echoes and excerpts out of the race's poetic past," from the Greeks and Dante to Hart Crane. It is a "strange, absorbingly fateful novel," with "a nice touch in the handling of animals." The dachshund and stallion "are as vividly alive as any other personalities in the novel."

5 M., L. S. "It's Like O'Neill." Springfield (Mass.) Republican (4 June), p. 4d.
Reviews The Women on the Porch. Discusses briefly the author's use of "the experimental methods once used by Eugene O'Neill with the result that her novel seems a pale copy of O'Neill's Greek complex posturings." The grandmother, aunt, and cousin assume "the cryptic poses of the three fates." Catherine's affair with Tom Manigault is "a decidedly commonplace affair...which not even 'atmosphere' can save from being dully banal." Italicized writing represents "Catherine's subconscious divinings." Despite "some very lovely and lush moments," the novel is "warmed-over O'Neill."

6 PRUETTE, LORINE. "Shadows in Dixie." NYTBR (21 May), p. 6.
Reviews The Women on the Porch, a novel in which "the shadows of the past" sometimes obscure "the lineaments of the present." Gordon's situation is an important, contemporary one: "how shall the reasonably cultivated Southerner make peace with his past, work with his present, live--with some tolerable efficacy--today?" Jim Chapman "is actually much better realized as a character than is Catherine, whose actions seem not so much motivated within herself as shaped by the most casual of circumstances." The "most touching episode...is the one in which Aunt Willy shows the stallion at the fair." Gordon uses "modified stream-of-consciousness technique" to take the reader back and forth in the minds and histories of the characters: this generally diffuses interest. Moreover, the characters

"seem to have been hopelessly damned in their several ways from infancy," though Jim Chapman occasionally seems to matter to the reader; Gordon's writing is the "most sensitive" in the passages devoted to him. The novel is "not quite as heroic as it might have been in its picture of man's fate."

7 ROTHMAN, NATHAN L. "'Escape' to Tennessee." SatR (27 May), p. 24.

Reviews The Women on the Porch, a novel "for those who like fine and evocative writing" ranging "far out to the periphery of experience." Because it is a "rare treat" one will "forgive its limitations" [e.g., the story is very slight and "told neither consecutively nor thoroughly"]. The story-line peeps "in and out of the book like a meandering stream going nowhere, or, better, like a convenient thread, unimportant in itself, with which to tie up" observations, personalities, and "the brilliant single strokes of poetic realization that make up the book." Gordon lavishes upon even minor characters "the ultimate powers of her perception" and in her characterization resembles Joyce and D. H. Lawrence. Her poetry appears "sometimes in a sentence," in a "sustained lyricism" [e.g., a character speaking in solitude], or at a chapter closing [e.g., Chapters 9, 13, 15, 17]. Every page is "marked with her devotion to the craft of writing."

8 STROBEL, MARION. "An Unhappy Marriage." Chicago Sun Times Book Week (21 May), p. 3.

Reviews The Women on the Porch, a "far from casual" novel that invites comparison with the novels of Virginia Woolf. The characters "are illuminated from within." This "vision turned inward" would, "in the hands of a lesser artist, result in confusion. Here, there is none." But the "sterile fascination of the past" and "the brooding retrospect of many eyes looking back on it" may prevent the novel from having a wide appeal, though this will be due chiefly to the fact that the characters "are all neurotics." Only Red, the horse, "has enough heart to win a race."

1945 A BOOKS - NONE

1945 B SHORTER WRITINGS

1 ANON. Review of The Forest of the South. Booklist 42 (1 December), 110.

Brief mention. Most of the stories "have a mood of reminiscence rather than a sense of the present."

1945

2 ANON. Review of The Forest of the South. Kirkus 13:375.
Gordon is "at her best in recapturing that phase of life in the South...where fishing and gunning seem infinitely preferable to the serious business of life." The best stories in this collection are "vignettes of that phase"--that is, the Aleck Maury stories, which "ring a bell of authentic characterization."

3 ANON. Review of The Forest of the South. New Yorker (22 September), p. 78.
Very brief note. "Pace has never distinguished Miss Gordon's work, but on the other hand, few writers have so admirable a talent for creating by suggestion." Gordon makes you "sense a great deal more than she tells."

4 ANON. Review of The Forest of the South. U. S. Quarterly Book List 1 (December), 10.
The three stories dealing with the Civil War "are rather melodramas than fictional achievements." Gordon's South is "a timeless one, marked as it is throughout by a peculiar mode of speech and a fixed set of values [courage, fidelity, and love of nature], the virtues she unobtrusively admires." Into this collection have gone a "delicate ear for the rhythms of Southern speech, subtle accretion of detail, rich inventiveness of incident, and rigid subjection of the material to the point of view." The best of these stories are those in which values express themselves in action, such as "The Captive" and "Her Quaint Honour"; in "The Last Day in the Field" this method is united to natural symbolism.

5 CARRUTHERS, OLIVE. Review of The Forest of The South. The Chicago Sun Book Week (23 September), p. 17.
A capsule review. All the stories are "rich in detail, in verisimilitude, in colloquial idiom, and as charming as one could find in a day's browsing."

6 DANIELS, JONATHAN. "Tales of the South." SatR (27 October), p. 40.
Reviews The Forest of the South. "Even when they are trivial as stories and become mere anecdotes," there is a "flowing vividness about grand folk and plain ones in these stories" that "lifts them into high quality by contrast with most American short stories now being written." However, it is doubtful whether "Miss Gordon is at her best in the short story." Here, "The Captive" is the most effective. Gordon's strength is in the creation of attractive characters; her weakness is that her characters' "exits are often

not quite satisfying." "The Forest of the South" is the "most enjoyable"; though "it is not a great short story," it is almost perfect as an expression of "the dark beauty of the mood of grandeur and grace which disappeared long ago in the American South," or perhaps never existed. Gordon "has coupled a sort of mad majesty with such meticulous realism" that her world seems "more tragically true than any past could have been." Whereas Gordon is "particularly skillful" in characterizing women and boys, only her stories of Aleck Maury were boring: "there I felt a thinness of character, not of story." Maury seems to be "an almost too familiar character" in fiction about "courtly but shrewd elderly men down in Dixie."

7 ENGLE, PAUL. Review of The Forest of the South. Chicago Sunday Tribune (23 September), p. 9.

"A very fine book of short stories. There is ease in the telling, restraint in the planning, and care in the phrasing. Never is the intention of the story compromised for the sake of popular appeal or cheap effect." Each story has "a richness of conception and a measuredness of meaning which makes the book solid, varied, delightful, and original." In "The Ice House" there is "none of the superficial scorn for the carpetbagger which would have made the story simply another example of the southerner's resentment at the exploiting post-war Yankee." Jinny in "The Captive" seems "to have the quality of a gray and ghostly figure in a savage and timeless world, rather than the personality of a plain woman." Aleck Maury is as fine and as forceful in the stories about him as he was in the novel. "Old Red" is especially "handsome" writing. "For the most part the writing [in the collection] is wholly admirable."

8 FARBER, MARJORIE. "Recent Fiction." New Republic (22 October), pp. 543-44.

Includes a review of The Forest of the South. "Preserving certain values indispensable to life and art," the collection "shows how nearly these have disappeared from the urban jungles of the North": namely, a dramatic sense, a sense of character, a sense of history, a tragic sense--all associated "with agrarian life, large families, ancestral piety." Cities cannot develop these "sensuous qualities" which enable Gordon to "treat certain themes long ridiculed in melodrama." The best of the stories "are perhaps the least formal of these anecdotes, concerning the piety and erudition of the sportsman." "Occasionally a formal story fails--by comparison with Miss Gordon's own standards--when it relies on abstract symbol rather than

(FARBER, MARJORIE)
experience"; but, on the other hand, "there is never a pretentious 'success' based on the _idea of experience_" as in the case of writers who so hanker to create works that are "absolutely real and life-like" that like German clock makers they produce works that "tick rather loudly." Gordon is "less ambitious." "All Lovers Love the Spring" is a "miraculous six-page story" of "the felt quality of spinsterhood" and of the tragic limitations of "life on earth, bound in time and defined in death." All this is projected through the "absolute rightness, in context" of the understatement in the camphor reference and through "one vision of pear branches rising up like wands, their petals like festoons of little sea shells still unfolded."

9 KOCH, VIVIENNE. "Regions of the Heart." _Briarcliff Quarterly_ 1:222-27.

Reviews four novels including _The Women on the Porch_, Saul Bellow's _Dangling Man_, Harry Brown's _A Walk in the Sun_, and Jean Stafford's _Boston Adventure_. All "share a basic obsessive quality," and "at least three of them are cast in emotive images of a valued past." In _The Women on the Porch_, Gordon "continues to reveal her absorption in the Southern materials handled so magically" in _Aleck Maury, Sportsman_, and _Penhally_, but here "her frame of reference is extended" from New York to Tennessee and back again. Gordon's New York is "shadowy" compared with her South. Similar to Marianne Moore in authentic knowledge and sensitivity, Gordon writes prose that is "perhaps the most unaffected and yet the most classically accomplished written by any American woman today." Unfortunately, _The Women on the Porch_ "has neither the integration of tone nor of material which gave _The Forest of the South_ its haunting and evocative beauty." It is too ambitious and introduces an "allegorical sociology" which seems extraneous. Jim "is not developed sufficiently as a character for us to judge whether, in his case, deracination was really a cause or an effect of his temperament." Gordon seems to be arguing for "possession by the land"; since this is always an accident of birth, how can a "spiritual imperative" be derived from it? The Catherine-Jim conflict seems "much ado about nothing," whereas "the more fundamental rivalry Miss Gordon meant to draw" is that between the two cultures represented by them. Yet it is "an interesting novel, beautifully written," though the final outlines are "somehow blurred" and unsatisfying. Some of the material in this essay reappears in 1953.B2.

10 MARIELLA, SISTER. Review of The Forest of the South. Commonweal (26 October), pp. 50-51.

Although The Forest of the South is her first volume of short stories, Gordon "has long been recognized as a skilled craftsman of the shorter form of fiction." All that Gordon "does supremely well stems from a single gift: a Thoreau-like passion for the sweet world of her native South." She never points, never exclaims. The best in this collection are "her three superb stories" about Aleck Maury, just as Aleck Maury, Sportsman is "the finest novel of sports and fishermen in American literature." Yet "distinguished" as are the stories in this collection, "they are forgotten almost as soon as the book is closed. It is well to remember that an almost infallible test of greatness is the way a story sticks in the memory." "Summer Dust," for example, "is a series of sketches giving no more than its title promises."

11 MAXWELL, WILLIAM. "Of Southerners and the South." New York Herald Tribune Weekly Book Review (23 September), p. 4.

Reviews The Forest of the South. "Four of the stories in this collection--'The Ice House,' 'The Long Day,' 'The Brilliant Leaves,' and 'All Lovers Love the Spring'--are good. 'Her Quaint Honour' is excellent. The others are slight or, more often, exasperating." Where suspense and surprise are missing, they should be replaced by "smaller tensions, so that the reader, abandoning his interest in the outcome of the story, is completely held by every detail of its architecture." No such tensions occur in these stories. There is a "fundamental honesty" in the writing and in the conception, but this is "frequently canceled out by an equally fundamental dullness": few characters "ever seem to be alive," though "Miss Gordon can create character." Frequently, "one crabbed unwieldly sentence follows another" as if she were trying to "keep her writing low in key, unexciting, unemotional, factual and flat." Admirable effects are gained from this, but not when "carried on ad infinitum." There is also "a regrettable lack of clarity" by "virtue of Miss Gordon's inexplicitness." However, "the action of all these stories is carefully motivated...and the ideas, once they are recognized, are simple and direct." The author also handles "special and exclusively masculine interests" with "absolute first-hand knowledge and as a man would handle them." The woman remembering her girlhood in "All Lovers Love the Spring" may well be Caroline Gordon and her aside may be a key to why some stories are "well written and moving" and "others so unsatisfactory." The little girl tagging along after boys, learning "the secrets

1945

(MAXWELL, WILLIAM)
of the world she is never going to be accepted into, must ultimately pay for knowledge thus acquired by not knowing, at times, what use to make of it."

12 SPENCER, THEODORE. "Recent Fiction." SR 53:297-304.
Reviews fourteen books, among them The Women on the Porch [three paragraphs]. "Not many--if any at all" of these books describe experience "so richly that the experience described is not merely seen as something that happened at one time and in one place, but something that is seen as always happening at all times and in all places." The Women on the Porch "is a serious book, and one applies stiff standards to it in appreciation of the talent and ambition of the author." It is "the best novel that Miss Gordon has written"; its technique is "really professional and fine." However, there is "no catharsis in it, if by catharsis we mean a purgation somewhat different from that of Aristotle." The characters here are victims, whereas "first rate fiction needs a hero or a heroine, however out-of-date it may sound to say so, not a victim."

13 SULLIVAN, RICHARD. "Out of the 'Near South.'" NYTBR (7 October), pp. 6, 26.
Reviews The Forest of the South, a "carefully arranged exhibit of work by a serious artist in prose," and a collection having "almost ponderable integrity" leaving "no gaps." Gordon's writing is "beautifully American" and each story gives a facet of the "near" South. "The Captive" is a "notable" story that deserves "wide recognition" as a "swift narrative rendering of heroic human experience." The grim reality in such a story is "emphasized by the paradoxical expression of violence in matter-of-fact understatement." "The Captive," the Civil War stories, and a few others in the book, particularly "Tom Rivers," represent "the highest accomplishment of that specialized fiction called 'historical.'" Conviction runs through everything in the book; all necessary details of background seem fully known and are, therefore, treated casually. "The Last Day in the Field" is "sound and excellent"; in "The Brilliant Leaves" one can hardly separate the "fatal clumsiness" from the "somber poetry of the setting." In all the stories, there is a "wonderfully indirect handling of frustration." There are "no standardized short story patterns in this book." "Occasional little perversities" [digressions, over-concentrations, obscurities and the like] momentarily break the flow of several stories but do not affect "the solid goodness of the work."

14 VAN DORE, EDRIE. Review of The Forest of the South. Springfield (Mass.) Republican (12 October), p. 8.
Brief mention. "There is not much to distinguish" this collection, except the "bird-hunting atmosphere" and the "poignant" first story. The stories "leave remarkably little imprint on the memory." In "The Captive" monotone is "more effective than any hysteria." The other stories "have an air of cohesion as if they should have been made into a novel." If they had been, the reader might hold in his mind a "more vivid picture."

1946 A BOOKS - NONE

1946 B SHORTER WRITINGS

1 KOCH, VIVIENNE. "The Forest of the South." SR 54:543-47.
Discusses in detail seven stories in this collection which represents a "cross-section" of Gordon's "development as a prose artist." The stories have a "curious psychological depth" and the "invisible canvas of the past" serves as a backdrop "against which the theme is played." Gordon's perspective is "more than merely nostalgia for a lost grandeur"; rather, she fuses the surface, structure, and sensibility of the past in such a way that the past itself acts as "protagonist or agent...always accrueing upon itself." "The Captive" illustrates "the growth of her resourcefulness in dealing with the past"; its particular brilliance is the "subtle blending of the natural and the supernatural." "Old Red," in which the "plot is Time," is representative of "the more mature habits of Miss Gordon's art." "The Forest of the South" illustrates the "heightened connection between interior and exterior event, between environment and character which can only be vaguely suggested by the term symbolism." "Her Quaint Honour" is a powerful example of Gordon's "extraordinarily keen insight into the caste structure of the South." No prose writer except Faulkner "has remained so purely identified" with the forest of the South for "almost two decades."

1947 A BOOKS - NONE

1947 B SHORTER WRITINGS

1 RAGAN, DAVID. "Portrait of a Lady Novelist: Caroline Gordon." Mark Twain Quarterly 8:18-20.
A portrait/interview of Gordon which sees her as conservative, and the "most literary" of Tennessee's novelists.

1947

(RAGAN, DAVID)

Discusses Gordon's physical appearance, her home in Sewanee, her hobbies (gathering mushrooms, gardening, painting), and her interest in the Civil War. Gordon has no favorite among her novels, but Aleck Maury is her favorite character, "'doubtless because the book purports to be an autobiography of my father.'" Gordon does not subscribe to a clipping bureau and so "hardly knows what the critics have to say about her work." She claims: "'My work has never had any serious critical attention, except a few private letters from friends,'" and adds: "'The historical novel cannot be written [now]. Or rather it cannot be read'" because people want twentieth century psychology in novels, not that of an earlier age. "'The majority of novel readers are not capable of the effort it takes to translate yourself into another age.'" Gordon says The Women on the Porch does not symbolize Southern decadence but what happens to old women "'just as often in Michigan and Massachusetts.'" She finds Faulkner "'the only contemporary American novelist who approaches major stature,'" sees Flaubert's influence in Faulkner's work, and thinks the recent renaissance of Southern letters at an end, though it has "'the kind of extra vitality an organism sometimes musters just before death.'"

1949 A BOOKS - NONE

1949 B SHORTER WRITINGS

1 LYTLE, ANDREW. "Caroline Gordon and the Historic Image." SR 17:560-86.

Discusses, in detail, "The Brilliant Leaves" (as an example of the thesis), and six novels: Penhally, Aleck Maury, Sportsman, None Shall Look Back, The Garden of Adonis, Green Centuries, and The Women on the Porch, in terms of the functioning of their particular "historic images." The "legitimate illusion," the creation of which should be the goal of the writer of fiction, "once established, will always give the sense of contemporaneity, of happening before the reader's eye." For this to occur successfully, "the author must first absorb the period of his scene so thoroughly that the accidental restraints of manners and customs become the medium of representation of what is constant in human behavior. The tension between form and subject then becomes right in its strain. But the sense of watching the action as it is taking place, although the primary test, is not enough. There must be for the definition under consideration also some historic image of the whole, which will serve as a center of reference and the selective cast to the author's vision." Writers of Gordon's vision, "have but one subject. On one level hers is in the fullest sense traditional and historic. By this I do not mean what is commonly understood as the 'historic novel': that is, the costume piece or the arbitrary use of certain historic periods dramatized through crucial events." Rather, the "legitimate illusion," as in Gordon's work, is distinguished by the "sense of contemporaneity." The "historic image of the whole allows for a critical awareness of a long range of vision, by equating the given period to the past and the future, sometimes explicitly, sometimes implicitly. This makes the period at once the setting and the choral comment. Such a restriction upon the imagination adds another range of objectivity to the post of observation, another level of intensity to the action [as if the actors while performing expose to the contemporary witness, the reader, the essential meaning of their time]. This is literary irony at a high level. It is the nearest substitute for the religious image." This "historic image" gives the writer "balance and lessens the risk of a faulty vision in that it keeps the scale of observation from being entirely private, or of seeming so." The "historic image" is the "concrete surface" of the writer's myth. "The historic image which is so integral to Miss Gordon's work is not static. Behind it is a myth and the process of rendition [is] dynamic in the sense that the image enlarges as the development of the complication grows." In her novels this sense of growth "distinguishes what is permanent and what there is of change, but always in terms of the human predicament." Reprinted in Lytle's The Hero with the Private Parts. See 1966.B3.

2 WEST, RAY B., JR., and ROBERT WOOSTER STALLMAN, eds. The Art of Modern Fiction. New York: Holt, Rinehart, and Winston, pp. 422-23.

Offers questions and brief comments on "Her Quaint Honour" which is included in this anthology of short stories, short novels, and analyses of longer novels. "We are a rather long while getting into the central scene of this story," which takes its title from Andrew Marvell's "To His Coy Mistress." A key statement in the story is: "It's the curing that tells the tale." The "process of tobacco curing has symbolic significance." Gordon "manipulates her material into symbol."

1950

1950 A BOOKS - NONE

1950 B SHORTER WRITINGS

1. CROMIE, ROBERT. Review of The House of Fiction. Chicago Sunday Tribune (16 July), p. 6.
   Very brief mention. Discusses the contents of the book. The commentaries and biographies "add to the worth of the volume" for the "serious student of the short story form."

2 DAVIS, ROBERT GORHAM. "Inside the Short Story." New York Times Book Review (30 July), p. 4.
   Reviews The House of Fiction, an "admirable anthology," especially the appendices on the art of fiction and the analyses of fifteen stories. The authors' "standards are moral as well as artistic," following their belief that "failures of form are usually also failures in moral sensibility or moral intelligence." Their criticisms of the faults in certain Hemingway, Maugham, Hawthorne, and James stories "do not seem tendentious or dogmatic"; the total effect of the book is affirmative. The authors "try to do for the short story what Aristotle in the 'Poetics' did for Greek tragedy." The collection is "thoroughly traditional," authoritatively representing "the intensive technical and symbolic analysis that the New Criticism developed for poetry." The authors, for example, favor naturalism and symbolism, with the symbols operating "dramatically and descriptively on the naturalistic level." Thus, "purely romantic or allegorical art is rejected," and "because of the emphasis on moral responsibility, the stories are predominantly pathetic or tragic." Six of the nine living American writers included are Southerners.

3 LIND, SIDNEY E. "Advice to the Hungry Reader." New Republic (11 December), p. 22.
   Lists The House of Fiction with very brief comment. This anthology "is probably the first to be grounded avowedly and almost entirely on the principles which Henry James enunciated or implied in the prefaces." The list of authors "is almost definitive for all aspects of the short story." The fifteen appended commentaries are "perceptive" and "the bibliography reflects the direct critical line from James."

4 PEDEN, WILLIAM. "From Poe to Welty." SatR (17 June), p. 18.
   Reviews The House of Fiction. The editors' "selections, without exception, are distinguished," though the section devoted to more recent writers is "the least satisfying of

the entire volume." The appended analyses and criticisms of individual stories, based largely on the views of Henry James, "are occasionally irritating, frequently controversial, and always stimulating." "The editors tend to identify their own critical evaluations with absolute facts and consequently are often unnecessarily dogmatic." [Examples of such declarations are given.] As opinions their comments deserve respect, but they cannot be regarded as categorical statements of fact. Otherwise, The House of Fiction is an "admirable book," perhaps "the best" of similar recent anthologies, all indebted to the work of Cleanth Brooks and Robert Penn Warren. Finally, the essays on certain fictional elements such as point of view or tonal unity are "excellent." The volume should be enjoyed by any reader "who respects integrity and artistry" in short fiction.

1951 A BOOKS - NONE

1951 B SHORTER WRITINGS

1 ANON. Review of The Strange Children. Atlantic Monthly (November), p. 97.

The Strange Children is a "deceptively quiet" novel. "No scene, no dialogue is recorded that falls outside [Lucy's] orbit." The novel is both dramatic and subtle, and "suggests without special pleading the contrast between the aimless and the consecrated life."

2 ANON. Review of The Strange Children. Bookmark 11 (November), 34.

A capsule précis. "Through the eyes of a precocious, nine-year-old girl, visitors to her home on the Cumberland river are seen impressionistically, while a Holy Roller meeting heightens complex emotions and leads to an elopement."

3 ANON. Review of The Strange Children. Kirkus 19:403.

Briefly summarizes plot. The lives of the characters "seem to become fuzzy in outline, confusing in direction, although each character seems to know what he wants." The tone of the novel is "detached, worldly wise." "Placed against the aimless vegetating and religious fanaticism of the native neighbors, the tiresome round would lack any solidity were it not for the character of Lucy" whose cynicism and romanticism provide satiric perspective.

1951

4 ANON. Review of The Strange Children. New Yorker (15 September), pp. 131-32.

A brief note on The Strange Children. In this "novel of conversations," the relationships among the characters, "even among the married, remain unclear and watery to the end." Lucy is spoiled and "something of a pest," making interpretations of adult talk that are "more stupid than childlike." "The atmosphere is consistently fascinating, but one cannot help feeling that if little Lucy could be got out of the room, all the grownups would breath easier and speak more freely."

5 CAVENDISH, HENRY. "More Style Than Clarity in This Tale." Chicago Sunday Tribune (23 September), p. 10.

Reviews The Strange Children. Discusses the "distinguished" novelist's "bent toward cerebrational motivation and activation" pushed in this novel "to a point where many readers...will probably be wondering what it's all about long before the rewarding clarification which comes at the end." The novel develops "along a series of more or less straight lines which only converge with the belated--but intellectually battering--punch of the climax and swiftly following conclusion." With the elopement of Tubby and Isabel, "the insubstantialness of Isabel's nature... becomes clearly similar to the insubstantialness of Undine" and "the elopement becomes inferentially as fatal for Tubby as the embrace was for Sir Huldbrand." Similarly the snake handling scene reveals the purpose of the line of action involving Catholicism, the Holy Rollers, and Agnosticism. "Other seemingly disconnected developments are introduced very much after the fashion of ornamental filigree." Only at the end are "these apparently conflicting currents and cross-currents seen clearly to be coordinating parts of a unified whole." The import of the novel is that "all we creatures on this mundane earth, rather than just Lucy herself, are more or less in the nature of 'strange children.'" The tale is characterized more by an "extremely polished style" than by "highly distinct lucidity in the narrative itself."

6 CHAPIN, RUTH. "Twilight of the South." Christian Science Monitor (4 October), p. 15.

Reviews The Strange Children and Styron's Lie Down in Darkness. Gordon's "tidy economy and cool ambivalence" contrast with Styron's "complex and even turgid" first book. Where Roman Catholicism, "although partly considered as a refuge, is nevertheless just another facet of the whole sterile concern with form and human myth" in The Strange

Children, formal religion is of "dubious effectiveness" as a "possible means of surcease" from torment in Styron's novel. The Strange Children is written with "dispassionate control," and successfully epitomizes a way of life. Yet it offers "no unique insight: neither explanation nor explicit condemnation. Technically skillful, the book is without a concrete moral focus."

7 DAVIS, ROBERT GORHAM. "An Evil Time for Lucy." NYTBR (9 September), pp. 5, 20.

Reviews The Strange Children. The "children" are the grown-ups "living in spiritual aridity" who "talk too much, drink too much, know too much." Life is deflected with words. Lucy is "sophisticated like her parents, but without loss of passion, imagination, will." The love triangle [Kevin-Isabel-Tubby] "reaches a climax--perhaps a little theatrically--just as a Holy Roller revival meeting...comes to its own violent conclusion." Lucy is "less complexly naive and innocent" than Henry James' Maisie. Gordon is "more interested in the adult relationships" than in what they mean to Lucy; hence, the "long, revelatory, allusive conversations to which a child like Lucy would automatically shut her ears and mind." However, Lucy shares in evil, betrays and is betrayed. "The treatment of evil is explicit" in the novel and "the ultimate concern of most of the characters...is religious." The novel has more "symbolism, high dramatics, and elaborate interweaving" than it is capable of absorbing, fusing, or "causing to seem imaginatively necessary."

8 FREMANTLE, ANNE. Review of The Strange Children. Commonweal (16 November), pp. 155-56.

Though Lucy is odious--"of all American brats in fiction she is outnastied only by Carson McCullers' megalomaniac heroine in The Member of the Wedding--her elders are infinitely worse." Gordon "conveys beauty admirably" but though she "shows beauty as truth, she knows it is not love, at our level." Contrasts Gordon's The Strange Children with Stark Young's The Pavilion. In her South Gordon "shows how all that spirit or heart could desire of perfect setting and 'gracious living' are [sic] wasted by those who don't obey the first commandment." Stark Young's South is one in which slavery is practically present, and "he shows how good can come even out of evil."

9 GAITHER, FRANCES. "Disillusionment of a Child." SatR (15 September), p. 13.

A précis of The Strange Children with hardly any critical comment.

1951

10 GARDINER, HAROLD C. "Two Southern Tales." America (6 October), p. 18.

Reviews The Strange Children and Faulkner's Requiem for a Nun. Faulkner's novel is not "top-drawer"; rather it is meandering and displays "a positive contempt for style." On the other hand, The Strange Children "is limpidity itself in comparison. Not that it's an easily analyzed affair; it isn't, but the style is crystal clear and the import rather simple"--"another of those 'adults as seen through the eyes of youngsters' stories." The novel is characterized by little exterior action, with emphasis "exclusively on interior strains and stresses." The symbolism of the crucifix runs throughout. "Perhaps Miss Gordon means that until people like these modern beautiful and damned learn the meaning behind the little crucifix, they, too, will continue to be very strange children, indeed." Reprinted in 1959.B2.

11 HAWTHORNE, HAZEL. "Varieties of Experience." New Republic (29 October), p. 28.

Reviews The Strange Children. Though V. S. Pritchett says "The South is America's richest artistic soil," Gordon here "but lightly works this soil." In The Strange Children, which studies the effects of religious experience, and of the lack of such experience, "it is the agnostics who are supposed to come off badly and [who] are the strange children of the title." But the problems of the adults are "humanistic," religious, and serious. Because as chosen narrator Lucy's power of judgment is beyond her power of statement, she cannot do justice to the expression of these problems which "would, one feels, have reached full stature had they been presented out of range of little Lucy." Gordon's style is good, "above a certain tedium of pastoral description."

12 JACOBS, ROBERT D. "Best of Its Kind." Hopkins Review 4:59-60.

Brief descriptive review of The House of Fiction, "one of the latest competitors" to Brooks and Warren's Understanding Fiction. Gordon is "a fictionist in her own right good enough to appear in several of the competing anthologies but modestly omitted from this one." The inclusion of certain pieces by Hawthorne, Poe, and Bowen "gives the book a variety that its guiding principle [the "tradition of naturalism"] does not suggest." The House of Fiction is "less burdened by critical apparatus than Understanding Fiction" though Appendix B "aimed at the faults of the beginning writer" is "an odd mark for these editors who comment that writing cannot be taught." In general, despite minor lapses, The House of Fiction is "the best of its kind so far"--of "greater scope" than Mark Schorer's The Story, and "with more adequate [though fewer] commentaries than Robert B. Heilman's Modern Short Stories."

13 ROSENBERGER, COLEMAN. Review of The Strange Children. New York Herald Tribune Book Review (9 September), p. 5.

Gordon's "most richly rewarding work" is "concerned with the abiding themes of man's destiny, his search for certitude, the littleness of his time under the sun, and the vanity of all his works" [Psalm 144]. The scene is explicit, the time "somewhat less explicit." Lucy is the "pivotal character," though the author retains the role of narrator and "the reader is not limited to Lucy's observations, perceptive as they are, or to incidents to which the child is a witness." The exploration of human destiny and vanity in the "complex characters" of Tubby, Isabel, and Kevin is "immeasurably enriched and illuminated" by juxtaposition with the MacDonough family and friends and the Holy Roller meeting.

14 RUBIN, LOUIS D., JR. "What To Do About Chaos." Hopkins Review 5:65-68.

Reviews The Strange Children and William Styron's Lie Down in Darkness. "A single theme, openly arrived at and stated again and again, runs through both these novels by Southern authors: chaos. Caroline Gordon finds it in seemingly sane persons who suddenly do violently insane things." The "author's answer in each case is religious faith." Gordon's answer is "Catholicism: the faith of Kevin Reardon, the one man who is able to stand up to chaos and cope with it." Except for Lucy, the Lewises are spectators in the drama. Isabel Reardon and Uncle Tubby "seemingly sane and intelligent and 'normal' have blundered into what is certain to be chaos." Only Kevin is in control of the situation. The final switch in point of view is "effective and not incongruous as far as the narrative goes." Objection to it might be made "on grounds of mechanical consistency" but since "mechanics are designed only to make the effect possible, I suppose that there is really no room for complaint." It is a successful, effective novel; "if it moves a little slowly at the beginning, one comes to see that the careful opening development is what makes the conclusion possible."

15 WEST, RAY B., JR. "The Craft of the Short Story: 1951." WR 15:84-86, 157-60.

Discusses The House of Fiction among a group of eleven volumes of short stories and three critical anthologies

(WEST, RAY B., JR.)
including short stories. "It is in the critical anthologies that 'influence' is most strongly felt. Criticism works most effectively after the fact, as elucidation and definition, its precepts drawn from examples before it." Allen Tate and Gordon are less concerned with distinctions between the short story, novelette, and novel, "but they do insist upon the need for an enclosing form within the concept of fiction itself. They see the form of the short story as organic and objective, and they see its principal means of achievement represented in a technical competency in dealing with the problem of 'authority.'" Thus, the "influence of Henry James is obvious" in The House of Fiction. "The question we need to ask, however, is whether the Jamesian concept (brilliant as it was) is sufficient to do justice to all of the fiction written since his day." Tate and Gordon imply a recognition of this problem "when they bring techniques other than Jamesian to bear upon certain stories in their anthology." In dealing with the short story today, "most of the criteria, the criteria afforded the highest critical respect, was supplied by Henry James." Yet we must not allow those criteria "to blind us to other values than those which James has pointed out."

1952 A BOOKS - NONE

1952 B SHORTER WRITINGS

1 BEATTY, RICHMOND C., FLOYD C. WATKINS, THOMAS D. YOUNG, and RANDALL STEWART, eds. The Literature of the South. New York: Scott, Foresman and Co., pp. 864-65.
An anthology of Southern writing, containing "The Captive." Gordon's "solid reputation is based upon her achievement in prose fiction, a form in which she has few superiors." The title of None Shall Look Back is ironic: "we are all looking back constantly, to discover what we are, and why."

2 HARTMAN, CARL. "Charades at Benfolly." WR 16:322-24.
Reviews The Strange Children wherein method is in excess of content, and yet paradoxically does not adequately serve the content. It is "a book consciously filled with fine things, most of them tremendously effective up to a certain point and within the limits of the discipline which contains them," but something is wrong here, and "the failing directly concerns method," the problem of "form in relation to the central morality it is intended to express." Specifically, it is the abandonment of Lucy's point of view in

the end: the "tremendously skillful shift" by which "we suddenly assume Stephen Lewis' terms" in a "sort of last minute denial, perhaps, of the framework that has been so carefully (we thought) established." Yet in the end Stephen cannot serve and "there is no other force present strong enough to make up for what we have lost." Thus, "the book as a whole fails ultimately to make clear the one thing it seems to have been concerned with revealing--the true nature of the relationships between its people."

3 HEILMAN, ROBERT B. "Schools for Girls." SR 60:299-309.
Reviews Faulkner's Requiem for a Nun, Gordon's The Strange Children, and Shirley Jackson's Hangsaman which focus on "the girl with a special sensibility--or at least the girl who is a special case of sorts" and "all of which, literally or metaphorically, send their heroines to school." In The Strange Children, "one senses the artist leaning, though unknowingly--perhaps struggling not to lean--on some background reality which is more vivid for her than for oneself." One is "set off on the inferior game of identity-hunting: what one may call the external relations of the book interfere with one's judgment of the internal relations, which are its only valid definition." Yet Gordon's book is superior to Jackson's in its transmutation of "the event in time into the timeless action...the case history into the universal case." There are "two recording minds": Lucy's and the author's, though in the end Lucy is reduced to the role of extra while her father "thinks out the envoi." The tensions of the book arise from the "varieties of religious experience." The diverse personalities share a common "fascination with the phenomena of spirit," and pursue "a truth, or a firmness, or a communion not possessed." The word "strange," meaning "foreign, alien, the world cut off from spirit," appears constantly and reaches a brilliant climax in the revelation that Isabel is insane, and that Kevin has borne this. In "this marriage of comedy of manners and parable with tragic implications," something "militates against adequate firmness and depth of character." Perhaps it is, in part, "the photographic habit and the tendency to parable."

4 HUGHES, RILEY. Review of The Strange Children. CathW (January), p. 313.
"In this perceptive, impressionistic, and finally unresolved novel the adults are the 'strange' ones." Lucy's life is substantial, contrasted with that of her parents and their friends: she at least "lives in the moment"; they "live for a moment to come." Lucy is "at the center

1952

(HUGHES, RILEY)
of the book" and "the author's revelation of the decay in personal values is aimed at the consciousness of the reader," for "what Lucy sees...has no intellectual message for her." Her "only positive act is to steal a crucifix, to participate for a time in the corruption which leads to the undefined moment for which her life is being prepared."

5 MORGAN, FREDERICK. "Seven Novels." HudR 5:154-60.
Reviews seven novels by different authors, among them Gordon's The Strange Children, "a novel that seems to have grown naturally and without strain." Gordon is recognized as "one of our best novelists" and this "seems to me to be her best book, possessing as it does a richness of substance beyond anything I have found in her earlier writing." The reader shares in the gradual "illumination" which Lucy experiences--"the small hard extra bit of understanding we can sometimes wrest" from ordinary everyday living. Crucial objects and events in the novel take on "natural overtones" of mystery and significance: the crucifix, the story of Undine, a game of charades, a pony, a revival meeting, the love-affair between Isabel and Uncle Tubby, their elopement--though these larger meanings "are not insisted upon by the author."

1953 A BOOKS

1 RUBIN, LOUIS D., JR., and ROBERT D. JACOBS, eds. Southern Renascence: The Literature of the Modern South. Baltimore: The Johns Hopkins Press, pp. 3-13, 112-25, 290-305, and 325-37.
Contains the following essays relevant to a study of Gordon's work; in each she is significantly discussed: Robert B. Heilman, "The Southern Temper"; Walter Sullivan, "Southern Novelists and the Civil War"; Louis D. Rubin, Jr., "Thomas Wolfe In Time and Place"; and Vivienne Koch, "The Conservatism of Caroline Gordon." See 1953.B1, 1953.B5, 1953.B2, and 1953.B3.

1953 B SHORTER WRITINGS

1 HEILMAN, ROBERT B. "The Southern Temper." In Southern Renascence: The Literature of the Modern South. Edited by Louis D. Rubin, Jr., and Robert D. Jacobs. Baltimore: The Johns Hopkins Press, pp. 3-13.
"The Southern temper is marked by the coincidence of a sense of the concrete, a sense of the elemental, a sense of the ornamental, a sense of the representative, and a sense

of totality. No one of these endowments is unshared; but their concurrency is not frequent. This concurrency is a condition of major art and mature thought." The sense of the concrete is "so emphatically apparent in Faulkner, Warren, and Wolfe, so subtly and variously apparent in Porter, Welty, and Gordon, and so flamboyantly so in someone like Capote." The sense of the elemental is seen in "the juxtaposing of life and death in Porter, the insistent awareness of death in Porter and Gordon, and a certain mystery of being inseparable from the closest factuality in Elizabeth Madox Roberts and Welty." "Ornamental" here means "non-utilitarian values; whatever comes from the feeling for rhythm, the sense of the incantatory, the awareness of style as integral in all kinds of communication; the intangible goods that lie beyond necessity; grace." The sense of the representative is present in Gordon's work where we see Everyman "as sportsman." Such work "boldly assumes as axiomatic the symbolic quality of all works." The sense of totality is "a sense of time, of the extent of human need and possibility, of world and of spirit." In this regard, "Gordon's stories expand into the myth of a recurrent character." In Gordon's "instinct for inclusiveness," she digs into and relies upon the past, for "the past is part master." Unwilling "to be uncritically content inside fashionable limits, the Southerners apparently find the religion of humanity inadequate. Not that any of them do not value the human; the question is whether the obligation to be human can be secured by a secular religion, and whether humanity alone can adequately engage the religious imagination." They are aware that "as Tate has put it, man is incurably religious" and that the critical problem is one "of distinguishing the real thing and the surrogates." The Southerners "have a surprisingly 'liberal' complexion; they are in the classical American tradition of 'protest.'" It is in "the strength and the combination of the qualities enumerated that the Southern temper is distinctive." Reprinted in 1961.B4.

2 KOCH, VIVIENNE. "The Conservatism of Caroline Gordon." In Southern Renascence: The Literature of the Modern South. Edited by Louis D. Rubin, Jr., and Robert D. Jacobs. Baltimore: The Johns Hopkins Press, pp. 325-37.

Discusses in some detail five or six novels but focuses primarily on The Strange Children wherein Gordon's "fidelity to the tradition of 'naturalism' as she has defined it emerges with a mature authority." By contrast with Eudora Welty whose acclaim is merited, and with Katherine Anne Porter and Carson McCullers whose fame exceeds their

(KOCH, VIVIENNE)
achievement, Gordon has "suffered a curious lack of appreciation." Her "unmodishness" may be responsible for her lack of wider recognition. Gordon is "the conservator in contemporary Southern fiction of the great classical tradition of the nineteenth century novel as formulated by Stendhal, Flaubert and somewhat later, Henry James." The Strange Children is a "finely thoughtful work." Here Gordon is "most powerfully" the conservator of "the heritage of 'naturalism' and thus of the mainstream of the great fiction of the western world." Discussions of Penhally, Aleck Maury, Sportsman, None Shall Look Back, The Garden of Adonis, The Women on the Porch, and Green Centuries prepare the way for the claim that in The Strange Children Gordon achieves with "dazzling effect--something that the romantic agony of the early novels only timidly hinted": the novel of manners in which "social comedy is complicated and, in the end, dominated by the perilous likeness it bears to tragedy." The novel of ideas is Gordon's "proper domain"; here she gives rein to a "powerful intellectual scrutiny suppressed in the earlier novels in favor of an ambivalent mystique of localism and historicism." Includes some of the material on The Women on the Porch used in 1945.B9.

3 RUBIN, LOUIS D., JR. "Thomas Wolfe In Time and Place." In Southern Renascence: The Literature of the Modern South. Edited by Louis D. Rubin, Jr. and Robert D. Jacobs. Baltimore: The Johns Hopkins Press, pp. 290-305.

Certain characteristics "are not confined to Southern writers; but the unusual emphasis placed upon them by most Southern writers causes them to be considered indigenous to the Southerners." These characteristics are: "the element of rhetoric"; "a sense and awareness of time, of past and future as well as immediate present," including the consciousness of race and family; and a "devotion to texture, to what Ransom calls 'things as they are in their rich and contingent materiality'" which involves, for Southern writers, the "contemplation of death" and a "taste for detail." Gordon's prose "abounds in rich, variegated textural imagery." "Such textural composition of place as Wolfe displays is assuredly a characteristic common to almost all modern Southern writers. In the poor ones, the odor of magnolia reeks; in work by Faulkner, Wolfe, Gordon and others, the prose is made rich and sensuous thereby."

4 SULLIVAN, WALTER. "Southern Novelists and the Civil War." Hopkins Review 6:133-46.

As part of a symposium on Modern Southern Literature, this essay deals principally with novels of Stark Young,

Allen Tate, Andrew Lytle, William Faulkner, and Caroline Gordon. Gordon's None Shall Look Back "is perhaps of all Southern novels the sternest and most unrelenting in its treatment of the Civil War" for every single character who remains faithful to the Southern ethic is in the end "killed or sadly broken." In the novel "the principal image is the family and...the public and private moralities coincide until the status quo is ruptured by the War." The chapters dealing with Fount Allard's ride over the plantation at Brackets and his investigation of the overseer's cruelty at Cabin Row "superbly" convey Allard's sense of the good. More important is the "superb development" of Rives Allard: "he refuses to live beyond the failure of his inherited moral code." The sense of morality in the novel "is developed through the consciousness of Lucy," and she participates repeatedly in "the novel's constant concern with death." The center of the novel is Rives' rejection of his chance to live, "not because he loves death but because he is devoted to the civilization which he is defending." "Much of the strength of the image is personified in the man, and among views of history, Miss Gordon's is perhaps the shortest one of all." Reprinted in 1953.B5.

5 ____. "Southern Novelists and the Civil War." In Southern Renascence: The Literature of the Modern South. Edited by Louis D. Rubin, Jr., and Robert D. Jacobs. Baltimore: The Johns Hopkins Press, pp. 112-25.
Reprint of 1953.B4.

1955 A BOOKS - NONE

1955 B SHORTER WRITINGS

1 KING, LAWRENCE T. "The Novels of Caroline Gordon." CathW (July), pp. 274-79.
Discusses seven novels focusing especially on The Strange Children which "marks a definite departure for Miss Gordon," her "best--and also her most profound--work." Many critics were at a loss to evaluate its theme: "the necessity of spiritual regeneration or re-birth through suffering or immolation." A "moral and philosophical attitude informs the entire novel." Gordon's is "a talent already recognized as one of the finest that contemporary American writing has to offer."

1956

1956 A BOOKS - NONE

1956 B SHORTER WRITINGS

1 ANON. "Ode to the Expatriate Dead." Time (12 March), p. 124.
Reviews The Malefactors. Gordon, an expatriate herself for a time, has made this a "lost-and-found generation novel." Here is "a kind of purgatory on the road to religious serenity." With its "semi-autobiographic overtones" (Gordon's recent conversion to Roman Catholicism), the book is "one of those Mary McCarthy-like exercises in intellectual cattiness in which one claws one's literary coterie in public." "Tom holds a running bull session with 1) the spirit of his rakehell father, 2) the voice of his moral and artistic conscience (it speaks in italics), 3) the bittersweet memories of expatriate days centering on...Horne Watts, who is clearly modeled on the late Hart Crane." Marcia Crenfrew's mind is "an ambush out of which Freud continually jumps." True, "the moral and intellectual striptease is a legitimate novelistic device for baring some universal truth," but here "it becomes an end in itself, exposing only cliquish gossip." The novel is "written with sensibility, if debatable sense" and may inadvertently reveal that the Lost Generation was "born to be led astray and taken in." Photograph of Gordon by Charles Henri Ford.

2 ANON. Review of The Malefactors. New Yorker (17 March), p. 180.
Reviews a "tedious novel." "Miss Gordon's tone is earnest and provokes echoes that sound as though they ought to be significant, but there is always the possibility that she intended her work to be taken as a satire."

3 ANON. Review of The Malefactors. Kirkus 24:16.
Sees the novel as "similar in caste" to The Strange Children: again, "an ambient, sometimes aimless portrait of some rather liberated literati and aesthetes, which shares with its characters the lack of definition of their lives." Here, also, "Catholicism is an intermittent influence." The Malefactors is "a strange book, dealing as it does with spiritual and emotional deviates" and "for some it will also be bewildering."

4 BENÉT, ROSEMARY G. "Neurotic People." SatR (17 March), p. 15.
Briefly reviews The Malefactors. "There is scarcely a suffering character in [the novel] who is not deeply neurotic." Reviews the story-line and then concludes: "As a picture of sick intellectuals [the novel] is indeed a bitter

dose and, despite some spots of excellent writing, one is inclined to agree with Tom when he finally says, 'I'm tired of incest.'"

5 BLUM, MORGAN. "The Shifting Point of View: Joyce's 'The Dead' and Gordon's 'Old Red.'" Crit 1:45-66.

The "skillful manipulation of point of view has helped to create" the "freedom, power, and humanity--as well as great subtlety" of the work of James Joyce and Gordon. Discusses in great detail the shifts from the "sustained point of view" in "The Dead" and the shifts from Maury's point of view in "Old Red." "We may ask the question why are these shifts made, and [with respect to each story] ask it for similar reasons. But the question of how they are made is for our present purposes prior and possibly as rewarding." Examines with close attention the method of the transitions of point of view employed in "Old Red." The purposes of these transitions are varied but related: to ease "the reader into Maury's point of view with precision and economy"; to introduce "the theme of readiness for flight and the implied pursuit"; to supplement "the limited authority that attaches to any man's view of himself"; to support, by the introduction of Sarah's unresentful attitude, Gordon's central insight about Maury's "own satisfaction in his life." Of all living persons in the story, Sarah is "the one with the greatest apparent cause for resentment." Yet the transition to her point of view reveals her tolerance and realism, and tells us something about Sarah "as a moral being." Whereas "Joyce turns to omniscience at the story's reversal--that is, at a moment which is central to the story's structure as well as to its meaning," Gordon's shift "seems at first glance significant for meaning only; it apparently does nothing to bring about the identification with the fox, the discovery that ends the story." But a "first glance" is not sufficient. The words Sarah hears her father say--"Little West Fork...my first love"--"prepare us for the more difficult portion of the story's resolution." The "identification with Old Red the fox cannot by itself end the story successfully," for this is "first of all a story of fishing, not of hunting. Fishing here is action: hunting is reminiscence." The key passage "immediately precedes the final identification with the fox." Here the merging streams of water "become themselves pursuers. But for this to be a meaningful reversal, we must have first seen them as pursued." Here the words Sarah heard "make their structural contribution. In them we see how a stream can obsess consciousness; more than this, we hear the pre-emptive word 'love.'" The merging

1956

(BLUM, MORGAN)
streams in this story remind the reader of "the tributaries that pursue, and merge with the Po [River] as it passes [Francesca's] place of birth in Dante's The Divine Comedy." Allen Tate's article "Tension in Poetry" which deals with this passage from Dante's work was published "some five years after 'Old Red.'" This literary relationship is not one of "conventional, or demonstrable, influence. But the familial relationship has a symbolic rightness."

6 COWAN, LOUISE. "Nature and Grace In Caroline Gordon." Crit 1:11-27.

There are "two opposite attitudes toward the artist's function"; he can conceive of himself: "as subject to the creator and the laws of his creation or as artificer of an independent order." Gordon and "Modern Southern writers in general have regarded their task as the discovery of an already existent pattern in actual experience rather than as the imposition of an ideal pattern upon experience." For the Southerner matter is sacramental. "Objects and creatures are real in themselves, and yet they are also mysteries, reflecting God and each other in a network of resemblances which at times illumine and at times veil the relationship between the creator and his creation." Discusses at length "The Brilliant Leaves" which is "almost parabolic, so clear, hard, and precise are its analogical formulations." It is also "a dumb-show in which the events of the novels are acted out in shortened and pantomimic version. The constant set of events in all the novels revolves around man and woman, caught in mortality and seeking self-realization." Two possibilities are open to the women in Gordon's fiction: "to fall over the precipice into utter destruction...or to become one of the women on the porch." The men "must engage themselves in perpetual flight." Both sexes face "the common enemy Death," who is "constantly at hand" and increasingly "bold in revealing himself." This same story is in all Gordon's works, against various backgrounds and from many perspectives. Discusses the novels before The Women on the Porch; in these "nature itself is the inadequate garden, since it cannot sustain and nourish man, the essentially rootless plant." In The Women on the Porch "can be seen for the first time the proper order and arrangement of events to form the complete pattern of Caroline Gordon's 'plot.'" Here the temporal pattern--which in her earlier works Gordon has shown "as ending in the observable motifs of withdrawal, flight, and death"--is seen "to have its roots in eternity." Discusses at length The Women on the Porch. Though here Gordon "does not desert her naturalistic method," nonetheless "something supernatural enters into the dramatic framework of the novel." The symbol of water "as both destruction and salvation permeates the novel." The death of the stallion suggests "the carnal element that must be shattered before grace can grow." The events of the novel are "agonies of child-birth rather than of death." Gordon's "one story" all along has been: "man's search for grace in a fallen world." In her work nature without grace cannot "afford man a path to salvation." A slightly revised version of this essay appears in 1971.B6.

7 GRISCOM, JOAN. "Bibliography of Caroline Gordon." Crit 1: 74-78.

Includes works by and about Gordon and aims to be fairly complete prior to 1956. Excludes reference to The Malefactors. The writings about Gordon and her work are "surprising and disappointing; the majority of reviews are either negligible or inadequate as criticism, and, considering the extent and excellence of her work, the fact that there have been only four general articles devoted to it is something more than surprising." "Especially valuable and perceptive" writings are marked with an asterisk; some entries have descriptive or evaluative notes. All items about Gordon's work listed in this Bibliography are contained in this Reference Guide.

8 HOFFMAN, FREDERICK J. "Caroline Gordon: The Special Yield." Crit 1:29-35.

Aleck Maury, Sportsman is "the most illuminating" of Gordon's works of fiction. The character of Aleck is "of special interest because the singleness of his dedication to a way of life acts as a major paradigm of explanation"; to see him as he sees himself is to realize Gordon's "special vision of the South as well as her relation to certain of her Southern contemporaries." Maury is "the priest attending with an almost fanatic persistence to his rituals. The religion is itself a worship of nature, a worship conducted according to clearly defined limits of definition and significance." The most important reason for Gordon's "persistent and patient attention to the details of Maury's obsessions" is that "it offers a fixed image of reality, a spatial image which incorporates all time and history within its range and scope." For her this nature image is "the very last word in a pre-civilized or supra-civilized vision." For Gordon "life needs to move in an orderly fashion from a fixed point of a patterned and naturally pure world toward a more stylized, a more formally ordered world." The proper principle of

1956

(HOFFMAN, FREDERICK J.)
"architecture" and the "best means of governing taste"--whether of house, families, or tradition--is "to civilize according to need and never beyond the limits set by need." In this building "memory and need are the sinews of tradition." Of course this "can lead to awkward confusions in historical narrative," and a "more than negligible fault" in Gordon's fiction "comes from a double view": the place is understandably simple but the people of her fiction "are often a scarcely differentiated mass; they are held to lines of descent from the world's human beginnings, and they lack complexity." Some of her novels "have a clutter of personalities instead of a wealth of characters." Often her personalities simply "add to an inventory of themes," as various and conventional as Gordon's concerns. "These are not necessarily damaging circumstances"; indeed, "they are valuable rehearsals of the human drama. But they are too often insufficiently explored; the line of narrative development is not always as deep or as complex as it might have been." The "most satisfactory" of Gordon's thematic concerns is the "conflict between the sportsman and the intellectual": in extended form, "the range of dissimilarity affecting the agrarian theorist and the urban sophisticate," and the child's "contemplation of adult absurdities." At the basis of all this is "the temperament of Aleck Maury." Gordon's fiction "describes a remarkable range of achievement and failure" from the "wonderfully sharp and wise" fiction of Aleck Maury and the "extraordinarily restrained" Green Centuries to the "hopeless mélange" of Penhally and the "similarly handicapped" None Shall Look Back. Nevertheless, "the eight books leave a remarkable impression" and form "a fictional parallel of John Crowe Ransom's poem 'Antique Harvesters' [in which] Ransom speaks of 'one spot' of the land as having 'a special yield'...the 'yield' of a tradition aesthetically realized and obstinately treasured, imaged in the ritual fox hunt and the worshipful gestures of harvesting in the later stanzas." Gordon "acknowledges a similar 'yield' from tradition. It comes from a vision of life seen often in starkly simple terms and thus made the focus of an historical interpretation of human society." Some of the material in this essay reappears in 1967.B1.

9 KOCH, VIVIENNE. "Companions in the Blood." SR 64:645-51.
Reviews The Malefactors, a "profoundly conceived, incandescent story" wherein Gordon emerges "as the best woman novelist we have in this country at this time." Here, again, alienation is "a removal from God to whom we have become strange children." The "terms of the organizing

dynamic of the spirit" are "innocence, knowledge, salvation through grace, and the renewal of innocence." The novel is not simply "another witty and malicious roman à clef"; the malice, as the title hints, "is a function of its personae, not a personal vendetta of the author's." Gordon's moral attack has many opponents in the novel, but "the slipperiest antagonist of all" is the protagonist, Tom Claiborne. "The symbolic force of her characters' names...deserves critical treatment." The central problem of the novel--"the problem of redemption--is unpersuasively resolved." Tom's "reclamation" seems implausible: he is "seemingly incapable of love." "Can one who has been so long blind suddenly be made to see?" Gordon says yes: "Revelation is mysterious and grace is sudden." Homosexuality is one of the "sub-themes, or rather, counter-themes" of the novel, and is given "original treatment" in the claim, through the Irish nun, that "homosexuality is akin to sainthood," part of man's larger agony: the "external search for wholeness." This "strange chapter" is "surely one of the most extraordinary in modern fiction." The "artificial insemination issue" present in the opening of the novel is "a parable" of "the desire to isolate and identify the creative element in man" which is one of Gordon's concerns, and prepares for the final correlation between increasing nearness to "the divine in themselves which is God" and the renewal of creative powers.

10 LYTLE, ANDREW NELSON. "The Forest of the South." Crit 1:3-9.

The process of using the tools of the craft is "the fundamental mystery of the art of fiction." The critic watches "the way the technique works," the "way the words are put together." Up to The Strange Children, the action of Gordon's novels "had always been cast against an explicit understanding of a sense of history" though "there is a difference of approach between the novelist using past time and the historian." To the novelist "the past is contemporaneous or almost," and the historical cultural pattern becomes "the enveloping action against which, and out of which, the action proper complicates itself." Gordon's structure "depends upon a cultural loss, caught in a succession of historic images, a loss which impairs the possibilities of human nature. This impairment, made concrete in the action proper, makes explicit the meaning of history. The controlling image, therefore, is a double clue to meaning, through the action to the enveloping action, and vice versa." In the Arthurian saga, when Merlin withdrew with Niniane into the forest, she "understood only one verse [of the songs of knights and ladies]: 'Bitter suffering

(LYTLE, ANDREW NELSON)
ends the sweet joys of newborn love.' This is the oldest song. It is Miss Gordon's song [in Green Centuries], accompanied by the discords of history." It is also the subject of her stories in The Forest of the South. In the title piece, "the conquest of the South is the destruction of a society formal enough and Christian enough to allow for the right relationships between the sexes." The theme is the same in "Hear the Nightingale Sing." The most extreme statement of this theme and of the reversal of roles "results from the complications in 'The Ice House,'" one of the few stories "where the complication lacks a woman." These stories involving, for example, Aleck Maury, Tom Rivers, and Ladd are stories of "dispossessed men." The world "in which they would function best has been destroyed." Nonetheless these stories deal indirectly with Gordon's theme. "With one or two exceptions the other stories in the book deal more directly with 'bitter suffering ends the sweet joys of newborn love.'" In all the stories Gordon's "use of history is the right use. It recovers it as a living set of deeds, whose actions as they represent the universal predicament also interpret the changing flow of history. Now that she has joined the Catholic church, her material will receive a new emphasis and history another focus."

11 MIZENER, ARTHUR. "What Matters with Tom." NYTBR (4 March), pp. 4, 32.

Aleck Maury, Sportsman was a "minor classic," and Gordon's books "have grown more skillful with time" but "not many people seem to notice." While "temporary immortals" accumulate reputations, "Miss Gordon goes on being unnoticed"--e.g., The Oxford Companion to American Literature gives her one sentence at the end of its entry on Allen Tate. The Malefactors is her "most ambitious novel," a work of "great intelligence"; its life is in its "observed detail" and "fine structure." Gordon creates "daily life... as few writers have," in order to "give authenticity to her perception of its meaning, a perception which controls every detail in the novel." In this novel, the perception "is Roman Catholic; but it is a perception, not an argument," and "accounts for everything" in Tom's experience, as well as for the "world's lost and twisted people."

12 O'CONNOR, WILLIAM VAN. "The Novel of Experience." Crit 1: 37-44.

Henry James wrote "what might be called the novel-of-experience" which is quite distinct from the Conradian or

Joycean novel. This term, though perhaps too loose, "helps to define a line of 20th century American fiction that is quite as distinct, and is perhaps equally as important, as the novel-of-violence." Henry James, Edith Wharton, Willa Cather, Katherine Anne Porter, and Caroline Gordon are of this line. Their protagonists, like James', "come to understand deceit, the seamy side of motives, the urgency of time, the importance of vivid experience--they reconcile their innocent vision with the world as it is, and they compromise with the high expectations they had had for themselves." Gordon "is able to cast a cold eye on excesses, to compare expectation with event, theory with experience, and especially to show us Time as antagonist. Her fine novel Aleck Maury, Sportsman may be considered as almost the prototype of the novel-of-experience." One might infer that "the novel-of-experience is most frequently written by women" but there are a number of other men novelists "who also fit the category, notably Glenway Wescott and James Gould Cozzens." The novel-of-experience "stands or falls by the very quality of its thoughtfulness."

13 ROSENBERGER, COLEMAN. "Artists, Writers, and Their Problems In Miss Gordon's Comedy of Manners." New York Times Herald Tribune Book Review (25 March), p. 3.

Reviews The Malefactors, "a novel of ideas and manners, a literary form in which Caroline Gordon has few contemporary peers." It is also clearly a roman à clef: Horne Watts is Hart Crane; "the other characters may no doubt be equally easily identified by the initiate." Tom Claiborne resembles Stephen Lewis of The Strange Children. Catherine is "a sort of medieval abbess in the Bowery." Tom's final recognition of "meaning and order and grace in Roman Catholic values...if it is in the nature of conversion, comes by as extraordinary a route as any in recent fiction." Gordon "recreates with mastery one intellectual milieu in which a concern for such values might develop." It is a highly individual group "with its own special wit and argot" built up over the years. In fact the milieu is here presented more clearly than "is any achievement of certitude on the part of Claiborne or his circle." The Malefactors "remains at its most rewarding a comedy of manners."

14 ROSS, DANFORTH. "Caroline Gordon's Golden Ball." Crit 1: 67-73.

Gordon's approach to the teaching of writing is disciplined and intolerant of looseness; she insists that students construct "from the center out, as against from the periphery in"; that they start from a core and then wind

(ROSS, DANFORTH)
string around it. If the center is solid and "can't be pricked" then a writer has "something worth winding on" and the "finished ball" can be of any size. Though she believes there is a part of writing which cannot be taught, Gordon dogmatically insists that students master the "teachable part"; though this part is less important, it is "not entirely without interest." The student of writing must in her view: "get his story down cold"; "render it, detail by detail, not simply report it"; "get the detail physically, get its physical essence"; and look "for the dynamic relations between objects." In her teaching Gordon "doesn't stress plot" but she does insist on the necessity of driving down a stake from which the novel or story can unfold: "'You must drive it down firmly at the beginning.... Everything has to swirl around the stake. You must never let the stake get away from you.'" Each new character must be fed in in such a way that the reader realizes about the stake. Gordon's "original contribution to the teaching of writing" is in the matter of point of view: she distinguishes between the "long view" (the story from a distance) and the "short view" (the close-up: as the scene "would occur on the stage or in a flash back through a person's consciousness"). The omniscient narrator is "prone to use the long view"; the first person narrator tends toward the short view; when the author is identified with a character other than a first person narrator, he is involved with "essentially a short view approach." The Technique of the Central Intelligence "combines the advantages of the three others and involves the artist in fewer of their disadvantages than any other technique."

15 SIMONS, JOHN W. "A Cunning and Curious Dramatization." Commonweal (13 April), pp. 54-56.
Reviews The Malefactors as a novel dealing with the theme of conversion. Gordon's works "have always been remarkable for their subtle poetic essence and vigilant craftsmanship." The Malefactors features "a poet who, approaching middle age and seemingly forsaken by his muse, makes the discovery of Christ"--and this, in Pennsylvania's Bucks County, "the penultimate of Eden, it would seem, of reflective or refuted artists." Tom Claiborne's poetry-mentor Horne Watts "is the literary evocation and transmutation of the actual poet Hart Crane." The novel is "cunningly and curiously wrought"; "nothing fortuitous or gratuitous is allowed entrance." "From the point of view of art, however, what matters is less what happens than the strategy by which it is accomplished--the power of poetry by which the

originating vision is sustained and subdued, and through which the reader is compelled to a clear-eyed acquiescence." Since "a conversion is admittedly a special invasion of Grace into a particular life," the artist is often caught in one of two extremes: overdrawing the motivations and thereby reducing "the essentially free character of Grace"; or giving "maximum permissiveness to Grace" and thereby "making his character seem a puppet of Grace." Only Bernanos has come close to accomplishing the balance. Gordon's epigraph for the novel--"It is for Adam to interpret the voices which Eve hears" (Maritain)--specifies "the relationship between the practical or critical intelligence and poetic intuition." Hence man's critical intelligence is "situated between a lower and a higher intuition" which "can be mistaken for each other," for "one has an obscurity 'by excess of opacity'; the other, an obscurity 'by excess of transparency.'" Consequently, "the poet is nourished by his intuitions, but it is the critical intelligence (Adam) which must decide on the authenticity of what the soul (Eve) experiences." In the novel, Claiborne's "critical spirit has in the course of years gained ascendancy over the creative spirit" yet ironically "is powerless to probe his own _malaise_." In all this Gordon "handles the voices superbly, locating each with its distinctive intonation," and exhibiting "an admirable virtuosity in the deployment of symbols and echoes." Finally it is people, not memories or dreams, "who, wittingly and unwittingly, bring Claiborne to the edge of self-realization." Even the host of minor figures "have their function" and "the dead, too, possibly even more than the living, join in that skillfully discordant choir which, at one level of meaning, constitutes the Adam who interprets the voices of Eve." In the end, Tom was "obviously and not too implausibly in the toils of Grace" and Gordon, avoiding cliché, had come closer than any vernacular writer to encompassing the elusive miracle" of conversion, though "it may be that the ghost of Hart Crane was over-intrusive," and the nun's exegesis [of _Pontifex_] "not merely ingenious to excess, but unassimilable to the intent of St. Catherine's _Dialogo Divino_."

16 SULLIVAN, RICHARD. "A Precise, Profound, Sensitive Novel." _Chicago Sunday Tribune Magazine of Books_ (18 March), p. 4.
Reviews _The Malefactors_, a book that is "really 'written.'" Such a book is "a composed thing, a work of form and texture impeccably manifested in the rendering of complex material. It is a mastering in words of a certain stretch of human experience, so that everything that needs telling is richly told, but without frills or fuss." Tom

1956

(SULLIVAN, RICHARD)
Claiborne's point of view is "expertly sustained." The novel "perceptively and convincingly" deals with "a most difficult subject": "the progress of a religious conversion." Gordon's characterization is "precise and profound" and her writing "has a sensitive, sharp, even critical authority." Photograph of Gordon.

17 THORP, WILLARD. "The Redemption of the Wicked." New Republic (30 April), p. 21.
Reviews The Malefactors, a novel "that in time...will make its way." It is "beautifully contrived...weighted with curious but fascinating learning." For lazy readers its virtues will be "high hurdles"; for others, there will be "too much religion or too much (concealed) Jung." But in terms of the craft of fiction, The Malefactors with its "nearly faultless" construction "will be judged the finest of Miss Gordon's eight novels, though not her most ingratiating." The complex story has a plot "almost as simple, in reduction, as that of The Golden Bowl." It is Tom's story, though Catherine is the dominating figure. Vera must learn disinterested love; Tom, forgiveness of others. Gordon "accomplishes all she has to do" through "subtle and suitable devices"; e.g., Tom's poetic but unproductive consciousness, and the "technical triumph" of the "three-fold movement of the novel, which accords perfectly with the movement of Tom's mind": his hyperintensive staring at his present world, his imaginative return to its past causes, and the forward thrust exerted by "the characters who act on Tom." "I know of no modern novel in which this polyphony of present, past, and future is so skillfully composed."

18 _____. "The Way Back and the Way Up: The Novels of Caroline Gordon." Bucknell Review 6 (December), 1-15.
"Because of its absolute perfection of form," The Malefactors is the culmination of Gordon's "unremitting search for suitable techniques with which to project the inner lives of her complex and fascinating characters. It may also prove to be a turning point in her choice of themes and locale." Gordon's fiction "invites comparison with that of Elizabeth Madox Roberts," though there are "marked differences," including Gordon's superior ability to create male characters. Tolstoi was Gordon's master when she was working on Penhally and None Shall Look Back; the method of the "later" Henry James influenced The Women on the Porch and The Strange Children. Gordon "never seems to have to 'get up' anything" for her novels, except for Green

Centuries which required much research. Aleck Maury, Sportsman is a tour de force. Though None Shall Look Back and The Garden of Adonis "have some structural faults, they are more ambitious works than the first two." In Green Centuries the means by which the two stories of Rion and Archy are united "help to give the novel an extraordinary depth." In The Women on the Porch, Gordon "turned to a different kind of novel, concentrating on a few characters and the modern scene." The myth of Orpheus and Eurydice informs that novel. Though The Malefactors "marks a new departure" in Gordon's fiction, it "does have a connection with four novels which precede it," and "illustrates strikingly a change in outlook which these novels represent." The earlier novels are "full of regret for the vanished order of the Old South"; with The Garden of Adonis Gordon moves into "the modern Southern world which has lost its connections with the old order." For the men and women in these later novels "there is no way back, not even through nostalgia and grief." In The Strange Children "a new note is faintly sounded." At the end, Lucy "stands with her father looking up at the stars." This "muted emphasis on a religious theme prepares us for its full development in The Malefactors" where at least Tom and Vera "discover the way up and are re-born." As the South has faded from Gordon's novels, "religion has taken its place, and the way is up." Some material in this article is repeated in a later essay: See 1960.B1.

19 VAN GHENT, DOROTHY. "Technique and Vision: Some Recent Fiction." YR 45:625-33.

Reviews eight current novels, among them The Malefactors, an "absorbing" book if "one is patient enough...to get beyond the first 150 pages" where flashbacks in pluperfect tense ("the most tedious tense for narrative") stultify and congest. Tom, the "pluperfect rememberer," isn't sufficiently individuated in the first part of the book for the reader to be interested in his "remembered people's names and vermiculated cross-chronological sequences." Here a "device" (the flashback of memory) nearly crowds to death "the fundamental psychological 'technique' upon which all fiction depends, the technique of persuading the reader's imagination into an illusionary reality." But after this, "the book becomes suddenly powerful and streamlined," a "fairly transparent roman à clef, and Miss Gordon has not worried very much about obscuring the key" (Hart Crane, Dorothy Day). The novel is "an 'imitation of nature' in the oldest sense of that critical criterion, where 'nature' means the human essence, not its accidents. Yet Miss

1956

(VAN GHENT, DOROTHY)
Gordon mirrors the essence in its accidents, as a fiction writer must, finding the universal in the local." "The probity and range of the story are classical, with the sublime red bull, ancient double-image, munching in the middle of it."

1957 A BOOKS - NONE

1957 B SHORTER WRITINGS

1 ANON. Review of How to Read a Novel. Booklist 54:162.
"Despite a somewhat overblown style and a tendency to ridicule whatever is not to her taste, a practicing novelist advances stimulating theories both on the novel and on its enlightened and pleasurable reading." Gordon criticizes "readers who demand what she feels are the wrong satisfactions from fiction--that it be amusing, moral, superficial, or ideological."

2 ANON. Review of How to Read a Novel. Kirkus 25:623.
Briefly discusses the book as "a visiting tour of master craftsmen from Sophocles to Hemingway, pointing to this, steering away from that." Claims "the goal of the author [of any novel] and the reader is the same--the perception of life as it really is, in other words, the grasp of truth," and that the "key-note approach for both is that of humility." How to Read a Novel explains the development of the novel, citing practitioners and critics and yet it is "an unacademic, informal study" directed toward the laying aside of "preconceived notions of what a novel must be."

3 ANON. Review of How to Read a Novel. New Yorker (2 November), p. 197.
Very brief mention. "The impact of art" is the "stimulating, if not wholly unfamiliar, subject" of this book. Gordon "distinguishes with the utmost nicety between reading for 'enjoyment,' for 'amusement,' and for 'recreation.'"

4 BITTNER, WILLIAM. "For the Ladies." SatR (16 November), pp. 20-21.
Reviews How to Read a Novel which "certainly is not much help in illuminating the complex problem of the novel." The book attends too heavily to Henry James, and simply tidies up work already done by critics from E. M. Forster to Joseph Warren Beach, without approaching their clarity or comprehensiveness. Rather, How to Read a Novel seems to

be "a series of lectures aimed at the kind of women's club whose members want to be 'challenged' without having their ignorance remotely violated." The chapter on "Complication and Resolution" is "typical of this kind of uninformed academic piddling," where Gordon doesn't appear to recognize the Renard fable in the children's story "Jemima Puddle-Duck." The "serious flaw" in How to Read a Novel is Gordon's effort to reduce novels to some "one thing," when actually novels are "vastly different"--with "infinite combinations and variations," all "derived from the three prime ingredients: Swift, Defoe, and Sterne." The book will not help one to discriminate among novels and alleged novels, "good" and "best" novels; the work itself is "all derivative"--"from Lubbock, or Beach, or Forster," or others. Gordon "offers no sense of purpose in fiction" and "provides no stimulation to the reader's understanding of fiction." However, there is one provocative chapter, the first: "How Not to Read a Novel"; it should be "required reading for all who think that novels are supposed to soothe rather than to arouse." Photograph of Gordon by Willard Starks.

5 DAVIS, ROBERT GORHAM. "It Isn't Life That Counts." NYTBR (27 October), p. 6.

Reviews How to Read a Novel, claiming that Gordon's answer is that "art is a matter of rules, principles, techniques," which must be learned before novels can be read intelligently. In this book the author "does not try to be original," relying rather on "other practitioner-critics." She attempts only to present what is "orthodox in the best American colleges in the last twenty years." The "key is the 'great technical secret'": the central intelligence, which combines narrative techniques and dramatic techniques, as, for example, those in Oedipus Rex. The book "puts a rather heavy burden on technique and appreciation of technique." For the wider audience she has in mind, the author "does not explain fully enough or originally enough how an author's concern for life finds expression in and is modified by the nature of his art and how both ultimately are to be judged."

6 KELLEY, MARY E. Review of How to Read a Novel. LJ 82:2127.

Brief review of "a book for the better reader." "The analysis of well-known novels makes this double as a work of literary criticism."

1958

1958 A BOOKS - NONE

1958 B SHORTER WRITINGS

1 BRADBURY, JOHN M. The Fugitives: A Critical Account. Chapel Hill, N. C.: University of North Carolina Press, pp. 105, 118, 170, 271-72.

Gordon is mentioned only a few times in passing in this volume which deals with major and minor Fugitives, among whom she is not discussed. Gordon is listed as one of the "newer group of Southern women writers" who "found an important outlet" in The Southern Review after it was established in 1935. In a discussion of Tate's "The Buried Lake," the author suggests parenthetically that the poem and Gordon's The Malefactors "seem to project imaginatively, and at a small remove from fact, a joint experience which involved Dorothy Day."

1959 A BOOKS - NONE

1959 B SHORTER WRITINGS

1 COWAN, LOUISE. The Fugitive Group: A Literary History. Baton Rouge: Louisiana State University Press, pp. 98, 171, 206, and 217.

Discusses in passing Gordon's praise of the Fugitive writers when she was a writer for the Chattanooga News; the newly married Tates' frequent conversations with Hart Crane on such aesthetic matters as "the problem of the poet's relationship to society, which in turn hinged on the problem of the structure of social values"; and their association with Laura Riding Gottschalk in New York.

2 GARDINER, HAROLD C. "Two Southern Tales," in his In All Conscience: Reflections on Books and Culture. Garden City, N. Y.: Hanover House, pp. 128-29.

Reprint of 1951.B10.

1960 A BOOKS - NONE

1960 B SHORTER WRITINGS

1 THORP, WILLARD. "Southern Renaissance," in his American Writing in the Twentieth Century. Cambridge: Harvard University Press, pp. 233-74.

Within this chapter, Gordon is listed as one of the number of "excellent writers" among the Fugitives. Though

Gordon never signed any manifestoes of the Agrarians, she was present at their meetings, and fed and lodged their members. "Northern readers who wish to learn about southern ways should go to school to her fiction" for its detail. Penhally commits events to the consciousness of three men. Green Centuries is "one of the few first-rate American historical novels." The Strange Children is a parable of search for "a way out or a way up." The Malefactors is essentially a religious novel. "It is too early to say whether, because of Miss Gordon's conversion to Roman Catholicism, religion will replace the south in her fiction." The treatment of Gordon's work within this chapter is similar to though not identical with Thorp's longer earlier essay. It is not a reprint though some passages are identical. See 1956.B18.

1961 A BOOKS

1 RUBIN, LOUIS D., JR., and ROBERT D. JACOBS, eds. South: Modern Southern Literature in Its Cultural Setting. Garden City, N. Y.: Doubleday and Co., Inc. Reprinted: Westport, Conn.: Greenwood Press, 1974.

Contains three essays dealing significantly with Gordon and her work: Robert B. Heilman, "The Southern Temper," pp. 48-59; Frederick J. Hoffman, "The Sense of Place," pp. 60-75; and William Van O'Connor, "Art and Miss Gordon," pp. 314-22. See 1961.B4, 1961.B5, and 1961.B6.

1961 B SHORTER WRITINGS

1 BOOTH, WAYNE C. The Rhetoric of Fiction. Chicago: University of Chicago Press, pp. 23-33, 201-203.

Takes issue with some aspects of Gordon's theory of fiction. Unfortunately, in "serious college textbooks one soon found and still finds the telling-showing distinction presented as a reliable clue to the miraculous superiority of modern fiction." Gordon is mistaken in "treating Poe and Hawthorne primarily as sincere forerunners of the moderns" and in employing this "dialectical opposition between artful showing and inartistic, merely rhetorical, telling." Efforts "to find what is common to all works [of literature] or all good modern works" can be useful, but "a criticism that begins with such general definitions [e.g., Gordon's "search for the 'constants' which 'all good fiction, from Sophocles and Aeschylus down to a well-constructed nursery tale' will show"] is peculiarly tempted to move into value judgments without sufficient care about

(BOOTH, WAYNE C.)
whether those judgments are based on anything more than the initial arbitrary exclusiveness of the general definition." Hence, "we cannot be surprised at [Gordon's] manner of dismissing the works of Aldous Huxley and, indeed, all 'novels of ideas.'" In judging Huxley's "kind of satiric fantasia we must appeal to criteria very different from those appropriate to Miss Gordon's own excellent stories--stories which display, one need hardly mention, all of her constants." A critic should avoid letting his descriptive definitions become normative. With respect to another element of fiction--commentary--"it does not follow that commentary is always effective so long as it is spoken by a character in a story or that this story would be further improved by revealing more and more of its tone through dramatized detail and less and less through narrative statement," as Gordon and Allen Tate suggest by viewing Poe's "The Fall of the House of Usher" as "only half-realized" since "the story has 'not one instance of dramatized detail.'" Gordon and Allen Tate are really asking "that all general commentary, unrelieved by irony, should be eliminated." Their theory "seems to me a demand that springs from the prejudices of an age desiring effects basically different from Poe's." Many great authors have used mood-setting commentary "and used it well."

2 BROWN, ASHLEY. "A Note on 'The Dragon's Teeth.'" Shenandoah 13:20-21.
Reviews "The Dragon's Teeth," the "second chapter in Miss Gordon's work-in-progress which is to be called A Narrow Heart: The Portrait of a Woman." "The title...was also given to the first chapter, published last year in the new Transatlantic Review." The "second chapter" moves on two planes: "in the foreground we have the child's sharp perception of small events"; on "another plane," the child's father introduces Heracles as "an archetypal hero of salvation." The reader might compare this chapter to the opening chapter of James Joyce's A Portrait of the Artist as a Young Man. A Narrow Heart "will be 'autobiographical,' and consciously based on the action of a myth"; perhaps Heracles "will figure...as the symbol of salvation for the heroine."

3 CHARLES, NORMAN, ed. "Recent Southern Fiction: A Panel Discussion." Bulletin of Wesleyan College 41:1-16.
The text of a panel discussion held at Wesleyan College on October 28, 1960. The participants are Katherine Anne Porter, Flannery O'Connor, Caroline Gordon, Madison Jones,

and Louis D. Rubin, Jr., Moderator. They respond to such questions as: "Who qualifies as a Southern writer and on what grounds?" What are Southern characteristics? "How is the work of the present generation of Southern writers related to that being done in the 1920's and 1930's?" Among the specific matters discussed are the following: the physical conditions for writing, the sense of place, naturalism, the Southern sense of defeat, story-telling, religious symbolism, symbolism in general, the historical novel, the "moonlight and magnolias" stereotype, and the sense of man's guilt. Southern writing is "the combination of a certain number of qualities at one time."

4 HEILMAN, ROBERT B. "The Southern Temper." In _South: Modern Southern Literature in Its Cultural Setting_. Edited by Louis D. Rubin, Jr., and Robert D. Jacobs. Garden City, N. Y.: Doubleday and Co.; Westport, Conn.: Greenwood Press (1974 reprint), pp. 48-59.

Reprint of essay that appeared earlier. _See_ 1953.A1 and 1953.B1.

5 HOFFMAN, FREDERICK J. "The Sense of Place." In _South: Modern Southern Literature in Its Cultural Setting_. Edited by Louis D. Rubin, Jr., and Robert D. Jacobs. Garden City, N. Y.: Doubleday and Co.; Westport, Conn.: Greenwood Press (1974 reprint), pp. 60-75, passim.

Discusses the value to characterization and scene of specificity of place and time, in terms of identifying and communicable tradition and idiom. The role of place, as distinguished from scene, in literature is "to attach precise local values to feeling." In Gordon's work, as elsewhere, "the place metaphor persists as a symbol of a value regionally preserved. It is always a place in which... humanity is a concern, and its formal, even ceremonial, values are treasured. Implicitly at least, often quite openly, this metaphor is threatened by an inhuman, impersonal agent which exploits and destroys nature without love of it or respect for the ceremonies of man's living with it." The moral implications of certain Southern fictions "have to do with the problems of using space" and this involves "the difference between Northern sparseness and Southern abundance of natural imagery." In _Green Centuries_, Gordon emphasizes the "moral relationship of man to nature" and Daniel Boone serves here as a "symbol of human discretion and an unspoken code of manners." Her historical novels "define the progress of a fine balance of man and nature--the gradual and natural evolution of families, houses, estates, and communities." Thus, place achieves

1961

(HOFFMAN, FREDERICK J.)
"its status as metaphor" in Southern literature by "a finely balanced movement into and through nature, which is not a 'temple' so much as a dwelling place"--the land on which one may "respectfully and sensibly live." Gordon's work, as well as that of other authors discussed, belongs to that category of Southern literature which "defines, describes, and preserves the tradition without abstracting it." Some of the analysis in this essay is repeated later in 1967.B1.

6 O'CONNOR, WILLIAM VAN. "Art and Miss Gordon." In South: Modern Southern Literature in Its Cultural Setting. Edited by Louis D. Rubin, Jr., and Robert D. Jacobs. Garden City, N. Y.: Doubleday and Co.; Westport, Conn.: Greenwood Press (1974 reprint), pp. 314-22.

Analyzes the "best of Miss Gordon's stories": "The Brilliant Leaves," "The Forest of the South," and "Old Red" which is "undoubtedly one of the finest short stories written in our time." The fox is the central symbol in "Old Red" leading gracefully to the "identification of fox and man." Then discusses four of Gordon's novels. Gordon's work is vibrant; she is unwilling to "describe essentially inert situations"; rather "she wants the reader to look into the eyes of the characters--she wants the characters to look back at the reader, to have a light radiating from the page." Her prose aspires to and often exhibits "a fine ear for conversation," the "simplicity of good taste," impersonality, "firmness of surface," and where present, a never pretentious, always justified rhetoric. Her subject matter is "essentially simple": for the most part, the relationships of men and women. Her stories usually have to do with feminine self-giving and masculine fidelity, or the failure thereof. The Women on the Porch is typical, in treatment and subject. Here the young stallion "provides the central symbolism"; and water, cloud, and leaves form the pattern of imagery. Yet a male reader might feel that the novel is "a woman writer's dream," or that the "cold pastoral," with the author "dissolved into the atmosphere," is inappropriate. In None Shall Look Back, "artistry seems to deaden the subject; there are too many scenes, too many pictures--e.g., of handsome soldiers on their horses, of "young women crying in their darkened rooms." One gives the novel the credence given to "an excellent book of Civil War pictures." The author's "Southern piety" may have interfered with the dramatic possibilities of the subject: "the human heart in conflict with itself." She has brought "too much respect and too little skepticism to her Civil War novel." Her best works are Penhally and Aleck Maury, Sportsman; the latter, a quiet "masterpiece." Penhally has "an inner life growing out of two ideas in conflict": nostalgia and change. In Aleck Maury, Gordon's "detached and loving irony" has "never served a happier subject." Gordon's subjects are Southern; is her "preoccupation with Art also Southern?" Perhaps. But "her style is closer to Willa Cather's than it is to Southern rhetoric" and is "related to the nineteenth-century European heritage" with which "she has clearly identified herself" (Flaubert, James, Chekhov, Stephen Crane, Joyce, Ford, Hemingway). In this style, writing about simple things, Gordon often is "an excellent fiction writer." When the subject matter arouses her sympathy she is better than when it arouses her anger or leads her into "large theoretical conclusions about men and women or the social order." There are two novels "of a very high order and a half dozen excellent short stories." Reprinted in 1962.B1.

1962 A BOOKS - NONE

1962 B SHORTER WRITINGS

1 O'CONNOR, WILLIAM VAN. "Art and Miss Gordon," in his The Grotesque: An American Genre and Other Essays. Carbondale: Southern Illinois University Press, pp. 168-76.

Essentially a reprint of the article in South (1961.B6) with only a few stylistic changes. However, one change which may be only a printing error should be noted. It reads: "'The Forest of the South' and 'Old Red' are also excellent examples of Miss Gordon's willingness [sic] to describe essentially inert situations, to create what Joyce called 'mere literature.'" "Unwillingness" was the word used in the earlier version of this sentence. See 1961.B6.

1963 A BOOKS - NONE

1963 B SHORTER WRITINGS

1 ANON. Review of A Good Soldier: A Key to the Novels of Ford Madox Ford. TLS (4 October), p. 794.

Briefly reviews the "pamphlet, the first of a series of chapbooks to be published by the University of California," which contains Gordon's lecture on the novels of Ford as well as a selected bibliography of works by and about Ford. "Miss Gordon argues that Ford's early romance, The Young

1963

(ANON.)
Lovell, is the key to his life work and finds in that forgotten book a mythic vision of Archetypal Woman which anticipates later characters like Sylvia Tietjens in Parade's End, and which puts Ford among the followers of Robert Grave's White Goddess." Gordon's "key does not in fact open many doors. Nevertheless, she does direct attention to a recurrent treatment of beautiful, cruel women which is an important strain in Ford's novels, even though it is not quite so central or so mythic as she proposes."

2 BARO, GENE. "A Leisurely Hunter, a Man at Bay." NYTBR (20 October), p. 4.
Reviews Old Red and Other Stories. The best of the stories have "an unerring sense of place." When Gordon "is dealing with the rural South...she can scarcely be faulted." The "rhythm and detail of Southern middle-class life is her intimate possession" and she is "able to draw the proper degree of feeling from the commonplaces of that existence." Gordon "occasionally demonstrates that there is no substitute for sympathetic understanding of the intricacies of a way of life," for when she "works up" a story or writes from intelligence merely [as in "One Against Thebes" or "Emmanuele! Emmanuele!"] the stories are less successful. In this collection the most striking successes are the stories of Aleck Maury--"the sensual, the natural, man at bay." Maury "is unable to realize his gifts in worldly terms." Increasingly "his way of life is an indulgence, a leisured pursuit, out of step with individual progress and material ambition." Paradoxically, his life-style is an "evasion of responsibility and a confrontation of reality." The characterization of Maury is "wholly convincing" in "widely varying circumstances." In the Maury stories objects are "felt as well as perceived." Here, there is "the impact of environment, not the rhetoric of staging." Hence, the reader is a participant, not just an audience. There is slightly less empathy in the stories out of the historical past [e.g., "The Captive"].

3 BRADBURY, JOHN M. Renaissance in the South: A Critical History of the Literature, 1920-1960. Chapel Hill: University of North Carolina Press, pp. 57-63.
"Of the Fugitive group proper, those whose names appeared on the masthead of The Fugitive magazine" and "of those closely associated with the group," Gordon was the "first to print fiction." Unlike her associates, Gordon "went directly to fiction, without preliminary apprenticeship to poetry." Her fiction "belongs close to the heart of the

new tradition"; with Allen Tate, she is "responsible for the term, symbolic naturalism, and for its definition." Lacking the "spontaneity and originality of the more widely read artists in the mode," she has been "one of the most conscientious students of technique." Her "instinct is for pattern; she works most effectively, therefore, with the historical movement, the family group, the typical, rather than the individual, character." Only in her later novels "does she attempt any deep penetration into her protagonists' minds or psychological processes and seldom then does she enter into them with any strongly participative warmth." "Perhaps largely for this reason, she has never achieved great popular success, though her work has stood high in critical esteem." The life of Penhally is "rather thin" but "accomplishes its purpose through a completely honest objectivity, unmarred by sentimentality or melodrama." Her historical novels have "realistic detail and absence of traditional sentimentalities" but "on the human and symbolic levels" are "less effective." Green Centuries and Elizabeth Madox Roberts' The Great Meadow illustrate "the development of symbolic naturalism in a decade." In The Garden of Adonis, and contemporaneously with Allen Tate's The Fathers, and again in The Women on the Porch, Gordon adopts James Joyce's device of extended application of myth and ritual to modern literature. The Garden of Adonis is strained, but The Women on the Porch exhibits Gordon in "full control of her method and at her best as well in evocation of scene and country people." Yet the final resolution of The Women on the Porch "fails, as indeed the characters of the protagonists, and particularly of the vaguely realized Jim, themselves fail to carry the requisite conviction." The Strange Children and The Malefactors mark a third stage in Gordon's development wherein "she has abandoned mythic reference and substituted religious values for those of the agrarian tradition." Despite its limitations, The Strange Children "displayed a new talent for capturing the flavor of modern intellectual and spiritual dilemmas." The Malefactors is "somewhat ponderously and confusingly Jamesian in the early series of flashbacks." This novel "can have little appeal for the uninformed" and presents "all but insuperable difficulties" for the informed, the "chief of which is a sense of constant embarrassment" as the book "takes on the nature of a public confessional" through its parallels with widely known persons and facts. Moreover, The Malefactors lacks "the remove which the child-narrator provided in The Strange Children." "One is always left in a Gordon novel with admiration for her technique, her ironic revelations, her

(BRADBURY, JOHN M.)
accuracy in observation, but it is difficult to participate in the lives of her characters and to warm to them." Her "most complete success" is achieved in the short story "where her impeccable technique and command of symbol can operate freely with characters sketched in rather than presented in their full complexity." "Old Red," "The Brilliant Leaves," and "The Forest of the South" are "finely underplayed stories." Only where the stories "appear to have been pared from her novels," does The Forest of the South "fall off from Miss Gordon's masterful best."

4 BUCKMASTER, HENRIETTA. "'Condition of Kinship.'" Christian Science Monitor (31 October), p. 7.
Reviews Old Red and Other Stories, a collection which is "technically very winning; thematically less commanding." The "fictionalized speculation on André Gide and his wife" seems "to lack the tragic pathos necessary for either human or artistic relevance." The southern stories have "sight, smell, intonation, phrasing, but--for my taste--little depth." One senses that Gordon "is not very interested in the why or the wherefore of this stifling, parochial way of living" which perhaps is not so to her. The "constant Negro and white awareness of each other" is "never stressed (as in average day-by-day experience)." There is an odd detachment: "a heart seems, to me, left out." "Old Red" and "The Presence" are the most poignant stories because there is "a deeper involvement in compassion, a more effective probing of those sorrows which...connect the human family with some measure of concern." Gordon has probably "given these stories exactly the tone and touch she desired." But "is that sufficient when sensibilities are invoked?"

5 CASSILL, R. V. Review of Old Red and Other Stories. New York Herald Tribune Book Week (20 October), p. 22.
Brief review and portrait of Gordon, "one of the purest and best disciplined talents of the last 30 years. Her range is not very great--it isn't even as broad as she thinks it is--but the present sampler...shows a lapidary skill that can be admired even when she's polishing chestnuts." The best stories are "Old Red," "The Presence," and "The Last Day in the Field." "The Presence" is cunning in strategy; "The Last Day," as "true as a tuning fork." "The Captive" and the Civil War stories are less rewarding; their manner "seems dated." The "most bewildering story" is "Emmanuele! Emmanuele!" There seems no real reason for telling it "since the story is about André Gide" who is

"not very cutely" renamed by Gordon. "Gide tells the tale more poignantly in 'Et Nunc Manet in Te.'"

6 CHENEY, BRAINARD. "Caroline Gordon's Ontological Quest." Renascence 16 (Fall):3-12.

Discusses Gordon's fiction seen as a totum, the "composition of an epic ordeal." The Malefactors is not only "the culmination of her work" but also "the final flower of the quest that has ordered Caroline Gordon's whole artistic career. It is an answer to unremitting prayer. It is the revelation of ontological motivation." The dramatic conflict in sex relationships "constitutes the axis on which her fictional world turns.... It is the creative core in nature by which she intuits life's meaning. And it is the key by which she eventually unlocks a material world to the Christian spirit." Moreover, Gordon "succeeded in illuminating the flaw in the American myth of the frontier" which others came to perceive only a quarter of a century later. In Green Centuries "it was the odor of sanctity about an Indian society...by which she was able to render godless the smell of the sweat of the violent ever moving frontiersman." In the love-relation of Rion and Cathy "we find the core of the action that delivers Caroline Gordon's meaning. Their love has broken down under the unbearable burden of the westward movement." In The Women on the Porch, Gordon "brings this disease to definition." In a sense, all her novels before The Malefactors "were exploratory and transitional," attempts to "find the terms of moral conviction and Christian salvation in the context of contemporary life." Finding these terms was her ontological quest. Moreover, she "had to invent a strategy and tactic to give them dramatic weight, to make the action real." Even The Strange Children is prefatory: at once "her cleverest and slightest work." Here she "brings today's strange children from their cynical mirth into the light of Christian reality," and dramatically "presents the nature of conviction and the way to salvation." Yet all Gordon's work is a "progress toward The Malefactors," which is, categorically, "a story of Christian conversion." John W. Simons (See 1956.B15) fails to perceive Gordon's "greater achievement": the revelation of "Grace in Action" and "the Action of Grace." The truth of what Gordon has done in The Malefactors lies in "our realizing what Tom Claiborne finally found" in Horne Watt's poem: a recognition of man's ontological motivation toward God, "however impaled in flesh he may be." As early as "Summer Dust" [The Gyroscope, November, 1929] virgin-girlhood "becomes the antagonist of Caroline Gordon's panoramic dramas of

1963

(CHENEY, BRAINARD)
disintegration and remains at the center of the ordeal of rediscovery as well."

7 EISINGER, CHESTER E. "Caroline Gordon: The Logic of Conservatism," in his Fiction of the Forties. Chicago: University of Chicago Press, pp. 186-93.

"Caroline Gordon: The Logic of Conservatism" is a subsection of a chapter entitled "The Conservative Imagination." It is not surprising that in Gordon's "quest for the universal myth she should have come to Catholicism.... the entire, combined force of her need--for order, for tradition, for piety, for absolution and grace, for a shaping world view that would take the place of the shapeless chaos of the world--forced her inevitably and logically" in that direction. Before this she was elegiac toward the South and the past, and a "pervasive sense of cultural loss flows through her work." Neither urban culture nor the world of nature is "in itself sufficient." In technique, as well as in themes, the new fiction for her "means largely a turning back to models who had that same dedication to the craft of writing that is apparent in her own work" [James, Flaubert, Joyce]. Ironically she both admires dramatic structure and "frequently falls short in precisely this respect." Discusses Green Centuries in which Gordon subjects "to hard examination the great myth of the West"; The Women on the Porch, "somewhat disappointing in the commonplace quality of its conception," based as it is on two themes: the "death of the South" and "the spiritual corruption inherent in the metropolis"; The Forest of the South which may be seen, "at least in part, as a kind of supplement to The Women on the Porch": a set of stories that explain why the South has been despoiled; and The Strange Children, "the most satisfying volume that Miss Gordon has published." In the latter, she "gives full play to the substantial body of ideas demanded by the conflict she poses: the life of religious faith and the pursuit of regeneration versus intellectualism and cosmopolitanism." Here her style "takes on a richer quality" and "her manipulation of the point of view...is especially worthy of remark." The irony that adoption of Lucy's point of view affords "enriches the book throughout." Kevin "stands for the true religion, but unfortunately this is more apparent in the intention than in the performance." Gordon does not "demonstrate to us the life-giving force of religion in the man she selects to stand as its witness." On the other hand, the Lewises "suffer from the curse of the abstract and the immobility of the objective stance." In Tubby,

Gordon "makes her case for the pressing need for religion to counteract the decadence of Western man" and underlines this "by viewing it, stark and unmodified, in the light of a child's holistic morality." Though The Strange Children is "the most readable" of Gordon's novels, it is "not wholly successful," but rather "suffers from a failing apparent in all her work: she seems to lack a kind of dramatic nerve." She "cannot rise to the controlled passion, to the directed frenzy that will channel her action into the revelation of its essential meaning"; she seems to lack "the calculated abandon necessary to create the grand effect. She muffs or muffles her big scenes." "At the crucial moment she tends to be static."

8 LEONARD, JOHN. "Monsters, Butter-Pastry, Saltines." NatR (31 December), p. 571.

Reviews three books, including Old Red and Other Stories. Gordon is "always in complete control, reworking her materials to achieve a dream-like quality of large, nebulous softness, of sustained tension never quite relieved." She writes well of "the small stealthy death, the squandered opportunity, the unconsummated caress, the unacknowledged desire or disguise or defeat." "Emmanuele! Emmanuele!" is her best though Fäy "is modeled too obviously on Gide." Of the stories of the Maury family, only "Old Red" seems "really satisfying"; "the others are the stuff of a novel, left irritatingly unresolved and out of focus." Gordon is "good at child-stories." Her South "rings true" but "too many of her young men cry out or sob shudderingly over the beauties of nature," and "too many different people 'laugh like a child'"; too much "is 'unbearably sweet.'"

9 PINE, JOHN C. Review of Old Red and Other Stories. LJ 88:3224.

"Miss Gordon's unobtrusive style is so deceptively simple that it is easy to call it artless." This volume "constitutes a fine sampling of her work in the short story form." The best stories have to do with her own milieu: the "purely literary exercise ["Emmanuele! Emmanuele!"] is much less successful." Gordon has an "uncanny ear for local speech patterns." "Stories such as 'One More Time' and 'The Ice House' actually remind one of Hemingway in their purity and intensity."

10 RUBIN, LOUIS D., JR. The Faraway Country: Writers of the Modern South. Seattle: University of Washington Press, pp. 13, 196, and 240.

Mentions Gordon in passing on three pages. She "has not resided in the South for years" though she was a member of

1963

(RUBIN, LOUIS D., JR.)
"the previous generation of Southern writers, the generation of the high renascence," that prior to Styron and Agee. Though none of the younger generation of Southern writers "seems to be of quite such major stature" as Faulkner, Wolfe, Warren, Welty and others, "what is important is not what might happen, but what has happened: a literary renascence, a rich outpouring of artistic genius such as few times and places have ever enjoyed." Gordon is listed in this "incredible galaxy of talent."

1964 A BOOKS - NONE

1964 B SHORTER WRITINGS

1 ALLEN, WALTER. The Modern Novel in Britain and the United States. New York: E. P. Dutton and Co., pp. 113-14.
None Shall Look Back is "perhaps the most austere and uncompromising novel about the Civil War that we possess," a "heroic novel in the strict sense." It may "appear even fanatical in its author's complete acceptance of the image of the South in its antebellum period." Yet "one cannot help wondering whether life has ever been lived at the constantly heroic pitch described in this novel" where the conception of life as described seems "a literary abstraction," and the characters seem "static" and unaware of the "moral corruption that was fundamental to Southern society." The novel is "a heroic story--but nothing more." The achievement of Faulkner's novels is perhaps revealed by contrast with None Shall Look Back; Faulkner's treatment of the South "is infinitely more complex."

2 BROWN, ASHLEY. "The Novel as Christian Comedy." In Reality and Myth. Edited by William E. Walker and Robert L. Welker. Nashville: Vanderbilt University Press, pp. 161-78.
Discusses The Malefactors as Gordon's re-creation of "the Dantesque experience in her own terms, in images which we recognize as being peculiar to our own generation," and as "the culmination of her work." Her subject here is "the actual experience, not the mere fact, of religious conversion." In The Malefactors Gordon adopts "the same convention of social comedy that she used in The Strange Children, but she has informed it with a scheme that is far more ambitious than anything in the earlier novel": "a Commedia that follows something of the plan of Dante's poem. (The Malefactors was originally subtitled A Comedy)." The Purgatorio is that part of Dante's Commedia which is "most

inclusive in its reach of experience." In The Malefactors, Tom Claiborne "undergoes a spiritual experience like that of Dante in the Purgatorio: his state of mind allows him to reach far into the past to reconstruct the events which have brought him to his present condition, and at the end he has a vision which anticipates the Paradiso Terrestre." Vera is "the Beatrice of the novel"; George Crenfrew, the Vergil; Cynthia, the Siren of Purgatorio XIX; Catherine Pollard, the Matelda; and Horne Watts, the Arnaut Daniel of Purgatorio XXVI. "The bull is a major symbol of the action," ambivalently representing both fecundity and mechanical bestiality. The novel corresponds, in its parts, to Dante's days and nights on the mount of Purgatory. Toward the end, Tom "passes through a wall of flame himself" and learns "that he must forgive these dead men [Horne Watts and Carlo Vincent] whom he has resented so long." This is the limit of the secular wisdom Crenfrew (Vergil) can offer him. The scene in the chapel is "perhaps modeled" on Chapter XVI of Henry James' The Ambassadors. "The experience depicted in [Dante's] Commedia is an archetypal one, freely available to succeeding generations, and naturally it would be adjusted to the scope and limitations of a particular form." Knowledge of the Dantesque scheme in The Malefactors "adds another dimension to the action, which is thus played out against something larger than itself."

3 RUBIN, LOUIS D., JR. "The Image of an Army: The Civil War in Southern Fiction." In Southern Writers: Appraisals in Our Time. Edited by R. C. Simonini, Jr. Charlottesville: University of Virginia Press, pp. 50-70.

Of more than a thousand novels on the Civil War by Southerners, only a few, among them Gordon's None Shall Look Back, are "interesting, often of high literary excellence, and well worth reading." But, though good, these Civil War novels are not equal to their authors' greatest work, and "the war itself awaits its fictional chronicler." None Shall Look Back "has not the strength or scope" of several of Gordon's novels about the modern South. "So little really good fiction has been produced about the Confederate army" and "there has not been really outstanding work of fiction about the Confederate soldier, and his times." Herbert Marshall McLuhan's diagnosis that in the Southern novel there is "a vacuum where we might expect introspection" ["The Southern Quality," in Allen Tate, ed., A Southern Vanguard (New York, 1947), p. 117 , is "certainly true of a writer such as Caroline Gordon." In the portrayal of Rives Allard, there is no introspection,

1964

(RUBIN, LOUIS D., JR.)
no meditation, no sense of "the impact of a Confederate soldier's first realization that the war might be lost." In place of self-revelation there is symbol: "slight human gestures, external events." Gordon's characters are "mostly silent about the events of the war." Rives is intended "to exemplify a social system, a school of character, the region." Gordon's intention is "patriotic; Rives Allard is the prototype of a society." It is this purpose that "determines the form that numerous Southern war novels have taken," and their limitations. "This rules out such themes as the personal impact of war on an individual sensibility, the hammering out of the individual soul on the anvil of conflict, the growth of compassion and understanding amid the cataclysm of suffering," the themes that "make up the chief concern of War and Peace." Only in Southern nonfiction of the Civil War period (diaries, letters, memoirs) do we find the War treated "as an ordeal in itself" for individual persons, not just as a social "catastrophe that destroyed antebellum life." To write of the Civil War "with the breadth and penetration of great literature" would require the Southern novelist "not to foresake his sense of society and history, but [to] add to it the ability of a Crane [The Red Badge of Courage] to see the lonely individual soul as well." The War "happened not to waxen images but to men, in a region peopled by individuals who are not stereotyped as social exemplars but released by a social code into their full stature as men." "Through the perceptions of such a protagonist, the full tragedy of the Civil War might be captured in fiction." Reprinted in 1967.B2.

1965 A BOOKS - NONE

1965 B SHORTER WRITINGS

1 COWLEY, MALCOLM. "The Meriwether Connection." SoR N.S. 1: 46-56.

A biographical account of Cowley's visit to the Meriwether's home at Cloverlands in May 1933, with discussions of the countryside, the estate (built in 1830), the family (Caroline Gordon's cousins on her mother's side), the lifestyle, the habit of story-telling, the almost daily visits with Caroline Gordon and Allen Tate (married since 1924 and living then with Caroline Gordon's grandmother at Merry Mount), the presence of literary friends from Nashville, the local economy, the attitudes toward the land, the Southern heroes, and the defense of the agrarian way of life. A May reunion of the Fugitive group includes a dinner at John Crowe Ransom's. Among the figures portrayed are Andrew Lytle, Sidney M. Hirsch, J. C. Ransom, and John Gould Fletcher. The agrarian way of life was threatened both by industrialism and by its own meager treatment of sharecroppers: "The question of social justice was one that was avoided in their symposium, partly...because they could not agree on what to say about it." In 1933 "the injustice of the system appeared to be economic more than racial." Cowley, in 1933, "could not see much future for Southern Agrarianism....the Agrarians themselves had been forced off the land by their talents and training, which they had no scope to exercise in rural life." Like sharecroppers gone North, they too belonged now to "the underpaid white-collar staff of the new educational factories."

2 STEWART, JOHN L. *The Burden of Time: The Fugitives and Agrarians*. Princeton: Princeton University Press, pp. 41-42, and 184-85.

The distinctive image of man of Southern writers, including Gordon, is mythopoeic. In the work of leading writers of the "Renaissance," beneath the details of the regional material and far beyond the aims of mere local colorists, is "an image at once essential and definitive and it constitutes the special contribution of contemporary Southern writing to American literature." It is anti-progressive, anti-rationalist, anti-humanist, and "insists on the irreducible mystery in life, the all-pervasiveness of evil in human affairs, and the limitations of man's capacity to understand and control his environment and his own nature." Particularly "Southern" evil goes back to the Old Testament, to Original Sin, and to "the Protestant habit of searching the private heart," thus resembling New England writers up to Melville. The Southern image of man "was projected not only in religious terms but historic as well. And the view of history was curiously bifocal": life as blurred and blurring flux, and life as changeless permanence. Stewart discusses "*the* problem for Southern writers of the Fugitive-Agrarian generation such as Faulkner, Katherine Anne Porter, Eudora Welty, and Caroline Gordon": namely, the dangers and risks of regionalism [e.g., programmatic literature and the "dogma of the appropriate subject"]; and the writer's corresponding need to "establish an effective connection with the culture of his region" and to "think long and deeply" before writing. Gordon is "an interpreter of the Southern past," looking at her region in the light of history--and belongs thus, with Faulkner, Warren, Porter, and the later Davidson.

1966

1966 A BOOKS

1 McDOWELL, FREDERICK P. W. Caroline Gordon. University of Minnesota Pamphlets on American Writers, No. 59. Minneapolis: University of Minnesota Press, 48 pp.

Discusses at some length Gordon's life, critical views, selected short stories, and eight novels published before 1966. Her work "is more impressive in its totality than each book seemed to be on publication....only recently have critics felt the full impact of her work and been able to see its unity." The late Jamesian "central intelligence operates at its purest in her two latest novels." Her "use of symbolic naturalism is most clearly seen in her short stories," six of which are "some of the best written in the present century." None Shall Look Back has "the massive proportions associated with the epic"; Gordon's "model throughout seems to have been Tolstoi's epical War and Peace." Yet some of the battle scenes "reveal the weakness of the panoramic method." The Women on the Porch represents a turning point in Gordon's manner. In The Strange Children the reader does not see the truth of Kevin Reardon's heroism soon enough "for the novel to center upon him as well as upon Lucy." Gordon solves this problem in The Malefactors "by making Catherine Pollard spiritually central to the novel from the first time she appears." Here, Gordon's "notable achievement is to keep us interested in the culpable Claiborne," whose dreams are "most effective in extending the perspectives of the book." In all her novels Gordon "reaches a just balance between the idea and the fact, the abstract and the concrete, the metaphysical and the physical." Her books have an "even quality" and "consistent excellence." They deal with the "tragic dimensions of human life, the aborted aspirations of most human beings, the sense of evil infecting the good and the true, the glories and the burdens of a legendary past, the sense of cultures and individuals in conflict, and a feeling for place that becomes a muted passion." Her work is continually suggestive: hence, "the significance of any one of her books enlarges constantly as one reviews it." She suggests the ineffable through "a discerning use of myth." As a writer, Gordon is "the inquiring moralist even before she is the religious writer." Her work "impresses always by its comprehensiveness and strength." Includes a Selected Bibliography.

1966 B SHORTER WRITINGS

1 EISINGER, CHESTER E. "Class and American Fiction: The Aristocracy in Some Novels of the Thirties." In Americana-Austriaca: Festschrift des Amerika-Instituts der Universität Innsbruck, anlässlich seines zehnjahrigen Bestehens. Wein-Stuttgart: Wilhelm Braumüller, pp. 131-56.

Discusses Penhally and The Garden of Adonis for approximately two pages. For Gordon "the aristocratic way of life was good in the beginning; its disintegration in modern times leads to tragic consequences and its death can only be mourned. A heavy, ominous, dirge-like tone pervades Miss Gordon's novels. It never occurs to her that the modern, decadent aristocracy is an object for satire." Penhally "illustrates the nearly savage tone of Miss Gordon's elegy for a long-departed life." Her conception of aristocracy does not depend on money alone, but also on the patrician ideal. Chance so cherishes the patrician ideal that he is "compelled to kill his brother who violated it." The Garden of Adonis says very little that is different from the view expressed in Penhally, but "two observations [about The Garden of Adonis] are worth making": the Carters' inability to understand the Camps' "abandonment of name and identity" for the importance of family persists even in the absence of money; and Gordon's "almost uncontrolled" imagination in here depicting moral decay and the failure of human relationship.

2 HOLMAN, C. HUGH. "Her Rue with a Difference: Flannery O'Connor and the Southern Literary Tradition." In The Added Dimension: The Art and Mind of Flannery O'Connor. Edited by Melvin J. Friedman and Lewis A. Lawson. New York: Fordham University Press, p. 83.

Makes one brief indirect reference to Gordon. Allen Tate "was, with the exception of his wife, Caroline Gordon, and Ransom, unique in [a] persistent cry for a religious structure in his world."

3 LYTLE, ANDREW. "Caroline Gordon and the Historic Image," in his The Hero with the Private Parts: Essays by Andrew Lytle. Baton Rouge: Louisiana State University Press, pp. 148-70.

Reprint of 1949.B1, except for the deletion here of an illustrative sentence referring not to Caroline Gordon's work but to War and Peace.

4 TRAUTMAN, FREDERICK. Review of How to Read a Novel. Quarterly Journal of Speech 52:222.

(TRAUTMAN, FREDERICK)

For teachers or students, "Miss Gordon's advice is the most helpful in print today." The book "attempts to answer two questions: 'What is a novel?' and 'How should it be read?'" Gordon achieves her purpose with "the profundity, lucidity, and readability gained in a long career of successful writing."

1967 A BOOKS - NONE

1967 B SHORTER WRITINGS

1 HOFFMAN, FREDERICK J. The Art of Southern Fiction: A Study of Some Modern Novelists. Carbondale: University of Southern Illinois Press, pp. 5, 6, 11, 18, 19, 28, 36-39.

Gordon transmutes "the folk narrative into an examination of a universal moral circumstance." In her treatment of the Southern historical metaphor "inner weakness [in the character] conspires with external forces to threaten the center of the metaphor." Aleck Maury, Sportsman is her "most illuminating" work and deals with "her primary concerns," as well as with "the major symbols she employs to bring them to realization." Maury's acts and eccentricities are "intimately related to [her] special vision of the South and to her relation to a few of her contemporaries." "Maury's life as sportsman offers a fixed image of reality": a deep "pool" in an "out-of-the-way place" fed by cool streams--i.e., reality as "still movement." In this novel the hunt is converted "into a very special kind of experience," a search for reality. Maury is "the true heir of the 'whole man' of Southern history. The point of difference comes in the fates of the children," and the grandchildren. Gordon's "view of the adult intellectual has always been sharp"; he is "a person of limited experience," haunted by inadequacy: the intellectual's words interfere with "past and present experiences." Her fiction forms "a fictional parallel of Ransom's poem, 'Antique Harvesters'" and "its value lies in the emotional commitments and attitudes which stir it into being." Contains verbatim some of the analysis that appeared in 1956.B8, and in 1961.B5, though it is not strictly a reprint of either essay.

2 RUBIN, LOUIS D., JR. "The Image of An Army," in his The Curious Death of the Novel: Essays in American Literature. Baton Rouge: Louisiana State University Press, pp. 183-206.

Reprint of 1964.B3.

1968 A BOOKS - NONE

1968 B SHORTER WRITINGS

1 BROWN, ASHLEY. "The Achievement of Caroline Gordon." SHR 2: 279-90.

Gordon has "the most elusive reputation"; her novels "have not yet had a full-length critical presentation." She is "a conscious heiress to what is probably the central tradition of modern fiction...the Impressionist novel." Discusses Gordon's life, her debt to Ford Madox Ford, her method, and the eight novels to date. Gordon "obeys the ancient rhetorical principle of decorum." Penhally is "a completely 'rendered' novel" though its outcome is not tragic. Aleck Maury is "an Aeneas, who will leave the ruins of his father's house, but not under the aegis of any Venus who will guide him to another Troy." Like certain Southern poets, Gordon identifies "the 'lost' cause of the Old South with the cause of Troy, and thus the Southern attitude is placed within a larger perspective." None Shall Look Back and The Garden of Adonis "complement each other" and both "pose certain problems of structure and meaning." Of Gordon's novels, only None Shall Look Back contains a complete tragic movement. The Garden of Adonis is her Agrarian novel, yet here there is "no true center of action" and the novel, "though on occasion brilliant, suffers from long stretches of banality." The Adonis myth "remains external to the action." Green Centuries is the "most intelligent novel" written on the Westward migration, yet the length, accretion of detail, and austere prose preclude concentration and leave the novel "less satisfying." "The Captive" is a "masterpiece of sustained style": the experience portrayed there is "cut loose from the day-to-day 'realism' that clogs the longer work." The mode of Gordon's next group of novels--The Women on the Porch, The Strange Children, and The Malefactors--is Christian comedy. With Gordon's growing "complexity of subject has come a new boldness of technique"--more Jamesian, with the point of view "more strictly controlled." These later novels also "draw extensively on the resources of poetry," such as The Waste Land and Dante's Purgatorio. The imagery of flight permeates her books and is countered by "the emblem of stasis, even of fulfillment." Most frequently this "takes the form of a tree." The "most 'typical' moments" in Gordon's fiction are those in which her heroes "contemplate the forest." "No other American writer has so patiently described the surfaces of trees, even the striations of leaves, or made so much of them." The tree is an image

(BROWN, ASHLEY)
of wholeness: "the moment of stasis can perhaps be an intimation of something divine." Gordon "has tried to use the full resources of a tradition to create an enduring fictional illusion." She assumes that "a public reality is accessible to a private vision."

2 FLETCHER, MARIE. "The Fate of Women in a Changing South: A Persistent Theme in the Fiction of Caroline Gordon." MissQ 21 (Winter 1967-1968):17-28.

For Gordon "ideally a woman should commit herself to a man completely and unquestioningly and he should be compelled by her commitment never to betray her faith." Discusses four stories and six novels. "The Brilliant Leaves" is "the best example in The Forest of the South of the theme of modern man's inadequacy before all womankind." By the time she writes The Malefactors Gordon "believes that social order can be recovered only after religious conversion of the membership. In the face of this new religious preoccupation, her interest in the question of woman's place in the world in which no men, or very few, are to be found has diminished," though it has not disappeared. Gordon's heroines search for "love and stability in the chaotic world which has replaced or is replacing the Old South." Failing to find this, they "usually have two choices--to withdraw from life to join the women on the porch or to fall from a precipice into complete destruction. If neither of these appeals to them, they may work to sustain a poor marriage or set out to be their own man." Their endurance is "without joy." In the most recent of her books Gordon "sees hope for the Southern women, and for all the South, in the framework of the paternalistic Roman Catholic Church." Social and religious hierarchies are "interdependent; one can recover with the other and neither will do by itself."

3 ROCKS, JAMES E. "The Christian Myth as Salvation: Caroline Gordon's The Strange Children." Tulane Studies in English 16:149-60.

Gordon's Catholicism is of "a rather special kind, one that advocates the practice of the highest theological virtue, charity or Christian love." Whereas pride negated "the kind of understanding and sympathy deficient in the characters of her earlier novels," her Catholics "pursue the contemplative life of service, very often and significantly in close contact with the land." Although "perhaps not her finest work," The Strange Children (its title drawn from Psalm 144:7-8) "does mark the transition in her thinking from the agrarian myth to the Christian myth" and "utilizes well those fictional techniques that are at the very center of her critical attitude," especially "the containment of materials within the ordering principle of a consistent narrative point of view." The Strange Children is one of her best examples of this and of her other favored fictional components. Hence, The Strange Children is a "highly representative work of Caroline Gordon's intellectual and artistic maturity." Gordon's "growth into Roman Catholicism and her conversion" help to explain "the emergence in her art of highly structured religious themes." Prior to The Strange Children she had sought "a stable order or morality, in short, a myth, to give coherence to the apparent flux and chaos of human existence." But the "agrarian life and its corresponding values can serve only as a provisional or complementary ethic." Hence, Gordon's "intellectual growth from agrarianism to religious orthodoxy represents the successful quest for a permanent morality." In The Strange Children, Gordon "bears witness fully to her conversion." That novel "possesses a coherence unknown in Miss Gordon's other novels" engineered in part by the unities of time, place, and plot, as well as by the complex symbolism including quest motifs, literary allusions (especially the repetition of Undine), water, eyes, light, and the place and objects of Benfolly. In a biographical reading, through a kind of double vision, Gordon is "dramatizing her own quest through Lucy" and her own past views through Sarah. "Kevin and Isabel initiate a change of direction in the novel; they precipitate the eventual catastrophe and dramatize before Lucy's vision the very values which emerge from the novel: damnation versus grace." The game of charades is a "scene of substantial importance" (Chapters V-VI) and "serves as a crisis" in Lucy's "descent from innocence." However, the shift in point of view (from Lucy's to Stephen's) in the last two paragraphs is "detrimental to the novel": the "story is Lucy's, only very incidentally that of Stephen," and "to change intelligence is to deny Lucy her final transformation from child to adult...--in fact, almost to invalidate the experiences which are at the very thematic center of the novel." This is "the one serious flaw of the novel."

4 _____. "The Mind and Art of Caroline Gordon." MissQ 21 (Winter 1967-1968):1-16.

Gordon is "a much neglected writer." This is due in part to her unpopularity. Discusses Gordon's idea of art, her methods, her development in style, the mythic character of her later work, her basic theme of Redemption, her creation

(ROCKS, JAMES E.)

of men and women characters, and her focus on "the conditions and attributes of virtuous love" and on the causes and consequences of failure to achieve such love. Gordon has suffered neglect for two reasons: the writer must "strike out on his own once he has profited from the teaching of his mentors"; and "one's art must define and not confine, the contents of one's mind." Gordon's technique "so rigidly informs her materials that much of the vitality is robbed from the emotions." Her "indirect, suggestive, elliptical manner" smothers rather than contains the intensity. Climaxes are "often disappointing because they are understated." Crucial scenes lack drama because Gordon's "limitations as an artist rest primarily with an inability to abandon herself during those scenes." Hence most of Gordon's characters, except for Aleck Maury, are "somehow dominated by technique." She "works best with the small unit, the short story." In her novels, "the totality is less than the sum of its parts." Gordon is "an author of second rank in the flourishing Southern Renaissance" though certain novels and stories "would suffice to place her in a high position among her distinguished confreres." She draws on a "rich cultural tradition" and a "foremost literary tradition" to produce works that, "for all their limitations, contribute significantly to modern Southern literature."

5 RUBIN, LARRY. "Christian Allegory in Caroline Gordon's 'The Captive.'" SSF 5:283-89.

Since Gordon's conversion to Roman Catholicism critics have been "trying to find signs of a religious orientation in her later work." Actually "the Christian vision, a sort of seventeenth-century Calvinism, appears much earlier" in her work, notably in "The Captive" published in 1932. Vivienne Koch (1953.B2) discusses Gordon's "significant use of the supernatural" in "The Captive" but there is "no attempt to offer a religious interpretation." Such an interpretation of the story is "not only plausible, but virtually unescapable." In this story Gordon presents "one form of the Christian vision of damnation and salvation, involving the familiar doctrines of original sin, predestination, justification by good works, and redemption through Christ's agony on the Cross." The Indians represent the "forces of Hell"; Mad Dog is a "literally diabolical figure"; Jinny's original sin delivers her into "the hands of these demons" and she is thus doomed. Her "fatalistic attitude at the beginning of the story" is "some form of the idea of predestination." The white youth "may be a Christ-figure" and for her he proves to be "a messiah" who comes to her in "a kind of dream-vision and shows her the way to safety--a safety analogous to salvation," if the Indian captivity is "a type of damnation." Jinny's physical hardships suggest "the familiar 'straitness' of the way to heaven." In the end her persistent poling of the raft across the river relates this incident to justification by good works in addition to faith. Finally, Jinny literally renders "her thanks to the Deity for saving her from hell-fire." Taken together these points "cohere into a single allegorical pattern that compels attention....the basically Christian view expressed in the story is unmistakable." Jinny is Everywoman.

1969 A BOOKS - NONE

1969 B SHORTER WRITINGS

1 CORE, GEORGE. "A Crossing of the Ways: An Afterword." In Southern Fiction Today: Renascence and Beyond. Edited by George Core. Athens, Ga.: University of Georgia Press, p. 93.

One reference: "In the last fifteen years Caroline Gordon, Tate, Davidson, Ransom, Warren and Lytle himself have turned some of their finest efforts to criticism, and today there is great evidence that younger men in the South have learned the lessons of the New Criticism. Yet one hastens to say that the criticism of Tate, Brooks, Warren, and Ransom is not as good as it was--and that the South no longer dominates the literary world as it once did in the early days of the Southern Review."

2 HOLMAN, C. HUGH. Introduction to Southern Fiction Today: Renascence and Beyond. Edited by George Core. Athens, Ga.: University of Georgia Press, p. viii.

Gordon is listed as one of those writers "whose absence from the rolls of contemporary American letters would so drastically change the picture of our national literature in the second third of the twentieth century that it is almost unimaginable that [she] should not be there."

1970 A BOOKS - NONE

1970 B SHORTER WRITINGS

1 ROCKS, JAMES E. "The Short Fiction of Caroline Gordon." Tulane Studies in English 18:115-35.

1970

(ROCKS, JAMES E.)

Gordon's "best work" has been in the short story form. She "is not very successful in controlling the larger form: the novels produce the effect of a series of parts that do not cohere into something larger." Rather than view her stories in chronological order, a "more meaningful approach" is to "arrange her stories by subject into three groups": "stories about history [the pioneer, the Civil War, and negro life], Aleck Maury, and the Christian myth." These three groups, "include almost every work of short fiction she has written," with one exception: "'The Brilliant Leaves,' probably her finest work in the short form, resists convenient labels." Discusses "The Brilliant Leaves" at length and then the following stories in these groups: 1) History: "The Captive," "The Forest of the South," "Hear the Nightingale Sing," "The Ice House," "The Olive Garden," "The Long Day," "Her Quaint Honour," and "Summer Dust"; 2) Aleck Maury: "The Petrified Woman," "To Thy Chamber Window, Sweet," "The Last Day in the Field," "One More Time," "Old Red," and "The Presence"; and 3) "her latest short stories," those concerned with the "problems of the Christian life": "Emmanuele! Emmanuele!", "A Narrow Heart: Portrait of a Woman," "Cock-Crow," and "One Against Thebes." This later group illustrate "her development from agrarianism to Catholicism and recapitulate earlier ideas that fit into the mold of her Christian faith." The "last three stories" are part of "an autobiographical portrait of the artist as a young woman, the aim of which is to recreate the past that formed [Gordon's] artistic vocation." As such, they "tantalize the reader," are "curiously open-ended and fragmentary." The novel-in-progress "will be a fitting confirmation of the attitudes which her whole career has fostered." As a whole, Gordon's short fiction illustrates her "spiritual growth" and "delineates the themes that constitute her mind and the techniques that form her art": "conflicts arising between dominant women and weak men, who fail to meet the test of woman as guide"; "initiation into a particular tradition or society and the resultant quest for identity"; and "the problems of the artist, as observer of and participant in his world." Gordon's short fiction contains her "search for order, stability and permanence--salvation, in fact."

2 TAYLOR, PETER, contributor. "Comments on Neglected Books of the Past Twenty-five Years." American Scholar 39:345.

When topicality and innovation seem to be everything, "such a masterpiece as Caroline Gordon's Aleck Maury, Sportsman...still exists." No one who has read it can forget "the superb craftsmanship, the profound character drawing, the poetry the novel finally achieves in the meaningful relationship of all its elements."

1971 A BOOKS - NONE

1971 B SHORTER WRITINGS

1 ANON. Review of The Glory of Hera. Kirkus 39:1330.
Sees the novel as "an impressive, if somewhat overwhelming statement concerning man's mass-mythic consciousness and the progressive evolution of the hero/deliverer through the legend of Heracles." Summarizes the divine-human entanglements of the action. "If you've left your Bulfinch in the fields of asphodel, you may feel insecure." Gordon's prose has "a cool acuity" and "exquisite control." The novel is "an Olympian effort which requires an equal one of the reader."

2 BAUM, CATHERINE B. and FLOYD C. WATKINS. "Caroline Gordon and 'The Captive': An Interview." SoR N.S. 7:447-62.
A tape-recorded interview with Gordon (1966). Prior to the interview Gordon "did not reread the story"; she "pulls her comments out of the pure material of memory--out of the past." The interviewers "have made editorial deletions, but no additions." Gordon discusses "The Captive" and comments on captivity stories, the donnée for her story, her attitudes toward her short stories and novels, the characterization of Jinny, pioneer ways, archetypes, dialects, Indian habits, point of view, the forest as menace, Dante's four levels of interpretation, allegory, the concept of theme, symbolism, and frontier culture.

3 BROWN, ASHLEY. "None Shall Look Back: The Novel as History." SoR N.S. 7:480-94.
The formal problem of the novel is: "how to unite several levels of action." Gordon solves this brilliantly; the novel is "an object lesson in the conversion of history into tragic fiction." Gordon arranges the novel in four parts and this is "one clue to her intention." Discusses at length the four parts which arrange the subject "according to history": I. The way of life of Fontaine Allard; II. The Confederate disaster at Fort Donelson and the burning of Bracketts itself; III. The peak of the Confederate effort: the Battle at Chickamauga; IV. The climax of the novel: the final desperate effort of the Confederates in the Battle of Franklin; and the Epilogue, with its

(BROWN, ASHLEY)
necessarily falling action. "At the climax of the novel, the two levels of action, public and private meet. Rives' tragedy is caught up in the larger action of which Forrest is the representative, and for this to be credible Forrest must participate in the pathos himself." Gordon "accomplishes this through her adroit shift in the point of view," from Rives' to Forrest's, "the technical feature peculiar to the novel." The effect Gordon gets "is tragic, and it has been well prepared for." For Lucy, "there is only bleak endurance, prefigured in her mother-in-law's mode of existence." This is the "most impressive" of Gordon's first group of novels.

4 CHENEY, BRAINARD. "Caroline Gordon's The Malefactors." In Rediscoveries: Informal Essays in Which Well-Known Novelists Rediscover Neglected Works of Fiction by One of Their Favorite Authors. Edited by David Madden. New York: Crown Publishers, pp. 232-44.

This essay is the same as that in SR 79:360-72 where it appeared first though it was written for this volume. See 1971.B5.

5 _____. "Caroline Gordon's The Malefactors." SR 79:360-72.

Fifteen years after the publication of Gordon's novel, Cheney reviews the neglect and positive and negative criticism accorded The Malefactors. The topical Catholic press ignored the novel with one exception: John W. Simon's review in Commonweal (See 1956.B15). The "formidable theme" of conversion evidently put off some reviewers. Moreover, "the roman à clef aspect of a piece of fiction has no direct literary or artistic importance." Dorothy Day was unwilling to have the novel publicly dedicated to her. More importantly, the novel reflects "a Catholic neo-medievalism of a generation ago" and is a stage in Gordon's "ontological quest of thirty years that had taken her from the heartland of economic absolutism to Christian mysticism," coming as she did in The Strange Children to the theme of "the actual experience, not the mere fact, of religious conversion." Following a synopsis of The Malefactors, a review of Brown's (1964.B2) and Simon's essays, and a discussion of Sister Bernetta Quinn's analysis of the parallel between Catherine of Siena's Divino Dialogo and Hart Crane's The Bridge, Cheney claims that "By leaving Pontifex a blank label, Miss Gordon intended surely to suggest to the reader the substitution of Hart Crane's 'Epic of America'--in all its richness, its power, and its weakness" and recalls that in 1937 Tate said Crane "was one of those men whom every age seems to select as spokesmen of its spiritual life." Cheney concludes that Gordon "is not yesterday's prophet, but tomorrow's." The Malefactors is the "climax" of Gordon's novels.

6 COWAN, LOUISE. "Nature and Grace in Caroline Gordon." In Studies in Medieval, Renaissance, [and] American Literature: A Festschrift [Honoring Troy C. Crenshaw, Lorraine Sherley, and Ruth Speer Angell]. Edited by Betsy F. Colquitt. Fort Worth: Texas Christian University Press, pp. 172-87.

Slightly revised version of the article originally published in Critique (See 1956.B6), and essentially the same except for the last paragraph where significant references to Gordon's work after The Strange Children are made. "The Strange Children and The Malefactors...delineate the workings of grace in the soul, since in them the religious theme is apparent and undisguised." At the time of her conversion to Catholicism Gordon "entered upon a stage of artistic productivity in which she examined openly and clearly those concerns which in her earlier work she had treated obscurely though powerfully." In her new novel, a chapter of which has been published in The Sewanee Review, Autumn 1969, Gordon "has begun a further extension of her range; and...one can now with some feeling of completeness survey the work leading up to this point."

7 LANDESS, THOMAS H. "The Function of Ritual in Caroline Gordon's Green Centuries." SoR N.S. 7:495-508.

The essential meaning of the novel is "the proper relationship between man and woman." Its true action "is archetypal rather than historical in its ultimate significance and is best traced in the relationships between the two pairs of lovers." Some critics have confused the enveloping action (historical) with the action: this distinction and the relationship between the two "can be better understood, perhaps, by examining the function of ritual in the narrative, a formal element which is of utmost importance to the dynamics of the novel." Gordon's concept of ritual is that "held by all traditional societies": it is "a means of definition--one which gives form and larger significance to man's archetypal actions in the ordinary world. As a participant in traditional rites and ceremonies the individual defines himself in relation to the three great realms of order within which he exists: those of nature, the community, and the supernatural." In Green Centuries the principal rituals "surround and contain the survival instinct in its two primary manifestations: the drive for food and the sex urge." The rituals of the hunt are associated with the

(LANDESS, THOMAS H.)
male, the hunter, the masculine principle; the rituals of sexual conduct and the generative spirit are associated with the female, the child bearer and sexual object, the feminine principle. Both represent the "idea of containing the animal spirit in ritual." These two groups of rituals are "normative and provide a key to the moral meaning of the action" of the novel. Gordon presents "two opposing societies: the amorphous, individualistic society of the pioneers, and the formalized communal society of the Cherokees.... The contrast between the two cultures is made explicit" in "analogous actions subtly designed to highlight the masculine and feminine roles in each society and their relationship to each other." Within the Indian society, rituals unite complementary spirits; in the white society, "the breakdown of ritual results in the dissolution of a marriage and, on a larger scale, the failure of two societies to live at peace in nature."

8 O'CONNOR, MARY. "On Caroline Gordon." _SoR_ N.S. 7:463-66.
A biographical memoir of Gordon. The wife of the late William Van O'Connor writes from two decades' friendship with Gordon. She discusses Gordon as one who assimilates and transmutes "the world of her personal experience into symbolic structures of the journey from innocence to the melancholy of knowing and the comforts of religious commitment, insight, hope. Over all her writing plays a shimmer, a luster of the classical Greek world deep in her consciousness and subtly patterning all her vision." Gordon's talent is "not all verbal": she paints, does needlework, cooks. "Fabulous beasts" and "the lives and relics of saints" interest her. "She has wrestled with her free thinker Meriwether heritage all the way" to Roman Catholicism, and "these contending strains serve her admirably in making whole the soul in its mortal dress." Gordon's work allows the reader "to live in the world but outside existing conceptions of it."

9 SQUIRES, RADCLIFFE. "The Underground Stream: A Note on Caroline Gordon's Fiction." _SoR_ N.S. 7:467-79.
Gordon's "interest lies in the descrescendos" of an earlier heroism. In _Green Centuries_ "we are given the origins of the dilemma and agony of such descrescendos." Rion Outlaw suffers from an "absence of intellect" which keeps him "from truly _possessing_ the land that he has only _seized_." The pain of his failure "arises from our feeling that the American wilderness constituted a second chance at Eden." In all the novels after _Green Centuries_, "a second

chance has already been thrown away." Aleck Maury represents the other side of the dilemma in Gordon's vision: "a dilemma between too much intellectuality and too little." Aleck "sees a modern tendency toward abstractness, dry intellectuality, as his adversary which he fights with a fierce insistence on tactile knowledge." His daughter and her husband are "victims of abstraction." With such characters as the Lewises, "menaced by mind and pride," Gordon in her mature fiction "finally chose to deal." In The Women on the Porch, "her concern shifts from objective realism toward subjective hallucination." The method shifts "from linear narration toward orbicular scenes folded within scenes; in fact, one almost feels that scenes rather than characters 'develop.'" In The Women on the Porch the social "decline has been perfected," and the novel "radiates from a problem of adultery," in a "very special gothic" mode. Chapman "is the perfect contrast to Aleck Maury" and Gordon is from this point on concerned with "writers who do not write": these historians and scholars are "really paralyzed poets" of several types. Aleck Maury, in contrast, "in some extended way comes to seem a metaphor for the vital poet whose inner being finds its perfect transfer in analogical action." The dangers of a world of decadence can be resolved only "by human contact, even violent human contact" and "by the water in the spring. Whatever the spring means." The meaning of the water "clarifies in her subsequent novel." In The Strange Children, Lucy's power is "counterpoised against the old enemy: the aridity of overweening intellectualism." Here "the stars are associated with 'intellect.'" Yet "water imagery recurs throughout the novel. Often it is underground water." It "represents salvation." Gordon believes "salvation runs like an underground stream" in man's being. Man's help is not that of a "vast power": he "needs no more than the eyes of a child, or the eyes of Aleck Maury." The surface water in Aleck Maury, Sportsman, the water that surrounds Swan Quarter in The Women on the Porch, and the water that runs beneath the burned pasture in The Strange Children are the same; the underground stream is "an arcane but always present element of human existence." It corrects the distortion or paralysis of our perception. The Malefactors does not succeed. It is "too logical." Gordon's attempt to combine "her feeling for the concrete, earthy life with her feeling for the underground stream of salvation" comes out as a "kind of impossible Fundamentalist-Catholicism." Yet this is "exactly the kind of work a serious writer often has to write before he can rise above his previous attainment" and return to the uncertainties, mysteries, and intricacies of "life."

1971

10 STANFORD, DONALD E. "Caroline Gordon: From Penhally to A Narrow Heart." SoR N.S. 7 (April):xv-xx.

Gordon "evaluates her material from the viewpoint of conservative, traditional Agrarianism which favors a dogmatic Christian faith and a stable, hierarchical society of landowners and workers over a liberal, urban, mechanized society." Hers is "some of the most civilized and moving fiction of our time," measuring up to "old but still viable standards." Her characters "come to life" and particularly her Southern characters "are treated with the compassion and irony of complete understanding." In her historical novels Gordon "has come as close to complete success as any twentieth-century writer in English." The action of Green Centuries is "absolutely convincing." "Entering into the mind of General Forrest and depicting a battle through his eyes is considerably more difficult than entering the mind of Rion Outlaw." Nevertheless, None Shall Look Back "is suspenseful and moving from beginning to end and is one of the best novels of the Civil War written in this century." The Garden of Adonis, The Women on the Porch, The Strange Children, and The Malefactors appear "to be somewhat less impressive" than Penhally, Aleck Maury, Sportsman, None Shall Look Back, and Green Centuries. One could well claim that Gordon is "one of the best half dozen or so writers of fiction in English in our century."

11 VALENSISE, RACHELE. "Tre scrittrici del Sud: Flannery O'Connor, Caroline Gordon, Carson McCullers." SA 17:251-89.

The narrative of the South as treated by these writers identifies its violent and grotesque cosmos with the human condition in an existential sense. Its repeated theme seems to be the desire of the divine, as a minister but above all as the ordering principle of a lost cosmological harmony, of a system of values that sees the individual as fully fixed in the social organism, and that organism, in the body of nature. The work of these writers gives to the ethical and social problems of the South solutions which even across varied alternatives present a thoroughly religious opening. In the view of these writers, the disturbed world of the modern South can be exorcized only by a code of values which reach a theological base. Each artist has been pushed toward a religious problem by environmental conditions; each has affirmed a common need for coherence and order in the face of the chaos which governs reality and threatens the identity of the individual: this exigency is interpreted in essentially religious terms evident in the use of biblical and mythological materials and in the use of recurring symbols; and each writer is similar to the others in the choice of a narrative filter: the grotesque (rare in Gordon) and other devices that suggest that the journey toward God is a torturing ascent toward Truth. Faith pervades the work of O'Connor and Caroline Gordon but remains frustrated in the case of Carson McCullers. In Gordon's work charity or love makes us regard one another as if each incarnates Christ, appeases harsh human solitude, and creates ties among creatures in the name of faith. Her women retain a strong attachment to the land, to family, to the traditional values of the South. Gordon has stigmatized the rejection of charity. In her work agnostic intellectualism often materializes in homosexuality as a visible manifestation of a corrupt spirituality or, in her later work, as a discarnate evil presence which leads the way to scepticism and materialism. For her, the reasons for the malaise of the South are rooted in the denial of God. Gordon was fascinated by strictly Catholic Christian material, the martyrology, and the works of the Church Fathers, as well as by the Bible. She used the lives of the saints as living metaphors of Biblical personages. Gordon's conversion to Roman Catholicism influenced her aesthetic position in that it gave her a point of thematic vision on which to found her judgment. Finally Gordon achieved a synthesis between the craftsman and the mystic. In Gordon's last works it is as if reality enriched by spiritual values can no longer be recognized and held within the conventions of realism and demands a more total dimension whence to embrace being in its spiritual and material duality. The wavering between a material reality and an ineffable dimension gives testimony to the fullness of her religious convictions and projects into her books, solidly anchored to everyday affairs, the flavor of the visionary and the mysterious. Her later narrative method is characterized by the fusion of symbolism and of a deep-seated realism in the observation of a precise social reality. The difference between the three writers remains marginal. The work of all three is characterized by a particular attitude toward reality on the basis of which phenomena are interpreted as signs or reflections of the divinity without alienating the concrete. This attitude may be defined as sacramental or reunited to a hypothetical Platonic tradition; it is, in either case, peculiar to the whole culture of the South.

1972

1972 A BOOKS

1 LANDESS, THOMAS H., ed. The Short Fiction of Caroline Gordon: A Critical Symposium. Irving, Texas: University of Dallas Press, 133 pp.

Contains: Thomas H. Landess, "Introduction"; Louise Cowan, "Aleck Maury, Epic Hero and Pilgrim"; Robert Scott Dupree, "Caroline Gordon's 'Constants' of Fiction"; Thomas H. Landess, "Caroline Gordon's Ontological Stories"; Jane Gibson Brown, "Woman in Nature: A Study of Caroline Gordon's 'The Captive'"; John E. Alvis, "The Idea of Nature and the Sexual Role in Caroline Gordon's Early Stories of Love"; Melvin E. Bradford, "The High Cost of 'Union': Caroline Gordon's Civil War Stories"; and Melvin E. Bradford, "Caroline Gordon: A Working Bibliography, 1957-1972." See 1972.B14, 1972.B10, 1972.B11, 1972.B13, 1972.B8, 1972.B1, 1972.B7, and 1972.B6.

2 STUCKEY, WILLIAM J. Caroline Gordon. Twayne's United States Authors Series. Edited by Sylvia E. Bowman. New York: Twayne Publishers, Inc., 159 pp.

To date the only full-length study in bound volume about Caroline Gordon and her fiction. Discusses Gordon's life, her theories of fiction, eight novels (exclusive of The Glory of Hera, 1972), and the two volumes of short stories. The approach is primarily explicative. The main focus of each detailed discussion is: "how the book or short story in question 'works,' what the major issues are," and "how it relates to other of Miss Gordon's fictions." The novels are treated in chronological order; the short stories are considered "according to subject or by theme." A seven-page final chapter places Gordon's fictions in critical relation "to her times and to the prevailing literary situation." Factual information is strengthened by conversations with Gordon during the year she was Writer-in-Residence at Purdue University (1963-1964) and by subsequent correspondence with her, though these associations rarely included discussion of her fiction. Gordon's work "though rigorously modern in technique is rigorously antimodern in attitude." Her aim in her fiction has been "to efface herself as a person as completely as she can." Her fiction "runs counter to the main drift of contemporary American literature." To regard her as "conservative" is irrelevant; for her, "fiction is universal, not temporal; her concern is with human emotions, not political opinions." The South she writes about is "as much the creation of her unique imagination as an actual physical place." Though her work can be related to various writers, movements, ideologies, and regions, it "almost defies categorizing." In concern for craft and technique, her fiction has much in common with James Joyce and Ernest Hemingway. In her choice of heroes and "in her view that the love of a man for a woman is an essential ingredient of fiction, she has more in common with Hemingway and Scott Fitzgerald than Joyce." Her attitudes toward the Southern past are similar to William Faulkner's. She is also significantly compared and contrasted with Eudora Welty, Katherine Anne Porter, and Flannery O'Connor, though the "important male writers of this period" are "the writers with whom Miss Gordon appears to have most in common." Yet she is separated from all the major writers of this period by a "deeper detachment" manifested in her lack of moral ambiguity. Whereas "moral ambiguity is one of the characteristics of our best fiction," Gordon "is perhaps our most unambiguous novelist" though "she is careful not to let her moral sense distort her presentation of reality." It is "possible that her techniques for achieving the illusion of objectivity were developed, in part, as a way of keeping her strong moral sense out of sight." Only in Aleck Maury, Sportsman and in "Old Red" "does she seem morally ambiguous; and, interestingly enough, these works have been her most popular ones." Gordon's novels and short stories "constitute a body of modern American fiction that must be seriously considered": in her fiction the reader receives "a sense of solidly created worlds in which men and women struggle to uphold something that is highly prized." The pleasure they offer is analogous to that which "a painter might get from studying the canvases of Vermeer or Chardin while the crowds hurry on to view those of El Greco and Picasso." Includes a Selected Bibliography of Primary Sources and briefly annotated Secondary Sources. All items listed in the Secondary Sources are included in this Reference Guide.

1972 B SHORTER WRITINGS

1 ALVIS, JOHN E. "The Idea of Nature and the Sexual Role in Caroline Gordon's Early Stories of Love." In The Short Fiction of Caroline Gordon: A Critical Symposium. Edited by Thomas H. Landess. Irving, Texas: University of Dallas Press, pp. 85-111.

Discusses at length "One Against Thebes," "The Petrified Woman," "The Brilliant Leaves," and "All Lovers Love the Spring." Gordon's stories of love "are not the least significant part" of her collected short fiction, yet "with a few notable exceptions [e.g., "The Brilliant Leaves"] these stories have not received the recognition and critical

(ALVIS, JOHN E.)
regard which their intrinsic excellence and their relevance to the understanding of Miss Gordon's total vision would seem to warrant." Much of Gordon's shorter fiction explores "the theme of sexual love, yet in none of her stories is the subject treated in an optimistic or uncomplicated manner." There are "no happy lovers" and "few characters who prove themselves adequate to the demands of love." Gordon is "peculiarly tough-minded in her treatment of sexual relationships, and her view of the conditions necessary for successful love seems highly exacting. Passion itself is rarely dwelt upon in the stories although it figures prominently" in her novels. The characters of the early love stories more often than not fail in the "worthy" but, in Gordon's view, "very hazardous enterprise" of virtuous love. The South as "forest" is an appropriate situation for these stories. In "her most popular story," "The Brilliant Leaves," Gordon manages "a more effective union of action and symbol" in her portrayal of the theme of inadequate love. Concomitant with Gordon's "vision of nature as forest" is her depiction of "a Dantesque 'dark wood' of human incapacity": thus, her portrayal of the human "as the only element [in creation] for which the proper fulfillment of sexual role poses a real problem."

2 ANON. Review of The Glory of Hera. Booklist 68:972.
Briefly reviews "a richly descriptive novel written from evident research." The novel which may be read as both adventure and philosophy defines "various parallels between Greek myths and Christian legends," and explores the psychological motives of Heracles and Hera.

3 ANON. Review of The Glory of Hera. Publisher's Weekly (3 January), p. 62.
The novel is "a retelling, at great and often tedious length, of Greek myths that succeeds in making the Olympians sound like characters in television's 'All in the Family.'" The research is meticulous but "the novel is terribly discursive and many readers grow weary of these gods without stature whose bickering and equivocations and backbiting are endless, petty and, quite often, boring." Only Heracles arouses sympathy in "an otherwise heavy, cerebral novel that makes few calls upon the emotions."

4 ANON. Review of The Glory of Hera. VQR 48 (Summer): xcviii.
Very short review. Gordon's new book is "written in her graceful style with enough persuasiveness to give life to the old legends and an air of credulity to the belief in supreme beings with anthropomorphic attributes."

5 BRADFORD, M[ELVIN] E. "Quest for a Hero." NatR (18 August), pp. 906-907.

Review of The Glory of Hera and a short commentary on Gordon's work as a whole. The Glory of Hera represents and completes a "more general development" in Gordon's work. "From the first, her search has been for the hero per se--the masculine figure of reference by whom the human (and not just the Southern) enterprise may be transformed." In her fiction, "the enemies of the hero are likewise consistent: the 'monstrous,' the 'powers of darkness'; death, in its final essence, as nullity." As in her much earlier work (especially The Garden of Adonis and Green Centuries), "she has once again located her exemplars in a classical, not a Christian, context" for here "the humanity of the hero may be most instructively explored; and it is the hero as man (rather than as demigod) which we most often misconstrue." In the novel the story of Heracles is "fleshed out and circumstanced so as to re-interpret its subject"; hence the novel is "more than a stylish updating of old mysteries." Here Heracles "personifies all the complete masculine exemplars, even the Son of Man" and "conscious moderns, accustomed to a Christ/Dionysus analogy, may be puzzled by this modest and yet formidable 'dragon slayer'" and "may quarrel with the honor given Heracles in his victory over death and in his rebirth as the child of Zeus and Hera"; yet Gordon intends this reaction: "the deliverance of her Heracles is a surprise even to him." Gordon compels us to recall that "there is no transcendence without such a basis in will [Heracles' putting up a "good fight all the way"], not knowledge."

6 ______. "Caroline Gordon: A Working Bibliography, 1957-1972." In The Short Fiction of Caroline Gordon: A Critical Symposium. Edited by Thomas H. Landess. Irving, Texas: University of Dallas Press, pp. 130-33.

The bibliography is "intended as a supplement to the listing published in Critique of Winter, 1956, and edited by Joan Griscom." It lists "Short Fiction by Caroline Gordon Since 1956" (5 items), "Criticism by Caroline Gordon Since 1956" (14 items), "Commentary on the Fiction and Criticism of Caroline Gordon Since 1956" (34 items; all these items are annotated in this Reference Guide), and "Interviews with Caroline Gordon Published Since 1956" (2 items; both are annotated in this Reference Guide). Of The Malefactors, Old Red and Other Stories, and The Glory of Hera "only a few brief reviews...are included in this gathering."

7 BRADFORD, MELVIN E. "The High Cost of 'Union': Caroline Gordon's Civil War Stories." In The Short Fiction of Caroline Gordon: A Critical Symposium. Edited by Thomas H. Landess. Irving, Texas: University of Dallas Press, pp. 113-29.

Discusses at length "The Forest of the South," "Hear the Nightingale Sing," and "The Ice House." The "three tales should be treated in conjunction. Each renders as action some portion of the many-sided enemy which the South faced from 1861 through 1865 and in lesser but more deadly struggles before and since." From this trio one can derive "some sense of the unbelievably desperate character of the conflict which turned a total culture aside from its natural course toward an imaginary tomorrow about which we now know more than we would like." These stories depict "a steady progression toward ruin." No other of Gordon's works of fiction, "not even None Shall Look Back (perhaps the most utterly 'unreconstructed' of Southern novels), is so severe upon the destructive innocence of that puzzle, the 'mind of the North,'" as "The Forest of the South." Its intersectional marriage at the end "is a deepening of conflict, not an armistice." In "Hear the Nightingale Sing," the Indiana soldier, "in his non-ideological Midwestern complaisance, betokens the political triumph" of Lieutenant Munford's breed. He "may be treated as a counter for the second stage in the North's self-conversion into Leviathan." Finally, "The Ice House" completes "the declension begun and extended" in the other two stories. In her Civil War stories Gordon is observing that "all unilinear, simplistic approaches to the human condition carry in themselves the potential of such fracturing" as the boys at the end of "The Ice House" have identified: "There ain't a whole man in ary one of them boxes [coffins]." The "only useful comment on this story" is Andrew Lytle's [See 1956.B10]: "Death is, of course, the final comment on the matter."

8 BROWN, JANE GIBSON. "Woman in Nature: A Study of Caroline Gordon's 'The Captive.'" In The Short Fiction of Caroline Gordon: A Critical Symposium. Edited by Thomas H. Landess. Irving, Texas: University of Dallas Press, pp. 75-84.

Discusses at length this short story which "has been either ignored or else misunderstood since its publication" in 1932. Some critics have classified it "as a tour de force of the 'adventure' story genre"; since Gordon's conversion to Roman Catholicism, some [e.g., Larry Rubin, See 1968.B5] have attempted to see it "as a Christian allegory almost sectarian in its emphasis." "Both extremes--the earlier condescensions and the later theological analyses--

do an injustice to the artistry of Caroline Gordon." Rather, "The Captive" is "a narrative of endurance and initiation in which the main character, a spirited and over-assertive woman named Jinny Wiley, learns the code of the wilderness while she is held captive by a group of Indian warriors who are the true inheritors of the land. It is through this ultimate understanding of the mysteries of 'a sacramental nature' that she achieves her heroic stature and her own salvation." Jinny eventually receives "the wisdom of the wholeness of nature, and her feminine function in the masculine world of the frontier is at last apparent to her."

9 CHARLES, JOHN W. Review of The Glory of Hera. LJ 97:515.

The novel's repetition of "essential incidents when a god or mortal is mentioned...can be tedious but does add to the deliberately timeless scene, since events appear to be constantly recurring." "Alternating between gods and mortals, Gordon achieves a stylistic tour de force"--treating the mortals with post-Jamesian resources, while heightening the estrangement of the gods by a "more formal, sometimes ponderous vocabulary which reads like a turn-of-the-century translation." The gods remain "incomprehensible and awesome, not amusing or rational." The novel is learned, and consistent with the Greeks' outlook; it is "a remarkable achievement."

10 COWAN, LOUISE. "Aleck Maury, Epic Hero and Pilgrim." In The Short Fiction of Caroline Gordon: A Critical Symposium. Edited by Thomas H. Landess. Irving, Texas: University of Dallas Press, pp. 7-31.

Discusses in detail five short stories: "The Burning Eyes," "The Last Day in the Field," "To Thy Chamber Window, Sweet," "One More Time," and "The Presence." Gordon's angle of vision "is primarily epic." In the epic genre, "everything is sacrificed to an essentially eschatological thrust; for nothing less than the outcome of the human enterprise hangs upon the success of its heroic quest." If Gordon's characters "hurtle into the abyss, they do so as epic and not tragic figures." Epic heroes do not struggle against the gods or within themselves but rather, "endeavor to maintain manliness and courage in a communal and cosmic realm, obeying whatever divine imperatives are given them, following a code of honor in a society that is in perpetual disorder." "No moral ambiguities must cloud" the epic writer's mind "if he is to depict the heroic." Gordon's chief effort as a writer "has been to find a usable sacral system--a myth--in a society increasingly secular and

(COWAN, LOUISE)
consequently detached from the major symbols within its own cultural heritage." The Christian master images "are to be encountered in their complete paradigmatic form in The Divine Comedy"; to this work Gordon and "most other serious artists," have "knowingly" turned. According to Erich Auerbach, "the story of Christ fundamentally changed [the European] idea of man's fate and how to describe it"; this transformation took place "far more slowly than the spread of Christian dogma." Gordon like "most other major twentieth-century writers" has tried to reconcile "the polarities of ancient myth and Christian mystery." In fact, "no writer in our time has been more concerned with this reconciliation" than she. In her early work this concern is not overt; gradually it becomes manifested. By The Women on the Porch the "union of myth and mystery, nature and grace" is signaled. "For the last fifteen years Miss Gordon has been working on a double novel, the upper pattern of which is to be entitled 'A Narrow Heart: The Portrait of a Woman' and the lower pattern, to be published first, to be called 'The Glory of Hera.'" The five stories are discussed in the light of this doubleness and of the development of Gordon's dominant angle of vision: "within this epic vision she sees life as manifesting a 'lower' and an 'upper' pattern--the first mythological and archetypal, the second historical and analogical." The Aleck Maury stories, "written for the most part in her early years (and admittedly here read in the light of her later work!), hold a paradigmatic position in her canon," partly because they demonstrate her chief theme: the futility of searching in nature to find the ground of being, but principally because they present "so clearly the character of the modern comic epic hero: Aleck Maury."

11 DUPREE, ROBERT SCOTT. "Caroline Gordon's 'Constants' of Fiction." In The Short Fiction of Caroline Gordon: A Critical Symposium. Edited by Thomas H. Landess. Irving, Texas: University of Dallas Press, pp. 33-51.
Analyzes in great detail the short story "Emmanuele! Emmanuele!" and, in much lesser detail, the uncollected story "The Olive Garden" [Sewanee Review 13 (1945):523-43]. In The Rhetoric of Fiction (See 1961.B1), Wayne Booth "misunderstands the nature of the critic's task when he goes so far as to claim that Miss Gordon's 'general definitions' [in How to Read a Novel] produce only value judgments without substance." On the contrary, Gordon "believes that the use of any given technique implies a moral position; she does not take the inhumanly 'objective' stance that Booth

attributes to the 'realistic' movement in modern fiction." Gordon "recognizes that neither sincerity nor technical skill alone is adequate for great art; they must be made indissolubly the same thing in order for fiction to possess conviction." In the light of this position, "Emmanuele! Emmanuele!" takes on "a peculiar significance. It is something more than a short story; it is perhaps a critical essay made flesh." This conte à clef based on the life of André Gide belies Booth's claim that Gordon "rejects fiction that deals with ideas." It is "perverse to see Fäy as anything other than a lost soul; but in order to understand the point of view which makes both condemnation and sympathy possible, we may turn to Dante" and to his "reluctant admission [with respect to Brunetto Latini] that even the greatest of poets cannot be saved from damnation if he does not adhere to the right forms of human behavior." Fäy's (Gide's) misbehavior is not primarily his homosexuality but his "contemplation of his own mirrored image." This is "the real sodomy which condemns him." Robert Heyward's "sensibility is the one that matters." In "The Olive Garden" also Gordon portrays "a young man who finds himself not in terms of his own actions but as a result of understanding the actions of another"--here, Deucalion and Pyrrha. In both stories the observed characters are mythological, "though the myth of Gide is one that is within living memory." Gordon's "constants" of fiction are not "merely technical devices" but rather those "normative terms" in a work that "are primarily indicative of a moral view of the universe and are more than vague generalities." A moral theme rather than pure technique "engages her attention" and "is the basis of her 'constants.'" Hence, "to approach her as either a critic or fiction writer without understanding the moral vision at the base of her work is to do her an injustice; at the least it is a distortion of her true position." Gordon "does not reject the novel of ideas, but she does insist that those ideas have to come alive through actions." Her "constants" are based on this premise, "whether she speaks of plot, narrative technique, or the character of the hero."

12 HOLMAN, C. HUGH. The Roots of Southern Writing: Essays on the Literature of the American South. Athens: University of Georgia Press, pp. 1, 117, 177, 184, and 219.

Gordon is mentioned only in an initial listing and elsewhere in passing. She is listed among the writers of the South which has "triumphantly taken possession of the American literary world." "Such a body of writers is unrivaled in a single region of America since the New England

1972

(HOLMAN, C. HUGH)
transcendentalists." With Allen Tate and John Crowe Ransom she has been "unique" in a "persistent cry for a religious structure" for her world.

13 LANDESS, THOMAS H. "Caroline Gordon's Ontological Stories." In The Short Fiction of Caroline Gordon: A Critical Symposium. Edited by Thomas H. Landess. Irving, Texas: University of Dallas Press, pp. 53-73.

Discusses at length four short stories: "Tom Rivers," "The Long Day," "Mr. Powers," and "Her Quaint Honour," which is "perhaps the best story in this group." Gordon's "later work has been characterized not only by formal properties which suggest her significant growth as a conscious craftsman but also by the discernible presence of philosophical patterns which inform the actions of her narratives and lend to them a dimension characteristic of the best in American literature." Yet her earlier stories are not "an achievement of a lower order," nor has her "essential vision of her fictional world changed in some radical sense over the years." Gordon's ontological assumptions in these stories "define man's place in the natural order of being" and may be summarized as follows: "God, a transcendent Being, exists and orders all things; man, a natural being, is in some measure an imperfect analogue of God; man's soul, therefore, partakes of the divine as well as of the earthly; for this reason, man occupies a 'middle position' in the hierarchical structure of being, and his noblest achievements involve the affirmation of the god-like portion of his nature at the expense of the merely animal, an affirmation realized most often through sacrifice or self-control." The four stories discussed here, in the light of these ontological assumptions, "were chosen primarily because they have not been discussed elsewhere in this volume, but other selections from The Forest of the South exemplify to a greater or lesser degree the same tissue of symbols supported by the same ontological assumptions." Each story discussed here "defines a different symbol of Southern ontology and does so in a way which suggests not only the presence of the daimon but also the mortal part as well."

14 _____. Introduction to The Short Fiction of Caroline Gordon: A Critical Symposium. Edited by Thomas H. Landess. Irving, Texas: University of Dallas Press, pp. 1-5.

"No more than a handful of modern writers have produced short stories which are both technically sound and rich in fictional values." Gordon is such a writer. Her stories contain: "the total experience of a region's history, the hero's archetypal struggle, the complexity of modern aesthetics." Classic simplicity characterizes most of her short stories: this quality is "a clue to the origins of Miss Gordon's narrative virtue," for "she is still in touch with the oral tradition which in her formative years was a vital element of family life." For her, the family is "a natural symbol of the order of existence, the basic analogue for everything of importance." It provides "a key to the meaning of community, history, politics, morality, the transcendent and timeless." Gordon's fiction "moves toward abstraction rather than proceeds from it, and is always symbolic rather than purely literal or purely allegorical." Her technique "is never used to distort or to oversimplify" and her irony "is classical in tone rather than modern, the irony of high seriousness." Compares Gordon's "All Lovers Love the Spring" with James Joyce's "Clay."

15 STANFORD, DONALD E. "The Fiction of Caroline Gordon: A Reissue." SoR N.S. 8:458.

Brief note celebrating the fact that Cooper Square Publishers are "reissuing eight of Caroline Gordon's long out of print titles." These volumes will "find their rightful place as being among the best fiction written by an American in this century as well as a distinct contribution to our understanding of the history and culture of the South."

1973 A BOOKS - NONE

1973 B SHORTER WRITINGS

1 BAKER, HOWARD. "The Stratagems of Caroline Gordon, Or, The Art of the Novel and the Novelty of Myth." SoR N.S. 9:523-49.

Reviews at length The Glory of Hera, a "matchless book" and a "peak" in Gordon's career, and discusses at length the nature of myth and mythic rendering. Whereas the ancients would argue that the "ineffable stuff [of myth] could never be captured by a writer of mere prose," Gordon has done this. Her Heracles is "no 'modernized' mythological figure like the Ulysses of James Joyce." The myth of Heracles' life ends "in a triumphant overriding myth" which "is one of the mysteries of The Glory of Hera." Gordon has "formed a lifelong habit...of filtering her stratagems as a novelist through a screen of mythology; for this reason she is much more an impressionist as a writer than a realist." Gives the circumstances of Gordon's writing of Penhally which was "instantly recognizable as a flawless, spirited exemplification of the sort of novel writing I have

(BAKER, HOWARD)
been trying to describe." Its opening reference to shadows that "shifted and broke and flowed away...like water" implies the "filtering consciousness" and persists in "the religious implications in the hidden waters which seem to lap at the pilings that support a number of the later books." Gordon's stratagems are "the stratagems of holding back, as if to get a firmer grasp on what is to come, of planning and timing, and of launching out finally in an unveering course." In this she is like Hemingway who revealed in A Moveable Feast the theory that "you could deliberately omit the key expository fact in a work of fiction 'and make people feel something more than they understood.'" Such lacunae as "unstated foreknowledge" and "omissions" can be "calculated devices." Penhally must "be viewed as a prelude to The Glory of Hera. I do not regard the Sophoclean culmination of family strife in fratricide as a matter of superficial resemblance." Gordon must have known "she was producing a local variant on an ancient theme"; another variant appears between Rion and Archie in Green Centuries. The important question as Tate suggests in "Sonnets of the Blood" is: "Who are the dead?" In Penhally Gordon offers a "reply," suggested in a description of water that has "the ring in it of a metaphor, of a way of saying that there is an almost inconceivable continuity running from life to life." The appearing, disappearing, and reappearing waters in Penhally are a key to the structure of the novel and to Gordon's stratagems as a writer of fiction: as she remarks, "Truth will seep out like water rising in marshy ground." In "no other fiction [than hers] is there quite so clear a projection of the living images and voices that belonged to another era, nor so tragic a completeness of the stories being told." With this projection and this completeness, The Glory of Hera is "the novel which I think is the best that has been written in something like the past half-century." Discusses the "crux in the problem of myth and mythology"--i.e., the fact that as expressions of Greek religion the "mythological stuffs" were "various and unsystematic," while viewed with historical perspective "the panoply of the Olympians is a first flowering" of Archetypal Religion. "The chief stratagem of Caroline Gordon is to see it thus, unerringly and as a whole." Thus, for her, Heracles' story contains "a promise of deliverance." Discusses the views of Claude Levi-Strauss and their correspondence with "the high art of Caroline Gordon's novel-making." The Glory of Hera is "the archetypal form of religious faith...without, at this time, a visible doctrine." Heracles' mission as Zeus's son is to "spend

himself in bringing to fruition the latent worth of his race." Gordon has "told it all, at length and in better form, I think, than it exists elsewhere in the surviving documents."

2 BROWN, ASHLEY. "Caroline Gordon's Short Fiction." SR 81: 365-70.

Reviews The Short Fiction of Caroline Gordon: A Critical Symposium (See 1972.A1), a "splendid idea well realized," but adopts a "slightly different position" toward Gordon's short fiction. Gordon is "one of the few living writers who seem to have grasped" the principle behind, the "historical vision that underlies," Flaubert's shifts of style: "one phase of history set against the others, as it were--and the whole matter of technique is given its rationale." This principle is at work in Gordon's short stories and "on a much larger scale in the novels." Each work "gives us a certain perspective" on preceding works. To view Gordon's fiction as "primarily epic" is "a brilliant way of regarding her work as a whole, though one should make certain exceptions, notably of None Shall Look Back (1937), which is finally tragic." Discusses Louise Cowan's views [See 1972.B10], and agrees with Mrs. Cowan that Gordon was "'Homeric' in her earlier books, but she has gradually become 'Dantesque.'" The Women on the Porch evinces this transition: the movement from oral folk-song or tale to spoken poetry with its "density of allusion." It is unfortunate that The Forest of the South has not been reprinted. The arrangement of its stories is chronological, whereas the arrangement in Old Red is reversed, as if Gordon "now wants us to look at the past by way of the present, or what history has come to." This "has its justification when you consider the development in her work." What is needed is a Collected Stories of Caroline Gordon, in chronological arrangement. "It would begin with 'Summer Dust' and end with 'One Against Thebes,' which in fact is the former story considerably revised." "Summer Dust" is "remarkable enough to preserve in its original form. In its immediacy of sensation it bears comparison to the opening chapter of A Portrait of the Artist as a Young Man. Furthermore, much of the author's subsequent work is implicity here, as her revision makes clear." The revised story "fully anticipates The Glory of Hera." A chronological arrangement of the collected short stories "might turn out to be something like that in Dubliners, with its progression from childhood to maturity and its sad wisdom. The historical design would then be implied, while the book would expand toward the big set-piece, which is 'Emmanuele!

(BROWN, ASHLEY)
Emmanuele!,' Caroline Gordon's version of [Joyce's] 'The Dead.'"

3 LEWIS, JANET. "The Glory of Hera." SR 81:185-94.
"Presumably since it is published first, the lower pattern [The Glory of Hera] of the double novel should be comprehensible without a knowledge of the upper pattern [Gordon's novel-in-progress]....but I confess to being considerably baffled by the lower pattern," though it "is the work of a writer who knows as much about the art of the novel and the practice of prose fiction as anyone living I can bring to mind." The confusion stems from "the conjunction of the quotations at the beginning and end of the story", and the method "which involves two different tones of narration and a great many different points of view. This method tends to break the movement of the story, preventing a build-up of momentum" though "presenting us with a number of vignettes, chapters which stand out clearly from the larger confusion and which are very fine in themselves." The shifting Central Intelligences prevent an adequate ending. The "problem of tone" is related to this: "How seriously are we intended to take this story, either when considering a baffled human being, Heracles, or when considering a well-meaning but inefficient deity, Zeus?" The beginning and ending quotations imply "that we are to take it very seriously; but such an air of mockery pervades the telling that the seriousness is largely cancelled out." The "jollity of the last scene"; the "air of irony, of detached amusement, whenever the gods are dealt with--or almost always"; "the humor which is bound to arise when allegory is treated as literal fact": all this creates one tonal attitude toward the gods. On the other hand, the scenes concerned with human beings are "moving and more warmly rendered" because of "the perpetual plight of humans bewildered by the intentions of the gods, attempting to understand and placate the non-understandable, the implacable, the whimsical. (This bafflement could be said to be the plot of the book.)" However, "these distinctions of tone are not absolute." Sometimes the mortals seem mocked; sometimes the treatment of Zeus "approaches the prophetic." Yet is is difficult to "shake off so quickly the effect of mockery implicit in all the preceding Olympian sequences." Heracles himself "does not seem to develop in character as a hero toward becoming a god; he has godhood thrust upon him." The "credibility of a god can best be solved, or perhaps can only be solved by giving the telling of the story to a believer in the god," as Mary Renault does with

Theseus in The King Must Die. In declaring that her novel takes place "outside of time," Gordon has "sacrificed this advantage of narration." Actually the novel "takes place both in and out of time." Finally, one is "left with a sense of inadequate comprehension of the ultimate intentions of the author." One does not know how to see the beginning and ending quotations or the quotation from Psalm 19 as suitable.

4 STANFORD, DONALD E. Review of The Glory of Hera. Michigan Quarterly Review 12:89-90.

The novel is "a vivid and sensitive re-telling of one of the great archetypal stories of Western Civilization," yet its "full symbolic import" will have to "await publication of Miss Gordon's companion volume, A Narrow Heart: The Portrait of a Woman" since "A Narrow Heart is the upper pattern of this double novel." The "lower pattern," The Glory of Hera, winds through the upper pattern of action and deals with the archetypal world which, according to Gordon, "Jungians and archaic Greeks inform us lies at the bottom of every human consciousness." Gordon relates the novel "with a cool, detached and at times slightly ironic realism." The literal story is written "with the wealth of perceptive detail and skillful arrangement of incident" noted in her earlier fiction. Gordon sees Heracles "as a God-like but still human champion who fights evil for the benefit of mankind but is himself destroyed (in a physical sense) because of imperfect knowledge of himself and of the will of Zeus."

1975 A BOOKS - NONE

1975 B SHORTER WRITINGS

1 SIMPSON, LEWIS P. The Dispossessed Garden: Pastoral and History in Southern Literature. Athens, Ga.: University of Georgia Press, pp. 75 and 94.

Brief mention. In Gordon's stories as well as in those of certain other Southern writers, we have "a struggle of revelation, an effort to achieve a vision of the meaning of the South in terms of the classical-Christian historical order of being in its twofold aspect": being in relation to transcendence, and being in relation to existence in time. To the extent that this vision is achieved, the resultant meaning amounts to "an almost unique discovery by modern American storytellers of the truth of historical existence," a realization that existence is dual: that it

1975

(SIMPSON, LEWIS P.)
is both a sacred and a profane history. Gordon is one of those who "are meditators on history more than imitators of it as in the case of conventional historical novelists."

Ph.D. Dissertations on Caroline Gordon

1946 CATER, ALTHEA C. "Social Attitudes in Five Contemporary Southern Novelists: Erskine Caldwell, William Faulkner, Ellen Glasgow, Caroline Gordon, and T. S. Stribling." University of Michigan.

1957 KIMBALL, WILLIAM JOSEPH. "The Civil War in American Novels: 1920-1939." Pennsylvania State University. (Discusses None Shall Look Back.)

1958 BROWN, SAMUEL ASHLEY. "Caroline Gordon and the Impressionist Novel." Vanderbilt University.

1963 FLETCHER, MARIE. "The Southern Heroine in the Fiction of Representative Southern Women Writers, 1850-1960." Louisiana State University.

1966 ROCKS, JAMES ENGEL. "The Mind and Art of Caroline Gordon." Duke University.

1967 SMITH, PATRICK JAMES. "Typology and Peripety in Four Catholic Novels." University of California, Davis. (Discusses The Strange Children.)

1973 CHAPPELL, CHARLES MILTON. "The Hero Figure and the Problem of Unity in the Novels of Caroline Gordon." Emory University.

1974 BROWN, JERRY ELIJAH. "The Rhetoric of Form: A Study of the Novels of Caroline Gordon." Vanderbilt University.

1975 RODENBERGER, MOLCIE LOU. "Caroline Gordon, Teller of Tales: The Influence of Folk Narrative on Characterization and Structure in Her Work." Texas A&M University.

Indexes to Flannery O'Connor and Caroline Gordon

Index to Flannery O'Connor

This index is a single, alphabetical listing of the titles of published writings on O'Connor, the authors of such writings, the titles of works by O'Connor, and two subject headings: Bibliography and Biography. Entries in the index are cited according to the code used throughout the reference guide, with each book and article or review on O'Connor being listed by number according to its place in the alphabetical listing by author for that year of publication. The "A" section for each year lists books devoted entirely to O'Connor; the "B" section lists reviews and articles on O'Connor as well as books where only a part of the book deals with her.

The entries cited next to the titles of O'Connor's works are intended to be a reasonably complete list of the published writings discussing that title, but no attempt was made to cite every brief mention of a certain title. Length or specificity of reference determined whether a work on O'Connor was included in the entries for a title. The reader should note that specific short stories, separate from their collections, are keyed only to material in the "B" section for each year, that is, to reviews, articles, and books not exclusively concerned with O'Connor. Furthermore, entries for specific short stories are listed only when a work treats a story apart from the rest of the collection in which it appeared or places its main emphasis on one or two stories. Other discussions of specific short stories will be found under the titles of the original collections in which the stories appeared, including all discussions in books devoted entirely to O'Connor. Thus, the works cited after _A Good Man is Hard to Find_ may include discussions of the collection as such and of several of the specific stories within it: "A Good Man Is Hard to Find," "The River," "The Life You Save May Be Your Own," "A Stroke of Good Fortune," "A Temple of the Holy Ghost," "The Artificial Nigger," "A Circle in the Fire," "A Late Encounter with the Enemy," "Good Country People," and "The Displaced Person." The same holds true for Everything That Rises Must Converge and the stories in that collection: "Everything That Rises Must Converge," "Greenleaf," "A View of the Woods," "The Enduring Chill," "The Comforts of Home," "The Lame Shall Enter First," "Revelation," "Parker's Back," and Judgement Day." References to Flannery O'Connor: The Complete Stories are only to that collection as a collection. While books devoted entirely to O'Connor are here indexed only to the novels and the collections of short stories, the reader should realize that most of these books emphasize some stories more than others, and he should check the index of each book if he is interested in discussions of particular stories. The only book that contains an extensive discussion of all the stories not contained in A Good Man Is Hard to Find or Everything That Rises Must Converge is 1976.A4.

In this index reprints of writings on O'Connor are not cited after the titles of O'Connor's works, but all reprints are cross-referenced with their originals within the guide itself. Titles in parentheses after the title of an O'Connor story indicate another title O'Connor gave to the story or to a different version of the story. Criticism of the story is indexed according to the title of the story used in the criticism, and the reader should check both titles to obtain a full listing of the criticism indexed for that story.

Index

Index

Index to Caroline Gordon

This index is a single alphabetical listing of titles of published writings about Caroline Gordon, the authors of those writings, the titles of works by Caroline Gordon, and two subject headings: Bibliography and Biography. The references in this index are to the entries in the Reference Guide proper and employ the code system used throughout. Thus, "None Shall Look Back 1937.B1" refers the reader to the first entry under "Shorter Writings" in the 1937 listing; and "1972.A2" refers the reader to the second entry under "Books" in the 1972 listing.

The entries cited after each title of Caroline Gordon's works direct the reader to books, articles or reviews which deal with that particular work of Caroline Gordon in a significant way. While these references are intended to be reasonably complete, no attempt has been made to cite all the published writings which mention that work. Italics are used for those references leading to the fullest information or discussion on that particular work of Caroline Gordon. In the case of individual short stories by Caroline Gordon, the reader should consult also the entries for the volume or volumes in which that story is collected since there the references cited are more complete. For example, in seeking references for the story "Tom Rivers," the reader should consult also The Forest of the South and Old Red and Other Stories. The volume or volumes in which each story is collected are indicated by abbreviation after each story listed in the index: (FS), (OR), or (FS, OR).

Index

INDEX